1 What is the surname of cop Maisie played by Pauline Quirke?
2 Michael French left which soap to become a Crime Traveller?
3 In "Murphy's Law", is Murphy named Mick, Pat or Tommy?
4 Which sleuth Jonathan was created by David Renwick?
5 Which early police serial is found at the end of the alphabet?
6 Which Yorkshire police series did Nick Berry leave in 1997?
7 In which county was "Dalziel & Pascoe" originally set?
8 "Dangerfield" deals with what type of police personnel?
9 David Suchet played which Belgian Agatha Christie detective?
10 In which English county does "Wycliffe" take place?
11 Which assistant to Morse was missing from the show in 1998?
12 Michael Gambon played which French detective in the 1990s?
13 How was "The Bill's" DC Lines, played by Kevin Lloyd, better known?
14 Which Glasgow detective was played by Mark McManus?
15 Which Hetty has a sidekick called Geoffrey?
16 What is the surname of detective Jack played by David Jason?
17 Which police station's blues were led by Captain Frank Furillo?
18 What is the first name of Commander Dalgliesh, created by PD James?
19 Which Jimmy starred in "Evita" and played Geordie Spender?
20 Which Victorian sleuth from Baker Street was played by Jeremy Brett?
21 In "Pie in the Sky", which profession did Henry combine with policing?
22 In which northern city was "City Central" set?
23 How is Cordelia Gray's creator Baroness James better known?
24 Which bald TV cop was "Friends" Jennifer Aniston's godfather?
25 In which series might DC Ben Jones be called on to help solve murders?
26 Where did Sonny Crockett aka Don Johnson sort out Vice?
27 Who has played Jack Regan and Morse?
28 In which city was "Cagney & Lacey" set?
29 Which crime buster show shared its name with insects?
30 In which city did Maigret operate?

1 What is usually sold at reduced prices during a happy hour?
2 What are the two main ingredients of a ploughman's lunch?
3 Whose 2005 collection of hits was called "Curtain Call"?
4 Which UK daily newspaper has the shortest name?
5 Dame Barbara Cartland is famous for what type of fiction?
6 In which city is the Louvre Museum?
7 What does the E stand for in the acronym TESSA?
8 Steve McClaren left which soccer club to become England boss?
9 Which surviving tombs were built for the Pharaohs of Egypt?
10 What type of animal was the first successful adult cloning?
11 Which Bill is the world's richest businessman?
12 Twelfth Night marks the end of which festive season?
13 On which river does Cairo stand?
14 What type of animal is a Chihuahua?
15 2006 marked the 40th anniversary of which Welsh mining village disaster?
16 Which county does TV detective Hetty Wainthropp come from?
17 In motoring terms, what does the second A in AA stand for?
18 What is the national emblem of Scotland?
19 What type of animal does BSE affect?
20 In which decade of the 20th century was Prince William born?
21 What sort of tickets would a bucket shop sell?
22 On which Isle is Parkhurst prison?
23 What is hopscotch?
24 Which actress Cate starred in the movie "Charlotte Gray"?
25 Which British colony returned to China in July 1997?
26 In which city did rhyming slang originate?
27 Which alpine peak's name means White Mountain?
28 Which food is traditionally eaten on Shrove Tuesday?
29 If August 31st was a Wednesday what date would August Bank Holiday Monday be in England?
30 In which city is Tiananmen Square?

Answers | TV: Cops & Robbers *(see Quiz 3)*

1 Raine. 2 EastEnders. 3 Tommy. 4 Jonathan Creek. 5 Z Cars. 6 Heartbeat. 7 Yorkshire. 8 Police surgeon. 9 Poirot. 10 Cornwall. 11 Lewis. 12 Maigret. 13 Tosh. 14 Taggart. 15 Wainthropp. 16 Frost. 17 Hill St. Blues. 18 Adam. 19 Nail. 20 Sherlock Holmes. 21 Chef. 22 Manchester. 23 PD James. 24 Kojak (Telly Savalas). 25 Midsomer Murders. 26 Miami. 27 John Thaw. 28 New York. 29 Bugs. 30 Paris.

1 Which movie actress's second marriage was to director Sam Mendes?
2 Raymond Blanc is famous for being what?
3 Which Betty became the House of Commons' first woman Speaker?
4 In 2006 where did Prince William start military training?
5 Which one time husband and wife actors were dubbed Ken and Em?
6 Which trendy homeware store did Terence Conran found in the 60s?
7 Which part of you would you ask Nicky Clarke to cut off?
8 How was Yorkshire-based murderer Peter Sutcliffe better known?
9 Which celebrity daughter was named after the song "Chelsea Morning"?
10 Which ex-Wimbledon champ did Andre Agassi marry?
11 Which 90s PM was in a university pop group called Ugly Rumours?
12 Who is taller, Kylie Minogue or Naomi Campbell?
13 Who launched Virgin Cola and Virgin PEPs ?
14 Which singer Sarah was once Mrs Andrew Lloyd Webber?
15 Which rock star became dad to Alistair at the age of 60 in 2005?
16 Which Monica was intimately associated with Bill Clinton?
17 Was Joan Collins born in the 1920s, 1930s or the 1940s?
18 Which ex-British party leader has the same first names as Bill Clinton?
19 Which model Jerry had a cameo role in "Batman"?
20 Did actress Gwyneth Paltrow call her daughter Apple, Banana or Peach?
21 Which London football club does David Mellor famously support?
22 Which Scot Andrew was the Sunday Times editor from 1983 to 1994?
23 John Prescott became Deputy Leader of which political party?
24 Which Prime Minister had twins called Mark and Carol?
25 The names Saatchi and Saatchi are associated with which industry?
26 Who was the last Beatle to marry twice?
27 What title does the brother of the late Princess Diana have?
28 What type of shops did Tim Waterstone found?
29 Which designer Vivienne is famous for her outrageous clothes?
30 What is the nickname of Royal "nanny" Alexandra Legge-Bourke?

Answers | Pot Luck 2 *(see Quiz 6)*

1 Donkey. 2 Italy. 3 80th. 4 Kirsty Young. 5 Poppy. 6 48. 7 Lah. 8 A calf. 9 China. 10 Frank Sinatra. 11 Chequered. 12 Gareth Gates. 13 C. 14 Bach. 15 Ellen MacArthur. 16 Orange. 17 11. 18 Blue. 19 Dublin. 20 Florence Nightingale. 21 Pumpkin. 22 Bill Haley & the Comets. 23 London. 24 Hans Christian Andersen. 25 The twins. 26 Shropshire. 27 Grapes. 28 Tennis. 29 Sound and noise. 30 Third World.

1 What kind of animal is Eeyore in the children's classic?
2 Which country produces Parmesan cheese?
3 The Queen celebrated which landmark birthday in 2006?
4 Which Kirsty replaced Sue Lawley on "Desert Island Discs"?
5 Which flower is linked with Remembrance Sunday?
6 How many sides are there in a dozen quadrilaterals?
7 Which note follows the musical note "soh"?
8 What name is given to a young elephant?
9 In which country was acupuncture developed?
10 Which singer was known affectionately as "Old Blue Eyes"?
11 Which flag in motor racing signals the end of the race?
12 Whose first album was "What My Heart Wants To Say"?
13 Which vitamin is found in oranges and lemons?
14 Which composer had the forenames Johann Sebastian?
15 In February 2005, who became the fastest female to sail solo around the world?
16 What kind of fruit is a satsuma?
17 How many players are in a hockey team?
18 What colour is the shade of cobalt?
19 The Abbey Theatre is in which Irish city?
20 Which nurse was called "The Lady with the Lamp"?
21 What was Cinderella's coach made from?
22 Who rocked around the clock in 1955?
23 Which zoo is found in Regent's Park?
24 Who wrote "The Ugly Duckling"?
25 What is the Zodiac sign Gemini also called?
26 Shrewsbury is the county town of which county?
27 Which fruit when dried produces raisins?
28 In which sport did Ivan Lendl achieve fame?
29 What is measured in decibels?
30 Underdeveloped countries are said to be which numerical world?

1 Messrs Docherty, Atkinson and Ferguson have all managed which team?
2 Who was the first football boss to marry one of her former players?
3 Who stood down at Charlton in 2006 after more than ten years as manager?
4 Which Stanley was first winner of the European Footballer of the Year award?
5 Which was the first Rovers side to win the Premiership?
6 Graham Taylor was likened to a turnip after a defeat in which Scandinavian country?
7 Whom did Ruud Gullit replace as manager of Newcastle Utd?
8 In which Asian country did Gary Lineker play club soccer?
9 What colour are the stripes on Newcastle Utd's first choice shirts?
10 Which side moved from Roker Park to the Stadium of Light?
11 Was Alan Shearer sold to Newcastle for £5 million, £15 million or £25 million?
12 In which country was George Best born?
13 What is the nationality of Dennis Bergkamp?
14 Which Premiership keeper fractured his skull in a game in 2006?
15 Which manager took Wigan into the Premiership for the first time?
16 Which Yorkshire side was involved in a plane crash in March 1988?
17 Which Paul was the first black player to captain England?
18 Who was known as El Tel when he managed Barcelona?
19 Who in 1997 became Arsenal's all-time leading goal scorer?
20 How is the Football Association Challenge Cup better known?
21 Which Welshman Ian said living in Italy was like "living in a foreign country"?
22 Which club Charlton were promoted to the Premier League in 1998?
23 Which colour links shirts at Liverpool, Middlesbrough and Southampton?
24 Which Brian managed Notts Forest for 18 years?
25 Gareth Southgate finished his playing career at which club?
26 Which Charlton brother was the first to be knighted?
27 Which Eric was the first overseas PFA Player of the Year winner?
28 Who was dubbed Duncan Disorderly?
29 Paul Le Guen took over as boss of which Scottish giants?
30 Which club did Martin O'Neill manage after Celtic?

Answers	Pot Luck 3 *(see Quiz 8)*

1 Austria. 2 Fawn. 3 Plums. 4 Fernando Alonso. 5 Ant & Dec. 6 Me. 7 Sand. 8 Beatrix Potter. 9 Hampshire. 10 La Marseillaise. 11 Lion. 12 Ebony. 13 Ireland. 14 Golf. 15 Aardvark. 16 Bull. 17 Bayeux. 18 Beef. 19 Lira. 20 Prince Edward. 21 Eight. 22 An angle. 23 Will Young. 24 Bury its head. 25 Or Nearest Offer. 26 A clear soup. 27 Purplish red. 28 Apple. 29 West Ham. 30 Nottinghamshire.

1 Vienna is the capital of which European country?
2 What name is given to a young deer?
3 Which fruit when dried produces prunes?
4 Who claimed the F1 motor racing world championship in 2005 and 2006?
5 Which duo won the NTA's Most Popular TV presenters five times at the start of this century?
6 Which musical note follows ray?
7 What do you find in a bunker on a golf course?
8 Who wrote "The Tale of Peter Rabbit"?
9 Winchester is the county town of which county?
10 What is the name of the French National Anthem?
11 Which animal was Androcles very friendly with?
12 Which black wood is used for piano keys?
13 Which island is affectionately called the Emerald Isle?
14 In which sport is the Ryder Cup competed for?
15 What type of creature is Arthur in the CBBC series of the same name?
16 Which animal is linked with the Zodiac sign Taurus?
17 Which town is home to the Bayeux Tapestry?
18 What kind of meat can be silverside and topside?
19 What is the unit of currency in Italy?
20 What is the name of the Queen's youngest son?
21 How many notes are there in an octave?
22 What do you measure with a protractor?
23 The album "Friday's Child" was a No. 1 for which artist?
24 What is it said an ostrich does, if it thinks it is in danger?
25 After a selling price, what do the initials O.N.O. stand for?
26 Which type of soup is a consommé?
27 What colour is magenta?
28 What type of fruit is an Orange Pippin?
29 Which London-based football club are known as "The Hammers"?
30 In which county is Sherwood Forest?

1 The art of self-defence aikido originated in which country?
2 Which Bank Holiday comes immediately before Easter Day?
3 In which country was the 2006 Ryder Cup held?
4 Where might you be entertained by a redcoat?
5 Which reptiles feature in a popular board game?
6 Which is bigger, Disneyland or Disneyworld?
7 What do you play baccarat with?
8 Which leisure park Towers are near Stoke on Trent?
9 In which game is the object to gain checkmate?
10 What is the minimum number of players in a cribbage game?
11 Which quiz board game involves the collection of coloured wedges?
12 Brass rubbing usually takes place in what type of building?
13 Charles and Camilla shared their wedding day with which major sporting event?
14 In which English city could you watch Rovers and City play soccer?
15 Which part of a pub shares its name with an area of a law court?
16 Which End of London is famous for its theatres?
17 Microlighting takes place in what sort of craft?
18 What name is given to the hours that a pub can open to sell alcohol?
19 What type of music is celebrated at the CMA awards?
20 What colour is the L on a normal learner driver's L plate?
21 What sort of accommodation is provided in a B & B?
22 Knitting needs needles, what does crochet need?
23 Which pier is to the north of Blackpool's central pier?
24 What type of castle do young children enjoy jumping up and down on?
25 "The dogs" involves races of which breed?
26 What colour are the segments on a roulette wheel?
27 Which Planet is a celebrity-founded restaurant chain?
28 What colour are Scrabble tiles?
29 Which gambling game's best hand is Royal flush?
30 What colour is the M on the McDonalds logo?

Answers | Pot Luck 4 *(see Quiz 10)*

1 Green. 2 Fish. 3 Friar Tuck. 4 Bananarama. 5 Leo. 6 Scissor Sisters. 7 Public Limited Company. 8 Switzerland. 9 Bear. 10 Alexandra. 11 April. 12 76. 13 Pancakes. 14 On board ship. 15 A snake. 16 Belgium. 17 Yellow/orange. 18 Apple. 19 George Orwell. 20 Isle of Wight. 21 1960s. 22 Before they're hatched. 23 Holland. 24 Saturday. 25 A pup. 26 Malta. 27 Dark. 28 Eucalyptus leaves. 29 White coffee. 30 The Tower of London.

1 If you mix blue and yellow paint what colour is made?
2 What is usually eaten with Tartare Sauce?
3 Who was Robin Hood's priest?
4 Which 1980s girl group came back in 2005 with "Move In My Direction"?
5 Which sign of the Zodiac is normally shown as a lion?
6 Which Sisters made the album "Ta-Dah"?
7 What do the initials plc stand for after a company name?
8 Berne is the capital of which European country?
9 What type of creature was Baloo in "The Jungle Book"?
10 Which London palace is also called "Ally Pally"?
11 St George's Day is in which month?
12 How many trombones led the big parade according to the song?
13 What are Crêpes Suzettes a type of?
14 Where does a purser usually work?
15 What is a black mamba?
16 Which country does tennis star Kim Clijsters come from – Belgium or Holland?
17 What colour is ochre?
18 What kind of fruit is a russet?
19 Who wrote the novel "Animal Farm"?
20 On which island is Osborne House, home of Queen Victoria?
21 In which decade did Yuri Gagarin become the first man in space?
22 When must you not count your chickens, according to the proverb?
23 Which country makes Gouda cheese?
24 What day of the week is the Jewish Sabbath?
25 What name is given to a young seal?
26 Which island was awarded the George Cross in 1942?
27 Is presenter Carol Vorderman's hair light or dark?
28 What does a koala have for its main source of food?
29 What is cafe au lait?
30 Where are the Crown Jewels kept?

Answers | Hobbies & Leisure 1 *(see Quiz 9)*

1 Japan. 2 Good Friday. 3 Ireland. 4 Holiday camp (Butlin's). 5 Snakes (& ladders).
6 Disneyworld. 7 Cards. 8 Alton Towers. 9 Chess. 10 Two. 11 Trivial Pursuits.
12 Churches. 13 Grand National. 14 Bristol. 15 Bar. 16 West End. 17 Plane. 18
Licensing hours. 19 Country music. 20 Red. 21 Bed & breakfast. 22 Hook. 23 North
pier. 24 Bouncy castle. 25 Greyhounds. 26 Red, black. 27 Hollywood. 28 Cream.
29 Poker. 30 Yellow.

1 Which Spice Girl advertised Milky Bars as a child?
2 Was Billie Piper 10, 15 or 20 when she first went to No. 1?
3 Which Tina sang the title song from "Whistle Down the Wind"?
4 Who put her famous Union Jack dress up for auction?
5 Who had a No. 1 single with "Toxic"?
6 How many girls made up N-Tyce?
7 Janet and La Toyah are from which famous family?
8 What is the first name of the Welsh singer from Catatonia?
9 Whose album "Always and Forever" gives a clue to their name?
10 Which 60s singer's first hit was written by the Rolling Stones?
11 Heather Small found fame with which band?
12 What is the surname of sisters Kylie and Dannii?
13 Who made the big-selling album "J.LO"?
14 Whose third No. 1 was titled "Day & Night"?
15 Where do Scary Spice and Princess Anne's daughter have a stud?
16 Who share their name with an Egyptian queen?
17 Which Aussie soap did Natalie Imbruglia appear in?
18 How many singers make up B*witched?
19 How did the Bangles Walk?
20 Shaznay is in which all-girl band?
21 Which 60s singer hosted "Surprise Surprise"?
22 Which Capstan sang with the B52s and guested with REM?
23 Who was the lead singer for Blondie?
24 Which musical instrument is Vanessa Mae famous for?
25 Which musical star Alicia sang before the 2005 Super Bowl?
26 Alanis Morissette and Celine Dion are from which country?
27 Who sang about "Baboushka" and "Wuthering Heights"?
28 In which decade did Bananarama have their first hit?
29 Miss Nurding dropped her surname and became known as whom?
30 Which singing star married Kevin Federline?

Answers | Pot Luck 5 *(see Quiz 12)*

1 July. 2 Bull/cow. 3 Cider. 4 Michael Palin. 5 A savoury snack. 6 1969. 7 Venice. 8 Mount Ararat. 9 Forbidden fruit. 10 A will. 11 France. 12 Norwich City. 13 Vincent van Gogh. 14 Aries. 15 Calligraphy. 16 Harley Street. 17 Pinocchio. 18 Tanks. 19 Friday. 20 A bird. 21 David Gray. 22 Cherry. 23 17. 24 September. 25 Devon. 26 Baptism. 27 Cameron. 28 Tottenham Hotspur. 29 Hippopotamus. 30 Colin Firth.

Quiz 12 | Pot Luck 5

1 St Swithin's Day is in which summer month?
2 Who or what is an Aberdeen Angus?
3 What drink did writer Laurie Lee share with Rosie?
4 Which ex-Python Palin published his diaries in autumn 2006?
5 What are pretzels?
6 Did man first land on the moon in 1966, 1969 or 1972?
7 In which Italian city is St Mark's cathedral?
8 On which Mount is the resting place of Noah's Ark?
9 Which fruit tastes sweetest according to the proverb?
10 What does a testator make, in law?
11 Which country produces Camembert cheese?
12 Which football team is known as "The Canaries"?
13 Which Dutch painter cut off his ear?
14 Which Zodiac sign is normally associated with the ram?
15 What is the study of handwriting called?
16 Which London street is associated with the medical profession?
17 Which wooden puppet was written about by Carlo Collodi?
18 Shermans, Grants and Cromwells are all types of what?
19 Which day of the week is the Muslim Holy Day?
20 What is a quail?
21 Who had a No. 1 album with "A New Day at Midnight"?
22 Which fruit is used to make kirsch?
23 How old should you be to apply for a car driving licence in the UK?
24 In what month is Michaelmas Day?
25 Which county has Exeter as its county town?
26 For which religious ceremony is a font normally used?
27 ROMANCE is an anagram of the surname of which political leader?
28 Michael Carrick joined Man Utd from which other Premiership side?
29 Which animal has a name which means "river horse"?
30 Which Colin starred in the movie "Hope Springs"?

Answers | **Musical Babes** *(see Quiz 11)*

1 Emma (Baby Spice). 2 15. 3 Tina Arena. 4 Geri Halliwell. 5 Britney Spears. 6 Four. 7 Jackson. 8 Nerys. 9 Eternal. 10 Marianne Faithfull. 11 M People. 12 Minogue. 13 Jennifer Lopez. 14 Billie Piper. 15 Tongue. 16 Cleopatra. 17 Home & Away. 18 Four. 19 Like an Egyptian. 20 All Saints. 21 Cilla Black. 22 Kate. 23 Debbie Harry. 24 Violin. 25 Alicia Keys. 26 Canada. 27 Kate Bush. 28 1980s. 29 Louise. 30 Britney Spears.

1 Which early Spielberg blockbuster was about a shark?

2 What was Daniel Craig's first movie as James Bond?

3 In which 1990s musical film did Madonna change costume 85 times?

4 What was the name of the movie based on TV's "The X Files"?

5 Which Julianne played opposite Anthony Hopkins in "Hannibal"?

6 Martin Scorsese made a film about the Gangs Of which city?

7 "The Fellowship of the Ring" was based on which book?

8 Which creatures dominated "Jurassic Park"?

9 What was "Crocodile Dundee's" homeland?

10 "Hook" was based on which children's book?

11 Which lizard-like monster's name is a mix of the Japanese words for gorilla and whale?

12 Who left Kramer in the 1970s movie with Hoffman and Streep?

13 "From Here to Eternity" is set before the Japanese attack on where?

14 "Raging Bull" was about which sport?

15 Which film was an abbreviation of Extra Terrestrial?

16 "The Empire Strikes Back" was a sequel to what?

17 "Raiders of the Lost Ark" was about which Mr Jones?

18 Robin Hood was Prince of what in the 1991 blockbuster?

19 Was "Snow White and the Seven Dwarfs" released before or after World War II?

20 Where was Gary Oldman Lost in the 1998 hit movie?

21 Which Caped Crusader was the subject of one of the top 1980s films?

22 Which watery film succeeded "Waterworld" as the most costly to make?

23 Gene Kelly was An American ... where in the Vincente Minnelli movie?

24 Which star of "Grease" and "Saturday Night Fever" is a qualified pilot?

25 Was "The Sting" a hit in the 1950s, 70s or 90s?

26 Which Disney animal movie was a 1994 blockbuster set in Africa?

27 "Amadeus" told the story of which composer?

28 "Home Alone" shot which child star to fame?

29 Was "Schindler's List" in colour or black and white?

30 Which Kevin played Mariner in "Waterworld"?

---

1 Which country produces Gruyère cheese?

2 Who was invested as Prince of Wales in 1969?

3 Francis Drake's ship Pelican was renamed what?

4 Which opera by Gilbert and Sullivan is set in Venice?

5 Did John Le Carré write thrillers or romantic fiction?

6 Which London Street was home to several British newspapers?

7 Which county has Ipswich as its county town?

8 What shape are the teeth on pinking shears?

9 Which Saint is commemorated on the 17th of March?

10 Which Zodiac sign is normally associated with two fishes?

11 In March 2005 who had three singles in the same US top five?

12 What is the minimum age for leaving school in England?

13 In snooker, how many points is the brown ball worth?

14 Who was the first cricketer to win TV's "Strictly Come Dancing"?

15 What kind of animals were Cupid, Donner and Blitzen?

16 In which sport would you use a caddie?

17 Which manager moved across London from Crystal Palace to Charlton in 2006?

18 According to the proverb, which Italian city was not built in a day?

19 What is the first letter of the Greek alphabet?

20 What is a Shih-Tzu?

21 Which country does the wine claret come from?

22 In tennis, what does the initial L in LTA stand for?

23 What kind of plants are sage, lovage and basil?

24 Which London park is the name of a colour?

25 Andrea Levy wrote the award-winning novel titled "Small" what?

26 If you bought "Le Figaro" in France what would you be buying?

27 An elver is a young what?

28 What is kelp?

29 Which film featured the Von Trapp Family?

30 What is the county town of Dorset?

| **Answers** | The Movies: Blockbusters *(see Quiz 13)* |

1 Jaws. 2 Casino Royale. 3 Evita. 4 The X Files. 5 Julianne Moore. 6 New York. 7 The Lord of the Rings. 8 Dinosaurs. 9 Australia. 10 Peter Pan. 11 Godzilla. 12 Kramer. 13 Pearl Harbor. 14 Boxing. 15 E.T. 16 Star Wars. 17 Indiana Jones. 18 Thieves. 19 Before. 20 Space. 21 Batman. 22 Titanic. 23 Paris. 24 John Travolta. 25 70s. 26 The Lion King. 27 Mozart. 28 Macaulay Culkin. 29 Black & white. 30 Costner.

1 Did Mourinho join Chelsea in 2000, 2002 or 2004?
2 Which club was Damian Duff sold to in 2006?
3 Mourinho was dubbed the "special" what?
4 Who was skipper of Jose's first Premiership-winning side?
5 Shaun Wright-Phillips was bought from which City club?
6 Which country does Claude Makelele play for?
7 Which midfielder was top scorer in 2005 and 2006?
8 Petr Cech keeps goal for which international Republic?
9 Who went to Arsenal when Ashley Cole came to Chelsea?
10 Mourinho joined Chelsea from which Potuguese club?
11 Who was not signed by Jose – Michael Ballack, Michael Essien or John Terry?
12 Does Crespo play for Argentina or Russia?
13 Joe Cole and Frank Lampard were at which other London club?
14 Carvalho and Ferreira play for which European country?
15 Who bankrolled Chelsea's success?
16 Which Carlo was number-two keeper in 2005 and 2006?
17 Does Andriy Shevchenko play for, Bulgaria or the Ukraine?
18 Was Mourinho born in the 1940s, 1960s or 1970s?
19 Which Claudio was boss before Mourinho?
20 Which English team dumped Chelsea out of 2005's Champions League?
21 Who, in November 2006, beat Chelsea at home for the first time in 19 seasons?
22 Scott Parker moved on to which club?
23 Does Michael Essien play for France or Ghana?
24 When did Chelsea last win the league before 2005 – 1930s or 1950s?
25 Which Chelsea player Wayne has a link to the ground name?
26 Which Liverpool boss was part of the "no handshake" row?
27 Adrian Mutu's contract was cancelled after a scandal involving what?
28 Did Mourinho first win the League Cup or the FA Cup?
29 Arjen Robben plays international soccer with which country?
30 Who was the Ivory Coast target man brought in in 2004?

1 What does T stand for in the initials V.A.T.?
2 What does a Venus fly-trap trap?
3 Which movement was founded by Lord Baden-Powell?
4 What day precedes Ash Wednesday?
5 In snooker, is the pink ball or the brown ball of higher value?
6 Which sign of the Zodiac is pictured by an archer?
7 "Dare" was the first No. 1 single for which band?
8 Which animal is often given the name Brock?
9 In which country was the first series of "Robin Hood" with Jonas Armstrong filmed?
10 Which Shakespeare play features the Capulets and Montagues?
11 Which country was called Albion by Greeks and Romans?
12 In which country is the battle site of El Alamein?
13 Great oak trees grow from what, according to the proverb?
14 Which town did Jesus grow up in?
15 What is the name of the dress worn by a ballerina?
16 Which long-running TV series features Marge and Homer?
17 Stratus, Cirrus and Cumulus are all types of what?
18 Where do mosquitoes lay their eggs?
19 What are clogs traditionally made from?
20 Which actor played Basil Fawlty in "Fawlty Towers"?
21 Toronto is the capital of which Canadian province?
22 Who wrote "Mein Kampf"?
23 Which football team plays at Stamford Bridge?
24 What do your arteries carry from your heart?
25 In which northern Italian city is the Doge's Palace?
26 If speech is silver, what is golden according to the proverb?
27 Which county cricket team plays at Edgbaston?
28 What is a natterjack?
29 Which Gladys sang the theme song to the 007 movie "Licence to Kill"?
30 Was Renee Zellwegger a blonde or brunette in "Bridget Jones's Diary"?

Answers | Mourinho's Chelsea *(see Quiz 15)*

1 2004. 2 Newcastle United. 3 "The Special One". 4 John Terry. 5 Manchester City.
6 France. 7 Frank Lampard. 8 Czech Republic. 9 William Gallas. 10 Porto. 11 Terry.
12 Argentina. 13 West Ham. 14 Portugal. 15 Roman Abramovich. 16 Carlo Cudicini.
17 Ukraine. 18 1960s. 19 Claudio Ranieri. 20 Liverpool. 21 Tottenham Hotspur. 22
Newcastle United. 23 Ghana. 24 1950s (1955). 25 Wayne Bridge. 26 Rafael Benitez.
27 Drug taking. 28 League Cup. 29 Holland. 30 Didier Drogba.

1 Which detective did Dr Watson assist?
2 The cover of Peter Kay's "The Sound of Laughter" is a spoof of which film poster?
3 Mrs Beeton was most famous for writing on what subject?
4 Are Penguin books hardbacks or paperbacks?
5 Was St Trinian's a school for boys or girls?
6 What type of animal is Winnie the Pooh?
7 What relation was Charlotte to Emily and Anne Brontë?
8 Who is Agatha Christie's most famous female detective?
9 What is the name of the book of scripts from "The Catherine Tate Show"?
10 In which building does the murder take place at the start of "The Da Vinci Code"?
11 Who's "Winter Collection" of recipes sold 1.5 million copies in just eight weeks?
12 What sort of Factory is associated with Roald Dahl's Charlie?
13 In which book are there four accounts of Jesus's life called gospels?
14 Which African president's autobiography was called "Long Walk to Freedom"?
15 Who wrote "Cook with Jamie"?
16 What was "Schindler's Ark" renamed when it was made into a film?
17 Where was Douglas Adams' Hitchhiker's Guide to?
18 What type of tales did the Grimm brothers write?
19 What is the nationality of novelist Maeve Binchy?
20 Which novelist Dame Catherine died in 1998?
21 Who wrote "And It's Goodnight from Him..." about himself and his late comedy partner?
22 Who was Ian Fleming's most famous secret agent creation?
23 Whom did Laurie Lee write of Cider with...?
24 Which soccer coach's World Cup Story 1998 caused an outrage over breaches of confidentiality?
25 Which Stephen is famous for horror writing such as "The Shining"?
26 What was Dick Francis's profession before he turned to writing?
27 What was Bram Stoker's most famous monstrous creation?
28 In which century did Charles Dickens live?
29 Which comedian Ben wrote "Gridlock" and "Popcorn"?
30 Which Frederick's first success was "The Day of the Jackal"?

Answers	Pot Luck 8 *(see Quiz 18)*

1 November. 2 The tail. 3 Elvis Presley. 4 An alkali. 5 A small wood. 6 Hamlet. 7 Angels. 8 Conservatives. 9 Afrikaans. 10 Kenya. 11 Willow. 12 Seven. 13 An eyrie. 14 Threadneedle Street. 15 Doncaster. 16 The Osbournes. 17 £1. 18 Ballet. 19 Violet. 20 Adder. 21 Nepal. 22 Agoraphobia. 23 Mercury. 24 Pasta. 25 Spencer. 26 The Hours. 27 Norwich. 28 A news agency. 29 Mars. 30 Bolton.

1 In which month is Thanksgiving celebrated in America?
2 Where is the rattle in a rattlesnake?
3 Whose "Are You Lonesome Tonight" was back in the UK charts in 2005?
4 What is the opposite of an acid?
5 What is a spinney?
6 Who said, "To be or not to be, that is the question"?
7 In the Bible, what were seraphim and cherubim?
8 Which political party had Benjamin Disraeli as a leader?
9 Which South African language derives from the Dutch settlers?
10 Which country has Nairobi as its capital?
11 Cricket bats are traditionally made from which wood?
12 How many colours are in the spectrum?
13 What name is given to the home of an eagle?
14 On which Street is the Bank of England?
15 The St Leger is run at which Yorkshire race course?
16 Which real rock family includes Ozzy, Sharon and Kelly?
17 Which coin was first introduced in the UK in 1983?
18 For what type of dancing did Anna Pavlova achieve fame?
19 What colour is an amethyst?
20 What is the only poisonous snake in Britain?
21 Which country is native homeland to the Gurkha troops?
22 Which phobia is the fear of open spaces?
23 Which chemical is also known as quicksilver?
24 Penne, rigatoni and tagliatelle are all types of what?
25 What did the initial "S" stand for in Winston S. Churchill?
26 Did Nicole Kidman win an Oscar for "The Days", "The Hours" or "The Weeks"?
27 Which Norfolk city stands on the River Wensum?
28 What is Reuters?
29 Who was god of war in Roman mythology?
30 Diouf and Anelka played for Liverpool and which other English soccer club?

| **Answers** | Leisure: Books *(see Quiz 17)* |

1 Sherlock Holmes. 2 The Sound of Music. 3 Cooking. 4 Paperbacks. 5 Girls. 6 Bear. 7 Sister. 8 Miss Marple. 9 Am I Bovvered. 10 Louvre. 11 Delia Smith. 12 Chocolate. 13 Bible. 14 Nelson Mandela. 15 Jamie Oliver. 16 Schindler's List. 17 The Galaxy. 18 Fairy tales. 19 Irish. 20 Cookson. 21 Ronnie Corbett. 22 James Bond. 23 Rosie. 24 Glenn Hoddle. 25 King. 26 Jockey. 27 Dracula. 28 19th. 29 Elton. 30 Forsyth.

1 Mark Spitz won seven Olympic golds at record speeds doing what?
2 Which South American soccer team has won most World Cups?
3 How many seasons did Alan Shearer play for Newcastle – 3, 6 or 10?
4 Lyn Davies broke the British record in which jump event?
5 David Campese was leading try scorer for which country?
6 Which Sally was a world record hurdler and 1992 Olympic champion?
7 Who was made England's youngest ever football coach in 1996?
8 Did Roger Bannister run the first four-minute mile in Oxford or Cambridge?
9 Was Martina Hingis 13, 15 or 17 when she first won Wimbledon doubles?
10 Who was the first Rugby Union player to win 100 England caps?
11 Which Nigel was the first to win both F1 and Indy Car world championships?
12 Which record breaker Sebastian went on to become a Tory MP?
13 Which Tony made the first televised hole in one in Britain?
14 Who won the 100m in Seoul in record time before being disqualified?
15 Which Steve was six times World Snooker Champion in the 1980s?
16 For which former Iron Curtain country did Marita Koch break records?
17 Jerry Rice set a career touchdown record in which sport?
18 How many events were in Daley Thompson's speciality event?
19 Which Pete equalled Borg's five Wimbledon singles wins in 1998?
20 Which Gareth became Wales's youngest ever Rugby captain in 1968?
21 Alain Prost was the first to win the F1 world title for which country?
22 Bob Beaman held which Olympic jump record for over 20 years?
23 Who was Britain's only Men's 100m world record holder between 1983 and 1993?
24 Which David did Graham Gooch overtake to become England's highest-scoring Test player?
25 World record breaker Kip Keino is from which continent?
26 Did Nadia Comaneci first score a perfect Olympic 10 at 14, 18 or 21?
27 Which golfer Jack was first to achieve 15 career professional majors?
28 Colin Jackson was a world record holder in which event?
29 Who was the first player to score 100 goals in the Premiership?
30 Duncan Goodhew held British records in which sport?

Answers | Pot Luck 9 *(see Quiz 20)*

1 Paul Hunter 2 Gin. 3 Taj Mahal. 4 Dingoes. 5 Actor/Actress. 6 Violins. 7 Greece. 8 June. 9 Bridges. 10 May. 11 U2. 12 A stipend. 13 Red. 14 Kite-mark. 15 New York. 16 Albatross. 17 Coronation Street. 18 Sherry. 19 The worm. 20 Paul McCartney. 21 Bread. 22 45. 23 In the mouth. 24 Andrew Lloyd Webber. 25 St Paul's Cathedral. 26 Vertical. 27 Sheffield Utd. 28 Sugar, almonds. 29 Evangelism. 30 Magpie.

1 Which snooker star Paul tragically died of cancer in October 2006?
2 Which alcoholic drink contains juniper as a flavour?
3 By what name is the mausoleum at Agra, India normally known?
4 Which dogs are a serious pest in Australia?
5 What would your profession be if you were a member of Equity?
6 Which instruments did Antonio Stradivari produce?
7 Which country is famous for moussaka?
8 In which month is Father's Day in the UK?
9 Pontoon and suspension are both types of which construction?
10 What did the "M" stand for in Louisa M. Alcott's name?
11 Who had the 2005 No. 1 single "Sometimes You Can't Make It on Your Own"?
12 What is a salary paid to a clergyman called?
13 What colour is cochineal?
14 The British Standards Institute uses what mark as a sign of approval?
15 Which American city is served by Kennedy Airport?
16 Which bird has the largest wing span?
17 Which soap is set in the city which hosted the 2002 Commonwealth Games?
18 What kind of drink is Amontillado?
19 What does an early bird catch, according to the proverb?
20 Which Beatle's daughter is a dress designer?
21 Bloomers and baps are both types of what?
22 How many years are there in four and a half decades?
23 Where are your incisors?
24 Who, together with Tim Rice, wrote "Evita"?
25 Where is Lord Nelson buried?
26 On a staircase are the risers flat or vertical?
27 Paddy Kenny was an ever present as which club reached the Premiership?
28 What are the two ingredients of marzipan?
29 Billy Graham is famous for which branch of Christianity?
30 Which black and white bird is usually accused of stealing?

Quiz 21

Science: Communication

Answers – page 30

LEVEL 1

1 Is 0207 the dialling code for central Manchester or central London?
2 Which mobile phone company shares its name with a fruit?
3 If you dial 1471 whose number are you given?
4 Which four letters preface access to an Internet website?
5 What is the normal size of a floppy disk?
6 NDR is a broadcasting company from which country?
7 What are held in the hands to communicate through semaphore?
8 The fingertips represent which five letters in sign language?
9 112 is an alternative to which number?
10 A modem connects a computer to what?
11 Qantas Airways originated in which country?
12 Which cross-Channel link has its French terminus at Coquelles?
13 Tresco airport links which Isles to the UK?
14 What does a letter c enclosed in a circle stand for?
15 Which country has most Internet users in the world?
16 What does D stand for in IDD?
17 Which character divides the person from the place in an email address?
18 Which type of clock works from shadows?
19 Numbers beginning with 0800 usually cost how much to the caller?
20 On a standard keyboard which letter is to the right of Q?
21 Combinations of which two signs are used in Morse code?
22 What country are PanAm based in?
23 In texting what does TMI stand for?
24 Which number do you ring to contact a BT operator?
25 Which country's airline has the code PK?
26 What is the American version of the British post code?
27 With BT calls when does daytime end Monday to Friday?
28 What does "I" stand for in IT?
29 What is the internet code for the United Kingdom?
30 Ryan Air is a budget airline from which country?

Answers | Pot Luck 10 *(see Quiz 22)*

1 Pastry. 2 Mr Hyde. 3 Jewellery. 4 Red. 5 Loudspeakers. 6 Marriage. 7 Flamingo. 8 Table Mountain. 9 The Rank Organisation. 10 Three. 11 Senorita. 12 Russia. 13 Wolves. 14 Disraeli. 15 Dame Edna Everage. 16 Hong Kong. 17 Church/Cathedral. 18 Agenda. 19 Andrew. 20 Three. 21 Pears. 22 Shrew. 23 The Mayflower. 24 Helen Mirren. 25 Green. 26 Wuthering Heights. 27 Bridgetown. 28 Sultana. 29 Penultimate. 30 Hammer.

1 Choux, puff and short are all types of what?
2 Who was the more unpleasant – Dr Jekyll or Mr Hyde?
3 Generally what is Hatton Gardon in London famous for?
4 What colour is carmine?
5 What are tweeters and woofers?
6 Which ceremony is associated with orange blossom?
7 Which pink bird sleeps on one leg?
8 Which mountain overlooks Cape Town, South Africa?
9 Which British film company used a symbol of a man striking a gong?
10 How many of Will Young's first singles made No. 1?
11 What is the Spanish word for a young or single lady?
12 Where was the news agency Tass based?
13 At which club did Mick McCarthy take over from Glenn Hoddle?
14 Who was the first Jewish Prime Minister in Britain?
15 Comedian Barry Humphries plays which female character?
16 Which colony ceased to be British in June 1997?
17 Where would you be if you were in a transept?
18 What is the list of the subjects to be discussed at a meeting called?
19 Which Prince served in the Falklands War?
20 In the old saying, how many makes a crowd if two are company?
21 Conference and Cornice are types of which fruit?
22 Which animal needs "Taming" in the title of the Shakespeare play?
23 Aboard which ship in 1620 did the Pilgrim Fathers sail to America?
24 Which Helen was a star of the movie "Gosford Park"?
25 What colour is angelica?
26 What connects singer Kate Bush with novelist Emily Brontë?
27 What is the capital of Barbados?
28 What is a wife of a sultan called?
29 What word describes something being next to last?
30 Which British studios were famed for their horror movies of the 1950s, 60s and 70s?

Answers	Science: Communications *(see Quiz 21)*

1 London. 2 Orange. 3 Last person to have called you. 4 http (not all have www).
5 3.5ins. 6 Germany. 7 Flags. 8 Vowels. 9 999. 10 Telephone. 11 Australia.
12 Channel Tunnel. 13 Scilly Isles. 14 Copyright. 15 USA. 16 Dialling. 17 @. 18
Sundial. 19 Nothing. 20 W. 21 Dots & dashes. 22 USA. 23 Too Much Information.
24 100. 25 Pakistan. 26 Zip. 27 6 pm. 28 Information. 29 .uk. 30 Ireland.

Quiz 23 | Pop: 70s

1 Which country did Abba come from?

2 Which 70s pop movie with John Travolta was re-released in 1998?

3 Which band did Diana Ross leave at the start of the decade?

4 T Rex was led by which singer?

5 What colour was Debbie Harry's hair which named her band?

6 "Maggie May" provided whom with his first No. 1?

7 Kiki Dee's biggest 70s hit was with whom?

8 Where did Supertramp have Breakfast in 1979?

9 Who was lead singer with the Boomtown Rats?

10 Who cleaned Wimbledon Common and cleaned up in the charts in '74?

11 What went with Peaches in the 70s charts?

12 Who had a posthumous hit with "Way Down"?

13 Song for whom was Elton John's first instrumental hit?

14 Which World Cup football squad did Rod Stewart have a hit with?

15 Which Rollers had two No. 1s in 1975?

16 Who had a single hit from the album "Bat Out of Hell"?

17 Izhar Cohen and Alphabeta won Eurovision for which country?

18 Which brothers included Wayne, Donny and Little Jimmy?

19 Whose first hit was "Wuthering Heights"?

20 Which 70s B side for Queen became a football anthem?

21 Which Abba hit became the name of an Alan Partridge spoof?

22 Which Gary's first hit was as Tubeway Army?

23 Which hostel did the Village People visit in the 70s?

24 How many performers made up The Carpenters?

25 Which soccer side had a hit with "I'm Forever Blowing Bubbles"?

26 "Tubular Bells" is credited with establishing which record label?

27 Which band were "Part of the Union"?

28 Which Bryan founded Roxy Music?

29 Who celebrated his "Ding-A-Ling" in song?

30 Who had the last 70s Xmas No. 1 with "Another Brick in the Wall"?

---

1 Played in 2005, which team won the first FA Cup Final decided on penalties?
2 Which British sausage is traditionally sold in a coil?
3 What is the luxury hotel and country club called in "The Archers"?
4 Which profession is associated with Savile Row?
5 What colour is the flower of an oil seed rape plant?
6 How many packs of playing cards are needed to play Canasta?
7 Bewick, Black and Whooper are all types of what?
8 Which pop star sang about his blue suede shoes?
9 Which animals live in a holt?
10 For which type of dance was Nijinsky famous?
11 In which country is the Algarve Coast?
12 Which voice is higher - a tenor or a baritone?
13 What colour is the St Andrew's cross on the Scottish flag?
14 Which University Is based in Milton Keynes?
15 Who in AD 434 was King of the Huns?
16 Who invented the dot system with which the blind can read by touch?
17 On whose feast day did King Wenceslas look out?
18 Which boy band made the No. 1 album "World of Our Own"?
19 An abacus helps you do what?
20 Which actress sang "A Spoonful of Sugar" in "Mary Poppins"?
21 Which musical does "Climb Every Mountain" come from?
22 The anaconda is native to which continent?
23 How many legs does a spider have?
24 Who wrote the waltz called "The Blue Danube"?
25 Who was the most famous dancing partner of Fred Astaire?
26 What are Gorgonzola, Dolcelatte and Pecorino?
27 On which board game are The Strand, Mayfair and Park Lane?
28 At which Scottish school was Prince Charles educated?
29 What colour is the spot on the Japanese flag?
30 Which Ali is one of the alter egos of Sacha Baron Cohen?

Quiz 25 | TV: Sitcoms | Answers – page 34

1 What is the profession of Geraldine Grainger of Dibley?
2 How do Men Martin Clunes and Neil Morrissey behave in the sitcom?
3 In which country is "Kath & Kim" set?
4 Alphabetically which of the characters in "Friends" comes first?
5 "Whatever Happened to the Likely Lads?" was the sequel to what?
6 Which sitcom classic was about self-sufficiency in Surbiton?
7 How did Hyacinth pronounce "Bucket" in "Keeping Up Appearances"?
8 Which show about Grace Brothers' store had a rerun in 1998?
9 What was the sequel to "Yes Minister"?
10 Which sitcom about the Trotters was originally to be called Readies?
11 Which series featured the character David Brent?
12 Which Penelope alias Audrey was "To the Manor Born"?
13 How many children feature in the sitcom about Bill and Ben Porter?
14 Which Ronnie played Arkwright in "Open All Hours"?
15 Ian McShane starred in which sitcom about a shady antiques dealer?
16 In which historical sitcom did Baldrick first appear?
17 Which show was originally to have been called "Your Bottom"?
18 Which Felicity was the star of "Solo"?
19 In which sitcom did Joanna Lumley play champagne-swilling Patsy?
20 What are the names of the Birds in "Birds of a Feather"?
21 In "Dad's Army", who called Sgt Wilson Uncle Arthur?
22 Frasier was a spin-off from which series based in a Boston bar?
23 Which Craig co-wrote and starred in "The Royle Family"?
24 Which wartime sitcom featured Rene and Edith Artois?
25 Who played Jean, husband of Lionel, in "As Time Goes By"?
26 "Goodnight Sweetheart" is set in the 1940s and which other decade?
27 Which series was based on Butlin's and Pontin's?
28 What was Anton Rodgers' legal job in "May to December"?
29 Which Family is a sitcom with ex-Mrs Merton Caroline Aherne?
30 What is Mrs Victor Meldrew's first name?

Answers | Pot Luck 12 *(see Quiz 26)*

1 Butterflies. 2 Pork Pie. 3 The Sahara. 4 Horse racing. 5 Wright Brothers. 6 John Ridd. 7 Medicines/Drugs. 8 50 Cent. 9 Fox. 10 Red/green. 11 Asp. 12 Three. 13 Davina McCall. 14 Small pieces of wood. 15 Their wedding. 16 Flower/Shrub. 17 Otter. 18 Flanders. 19 Baloo and Mowgli. 20 Australia. 21 Four. 22 1970s. 23 Italy. 24 Stamps. 25 Blue. 26 Peppermint. 27 Dove. 28 Tom Jones. 29 Soprano. 30 The English Channel.

1 Red Admirals, Fritillaries and Tortoiseshells are all what?

2 Which pie is Melton Mowbray renowned for?

3 Which has more rainfall, the Sahara or Antarctica?

4 Which sport would you see at Chepstow?

5 Which brothers made the first manned powered aero flight in 1903?

6 Who is the main male character in the novel "Lorna Doone"?

7 What was sold by an apothecary?

8 "Get Rich Quick or Die Tryin'" was the breakthrough album for which artist?

9 Which animals live in an earth or lair?

10 Along with white, what colours appear on the Italian flag?

11 Which snake is it said Cleopatra used to poison herself?

12 How many ships came sailing by according to the carol?

13 Who presented the very first series of "Big Brother"?

14 What is chipboard made from?

15 Catherine Zeta Jones and Michael Douglas sued about photos from which event?

16 What is a poinsettia?

17 In the novel what kind of animal was Tarka?

18 Bruges is the capital of which part of Belgium?

19 Which characters sang "The Bare Necessities" in "The Jungle Book"?

20 Which country did keeper Mark Schwarzer play for in soccer's 2006 World Cup?

21 How many wings does a bee have?

22 In which decade did Britain convert to decimal currency?

23 Sardinia is part of which country?

24 What are collected by a philatelist?

25 What colour is the background of the Scottish flag?

26 What flavour is crème de menthe?

27 What type of bird are Ring, Turtle and Collared?

28 Which veteran Welsh pop singer was knighted in the 2006 New Year Honours List?

29 Which is the highest female singing voice?

30 Which sea is called La Manche by the French?

| **Answers** | TV: Sitcoms *(see Quiz 25)* |

1 Vicar. 2 Badly. 3 Australia. 4 Chandler. 5 The Likely Lads. 6 The Good Life. 7 "Bouquet". 8 Are You Being Served? 9 Yes Prime Minister. 10 Only Fools and Horses. 11 The Office. 12 Keith. 13 2 Point 4. 14 Barker. 15 Lovejoy. 16 Blackadder. 17 Bottom. 18 Kendall. 19 Absolutely Fabulous. 20 Sharon & Tracy. 21 Pike. 22 Cheers. 23 Craig Cash. 24 Allo Allo. 25 Judi Dench. 26 1990s. 27 Hi-De-Hi! 28 Solicitor. 29 Royle. 30 Margaret.

Quiz 27 The Movies: Comedies

Answers – page 36

LEVEL 1

1 Which Mr Atkinson created the spoof spy character Johnny English?
2 Sarah Michelle Gellar starred in the movie about which ghost-hunting dog?
3 What was the name of Sacha Baron Cohen's Kazakhstan character?
4 "Addams Family Values" was the follow-up to what?
5 Which west London borough is associated with classic comedies?
6 What age group are the performers in the gangster film "Bugsy Malone"?
7 Which cartoon set in Bedrock starred John Goodman in the human version?
8 What type of Adventure did Bill and Ted have?
9 What sort of farm animal was Babe?
10 Which Tom starred in "Jerry Maguire"?
11 Which Hill in London was the location for a Hugh Grant / Julia Roberts movie?
12 Whose World did Mike Myers and Dana Garvey live in?
13 "A Fish Called" ... what was a John Cleese & Jamie Lee Curtis classic?
14 What was Whoopi Goldberg disguised as in "Sister Act"?
15 Which group sang the theme song for "Four Weddings and a Funeral"?
16 Which Jim was the shy bank clerk in "The Mask"?
17 Forrest Gump said life was like a box of what?
18 Which Julia was the "Pretty Woman" in the film's title?
19 Which British comedy duo were the stars of "The Magnificent Two"?
20 What did Robin Williams in "Mrs Doubtfire" and Dustin Hoffman in "Tootsie" have in common?
21 What unusual handicap did Bernie have as a host in "A Weekend at Bernie's"?
22 Which film of a Book featured "The Bare Necessities"?
23 Which Sid's first Carry On was "Carry On Constable"?
24 To whom did someone say "I Shrunk the Kids" in the film title?
25 Which spinach-loving cartoon character was played by Robin Williams?
26 Which Colin played Mark Darcy in the movie about Bridget Jones?
27 Was Patrick Swayze or Demi Moore the Ghost in the 1990 film?
28 "Look Who's Talking Too" was the sequel to what?
29 Who was the Queen of the Desert in the transvestite comedy?
30 Which Inspector played by Peter Sellers was in "The Pink Panther"?

Answers	Pot Luck 13 *(see Quiz 28)*

1 Sugababes. 2 Stop bleeding. 3 The King and I. 4 Canada. 5 Sir Cliff Richard.
6 Tower of London. 7 Blue/violet. 8 Suffolk. 9 General Strike. 10 Cricket. 11
Russian. 12 Australia. 13 24. 14 Sturgeon. 15 Heart. 16 White. 17 Man Utd and
Real Madrid. 18 Spirit level. 19 Anna Sewell. 20 Maundy money. 21 Kayaks. 22
Oranges. 23 All for one and one for all. 24 Like a Virgin. 25 Windsor. 26 A Sharp.
27 Rolf Harris. 28 Cambridge. 29 Red/white. 30 Men's Marathon.

Quiz 28 | Pot Luck 13

1 Who had hits in 2005 with "Ugly" and "Push the Button"?
2 What is a tourniquet used for in First Aid?
3 Which musical is based on a book called "Anna and the King of Siam"?
4 The chipmunk is native to America and which other country?
5 Who was pop's first Knight?
6 Where in London is the ceremony of the keys held each night?
7 What colour is indigo?
8 Which East Anglian county is often called "Constable Country"?
9 In 1926 which General crisis happened in England?
10 Which sport links Ted Dexter, Peter May and Ray Illingworth?
11 What was the nationality of composer Rimsky-Korsakov?
12 Budgerigars are native to which country?
13 How many carats in pure gold?
14 Caviar comes traditionally from which fish?
15 What does a cardiologist study?
16 What colour are Aylesbury ducks?
17 Ruud van Nistelrooy and David Beckham were at which two clubs together?
18 What is used to check something is level by a builder?
19 Who wrote the novel "Black Beauty"?
20 What does the Queen give out on the day before Good Friday?
21 What are the sealskin boats used by Eskimos called?
22 What did Nell Gwyn sell when Charles II first saw her?
23 What was the motto of the Three Musketeers?
24 Which Madonna song was performed by Jim Broadbent in "Moulin Rouge"?
25 Which castle is in the royal county of Berkshire?
26 If a musical note is lowered by a flat, what raises it?
27 Who was the first presenter of "Animal Hospital"?
28 In which city is the River Cam?
29 Apart from blue, what other two colours appear on the Dutch flag?
30 What was the final event of the 2004 Athens Olympics?

Answers | The Movies: Comedies (see Quiz 27)

1 Rowan. 2 Scooby Doo. 3 Borat. 4 The Addams Family. 5 Ealing. 6 Children. 7 The Flintstones. 8 Excellent. 9 Pig. 10 Cruise. 11 Notting Hill. 12 Wayne's. 13 Wanda. 14 Nun. 15 Wet Wet Wet. 16 Carrey. 17 Chocolates. 18 Roberts. 19 Morecambe & Wise. 20 Dressed in drag. 21 Dead. 22 The Jungle Book. 23 James. 24 Honey. 25 Popeye. 26 Colin Firth. 27 Patrick Swayze. 28 Look Who's Talking. 29 Priscilla. 30 Clouseau.

Quiz 29 — Geography: The UK

Answers – page 38

1 Is Holy Island off the east or west coast of England?
2 What is a native of Aberdeen called?
3 Is London's Docklands, north, south, east or west of the city?
4 The Angel of the North was erected next to which major road?
5 Which English gorge takes its name from a nearby village famous for its cheese?
6 Which county has the abbreviation Beds?
7 St Anne's lies to the south of which British seaside resort?
8 Which Royal residence stands by the river Dee?
9 In which country is the UK's highest mountain?
10 What sort of an institution in London is Bart's?
11 On a London Tube map the Central Line is what colour?
12 In which Scottish city did you find the Gorbals?
13 Which motorway links London to Winchester?
14 Which Isle off the south coast of England is a county in its own right?
15 What is Britain's most southerly country?
16 Norwich is the administrative centre of which county?
17 In which city did the National Trust buy the childhood home of Paul McCartney?
18 Which motorway runs almost parallel to the A4?
19 With which profession is London's Harley Street associated?
20 What is Britain's largest international airport?
21 In which county is Land's End?
22 What colour are most London buses?
23 Which motorway goes from Lancashire to Yorkshire east to west?
24 What is the background colour of road signs to tourist sites?
25 In which part of the UK is "Land of My Fathers" a traditional song?
26 Winchester is the adminstrative seat of which county?
27 Aston University is near which Midlands city?
28 Most of the Lake District is in which county?
29 What red flower does Lancs have?
30 In which city is the Barbican Centre?

Answers | Pot Luck 14 (see Quiz 30)

1 Harry Potter. **2** Mozart. **3** A peach. **4** Sark. **5** Brown. **6** He who laughs last. **7** 1953. **8** Carpets. **9** Diagonally. **10** Spain. **11** JCB Song. **12** Black/Yellow. **13** A vixen. **14** Cakes. **15** Edmund. **16** Afghanistan. **17** Colour. **18** Isle of Wight. **19** A fish. **20** 39. **21** Blackberry. **22** Zambezi. **23** Herring. **24** Marie Antoinette. **25** Spam. **26** Victor Hugo. **27** Puffin. **28** Red, yellow & blue. **29** Four. **30** Italy.

1 Daniel Radcliffe played which famous boy on screen?
2 Who composed the opera "The Marriage of Figaro"?
3 What type of fruit is a nectarine?
4 Which of the four Channel Islands is the smallest?
5 What colour is sepia?
6 Who, according to the proverb, laughs longest?
7 In which year was Everest conquered?
8 Which house furnishing is associated with the town of Kidderminster?
9 How does a bishop move in chess?
10 The drink sangria comes from which European country?
11 What was Nizlopi's Xmas No. 1 single in 2005?
12 What two colours other than red appear on the Belgian flag?
13 What is a female fox called?
14 What is sold in a patisserie?
15 Who is Peter's brother in "The Lion, the Witch and the Wardrobe"?
16 .af is the internet code for which country?
17 What can a chameleon lizard change?
18 The rocks called The Needles are close to which island?
19 What is a barracuda?
20 How many steps were there in the title of the novel by John Buchan?
21 A loganberry is a cross between a raspberry and what?
22 Which river are the Victoria Falls on?
23 Sardines and pilchards are part of which fish family?
24 Which French Queen was executed in the French Revolution?
25 What name was spiced ham given during wartime?
26 Who wrote "The Hunchback of Notre Dame"?
27 Which seabird is associated with Lundy Island?
28 What are the three primary colours in art?
29 How many wings does a moth have?
30 From which country does the football team Juventus come from?

Answers | Geography: The UK *(see Quiz 29)*

1 East. 2 Aberdonian. 3 East. 4 A1. 5 Cheddar. 6 Bedfordshire. 7 Blackpool.
8 Balmoral. 9 Scotland. 10 Hospital. 11 Red. 12 Glasgow. 13 M3. 14 Isle of
Wight. 15 England. 16 Norfolk. 17 Liverpool. 18 M4. 19 Medical profession. 20
Heathrow. 21 Cornwall. 22 Red. 23 M62. 24 Brown. 25 Wales. 26 Hampshire.
27 Birmingham. 28 Cumbria. 29 Rose. 30 London.

Quiz 31 | Sport: Who's Who?

1 Whom was tennis star Martina Hingis named after?

2 Which lauded soccer star was born Edson Arantes do Nascimento?

3 Which French footballer David advertised L'Oreal hair products?

4 Golfer Ernie Els is from which African country?

5 Which British tennis player was born on Greg Rusedski's first birthday?

6 Jonah Lomu plays for which international side?

7 Athlete Kelly Holmes was formerly a member of which armed service?

8 Which Paula had a hat-trick of London Marathon wins this millennium?

9 Which snooker champ Ray was nicknamed Dracula?

10 What sort of eye accessory does Chris Eubank wear?

11 At which sport was Nokolai Valuev a world champion?

12 Which Monica was stabbed in the back by a fanatical Graf supporter?

13 Was tennis's Michael Chang from Hong Kong or the USA?

14 Which racing driver was first to clock up more than 75 F1 wins?

15 Rahul Dravid captained which international cricket team?

16 Which four-legged, three-times Grand National winner died in 1995?

17 Which Greg rejected a maple leaf for a Union Jack in the 1990s?

18 Who founded the book known as the cricketer's Bible?

19 Rachel Hayhoe Flint is a famous name in which sport?

20 Who was Ben Johnson running for when disqualified in Seoul?

21 Which Princess won the 1971 European Three Day Event?

22 Which David has kept goal for Liverpool, West Ham, Manchester City & Portsmouth?

23 Which temperamental tennis player was dubbed Superbrat?

24 Which Jenny was the first woman to train a Grand National winner?

25 Who was Australia's cricket captain in the 2006 ICC Trophy final?

26 Which boxer's catchphrase was "Know what I mean 'Arry"?

27 Which disappearing horse last won the Derby in 1981?

28 Who founded the Stewart motor racing team?

29 What was cricket umpire Harold Bird's nickname?

30 Who became the first black manager of a Premiership club when he took over at Chelsea in 1996?

Answers | Pot Luck 15 *(see Quiz 32)*

1 Four. 2 Loire. 3 McFly. 4 Cornwall. 5 South-south-east. 6 Thomas Hardy. 7 Slavery. 8 King. 9 Red/White. 10 USA. 11 Seven. 12 Kew. 13 Hadrian's Wall. 14 Purple. 15 Mont Blanc. 16 Venice. 17 June. 18 Malta. 19 Grey. 20 Apple. 21 Queen's Counsel. 22 The Black Death/Bubonic Plague. 23 Cherie Blair. 24 A spring tide. 25 Argentina. 26 Daisy. 27 West Ham. 28 Pigeon racing. 29 Melon. 30 Switzerland.

Quiz 32 | Pot Luck 15

Answers – page 39

1 How many wings does a butterfly have?
2 Which river is the longest in France?
3 Who had 2005 hits with "I Wanna Hold You" and "Ultraviolet"?
4 In which county is Bodmin Moor?
5 Which compass point is opposite North-north-west?
6 Which Thomas wrote "The Mayor of Casterbridge"?
7 Which trade was abolished in 1807 in the British Empire?
8 Which chess piece should be protected at all costs?
9 What two colours are on the Austrian flag?
10 In which country was there a North v. South civil war from 1861–65?
11 How many players are in a netball team?
12 Where in Britain are the Royal Botanic Gardens?
13 Which ancient wall crosses England from Wallsend to Solway?
14 What colour is an aubergine?
15 Which mountain is the highest in the Alps?
16 The artist Canaletto was associated with which Italian city?
17 In which month is the Trooping of the Colour?
18 Which island is also called the George Cross Island?
19 Which colour is linked to Sir Ian McKellen's character Gandalf?
20 Cox, Braeburn and Gala are all kinds of which fruit?
21 In legal terms, what do the initials QC stand for?
22 Which disaster struck England in the 1340s?
23 Carole Caplin found fame as adviser to which famous wife?
24 What is the opposite of a neap tide?
25 Which country lies immediately east of Chile?
26 Who was asked to ride "a bicycle made for two" in the song?
27 Jermain Defoe joined Tottenham Hotspur from which other London club?
28 The National Homing Union is involved with which leisure pursuit?
29 What kind of fruit can be cantaloupe?
30 Which country as well as France is Lake Geneva in?

Answers | Sport: Who's Who? *(see Quiz 31)*

1 Martina Navratilova. 2 Pele. 3 Ginola. 4 South Africa. 5 Tim Henman. 6 New Zealand. 7 Army. 8 Paula Radcliffe. 9 Reardon. 10 Monocle. 11 Boxing. 12 Seles. 13 USA. 14 Michael Schumacher. 15 India. 16 Red Rum. 17 Rusedski. 18 Wisden. 19 Women's cricket. 20 Canada. 21 Anne. 22 David James. 23 John McEnroe. 24 Pitman. 25 Ricky Ponting. 26 Frank Bruno. 27 Shergar. 28 Jackie Stewart. 29 Dickie Bird. 30 Ruud Gullit.

Quiz 33 — Pop: The 80s

Answers – page 42

LEVEL 1

1 Who went straight to No. 1 in 1981 with "Stand and Deliver"?
2 What colour Door gave Shakin' Stevens an 80s hit?
3 Which ex-Beatle had a hit with Stevie Wonder in 1982?
4 Whose album "Thriller" provided several hit singles?
5 Who was KC's backing Band?
6 Which Scot had chart success after Esther Rantzen's "The Big Time"?
7 Which BBC Radio station banned "Relax"?
8 Ravel's "Bolero" charted because of which skaters' Olympic success?
9 Which actor Robert was named in a Bananarama song title ?
10 Which Superstar Rat sang "Love Me Tender"?
11 Which Alison's nickname was Alf?
12 Which Elaine and Barbara topped the charts in 1985?
13 Which Mrs Andrew Lloyd Webber had a hit with "Pie Jesu"?
14 David Bowie and Mick Jagger had a hit after which Concert?
15 Elton John charted with "Nikita" at the same time as Sting had which coincidental hit?
16 Who had hits as part of Visage and Ultravox?
17 Who told you that you were "In the Army Now"?
18 Who fronted Culture Club?
19 Graham McPherson of Madness was known as what?
20 Which Kim reached No. 2 in 1981, 24 years after dad Marty?
21 Which Spanish singer had the UK's first chart topper in Spanish?
22 David Sylvian was part of which Asian-sounding band?
23 Who was the first ventriloquist in the charts with Orville?
24 Who teamed up with Annie Lennox in The Eurythmics?
25 Who was the then oldest man in the charts with "New York New York"?
26 Who joined Cliff Richard for his 80s "Living Doll"?
27 Which TV puppets sang "The Chicken Song"?
28 Which red-haired Royal liked "Lady in Red"?
29 Which future England coach joined Waddle on "Diamond Lights"?
30 Who had a Xmas No. 1 in 1988 after 30 years in the charts?

Answers | Pot Luck 16 *(see Quiz 34)*

1 Eton. 2 Raymond Briggs. 3 13. 4 Soft fruit. 5 Peter Kay. 6 A soliloquy. 7 Isle of Man. 8 Soccer (Portsmouth v. Man City). 9 Oranges. 10 French. 11 Horse Guards Parade. 12 Drugs. 13 Your Old Kit Bag. 14 Hats. 15 Honey. 16 Five. 17 Distillery. 18 His tools. 19 The Jordan. 20 Needles. 21 Blackbird. 22 Richard I. 23 Whales. 24 American Football. 25 Capricorn. 26 Pears. 27 November. 28 Lisa. 29 Esther Rantzen. 30 Harp.

41

1 Which school did Prince Harry attend when he was 13?
2 Which cartoonist was the creator of "The Snowman"?
3 How many are there in a baker's dozen?
4 What would you find in a punnet?
5 Who featured on Tony Christie's 2005 smash hit "Amarillo"?
6 What is a Shakespearan speech or scene with only one actor called?
7 Douglas is the capital town of which Isle?
8 Pedro Mendes was knocked out by Ben Thatcher in which sport?
9 The Spanish city of Seville is famous for which fruit?
10 What is the nationality of pianist Richard Clayderman?
11 Where does the Trooping of the Colour take place in London?
12 Pharmacology is the study of what?
13 Where, according to the song, should you pack up your troubles?
14 What is usually kept in a band-box?
15 What is the main ingredient in the drink mead?
16 In music, how many lines are there in a stave?
17 What name is given to the building where whisky is made?
18 According to the proverb, a bad workman always blames what?
19 Jesus Christ was baptised in which river?
20 What are inserted into the body during acupuncture?
21 According to rhyme which bird pecked off the maid's nose?
22 Which King was known as the "Lionheart"?
23 Beluga, Sperm and Blue are all types of what?
24 Which sport is played on a grid iron?
25 Which Zodiac sign is known as the sign of the goat?
26 What is perry made from?
27 In which month is the State Opening of Parliament in England?
28 Who is Bart Simpson's older sister?
29 Which presenter was the star of TV's "That's Esther"?
30 Which musical instrument is a national emblem of Ireland?

1 Which batter mix is an accompaniment to roast beef?
2 Which chef replaced Fern Britton on "Ready Steady Cook"?
3 What colour wine is Beaujolais Nouveau?
4 What colour is the flesh of an avocado?
5 What is the traditional colour for the outside of a stick of rock?
6 Would you eat or drink a Sally Lunn?
7 What type of egg is covered in sausage meat?
8 Scrumpy is a rough form of what?
9 Which mashed vegetable tops a shepherd's pie?
10 Which food has given its name to a road network near Birmingham?
11 Is a Spotted Dick a first course or a pudding?
12 Which fruit is associated with tennis at Wimbledon?
13 Champagne originated in which country?
14 Is a Melton Mowbray pie sweet or savoury?
15 What is a pistachio?
16 What sort of fruit is in a teacake?
17 Which chef Antony appeared in "I'm a Celebrity Get Me Out of Here"?
18 Which is more substantial, afternoon tea or high tea?
19 If you ate al fresco would you be indoors or out of doors?
20 What is the usual shape of a Camembert cheese?
21 Which soft pulpy peas are eaten with fish and chips?
22 What type of food may be served clotted?
23 What would you make in a cafetière?
24 What type of drink is Bristol Cream?
25 Is chowder a soup or a pudding?
26 A "pinta" is usually a pint of what?
27 Should red wine normally be drunk chilled or at room temperature?
28 Is there milk in a cappuccino coffee?
29 Are you more likely to eat a croissant at breakfast or supper?
30 Does celebrity chef Nick Nairn come from England, Scotland or Wales?

1 Which English King was also called "The Confessor"?
2 Don't hum it, but who had a smash European hit with "Axel F"?
3 Which football team play their home games at Goodison Park?
4 PG, 15 and 18 are all classifications for what?
5 Which manufacturer was the first to achieve more than 100 F1 Grand Prix wins?
6 How is US lawyer Hillary Roddam better known?
7 In Cockney rhyming slang, what are your mince pies?
8 According to the proverb, who is soon parted from his money?
9 From which Disney film does Cruella De Vil come from?
10 What is the capital of Iraq?
11 Which letter describes a soft lead pencil?
12 How long is an American president's term of office?
13 The Azores are a part of which European country?
14 Which Michael began his TV chat shows back in 1971?
15 What are the bars on a xylophone made from?
16 What is a mud skipper?
17 What is the second letter of the Greek alphabet?
18 In medicine, what do the initials ENT stand for?
19 With which Italian town is Saint Francis linked?
20 Blanket, back and buttonhole are all types of what?
21 Which Zodiac sign is known as the sign of the crab?
22 Whose life story was called "Stand By Your Man"?
23 Which wire is live in modern three-core electric cable?
24 From which country other than Australia did Anzac troops come from?
25 Who is the patron saint of mountaineers?
26 In which state of the US is the resort of Palm Springs?
27 How many consonants are in the English alphabet?
28 In "Peter Pan" what are the names of Wendy's brothers?
29 The port of Bergen is in which European country?
30 Edwin van der Sar joined Man Utd from which London club?

Answers	Leisure: Food & Drink 1 *(see Quiz 35)*

1 Yorkshire pudding. 2 Ainsley Harriott. 3 Red. 4 Green. 5 Pink. 6 Eat. 7 Scotch egg. 8 Cider. 9 Potato. 10 Spaghetti (junction). 11 Pudding. 12 Strawberries. 13 France. 14 Savoury. 15 Nut. 16 Currants and/or other dried fruit. 17 Antony Worrall Thompson. 18 High tea. 19 Out of doors. 20 Round. 21 Mushy peas. 22 Cream. 23 Coffee. 24 Sherry. 25 Soup. 26 Milk. 27 Room temperature. 28 Yes. 29 Breakfast. 30 Scotland.

Quiz 37 | Jamie Oliver

1 What type of chef was in the title of Jamie's first TV series?
2 What is Jamie's wife called?
3 In his early TV series how did Jamie travel around London?
4 Which number names the restaurant set up to help under-privileged kids?
5 In which decade of the 20th century did Jamie Oliver first find fame on TV?
6 What were the twizzlers made from in his programme about school dinners?
7 Did Jamie's parents run a pub or work in the theatre?
8 Which Cheeky charity set up by Jamie trains and mentors young people?
9 Which supermarket chain did Jamie advertise in the early 2000s?
10 In which county was Jamie brought up?
11 On which Channel was Jamie's series about school dinners?
12 In which decade of the 20th century was Jamie Oliver born?
13 Who or what are Poppy and Daisy in Jamie's life?
14 What does Jamie's favourite word "pukka" mean?
15 In which county is Jamie's Fifteen restaurant in Newquay?
16 Which Corporation broadcast Jamie's first TV series?
17 Which honour did he receive in the June 2003 Queen's Birthday Honours?
18 How many of Jamie's books had Naked in the title?
19 In "Jamie's Great Escape" which European country did he visit?
20 What was the name of his programme which first criticised school meals?
21 In which famous London Café was he first spotted by a TV producer?
22 In 2006, parents in which county pushed food through the school fence as a protest at Jamie's healthy options?
23 In which city was Jamie's first Fifteen restaurant?
24 What was the occupation of Nora Sands in one of Jamie's TV shows?
25 Which type of oil does Jamie use extensively in his cooking?
26 Was the soundtrack of Jamie's early TV series, rock 'n' roll or classical?
27 In which city were the first "Naked Chef" shows filmed?
28 Which Antonio ran a London restaurant where Jamie did some early training?
29 How many million pounds was added to the school dinner budget after Jamie's campaign, 180, 280 or 380?
30 How many people feature on the cover of "Cook with Jamie"?

Answers | Pot Luck 18 *(see Quiz 38)*

1 Fishermen. 2 Doctor. 3 Nothing. 4 Siam. 5 H. 6 Scorpio. 7 Bones. 8 Helsinki. 9 Jamie Oliver. 10 You spoil the child. 11 Violin. 12 Lorraine Kelly. 13 Bean. 14 Queen of Sheba. 15 John Prescott. 16 Royal Albert Hall 17 The Shannon. 18 30th November. 19 Double bass. 20 Dr Zhivago. 21 Radio 2. 22 The Mall. 23 Islam. 24 Weather reports. 25 Wiltshire. 26 A thief. 27 Brown. 28 Shakespeare. 29 Knots. 30 A long spoon.

1 What job was done by Peter and Andrew before they were disciples?
2 Ex-MP David Owen previously followed which profession?
3 If you are in your birthday suit, what are you wearing?
4 Thailand was formerly known by what name?
5 Which letter describes a hard leaded pencil?
6 Which Zodiac sign is usually shown as a scorpion?
7 Osteoporosis affects which part of the body?
8 Which city is the most northerly capital in Europe?
9 On TV who was the main character in "Jamie's Kitchen"?
10 According to the proverb, what happens if you spare the rod?
11 Stéphane Grappelli is associated with which musical instrument?
12 Which Scottish presenter is the star of GMTV's "LK Today"?
13 Which vegetable can be dwarf, runner and broad?
14 Which Queen made a visit to Solomon in the Bible?
15 Who was Tony Blair's first Deputy PM?
16 At which London venue did Cream reunite for four nights in May 2005?
17 Which river is the longest in the British Isles?
18 On which date is Saint Andrew's Day?
19 Which is largest – cello, viola or double bass?
20 Which epic film had the theme tune "Somewhere My Love"?
21 Terry Wogan's daily show is on which radio station?
22 Buckingham Palace is at the end of which famous London road?
23 A muezzin is an official of which religion?
24 John Kettley and Sian Davies presented what type of reports on TV?
25 In which county is Salisbury Plain?
26 In Cockney rhyming slang, what is a tea leaf?
27 What colour is the skin of a kiwi fruit?
28 What does "S" stand for in RSC?
29 What can be granny, sheepshank and bowline?
30 What do you need to sup with the devil, according to the proverb?

Quiz 39   Nature: Living World   Answers – page 48   LEVEL 1

1 Glaucoma affects which part of the body?
2 Which flightless bird lays the world's largest egg?
3 What is a puffball?
4 What happens to a female butterfly after it has laid its eggs?
5 In what type of environment do most crustaceans live?
6 Which natural disaster is measured on the Richter scale?
7 What is the main ingredient of glass?
8 Does a millipede have more, fewer, or exactly 1,000 feet?
9 An ore is a mineral which contains a what?
10 Is the whale shark a mammal like the whale, or a fish like the shark?
11 Which bird is the symbol of the USA?
12 Are butterflies more colourful in warmer or cooler countries?
13 What sort of rock is lava?
14 Which is larger, the dolphin or the porpoise?
15 Which organ of the body has the aorta?
16 How many bones does a slug have?
17 Are worker ants male or female?
18 Altocumulus is a type of what?
19 What is the main source of energy in our ecosystem?
20 Which name for remains of plants and animals which lived on Earth means "dug up"?
21 On which continent is the world's largest glacier?
22 Kelp is a type of what?
23 What order of mammals does the gibbon belong to?
24 What is the staple food of over half of the world's population?
25 Which creatures are larvae and pupae before being adults?
26 Are most bats visible at night or by day?
27 Which part of a jellyfish has stinging cells?
28 Natural rubber is obtained from what?
29 What is the mother of all the bees in a colony called?
30 The giant sequoia is the largest living what?

1 What was made "On a Dance Floor" according to Madonna's album title?
2 What is sugar added to, to make meringues?
3 Which poet laureate Sir John died in 1984?
4 What can pass through something if it is porous?
5 In which Scottish city are the Rebus novels set?
6 How many Oscars did "Titanic" win – 6, 11 or 14?
7 In the Bible, which angel foretold the birth of Jesus?
8 What youth group took to wearing parkas?
9 What is the German word for the number three?
10 Which children's favourite bear said he had "very little brain"?
11 Which English king reputedly commanded the sea to retreat?
12 What is the letter "V" if A is Alpha and B is Bravo?
13 Who is famous for saying, "Nice to see you, to see you nice"?
14 What is a popular name for the flower the antirrhinum?
15 Which Yorkshire city were Pulp from?
16 In music what does presto mean?
17 What object was invented by Lewis Waterman in 1884?
18 Tuscany is in which European country?
19 In the world of flying, what do the initials ETA stand for?
20 What is retsina?
21 Which soccer striker Robbie returned to Liverpool in 2006?
22 Which monster first hit the headlines in 1933?
23 How many edges are there around a 20-pence coin?
24 What are the New Zealand rugby union team called?
25 According to the rhyme, who killed Cock Robin?
26 The Samba originated in which South American country?
27 Who wrote "It Shouldn't Happen to a Vet"?
28 The port of Gdansk is in which country?
29 Would you eat, play or sit on a sitar?
30 Which Des presented the 1990s version of "Take Your Pick"?

Answers	**Nature: Living World** *(see Quiz 39)*

1 Eyes. 2 Ostrich. 3 Fungus. 4 It dies. 5 Water. 6 Earthquake. 7 Sand. 8 Fewer.
9 Metal. 10 Fish. 11 Eagle. 12 Warmer. 13 Volcanic rock. 14 Dolphin. 15 Heart.
16 None. 17 Female. 18 Cloud. 19 Sun. 20 Fossil. 21 Antarctica. 22 Seaweed.
23 Primates (also accept apes). 24 Rice. 25 Insects. 26 At night. 27 Tentacles. 28 Rubber Tree. 29 Queen. 30 Tree.

1 Which ex-James Bond has "Scotland Forever" tattooed on his arm?
2 Which Jools starred in "Spiceworld: The Movie"?
3 Which Irish-born 007 starred in "Tomorrow Never Dies"?
4 Which Grease actor danced with Princess Diana at the White House?
5 Which sleuth did Albert Finney play in Agatha Christie's "Murder on the Orient Express"?
6 Which top-selling rapper made his movie debut in "8 Mile"?
7 Who was the star of "Moonwalker" after being in The Jackson Five?
8 Which bespectacled US actor/director directed the musical "Everyone Says I Love You"?
9 What type of hat was Charlie Chaplin most famous for?
10 Who is Emma Forbes' actor/director dad?
11 Who was named after her home town of Winona?
12 Which knighted pop singer wrote the music for "The Lion King"?
13 Hayley Mills is the daughter of which knighted actor?
14 Who separated from husband Bruce Willis in 1998?
15 Which newspaper magnate bought 20th Century-Fox in 1985?
16 Who was Sid played by Gary Oldman in "Sid and Nancy"?
17 What name usually associated with a schoolbag did Woody Allen give his son?
18 Which Welsh actor Sir Anthony bought part of Mount Snowdon in 1998?
19 Which pop star Tina starred in "Mad Max Beyond the Thunderdome"?
20 Which Ms Foster swapped her real first name from Alicia?
21 In rhyming slang what financial term is Gregory Peck?
22 Which child star was Shirley MacLaine named after?
23 Who appeared first at Madame Tussaud's, Harrison Ford or Hugh Grant?
24 Who starred as Steed in the film version of "The Avengers"?
25 Which boxer played himself in "The Greatest"?
26 Film buff Barry Norman is a member of which club with the same name as a Marx brother?
27 Who sang "It's Not Unusual" in "Mars Attacks!"?
28 Which actress appeared on the cover of "The Sound of Music" movie DVD?
29 Judi Dench played which character known by a letter in the Bond movies?
30 "There's Something About Mary" and "Gangs of New York" starred which actress?

Answers | Pot Luck 20 *(see Quiz 42)*

1 John Lennon. 2 Ian Fleming. 3 Cornwall. 4 Skeleton. 5 Oporto. 6 Green. 7 Diamond. 8 Pirates. 9 Deux. 10 August. 11 Wrestling. 12 Intelligence. 13 Draw. 14 Spain. 15 Rice. 16 Indianapolis. 17 Sylvester. 18 Dover. 19 Deer. 20 Light. 21 Blair. 22 42. 23 BBC. 24 Pierce Brosnan. 25 Japan. 26 Horse racing. 27 Orange/Yellow. 28 An elephant. 29 The sea. 30 Par.

1 In December 2005, which pop legend was remembered 25 years after his murder?

2 Who wrote the novel "You Only Live Twice"?

3 Which English county has a border with only one other county?

4 What collective name is given to the structure of bones in the body?

5 The drink port takes its name from which town?

6 What colour is normally associated with ecological groups?

7 What is the hardest substance known to man?

8 Which people are associated with the Jolly Roger flag?

9 What is the French word for the number two?

10 Alphabetically, which is the second of the 12 calendar months?

11 With which sport do we associate a half nelson?

12 In a Steven Spielberg movie if A stood for Artificial what did I stand for?

13 What was the result of the final Ashes Test match of the 2005 series?

14 Which country did the paso doble dance originate in?

15 What type of food can be pilau?

16 In which American city is a 500-mile motor race run annually?

17 Which cartoon cat never manages to catch Tweetie Pie?

18 What is Britain's busiest ferry passenger port?

19 What kind of animal is a hind?

20 What can pass through something if it is translucent?

21 Which Tony first became MP for Sedgefield in 1983?

22 How many sides do seven hexagons have?

23 Was "Crackerjack" shown on BBC or ITV?

24 Who played James Bond in "Die Another Day"?

25 Which country does the drink sake come from?

26 For which sport is Pat Eddery famous?

27 What colour is saffron?

28 In children's books and on TV, what kind of animal is Babar?

29 David Attenborough's "The Blue Planet" was about life in what type of location?

30 What term is used in golf to indicate the stroke rating for each hole?

| **Answers** | **The Movies: Who's Who?** *(see Quiz 41)* |

1 Sean Connery. 2 Holland. 3 Pierce Brosnan. 4 John Travolta. 5 Poirot. 6 Eminem. 7 Michael Jackson. 8 Woody Allen. 9 Bowler. 10 Bryan Forbes. 11 Winona Ryder. 12 Sir Elton John. 13 Sir John Mills. 14 Demi Moore. 15 Rupert Murdoch. 16 Vicious. 17 Satchel. 18 Hopkins. 19 Turner. 20 Jodie Foster. 21 Cheque. 22 Shirley Temple. 23 Harrison Ford. 24 Ralph Fiennes. 25 Muhammad Ali. 26 Groucho. 27 Tom Jones. 28 Julie Andrews 29 M. 30 Cameron Diaz.

Quiz 43 | Hobbies & Leisure 2 | Answers – page 52 | LEVEL 1

1 What is a bookmaker's licensed premises called?
2 What shape is the target in archery?
3 Where on a dartboard is the bull?
4 Which cubes are necessary for a game of craps?
5 Which direction do you go if you are abseiling?
6 What sort of Park is at Whipsnade?
7 Which locomotive identification hobby shares its name with a controversial 1990s movie?
8 In which game do you aim to call "House!"?
9 Yoga was developed from which nation's religion?
10 Is scuba practised above or below the water's surface?
11 From which part of a vehicle might you sell goods to raise cash?
12 What name is given to a small piece of land rented for growing food?
13 In the UK most Bank Holidays fall on which day of the week?
14 Which commodities would you buy at a PYO centre?
15 What does E stand for in NEC?
16 What colour is the baize on a snooker table?
17 Which word precedes sport to describe killing animals for recreation?
18 What type of weapon is used in fencing?
19 What is the name of a coach trip where few know the destination?
20 If you practised on a pommel horse where would you probably be?
21 The Chamber of Horrors is in which London waxworks museum?
22 Which weekly draw is run by Camelot?
23 Are bonsai trees smaller or larger than average?
24 Which club moved to The Riverside in the 1990s?
25 What sort of establishment is a greasy spoon?
26 Who is a tied house usually tied to?
27 What is the type of billiards played in pubs called?
28 The Summer Bank Holiday takes place in which month in the UK?
29 Which name for an expert in a particular hobby is the same as a padded jacket?
30 What does Y stand for in DIY?

---

1 Did Britain join the EEC in the 60s, 70s or 80s?
2 Which "Ground Force" presenter was the tallest of the original three?
3 The Rumba originated in which country?
4 Where do the cartoon Simpsons live?
5 How many edges are there around a 50-pence coin?
6 What type of vehicle is seen on the Cresta Run?
7 Which Biblical giant was killed by David?
8 Where would you find a useful junk?
9 Dictionary expert Susie Dent featured regularly on which programme?
10 Which animal does ivory predominantly come from?
11 Which London bridge opens upwards to let tall ships through?
12 Fish breathe through what?
13 What was sold at London's Smithfield market?
14 How many noughts are there in the written number one million?
15 According to the saying, what is "nine points of the law"?
16 What colour is earth in modern three-core electric cables?
17 What relation are Huey, Dewey and Louie to Donald Duck?
18 What is the German word for the number one?
19 What was the name of the Bollywood version of Jane Austen's tale of Mr Darcy?
20 Which firework is named after a saint?
21 Which Queen became Empress of India in 1876?
22 According to the Will Young title when should you "Leave"?
23 Vichy is famous for which drink?
24 Which "Blackadder" character had a fascination for turnips?
25 Which Ingrid was the mother of Isabella Rossellini?
26 How many centimetres are there in six and a half metres?
27 The Vatican City is within which other capital city?
28 What colour is the shade of jonquil?
29 In the Bible, who was found in the bulrushes?
30 How many points does a snowflake have?

1 Which ice dance pair have the freedom of the city of Nottingham?

2 In 2006 which Premiership club featured a pair of Bents in attack?

3 What sort of animal takes part in a point-to-point?

4 In snooker what colour ball scores least?

5 In which country did sumo wrestling originate?

6 What was the name of Damon Hill's racing driver father?

7 Mike Tyson was suspended for biting off which part of Evander Holyfield?

8 In which sport did Justin Rose become a pro after the 1998 British Open?

9 In which Channel does the Admiral's Cup take place?

10 Which Scot Stephen won five successive snooker world championships in the 90s?

11 The Winter Olympics held in Nagano took place in which country?

12 In which state is golf's US Masters played?

13 In athletics what is the shortest outdoor track race?

14 What is the national sport of Spain, known as corrida de toros?

15 How often is the Grand National normally run?

16 What would you ride in a velodrome?

17 Which sport has Australian Rules?

18 Which golfer Jack was known as the Golden Bear?

19 How long does the annual motor race at Le Mans last?

20 The "Golden Gloves" championship is in which sport?

21 The Fastnet Race is competed for on what type of surface?

22 Which youngsters run between the ends of the net during a tennis match?

23 How does soccer player Dennis Bergkamp refuse to travel?

24 In which sport do you try to play below par?

25 Which Frankie had seven wins at Ascot at odds of 25,095 to 1?

26 How was Sir Garfield St Auburn Sobers known as a player?

27 Which sport do The Barbarians play?

28 Which game can be lawn or crown green?

29 Which two continents compete for the Ryder Cup?

30 Turin was the centre of which global games in 2006?

Answers	Pot Luck 22 *(see Quiz 46)*

1 Greendale. 2 Bruce Forsyth. 3 25. 4 Hutchence. 5 Banned from British racecourses. 6 Travel agents. 7 Liver. 8 Grasshoppers. 9 A letter. 10 Oldest university. 11 Great Britain. 12 Heart. 13 Man City. 14 Peter Gabriel. 15 No. 16 Blue. 17 London and Birmingham. 18 Glasgow. 19 Lancashire. 20 Roxy Music. 21 Hoops. 22 Delilah. 23 Canada. 24 Cook. 25 The Lone Ranger. 26 East. 27 Alan Bennett. 28 16. 29 Aladdin. 30 Guernsey.

Quiz 46 | Pot Luck 22

Answers – page 53

1 Where are you if Mrs Goggins serves you in the post office?
2 Whose catchphrase was, "Didn't they do well"?
3 What percentage is half of a half?
4 Which late Michael was lead singer with INXS?
5 What happens if a bookie is "warned off Newmarket Heath"?
6 ABTA is concerned with which group of people?
7 In the body, which organ secretes bile?
8 In Switzerland, which famous soccer club has an insect name?
9 What is returned in Elvis's "Return to Sender"?
10 What will Harvard University always be in America?
11 Which country was the first to use postage stamps?
12 Which part of his anatomy did Tony Bennett leave in San Francisco?
13 At which soccer club did Stuart Pearce follow Kevin Keegan as manager?
14 Which Peter made the album "Solsbury Hill"?
15 Was the great racehorse Red Rum coloured red?
16 Traditionally, what colour is willow pattern?
17 Which two cities in Britain are linked by the Grand Union Canal?
18 Sauciehall Street is in which city?
19 Wasim Akram first played County Cricket for which county?
20 Which group was fronted by Bryan Ferry?
21 What is the distinctive pattern on Dennis the Menace's shirt?
22 In the Bible, who cut off Samson's hair?
23 The province of Manitoba is in which country?
24 Would you expect Antony Worrall Thompson to cook or dance on TV?
25 Which cowboy had a horse named Silver?
26 Is St Andrew's golf course on the east or west coast of Scotland?
27 Who wrote an autobiographical work entitled "Untold Stories"?
28 How many sides would four trapezium have?
29 "The Return of Jafar" was the sequel to which Disney tale from the East?
30 St Peter Port is on which island?

| **Answers** | Sporting Chance 1 *(see Quiz 45)* |

1 Torvill & Dean. 2 Charlton Athletic (Darren & Marcus). 3 Horse. 4 Red. 5 Japan. 6 Graham. 7 Ear. 8 Golf. 9 English Channel. 10 Hendry. 11 Japan. 12 Georgia. 13 100m. 14 Bull fighting. 15 Once a year. 16 Bicycle. 17 Football. 18 Nicklaus. 19 24 hours. 20 Boxing. 21 Water. 22 Ballboys/ballgirls. 23 By air. 24 Golf. 25 Dettori. 26 Gary Sobers. 27 Rugby. 28 Bowls. 29 Europe & America. 30 Winter Olympics.

Quiz 47 | TV: Famous Faces | Answers – page 56

1 Who travelled from "Pole to Pole" and "Around the World in 80 Days"?
2 Which "Newsnight" interrogator has the nickname Paxo?
3 Clive James hails from which Commonwealth country?
4 Who was born John Cheese and changed his name by one letter?
5 Would you expect Brendan Cole to cook, dance or sing on TV?
6 Which David and Jonathan hosted the 1998 Election coverage?
7 Which "Gardener's World" presenter wrote a novel "Mr MacGregor"?
8 Which Kate won an OBE for her reporting in Beijing and the Gulf?
9 Which famous part of her did Rachel of "Friends" advertise?
10 Anthony Worrall Thompson replaced Michael Barry on which food magazine show?
11 Which Sir David's catchphrase is "Hello, good evening and welcome"?
12 Who worked with amateur chefs on "Hell's Kitchen"?
13 Which Paula gave interviews on her bed in "The Big Breakfast"?
14 Which Irishman has presented "The Eurovision Song Contest"?
15 Which practical joker Jeremy first hosted "You've Been Framed"?
16 Which "big name" moved her talk show from ITV to BBC in 1998?
17 Is Paul Ross the brother, son or no relation of Jonathan Ross?
18 In 2006, which "Top Gear" presenter suffered a near fatal high-speed crash?
19 Which stock cube did Lynda Bellingham advertise?
20 How were TV cooks Clarissa and Jennifer better known?
21 What is Anthea Turner's TV presenter sister called?
22 Who was the footballing team captain on "They Think It's All Over"?
23 Who is actor Rafe Spall's famous TV dad?
24 Ian McCaskill retired from presenting what in 1998?
25 Which Gloria presented an "Open House" on Channel 5?
26 In "Ground Force" is it Charlie or Tommy who has long red hair?
27 What are the first names of Reeves and Mortimer?
28 Which Judith did Anthea Turner replace on "Wish You were Here"?
29 Which "Match of the Day" presenter took on a Radio 2 show in 1998?
30 Which veteran comic pulled out of "Strictly Come Dancing" for health reasons?

Quiz 48 | Pot Luck 23 | Answers – page 55 | LEVEL 1

1 Which female star is the most imitated performer on "Stars in Their Eyes"?
2 How many players are on a cricket field during normal play?
3 What fruit comes from the rose?
4 The River Danube flows out into which Sea?
5 Which gas puts the bubbles into bottled fizzy drinks?
6 What gift was forthcoming on the 10th Day of Christmas?
7 The Harlem Globe Trotters are famous in which sport?
8 Who is older, Richard Branson or William Hague?
9 "Supercalifragilisticexpialidocious" comes from which Disney movie?
10 How many noughts are there in the written number ten million?
11 Which month of the year in Britain includes the longest day?
12 Copies of the Bible are left in hotel rooms by which religious organisation?
13 Who wrote the play "A Winter's Tale"?
14 What do the initials M.B.E. stand for?
15 What have you betrayed if you commit treason?
16 Who was swallowed by a whale in the Bible?
17 Andriy Shevchenko left AC Milan to join which club in 2006?
18 Which musician had the nickname "Satchmo"?
19 Which Julie played Jamie Bell's teacher in the movie "Billy Elliot"?
20 What is the children's version of backgammon called?
21 Which Girls band were formed from "Popstars: The Rivals"?
22 Which scientific word deals with the structure of the body?
23 Debra Messing played which character in "Will and Grace"?
24 What does a chronometer measure?
25 Chichester is the county town of which county?
26 Jerez in Spain is famous for which alcoholic drink?
27 In crime what do the initials A.B.H. stand for?
28 In a bull fight, what name is given to the person who kills the bull?
29 Which is the Lower House in British politics?
30 What is the German word for the number five?

Answers | TV: Famous Faces (see Quiz 47)

1 Michael Palin. 2 Jeremy Paxman. 3 Australia. 4 John Cleese. 5 Dance. 6 Dimbleby. 7 Alan Titchmarsh. 8 Adie. 9 Hair. 10 Food & Drink. 11 Frost. 12 Gordon Ramsay. 13 Yates. 14 Terry Wogan. 15 Beadle. 16 Vanessa. 17 Brother. 18 Richard Hammond. 19 Oxo. 20 Two Fat Ladies. 21 Wendy. 22 Gary Lineker. 23 Timothy Spall. 24 Weather forecasting. 25 Hunniford. 26 Charlie. 27 Vic & Bob. 28 Chalmers. 29 Desmond Lynam. 30 Jimmy Tarbuck.

Quiz 49 | Celebs

Answers – page 58

1 Which pop band did Geri Halliwell leave in spring 1998?
2 What is the married name of Cherie Booth QC?
3 Who was the fiancée of Michael Hutchence at the time of his death?
4 What was Caroline Aherne's showbiz pensioner persona?
5 Which London store did Mohammed Al-Fayed buy in 1985?
6 What is the first name of politician turned author Lord Archer?
7 Who is the man behind the Virgin group?
8 Madonna courted controversy over adoption of a child from which country in 2006?
9 Jennifer Garner had a daughter with which star actor Ben?
10 Which Tory politician did Ffion Jenkins marry?
11 Which rock star did Texan model Jerry Hall marry in 1990?
12 In which country was Ulrika Jonsson born?
13 Which radio DJ has his own company, Ginger Productions?
14 Who left husband Peter Powell for Grant Bovey in 1998?
15 How is former Royal girlfriend Kathleen Stark better known?
16 Who founded the London nightclub Stringfellow's?
17 Which country did Earl Spencer move to in the mid-1990s?
18 Which Royal was Lord Snowdon married to?
19 What was Liz Hurley's infamous Versace dress held together with?
20 Which millionairess cook is a director of Norwich City Football Club?
21 Which chain of cosmetics shops did Anita Roddick found?
22 What was the sporting profession of Jemima Khan's husband?
23 Which singer's "Showgirl" tour resumed in 2006?
24 Which Rolling Stone celebrated his 70th birthday in October 2006?
25 Which celebrity actor Grant's middle name is Mungo?
26 Which nightclub was named after Lady Annabel Goldsmith?
27 What does John Galliano design?
28 Which 60s supermodel helped to revive the fashion fortunes of M & S?
29 Which Foreign Secretary did Gaynor Regan marry in 1998?
30 What is the first name of PR man Mr Clifford?

Answers | Pot Luck 24 *(see Quiz 50)*

1 Athletics. 2 Champion. 3 Dr John Reid. 4 Joseph. 5 Grievous Bodily Harm. 6 Like a lamb. 7 Ron. 8 Five. 9 Caribbean. 10 India. 11 Growing of crops. 12 Mae West. 13 On the shoulder. 14 King Charles. 15 Kenny Chesney. 16 Animal. 17 Boutique. 18 Member of the European Parliament. 19 Grand National. 20 Mg. 21 2000. 22 December. 23 USA. 24 Leather. 25 Five. 26 John Lennon. 27 Democrats & Republicans. 28 Fame Academy. 29 Dix. 30 Harry Corbett.

Quiz 50 | Pot Luck 24

Answers – page 57

LEVEL 1

1 For which sport is Paula Radcliffe famous?
2 In the TV song, who was the "Wonder Horse"?
3 Which doctor became Home Secretary in Tony Blair's government?
4 Which of Jacob's sons had a coat of many colours, in the Bible?
5 In crime what do the initials G.B.H. stand for?
6 According to the saying, how will March go out if it comes in like a lion?
7 Did Rupert Grint play Harry or Ron in the Harry Potter films?
8 After how many years must an election be held in Britain?
9 Jamaica is in which sea?
10 Which country does the musical instrument the sitar come from?
11 Which kind of farming is arable farming?
12 Which famous film star gave her name to a life jacket?
13 Where would you wear an epaulette?
14 Which kind of spaniel was named after a king?
15 Who married Renee Zellwegger in 2005?
16 Is a jellyfish a mineral, vegetable or animal?
17 In the 60s what was Biba?
18 In politics, what do the initials M.E.P. stand for?
19 In 1993, which horse race was made void after a false start?
20 Which two letters form the symbol for the element magnesium?
21 How many centimetres are there in twenty metres?
22 Which month of the year in Britain includes the shortest day?
23 Goalkeeper Tim Howard plays for which country?
24 What is prepared in a tannery?
25 How many lines are there in a limerick?
26 Which member of the Beatles sang "Imagine"?
27 Which are the two main political parties in America?
28 What sort of "Academy" did Cat Deeley co-host?
29 What is the French word for the number ten?
30 Did Harry Corbett, Harry H. Corbett or Ronnie Corbett work with Sooty?

| **Answers** | Celebs *(see Quiz 49)* |

1 The Spice Girls. 2 Blair. 3 Paula Yates. 4 Mrs Merton. 5 Harrods. 6 Jeffrey. 7 Richard Branson. 8 Malawi. 9 Ben Affleck. 10 William Hague. 11 Mick Jagger. 12 Sweden. 13 Chris Evans. 14 Anthea Turner. 15 Koo Stark. 16 Peter Stringfellow. 17 South Africa. 18 Princess Margaret. 19 Safety pins. 20 Delia Smith. 21 Body Shop. 22 Cricketer. 23 Kylie Minogue's. 24 Bill Wyman. 25 Hugh Grant. 26 Annabel's. 27 Clothes. 28 Twiggy. 29 Robin Cook. 30 Max.

1 What mighty hero did Prince Adam turn into with the aid of Greyskull castle?

2 Which Stephen narrates "Pocoyo"?

3 What was the follow-up to "How!"?

4 Tom Baker was the longest-serving Doctor in which sci-fi series?

5 Which children's favourite has the number plate PAT 1?

6 Which Linford presented "Record Breakers"?

7 Which Engine's friends were Terence the Tractor and Bertie the Bus?

8 Does Tom or Jerry have the furrier coat?

9 What cuddly creatures are Uncle Bulgaria and Orinoco?

10 What was Worzel Gummidge?

11 Are Smurfs blue or orange?

12 Which Street teaches about letters and numbers?

13 What sort of creature is Pingu?

14 Which family is headed by Homer?

15 What colour is Teletubby Laa Laa?

16 Which Bear was found in a London railway station?

17 What is Popeye's occupation?

18 What sort of creature is Children's BBC's Otis?

19 What is the most number of presenters "Blue Peter" has at once?

20 Matthew Corbett said goodbye to which puppet companion in 1998?

21 What sort of animal was Huckleberry?

22 Who is Maya's twin on the TV show?

23 Who is Dastardly's canine sidekick?

24 "On Your Marks" and "Art Attack" are about what subject?

25 Spot is chiefly what colour?

26 Is "Crush" a game show or a drama?

27 What sort of animal is Garfield?

28 What is Casper?

29 What does Rupert Bear wear on his feet in the 2006 series?

30 Are "Thunderbirds" birds, child actors or puppets?

Quiz 52 | Pot Luck 25

Answers – page 59

LEVEL 1

1 Which band were credited with the first cyberspace No. 1 single?
2 What's the greatest number of consecutive calendar months with 31 days?
3 What name is given to the calm area at the centre of a hurricane?
4 Which flower is the symbol of the Labour Party in Britain?
5 Kingston is the capital of which island nation?
6 Michael Ballack joined Chelsea from which German club?
7 Which actress links "Green Wing" and "The Archers"?
8 Complete the Oasis song title "Cigarettes and ....?
9 What is the French word for the number three?
10 Are sponges mineral, vegetable or animal?
11 For which sport is Jean Alesi famous?
12 According to the proverb, there's no smoke without what?
13 Which army bugle call is played to wake up the troops?
14 Which Irish town gives its name to a five-line humorous verse?
15 Who preceded Tony Blair as Labour Party leader?
16 Who is renowned for saying, "I wanna tell you a story"?
17 Which letter of the alphabet is used as a measure of the size of a computer's memory?
18 Which country produces the pine-scented wine called retsina?
19 In 2005 what became the smallest winning margin by England in an Ashes Test?
20 What name is given to a fox's tail?
21 San Salvador is in which country?
22 Which abbreviation means "and so on"?
23 What is a Portuguese Man-o'-War?
24 What do Whipsnade, Chessington and London have in common?
25 What is the English equivalent of the American "faucet"?
26 Alphabetically, which letter is the last of the vowels?
27 Which name links golfers Kite and Watson?
28 Who bowed out of "Blind Date" in 2003?
29 What are we not doing if we send someone to Coventry?
30 How many balls are used in billiards?

Answers | Children's TV (see Quiz 51)

1 He-Man. 2 Stephen Fry. 3 How 2. 4 Doctor Who. 5 Postman Pat. 6 Christie. 7 Thomas the Tank Engine. 8 Tom. 9 Wombles. 10 Scarecrow. 11 Blue. 12 Sesame Street. 13 Penguin. 14 The Simpsons. 15 Yellow. 16 Paddington. 17 Sailor. 18 Aardvark. 19 Four. 20 Sooty. 21 Hound. 22 Miguel. 23 Muttley. 24 Art & crafts. 25 Yellow. 26 Game show. 27 Cat. 28 Ghost. 29 Trainers. 30 Puppets.

1 Tikka is a dish in which country's cookery?
2 A strudel is usually filled with which fruit?
3 What relation is Albert to fellow chef and restaurateur Michel Roux?
4 Which pasta sauce originated in Bologna in Italy?
5 What is a frankfurter?
6 How are eggs usually cooked in the breakfast dish bacon and eggs?
7 What is fromage frais a soft type of?
8 Does an Italian risotto contain rice or pasta?
9 Over what would you normally pour a vinaigrette dressing?
10 Rick Stein's restaurant and cooking specialises in what?
11 What colour wine is a Valpolicella?
12 In which country did Chianti originate?
13 What is the main filling ingredient of a quiche?
14 Is a poppadum crisp or soft?
15 What sort of drink is espresso?
16 Is brioche a type of bread or a fruit?
17 What shape is the pasta used to make lasagne?
18 What is mozzarella?
19 What colour is fudge?
20 Which north of England county is famous for its hotpot?
21 Do you eat or drink a loyal toast?
22 What type of meat is found in a cock-a-leekie soup?
23 In restaurant chains, what type of food would you buy from a Hut?
24 What is the alcoholic ingredient of Gaelic coffee?
25 Which fruit is usually used in marmalade?
26 At what age can you legally drink alcohol in an pub?
27 What does G stand for in G and T?
28 Which country produces more wine – Bulgaria or France?
29 Would you eat or drink schnapps?
30 A Conference is what type of fruit?

Answers	Pot Luck 26 *(see Quiz 54)*

1 The mice. 2 Sports trophy (golf). 3 American Indians. 4 Questions. 5 Spanish. 6 The Pussycat Dolls. 7 David Schwimmer. 8 Six. 9 Advent. 10 A kimono. 11 Mount Sinai. 12 Johnny Depp. 13 Althorp Park. 14 Quotient. 15 Hiroshima. 16 Tottenham Hotspur. 17 Cook. 18 Germany. 19 Boxing. 20 Neuf. 21 Tiger. 22 Tuxedo. 23 Battle of Hastings. 24 Rabbit. 25 Terry Waite. 26 Yellow. 27 Victory in Europe. 28 168. 29 The eye. 30 Anne Frank.

Quiz 54 | Pot Luck 26

1 According to the proverb, what plays when the cat's away?
2 Did Harry Vardon give his name to a disease, a sports trophy or a fruit?
3 Which people wore moccasins originally?
4 What does Q mean in FAQ?
5 What is the main spoken language in Mexico?
6 "PCD" was the first album by which girl group?
7 Which "Friends" star was the voice of the neurotic giraffe in "Madagascar"?
8 How many noughts are there in the written number fifty-two million?
9 Which season comes just before Christmas in the Christian calendar?
10 Which long dress is traditionally worn by Japanese women?
11 In the Bible, on which mountain was Moses told the commandments?
12 Who was Captain Jack Sparrow in the movie "Pirates of the Caribbean"?
13 At which Park is Princess Diana buried?
14 What does the Q stand for in IQ?
15 Where was the first atomic bomb dropped on 6 August 1945?
16 White Hart Lane is home to which football club?
17 What does Bill Granger usually do on TV?
18 Hanover, Westphalia and Bavaria are all parts of which country?
19 For which sport is Chris Eubank famous?
20 What is the French word for the number nine?
21 Which animal in the poem by Blake was described as "burning bright"?
22 What do Americans call a dinner jacket?
23 In which battle was King Harold killed?
24 What type of animal can be Dutch, Angora and Chinchilla?
25 Who was a Beirut hostage with John McCarthy and Brian Keenan?
26 What colour was the "itsy bitsy teeny weeny bikini" in the pop song?
27 What do the initials VE stand for in VE Day?
28 How many hours are there in a week?
29 Which part of the body can suffer from an astigmatism?
30 Which Jewish girl kept a diary while hidden in Amsterdam in 1942?

Answers | Leisure: Food & Drink 2 (see Quiz 53)

1 India. 2 Apple. 3 Brother. 4 Bolognese. 5 Sausage. 6 Fried. 7 Cheese. 8 Rice.
9 Salad. 10 Fish. 11 Red. 12 Italy. 13 Eggs. 14 Crisp. 15 Coffee. 16 Bread.
17 Rectangular. 18 Cheese. 19 Light brown. 20 Lancashire. 21 Drink (toast to
the queen). 22 Chicken. 23 Pizza. 24 Whiskey. 25 Oranges. 26 18. 27 Gin. 28
France. 29 Drink. 30 Pear.

Quiz 55　The Movies: Greats

1 Which great screen dancer is on the cover of "Sgt Pepper"?
2 Which wartime classic starred Ingrid Bergman and Humphrey Bogart?
3 Who is Jamie Lee Curtis's actor father?
4 Cary Grant was born in which west country port?
5 Was Rita Hayworth a blonde or a redhead?
6 Was it Bob Hope or Bing Crosby who was born in south London?
7 Which monster was arguably Boris Karloff's most famous role?
8 How was dancer Eugene Curran Kelly better known?
9 Who was the original "Candle in the Wind" dedicated to?
10 Which Anthony starred as the lead character in "Psycho"?
11 Which Sir Alec starred in, and had a share of the profits of, "Star Wars"?
12 Who was taller, Rock Hudson or Mickey Rooney?
13 Which James starred in "Harvey" and "The Philadelphia Story"?
14 Which Italian-born actor is best known for silent movies such as "The Sheikh"?
15 Which Citizen was the subject of Orson Welles' first film?
16 Lauren Bacall was the wife of which Humphrey?
17 Tough guy Frank J. Cooper adopted which first name?
18 Which Joan starred in "Whatever Happened to Baby Jane"?
19 How was Ruth Elizabeth Davis better known?
20 Which Charlie was a founder of the film studio United Artists?
21 Bing Crosby had just finished a round of which game when he died?
22 William Claude Dunkenfield used his first two initials to become who?
23 Jane and Peter are the children of which screen great Henry?
24 Which Katharine enjoyed a long on and off screen relationship with Spencer Tracy?
25 Which Doris enjoyed popularity in films with Rock Hudson?
26 He was born John Uhler Lemmon III but how is he known in films?
27 Who is Michael Douglas's famous actor father?
28 In which German capital was Marlene Dietrich born?
29 Did Clark Gable die during his last film in the 40s, 50s or 60s?
30 Greta Garbo was born in which Scandinavian capital?

Answers　Pot Luck 27 (see Quiz 56)

1 1970s. 2 An ill wind. 3 Harvey Keitel. 4 Beef cattle. 5 Windsor. 6 Runnymede. 7 Washington. 8 Around your waist. 9 Neun. 10 Egypt. 11 J. 12 Jack. 13 Origami. Circus. 15 Dutch. 16 Krypton. 17 Trousers. 18 The teeth. 19 Spain. 20 900.

1 Charting again in 2004, in which decade was Abba's "Waterloo" first a hit?
2 What kind of wind blows no good according to the proverb?
3 Which Harvey starred in Quentin Tarantino's "Reservoir Dogs"?
4 What type of animal can be Charolais, Galloway and Simmental?
5 Which is the largest castle in Britain?
6 Where did King John sign the Magna Carta?
7 In which capital is the Capitol Building?
8 Where would you wear a cummerbund?
9 What is the German word for the number nine?
10 Which country had eleven kings called Rameses?
11 What appears most as the initial letter in calendar month names?
12 According to the rhyme, who fixed his head with vinegar and brown paper?
13 What name is given to the Japanese craft of paper folding?
14 Billy Smart and Chipperfields provided what type of entertainment?
15 What was the nationality of diarist Anne Frank?
16 What was the name of Superman's home planet?
17 Who or what are Oxford Bags?
18 What part of your body is covered by orthodontics?
19 Paella is a traditional dish from which country?
20 How many seconds are in a quarter of an hour?
21 Which "Friends" star has advertised L'Oreal?
22 Bridge Farm and Brookfield Farm feature in which long-running soap?
23 What type of person was Laughing in the famous portrait?
24 Which festival follows Lent in the Christian calendar?
25 What colour is the Financial Times?
26 Brittany and Picardy are parts of which country?
27 Which phobia describes the fear of spiders?
28 In medicine, what does a dermatologist specialise in?
29 Suffolk Punch, Shires and Clydesdales are all types of what?
30 David Attenborough celebrated which landmark birthday in 2006?

..h country would you find Jerez?

..would you travel if you left for France from a hoverport?

..which Sea is the island of Majorca?

..n which country is Cologne?

Does London or Rome have the higher population?

6 The province of Flanders is in which country?

7 Which landlocked country is divided into cantons?

8 In which city would you find the Parthenon?

9 Bohemia is part of which Republic, formerly part of Czechoslovakia?

10 Is Schiphol an airport or a river in the Netherlands?

11 Which island is in the Bay of Naples?

12 Where is the Black Forest?

13 What type of country is Monaco?

14 Andorra lies between France and which other country?

15 In which Sea does Cyprus lie?

16 Belarus and Ukraine were formerly part of which huge republic?

17 What is the English name for the city known to Italians as Venezia?

18 Is Sweden a kingdom or a republic?

19 Vienna lies on which river?

20 Is Ibiza part of the Canaries or the Balearics?

21 In which Circle does about a third of Finland lie?

22 The Hague is the seat of government of which country?

23 Crete and Corfu belong to which country?

24 Which Scandinavian country is opposite Norway and Sweden?

25 Is Europe the second largest or the second smallest continent?

26 Which country marks the most westerly point of mainland Europe?

27 The Iberian Peninsula consists of Portugal and which other country?

28 Which French city is mainland Europe's largest?

29 What are the Balkans, the Apennines and the Pyrenees?

3. Which island is known to the French as Corse?

1 Which Pamela featured in the "Borat" movie?
2 In Bruce Springsteen songs what goes before In The USA and To
3 Which famous cricket commentator died of a heart attack in Janua.
   1994?
4 Which Lou wrote and sang "A Perfect Day"?
5 Was Liz Hurley born in the 50s, 60s, or 70s?
6 What does England spinner Ashley Giles often wear on his face when
   bowling?
7 Which Tory MP earned the name Goldilocks?
8 Which Harry created the character of Frank Doberman?
9 Which insects include drones, queens and workers?
10 Has a violin four, six or eight strings?
11 Which actor Peter played crumple-coated cop Columbo?
12 Fuzzy Zoeller was linked with which sport?
13 Where did Peter Mayle spend a year of his life?
14 In which county was the Plymouth Brethren founded?
15 Athena, Nike and Zeus were all what?
16 The movie "Starter for Ten" is about a student's ambition to be on which
   TV show?
17 In soccer what is the real first name of the keeper unkindly nicknamed
   "Calamity" James?
18 Which Derby is run at the Curragh?
19 Who had a best friend with the politically incorrect name of Big Ears?
20 A lateen sail is what shape?
21 Revie, Robson and Taylor have all managed which team?
22 Which valuable things were made by Thomas Sheraton?
23 On TV, Sabrina is the name of the Teenage... what?
24 Which musical instrument does Larry Adler play?
25 Tony Banks was Minister for what in Tony Blair's first Cabinet?
26 What type of crazy cops were created by Mack Sennett?
27 What do XL stand for in Roman numerals?
28 What's the foodie stage name of sizeable singer Marvin Lee Aday
29 Brady, Macari and Stein have managed which Scottish soccer cl
30 What kind of animal is a fox terrier?

Answers | Geography: Euro Tour *(see Quiz 57)*

1 Spain. 2 Hovercraft. 3 Mediterranean. 4 Germany. 5 Lond
Switzerland. 8 Athens. 9 Czech Republic. 10 Airport. 11 C
Principality. 14 Spain. 15 Mediterranean. 16 USSR. 17
Danube. 20 Balearics. 21 Arctic Circle. 22 Netherland
25 Second smallest. 26 Portugal. 27 Spain. 28 Pa
Corsica.

gium. 7
Germany. 13
Kingdom. 19
24 Denmark.
tain ranges. 30

1 Where is water stored in a cactus plant?
2 Are most conifers evergreen or deciduous?
3 Ceps and chanterelles are types of what?
4 Flax is grown to produce which fabric?
5 Which drug is obtained from the coca plant?
6 Bamboo is the tallest type of what?
7 Which Mexican drink comes from the agave plant?
8 Is it true or false that laurel has poisonous leaves?
9 The petiole is on which part of a plant?
10 What colour is cuckoo spit?
11 What colour are the flowers on a gorse bush?
12 Which perennial herb can be grown to create lawns?
13 What goes before lavender and holly to make another plant's name?
14 What can be obtained from the cassava plant which would have gone in a typical school dinner pudding?
15 Harebells are usually what colour?
16 Does a polyanthus have a single or several blooms?
17 Which ingredient in tonic water comes from the bark of the cinchona?
18 Which plants would a viticulturist grow?
19 Wild cornflowers are usually what colour?
20 Which paintbrush cleaner is found in the resin of a conifer?
21 Which pear has the most protein?
22 In the garden what would you use secateurs for?
23 Do peanuts grow on trees or low plants?
24 What colour is chlorophyll?
25 In which Gardens is the Princess of Wales Conservatory?
26 Cacti are native to which continent?
27 What would you find in an arboretum?
28 Which fast grower is nicknamed the mile-a-minute vine?
29 Which yellow flower is nicknamed the Lent lily?
30 Which trees carry their seeds in cones?

| **Answers** | Pot Luck 29 *(see Quiz 60)* |

1 A will. 2 Four. 3 Corfu. 4 Lion & Unicorn. 5 Zwanzig. 6 Bryan Adams. 7 A cactus.
8 Cheshire. 9 Street-Porter. 10 Australia. 11 World War II. 12 Black. 13 Landscape
Gardening. 14 A size of paper. 15 Edward Woodward. 16 A herb. 17 River Niagara. 18
Snow White. 19 Horse racing. 20 Beef. 21 Purple. 22 Three. 23 Alaska. 24 Wigan. 25
Simple Simon. 26 Luke and Matt Goss. 27 A kind of plum. 28 Celebrity Big Brother. 29
Lizzie. 30 Flattery.

1 If you die intestate you have not made what?

2 What's the least number of Mondays that can occur in July?

3 In which resort did the tragic deaths of the Shepherd children take place in Oct. 2006?

4 Which two animals are featured on the front of a British passport?

5 What is the German word for the number twenty?

6 Who had a No. 1 UK hit with "Everything I Do, I Do It for You"?

7 What is a prickly pear?

8 In which county, beginning with C, is "Goldplated" set?

9 Media person Janet Bull changed her last name to what in her search for "yoof"?

10 Bob Hawke was prime minister of which country?

11 The movie "Enigma" was set during which world conflict?

12 What colour is sable in heraldry?

13 For what was Capability Brown famous?

14 What is foolscap?

15 On TV who played the Equaliser?

16 What kind of plant is marjoram?

17 On which River are the Niagara Falls?

18 Which Disney movie includes the song "Heigh-Ho"?

19 For which sport is Willie Carson famous?

20 Sirloin, Rump and Topside are all joints of which meat?

21 What colour is Tinky Winky in the Teletubbies?

22 How many leaves are on a shamrock?

23 Which American state is the largest in area?

24 When Birmingham were relegated in 2006 Emile Heskey moved to which club?

25 According to the nursery rhyme, who met a pieman going to the fair?

26 Which two brothers made up the group Bros?

27 What is a bullace?

28 On which show did Chantelle Houghton first find fame?

29 A Model T Ford was nicknamed Tin what?

30 According to the proverb, imitation is the sincerest form of what?

Answers | Nature: Plant World *(see Quiz 59)*

1 Stem. 2 Evergreen. 3 Fungi. 4 Linen. 5 Cocaine. 6 Grass. 7 Tequila. 8 True. 9 Leaf stalk. 10 White. 11 Yellow. 12 Camomile. 13 Sea. 14 Tapioca. 15 Blue. 16 Several. 17 Quinine. 18 Vines. 19 Blue. 20 Turpentine. 21 Avocado. 22 Cutting, pruning. 23 Low plants. 24 Green. 25 Kew. 26 America. 27 Trees. 28 Russian Vine. 29 Daffodil. 30 Conifers.

Quiz 61 | Sporting Chance 2

1 What type of sport is eventing?
2 Who celebrated 20 years as boss of the same top soccer club in November 2006?
3 Phidippides was the first runner of which 26-mile race?
4 Which Stephen was the then youngest ever winner of a professional snooker title in 1987?
5 Did Evander Holyfield box at heavyweight or welterweight?
6 Which country did Virginia Leng represent at the Olympic Games?
7 FC Porto play football in which country?
8 At the USA PGA Championships, what game is played?
9 Did Shane Warne first play English county cricket for Essex or Hampshire?
10 At which sport might you see the American Williams sisters play?
11 Does the Le Mans 24-hour race take place in summer or winter?
12 In swimming, is freestyle usually performed on the back or front?
13 Which country won the first 25 America's Cup trophies in yachting?
14 In which sport is there a Foil discipline?
15 How was boxer Rocco Francis Marchegiano better known?
16 Caber tossing is native to which country?
17 In 2006, where did the Cardinals come from who won baseball's World Series?
18 For which national rugby side did Gavin Hastings play?
19 Magic Johnson found fame at which US sport?
20 Which horse race is sometimes called just The National?
21 What was tennis's Billie Jean Moffitt's married name?
22 Which Jackie's record of Grand Prix wins did Alain Prost pass in 1987?
23 Which heavyweight Mike knocked out 15 of his first 25 pro opponents in the first round?
24 Which international rugby venue opened a new South Stand in November 2006?
25 In which sport is a ball hit through a hoop with a mallet?
26 What is Scottish long-distance runner Liz Lynch's married name?
27 What does the first F in FIFA stand for?
28 F1 driver Jacques Villeneuve is from which country?
29 Which winter sport can be alpine or Nordic?
30 Is the Oaks a race for colts or fillies?

| **Answers** | Pot Luck 30 *(see Quiz 62)* |

1 Two. 2 Mean. 3 Lettuce. 4 Five seasons. 5 An even number. 6 Green. 7 Little Britain. 8 The mirror. 9 Half a pound of tuppenny rice. 10 Eight. 11 Westlife. 12 Penny Black. 13 Judas. 14 Half a crown. 15 The Banger Sisters. 16 One. 17 The Alps. 18 Gold. 19 Pepper. 20 Westminster Abbey. 21 A knot. 22 Coffee. 23 Victory. 24 Bread. 25 Green. 26 The harp. 27 Blue. 28 White Star Line. 29 A filament. 30 Queen Victoria.

1 How many people perform a pas de deux in a ballet?
2 If T is time what is M in G.M.T.?
3 Cos and Iceberg are varieties of which salad plant?
4 Did Ruud van Nistelrooy play three, five or seven seasons for Man Utd?
5 What type of number will you always get if you add two odd numbers together?
6 In movies is Shrek blue, green or purple?
7 Which TV series featured the Thai bride Ting Tong?
8 Who told the Queen that Snow White was the "fairest of them all"?
9 What is mixed with half a pound of treacle in "Pop Goes the Weasel"?
10 How many furlongs are there in a mile?
11 Who had a 2003 hit with "Miss You Nights", made famous by Cliff Richard?
12 What was the common name for the first postage stamp?
13 Which biblical character had the second name Iscariot?
14 What was the name for two shillings and sixpence?
15 In which film are Goldie Hawn and Susan Sarandon a pair of 50 something ex-groupies?
16 How many hooks do you use for crochet?
17 The Matterhorn is in which European mountain range?
18 What did Fort Knox originally store?
19 Steak au poivre is steak covered in what?
20 Where did the Queen's Coronation take place?
21 If you asked a Scout to make a sheep-shank, what would he make?
22 What drink is the main export from Brazil?
23 What was the name of Admiral Nelson's ship?
24 Chapatti is a kind of Indian what?
25 What colour is the door of the pub the Rovers Return?
26 Which stringed instrument has the most strings in an orchestra?
27 What colour is connected with the River Danube?
28 Which shipping line did Titanic belong to?
29 What is the name of the glowing curly wire in a light bulb?
30 At the start of the 20th century who was Queen of England?

Answers | Sporting Chance 2 *(see Quiz 61)*

1 Equestrian. 2 Sir Alex Ferguson. 3 Marathon. 4 Hendry. 5 Heavyweight. 6 Great Britain. 7 Portugal. 8 Golf. 9 Hampshire. 10 Tennis. 11 Summer. 12 Front. 13 USA. 14 Fencing. 15 Rocky Marciano. 16 Scotland. 17 St Louis. 18 Scotland. 19 Basketball. 20 Grand National. 21 King. 22 Stewart. 23 Tyson. 24 Twickenham. 25 Croquet. 26 McColgan. 27 Federation. 28 Canada. 29 Skiing. 30 Fillies.

Quiz 63 | Pop: Karaoke | Answers – page 72

1 Which "Grease" classic begins "I got chills, they're multiplyin'"?

2 Which Madonna hit contains the words, "Ring, ring ring"?

3 What is the first line of "Nessun Dorma"?

4 What did Tina Turner sing after "Do I love you, my oh my"?

5 What follows the Beatles' "will you still need me, will you still feed me"?

6 Which song begins, "I feel it in my fingers, I feel it in my toes"?

7 In "Candle in the Wind 98" how are England's hills described?

8 How many times is "submarine" sung in the chorus of "Yellow Submarine"?

9 Which hit began "Oh my love, my darlin', I hunger for your touch"?

10 Which song's second line is "and so I face the final curtain"?

11 Which song begins "First I was afraid I was petrified"?

12 In which song did Tammy Wynette complain "Sometime it's hard to be a woman"?

13 Which Slade Xmas hit has the line "Everybody's having fun"?

14 In the "Titanic" song what follows, "Near, far, wherever you are, I believe..."?

15 What follows Bryan Adams' "Everything I do"?

16 Which Dire Straits hit begins "Here comes Johnny"?

17 What follows "Two little boys had two little....."?

18 Which charity hit has the line "Feed the world"?

19 What follows The Spice Girls' "swing it, shake it, move it, make it"?

20 Which Abba hit states "I was defeated you won the war"?

21 What do neighbours become in the original "Neighbours" theme song?

22 What follows "I believe for every drop of rain that falls"?

23 Which football anthem speaks of "Jules Rimet still gleaming"?

24 Which song's second chorus line is "I just called to say I care"?

25 Which Evita song begins, "It won't be easy, you'll think it strange"?

26 What did Boy George sing after singing karma five times?

27 Which "Lion King" song began "From the day we arrive on the planet"?

28 Which Simon & Garfunkel hit begins "When you're weary, feeling small"?

29 Which traditional song has the line, "The pipes, the pipes are calling"?

30 What are the last three words of Queen's "We are the Champions"?

Answers | Pot Luck 31 *(see Quiz 64)*

1 The Peril. 2 McFly. 3 Mint. 4 Soldier Sailor. 5 Calais. 6 Horse racing. 7 August. 8 Berkshire. 9 Trombone. 10 Tuesday. 11 VAT. 12 Bulb. 13 Yellow. 14 Cricket. 15 Andrew Lloyd Webber. 16 Boxing (heavyweight). 17 Minestrone. 18 Champagne. 19 Little girls. 20 Patience. 21 Melbourne. 22 Silver. 23 Ganges. 24 Tannic/Tannin. 25 Boots. 26 A house. 27 Please. 28 Red. 29 Nose. 30 Sherry.

1 If Dennis is the Menace what is Beryl?
2 Who had a 2004 No. 1 single with "5 Colours in Her Hair"?
3 Which sweet flavoured herb is often used to accompany roast lamb?
4 According to the rhyme, which two characters followed Tinker Tailor?
5 Which French port is closest to Britain?
6 To see which sport could you go to Towcester?
7 Lammas Day is in which month?
8 In which county is the Royal Military Academy at Sandhurst?
9 Which brass instrument has a sliding, adjustable tube?
10 Which day's child is "full of grace" according to the traditional rhyme?
11 Which present-day tax replaced Purchase Tax in 1973?
12 Is a snowdrop grown from a bulb or seed?
13 What colour is Laa Laa in the "Teletubbies"?
14 For which sport is David Gower famous?
15 Who composed the music for "Cats"?
16 Found dead in 2006, Trevor Berbick was a former world champion in which sport?
17 Which soup is made from a variety of vegetables and pasta?
18 What sort of drink is Moet & Chandon?
19 Maurice Chevalier "thanked heaven" for what?
20 Which has smaller cards, an ordinary pack or a patience pack?
21 Which Australian city stands near the mouth of the Yarra river?
22 What colour is argent in heraldry?
23 The city of Calcutta stands on which river?
24 Tea contains which acid?
25 Which High Street chemists shop opened its first store in 1877?
26 What are you probably buying if you are gazumped?
27 What does the Italian "per favore" mean?
28 What colour, together with yellow, is the Spanish flag?
29 The symbol for Comic Relief is a red what?
30 What kind of drink can be Bristol Cream?

Answers | Pop: Karaoke (see Quiz 63)

1 You're the One that I Want. 2 Wannabe. 3 Nessun dorma, nessun dorma. 4 River deep mountain high. 5 When I'm sixty-four. 6 Love is All Around. 7 Greenest. 8 Six. 9 Unchained Melody. 10 My Way. 11 I Will Survive. 12 Stand by Your Man. 13 Merry Christmas Everybody. 14 That the heart does go on. 15 I do it for you. 16 Walk of Life. 17 Toys. 18 Do They Know It's Christmas? 19 Who do you think you are?. 20 Waterloo. 21 Good friends. 22 A flower grows. 23 Three Lions. 24 I Just Called to Say I Love You. 25 Don't Cry for Me Argentina. 26 Chameleon. 27 Circle of Life. 28 Bridge Over Troubled Water. 29 Danny Boy. 30 Of the world.

1 Which is the female half of Mulder and Scully?
2 Who first presented "Deal or No Deal" on Channel 4?
3 What is the subject of the Channel 4 show "Hooked"?
4 "Torchwood" is an anagram of which series of which it is a spin-off?
5 What colour is Channel 5's logo?
6 Which Ally is a zany US TV lawyer?
7 What would Peter Cockcroft talk about on TV?
8 Who took over "Gardener's World" from the late Geoff Hamilton?
9 Which Australian co-presents "Animal Hospital"?
10 Maureen Rees found TV fame at what type of School?
11 GMTV is usually seen at what time of day?
12 Which letters does TV's Kavanagh have after his name?
13 What sex is the audience of Chris Tarrant's show "Man O Man"?
14 Which Adrian became a regular presenter of "Match of the Day 2"?
15 Which TV presenter is Johnny Ball's daughter?
16 Which Mary founded the Clean Up TV campaign in 1964?
17 Which female pop quintet launched Channel 5?
18 Does Oz Clarke specialise in food or drink?
19 Which Jerry hosts a controversial talk show?
20 In which work location was the series "The Hello Girls" set?
21 Which Carol took over from Anne Robinson on "Points of View"?
22 What links Terry Wogan, Les Dawson and Lily Savage?
23 Which part of the country is served by Anglia Television?
24 "Ground Force" offered a viewer a makeover in which part of the home?
25 On which day of the week was "Countryfile" broadcast?
26 "It's good to talk" was the ad slogan of which phone company?
27 Who is taller, John Cleese or Ronnie Corbett?
28 Which broadcasting corporation is known as Auntie?
29 How many studio judges are there on "The X Factor"?
30 Who is the human half of Wallace and Gromit?

Answers | Pot Luck 32 *(see Quiz 66)*

1 Steve Coppell. 2 The farmer's wife. 3 R.E.M.. 4 Diamonds. 5 Broken. 6 All Saints. 7 1984. 8 Apples. 9 Rutland. 10 Stupid Mistake. 11 Sussex. 12 Hops. 13 Pears. 14 Saviour's Day. 15 Jennifer Lopez. 16 White. 17 He was married. 18 The Doge. 19 Eight. 20 Dance steps. 21 A plant. 22 Richard. 23 Red. 24 Birmingham. 25 Three. 26 Bank of England. 27 Goodwood. 28 Champagne. 29 A bulb. 30 New York.

Quiz 66 | Pot Luck 32

Answers – page 73

LEVEL 1

1 Which manager took Reading into the Premiership in 2006?
2 According to the nursery rhyme, who cut off the three mice tails?
3 Whose best-of album from 1988–2003 was called "In Time"?
4 What is mined at Kimberley in South Africa?
5 What does a German mean if he says something is "kaput"?
6 Who had a No. 1 UK hit in September 1998 with "Bootie Call"?
7 Which George Orwell novel has a year as its title?
8 Cider is made from which fruit?
9 What was the smallest county in England until 1974?
10 What was in brackets in the title of Gareth Gates's "Anyone of Us"?
11 Chris Adams captained which side to cricket's County Championship?
12 What is dried in Kentish oast houses?
13 Which fruit can be served Belle Helene?
14 Which Day gave Cliff Richard a No. 1 for Christmas 1990?
15 In "Out of Sight" which Jennifer starred along with George Clooney?
16 What colour along with red and blue is the Luxembourg flag?
17 What happened to Solomon Grundy on Wednesday, according to the rhyme?
18 Historically speaking, who was the chief magistrate of Venice?
19 On the Union Jack, how many blue triangles are there?
20 What does a choreographer plan?
21 What is a yucca?
22 In pop music, who is Jagger's long-time writing partner?
23 What colour is Po in the "Teletubbies"?
24 "Crossroads" was set near which major city?
25 How many people are in a boat in a rowing coxed pair race?
26 What is sometimes called the "Old Lady of Threadneedle Street"?
27 Which race meeting is known as "Glorious"?
28 What was invented by Dom Peter Perignon, a French monk?
29 Is a tulip grown from seed or a bulb?
30 Which American city has the Yankees and Mets baseball teams?

Answers | TV Times 1 (see Quiz 65)

1 Scully. 2 Noel Edmonds. 3 Fishing. 4 Doctor Who. 5 Yellow. 6 McBeal. 7 Weather. 8 Alan Titchmarsh. 9 Rolf Harris. 10 Driving School. 11 Morning. 12 QC. 13 Female. 14 Adrian Chiles. 15 Zoe Ball. 16 Whitehouse. 17 The Spice Girls. 18 Drink. 19 Springer. 20 Telephone Exchange. 21 Vorderman. 22 Blankety Blank. 23 East Anglia. 24 Garden. 25 Sunday. 26 BT. 27 John Cleese. 28 BBC. 29 Three. 30 Wallace.

Quiz 67 | Sporting Chance 3 | Answers – page 76 | LEVEL 1

1 What is the surname of German F1 drivers Ralf and Michael?
2 Which jump event did Carl Lewis specialise in as well as sprinting?
3 Did Man Utd's Gabriel Heinze play for Argentina or Germany in the 2006 World Cup?
4 Is professional badminton an indoor or outdoor game or both?
5 What was the professional name of boxer Joe Louis Barrow?
6 Which much-capped England Rugby star Matt took part in a TV dancing contest?
7 Did Asafa Powell become the world's fastest man at 100m or the London Marathon?
8 At which sport did suspended Irish Olympic gold medal winner Michelle de Bruin compete?
9 Which horned animal name does Leeds' Rugby Super League team have?
10 In which sport might you hit another living thing with a crop?
11 Peter O'Sullevan commentated on which sport?
12 Which Rugby side shares its name with stinging insects?
13 Which red flower is the emblem of the England Rugby Union team?
14 In which country is the golfing venue Valderrama?
15 Which motoring Grand Prix is held at the Hungaroring?
16 What's the highest score in darts from three different doubles?
17 In which country is the oldest football league in the world?
18 Which area of New York has a Globetrotters basketball team?
19 Which Bin was introduced for Rugby League players in 1983?
20 How many disciplines are there in a biathlon?
21 In which Sheffield theatre were the World Snooker Championships first held in 1977?
22 In which country was judo coincidentally added to the Olympic programme?
23 In badminton what were goose feathers used for?
24 What is the usual surface of the lane in ten-pin bowling?
25 Which German Men's Wimbledon champion was born on Billie Jean King's 23rd birthday?
26 Which Lennox of the UK became undisputed world heavyweight champ?
27 On what surface is curling played?
28 Which animal is on top of Rugby's Calcutta Cup?
29 In which sport would you wear a judogi?
30 What type of sporting event was The Rumble in the Jungle?

| **Answers** | Pot Luck 33 *(see Quiz 68)* |

1 Rise & Fall. 2 A hat. 3 Liver. 4 Julie Walters. 5 The Severn Estuary. 6 Music. 7 Swimming. 8 Tower of London. 9 Peter Sellers. 10 1950s. 11 A beetle. 12 Isle of Dogs. 13 Hastings. 14 African. 15 Dudley Moore. 16 Kate Winslet. 17 Antelope. 18 Moscow. 19 Red. 20 The Bill. 21 Saddam Hussein. 22 Two. 23 Vauxhall. 24 A bull. 25 Four. 26 Sheffield. 27 Chippendale. 28 None. 29 Trotters. 30 Australia.

1 Which Craig David hit featured Sting?
2 What is a tam-o'-shanter?
3 Which organ is particularly affected by hepatitis?
4 Who played the title role in the film "Educating Rita"?
5 On which river estuary does Swansea stand?
6 The letters F.R.A.M. mean a Fellow of which Royal Academy?
7 For which sport was Duncan Goodhew famous?
8 The raven is traditionally associated with which Tower?
9 Who played Inspector Clouseau in the original "Pink Panther" films?
10 Was Condoleezza Rice born in the 1950s, 1960s or 1970s?
11 What is a cockchafer?
12 Which animal isle is in the River Thames?
13 Where did a famous battle take place in 1066?
14 Which elephants are the larger - African or Indian?
15 Which English musician and comedian married Tuesday Weld?
16 Who was the female lead in the movie "Enigma"?
17 What kind of mammal is a chamois?
18 In which city is Pushkin Square?
19 Does coq au vin contain red or white wine?
20 Which TV series is set in Sun Hill police station?
21 During the Gulf War, who was the leader of Iraq?
22 How many members of the public join the chefs in "Ready Steady Cook"?
23 Which car maker has the same name as a London bridge?
24 Which animal should you take by the horns, according to the proverb?
25 How many pins are in the back row of a ten-pin bowling triangle?
26 Which city is further North – Bristol or Sheffield?
27 Which of Chippendale, Ming and Wedgwood is not a type of pottery?
28 How much gold is there in a one-pound coin?
29 What are a pig's feet called?
30 Of which country's coast is the world's largest coral reef?

Answers	Sporting Chance 3 *(see Quiz 67)*

1 Schumacher. 2 Long jump. 3 Argentina. 4 Indoor. 5 Joe Louis. 6 Matt Dawson. 7 100m. 8 Swimming. 9 Rhinos. 10 Equestrianism. 11 Horse racing. 12 Wasps. 13 Rose. 14 Spain. 15 Hungarian. 16 114. 17 England. 18 Harlem. 19 Sin bin. 20 Two. 21 Crucible. 22 Japan. 23 Shuttlecock. 24 Wood. 25 Boris Becker. 26 Lennox Lewis. 27 Ice. 28 Elephant. 29 Judo. 30 Boxing match.

1 What was the Spice Girls' first film?
2 Who with The Shadows starred in "The Young Ones"?
3 Which movie told of redundant steel workers becoming strippers?
4 "The Bridge on the River Kwai" prisoners are imprisoned by whom?
5 Nick Hornby's "Fever Pitch" is about which game?
6 Which Kenneth directed and starred in "Hamlet"?
7 "The Blue Lamp" preceded which TV series about PC George Dixon?
8 A BAFTA is a British Award for film and what?
9 What nationality was The ... Patient in the 1996 Oscar winner?
10 Which US food expert Loyd is the son-in-law of David Puttnam?
11 Mrs Blake Edwards won an Oscar for "Mary Poppins"; who was she?
12 What is the nationality of Sir Anthony Hopkins?
13 In which part of the UK was "Trainspotting" set?
14 Which one-time British Transport Minister twice won an Oscar?
15 Which Sir Richard directed "Chaplin"?
16 Which 1994 British hit shot Hugh Grant to superstardom?
17 Which Emma wrote the screenplay for "Sense & Sensibility"?
18 Jenny Agutter found fame in which movie about an Edwardian family?
19 Is Helena Bonham Carter a British Prime Minister's or a US President's granddaughter?
20 Elizabeth Taylor was twice married to this Welsh actor; who was he?
21 Who was born Maurice Micklewhite?
22 Which Julie was Oscar nominated in 1998?
23 Which Ewan plays the young Obi Wan Kenobi in Episode I of "Star Wars"?
24 In which film did Tom Conti play Pauline Collins' Greek lover?
25 Which blonde bombshell was born Diana Fluck?
26 Linus Roache's father has played which "Coronation Street" character since the soap began?
27 Who or what was the film "Wilde" with Stephen Fry about?
28 Which former James Bond became a goodwill ambassador for UNICEF?
29 In which part of the UK was Robert Carlyle born?
30 Hot Chocolate's "You Sexy Thing" was the theme for which 1997 film?

Quiz 70 | Pot Luck 34

Answers – page 77

1 The Dauphin was heir to which European throne?
2 Which castle was partly damaged by fire in 1992?
3 Which bear had a friend called Boo Boo?
4 What is another name for a linden tree?
5 Which sport is named after a place which is famous for horse trials?
6 The precious stone, a pearl, can be found in what?
7 Craig Bellamy joined Liverpool from which soccer club?
8 How many senior titles (excluding over-35 events) are contested each Wimbledon?
9 The movie "Walk the Line" was about which singer?
10 At which ceremony is a Monarch given their crown?
11 According to the saying, what do birds of a feather do?
12 Was Ted Hughes a dancer, painter or poet?
13 Elton John is an ex-Chairman of which club back in the Premiership in 2006?
14 For which sport is Tessa Sanderson famous?
15 Prince Charles is Duke of which English county?
16 What is a yacht with two hulls called?
17 Which character from "Winnie The Pooh" lost his tail?
18 What two initials did northern artist Lowry have?
19 What did William Tell shoot from his son's head with a crossbow?
20 Which continents are separated by the Urals?
21 Who was England's Queen when Shakespeare was alive?
22 Cowes on the Isle of Wight is famous for which sport?
23 Which country was formerly ruled by President Tito?
24 Which animal's milk is used to make cheese called Chevre?
25 Which city is further North – Lincoln or Leeds?
26 What flavour is Kendal's most famous cake?
27 Which is the only bird that can fly backwards?
28 What is John Major's favourite sport?
29 Which TV family featured on a No. 1 recording of "Spirit in the Sky"?
30 Which part of your body is a character in Shakespeare's "A Midsummer Night's Dream"?

Answers | **Movies: The Brits** *(see Quiz 69)*

1 Spiceworld The Movie. 2 Cliff Richard. 3 The Full Monty. 4 Japanese. 5 Football. 6 Branagh. 7 Dixon of Dock Green. 8 Television. 9 English. 10 Grossman. 11 Julie Andrews. 12 Welsh. 13 Scotland. 14 Glenda Jackson. 15 Attenborough. 16 Four Weddings and a Funeral. 17 Thompson. 18 The Railway Children. 19 British Prime Minister's. 20 Richard Burton. 21 Michael Caine. 22 Christie. 23 McGregor. 24 Shirley Valentine. 25 Diana Dors. 26 Ken Barlow. 27 Oscar Wilde. 28 Roger Moore. 29 Scotland. 30 The Full Monty.

1 What sort of security device is a Chubb?
2 An Entryphone would normally be found at the entrance to what?
3 What in the bedroom would have a TOG rating?
4 What colour is Copydex adhesive?
5 What is the abbreviation for volt?
6 Is pine a soft or hard wood?
7 Which machine tool is used for turning wood?
8 Do weft fibres run across the width or the length of a fabric?
9 What goes between a nut and the surface to protect it?
10 Soldering joins two pieces of what?
11 Cushions, curtains etc. are referred to as what sort of furnishings?
12 Should silk be washed in hot or cool water?
13 Which tool can be band, hand or hack?
14 E numbers refer to additives to what?
15 Is an emery cloth rough or smooth?
16 Which device turns off an appliance when a temperature is reached?
17 A rasp is a type of what?
18 Is Araldite a strong or light glue?
19 In which sort of bank would you deposit waste glass?
20 Canning, bottling and freezing are types of what?
21 What would a bradawl produce in wood?
22 Batik is a type of dyeing on what?
23 What would you normally make in a percolator?
24 Where is the door on a chest freezer?
25 A bedsit usually consists of how many rooms?
26 What type of electrical devices are "white goods"?
27 Is a kilogram less or more than two pounds in weight?
28 What colour does silver turn when it is tarnished?
29 Which wood is darker, mahogany or ash?
30 What does the ply of a yarn refer to?

Answers | Pot Luck 35 *(see Quiz 72)*

1 George Bush. 2 Sheffield. 3 Dock. 4 North Sea. 5 Angela Lansbury. 6 China.
7 Lines of longitude. 8 Scotland. 9 Australia. 10 Furniture. 11 Buttons. 12 Red
Rum. 13 Daisy. 14 Melinda. 15 Blubber. 16 Red. 17 Bob Dylan. 18 Birds of a
Feather. 19 Chocolate. 20 Roy Rogers. 21 Decathlon. 22 King John. 23 Scotland.
24 Macaulay Culkin. 25 Vodafone. 26 White. 27 At the beginning. 28 Sand. 29
Four. 30 Plane.

Quiz 72 — Pot Luck 35

1 Who was the last President of the USA elected in the 1980s?
2 Which city is further North – Cardiff or Sheffield?
3 Which plant helps to take away the sting of a stinging nettle?
4 The River Forth flows into which Sea?
5 Which actress plays Jessica Fletcher in "Murder She Wrote"?
6 Which country was ruled by Chairman Mao?
7 What name is given to the imaginary lines drawn from north to south on a map?
8 Where in Britain can you spend paper £1 notes?
9 Which country did Everton's Tim Cahill play for in soccer's 2006 World Cup?
10 Thomas Sheraton was a designer and manufacturer of what?
11 Which came first, zips, velcro or buttons?
12 Which horse named after a drink won the Grand National three times?
13 What was the name of Donald Duck's girlfriend?
14 What is the name of Bill Gates's wife?
15 What is the fat of a whale called?
16 Which is the warmest sea in the world, The Red, Med or Dead?
17 Who wrote the pop anthem "Knockin' on Heaven's Door"?
18 Who or what flock together according to the saying?
19 What is the flavour of a Devil's Food Cake?
20 Which cowboy had a horse called Trigger?
21 For which event is Daley Thompson famous?
22 Which King put his seal on the Magna Carta?
23 Which is nearest to Ireland, England, Scotland or Wales?
24 Who is Kieran Culkin's brother, famed as a movie child star?
25 Which company's name was on the shirts of the 2005 Ashes winners?
26 What colour balls were used at Wimbledon before yellow balls?
27 Where would you expect to hear the prologue in a play?
28 Which of the following will not dissolve in water: salt, sugar or sand?
29 How many teats does a cow have normally?
30 Was the Flying Fortress a plane or a train?

1 Which football anthem was co written by Skinner and Baddiel?
2 What is the surname of Oasis brothers Noel and Liam?
3 Whom was "Candle in the Wind" 1997 dedicated to?
4 Which Zoo sang "Spaceman" in 1996?
5 In which drama series did chart toppers Robson & Jerome find fame?
6 Isaac, Taylor and Zac make up which boy band?
7 Who said "Eh Oh" on the their first smash hit?
8 Whose album of "Urban Hymns" hit the top spot?
9 Which 90s band were named after an area of London?
10 "Knockin' on Heaven's Door" was released after which 1996 tragedy?
11 Which single was released by Robson & Jerome and two years later by The Three Tenors?
12 Who was "Older" in the 90s after a long-running battle with Sony?
13 Who were "Back for Good" in 1995 before disbanding?
14 Whose death propelled "Bohemian Rhapsody" back to the charts?
15 Which Peter had a No. 1 with "Flava"?
16 Who had a No. 1 with Nilsson's "Without You"?
17 Who backed Katrina on her 1997 Eurovision winner?
18 Which Damon fronted Blur?
19 Who starred in and sang on the soundtrack of "The Bodyguard"?
20 In September '98 Celine Dion released an album in which language?
21 Which toy provided Aqua with a No. 1?
22 Which country singer John died flying his plane in 1997?
23 Who had a daughter Lourdes Maria in 1996?
24 Which band's name is a US emergency number?
25 Dana International won Eurovision '98 for which Middle East country?
26 Oasis were formed in which UK city?
27 Who had a huge hit with "Drop Dead Gorgeous"?
28 Which Darren appeared in the 90s version of "Summer Holiday"?
29 In which county were Blur formed?
30 "My Heart Will Go On" came from which smash hit film?

Quiz 74 | Pot Luck 36 | Answers – page 81

1 Which Australian state is named after its discoverer Abel Tasman?
2 Which very soft wood is popular with model makers?
3 Which sport was played by Gabriela Sabatini?
4 According to the nursery rhyme, who joined the butcher and baker?
5 Do bananas grow pointing up or down?
6 Who wrote "Charlie and the Chocolate Factory"?
7 The River Ganges is sacred to the people of which religion?
8 Which Saint is the patron saint of Wales?
9 Which country was the 1994 football World Cup Final played in?
10 Was Terry Venables born in the 1940s, 1950s or the 1960s?
11 Which American hero wore a hat with a racoon tail hanging from the back?
12 Which sport is played on the largest pitch: cricket, football or polo?
13 What are or were winkle pickers?
14 Which part of an ocean shares its name with a musical?
15 Who was American president immediately before Bill Clinton?
16 Which Sean was was the star of "Sean's Show" on TV?
17 Does Nicole Kidman come from Australia or Austria?
18 What is the middle name of Sarah Parker, famed for "Sex and the City"?
19 Where was the person going, who met a man with seven wives?
20 Which Alan portrayed the character Jonathan Creek?
21 In the neck of a violin how many tuning pegs are there?
22 What were supporters of James II and his Stuart descendants called?
23 What is shouted by people when they make contact in fencing?
24 Which children's TV programme featured Bungle and Zippy?
25 Which English county shares its name with a beauty products range?
26 Man Utd's Alan Smith suffered a serious leg injury against which club early in 2006?
27 What colour is Rupert the Bear's scarf?
28 For which sport was Fatima Whitbread famous?
29 How many players take part in a game of patience at any one time?
30 Which city is further North – Bristol or Chester?

Answers | Pop: The 90s (see Quiz 73)

1 Three Lions. 2 Gallagher. 3 Diana, Princess of Wales. 4 Babylon Zoo. 5 Soldier Soldier. 6 Hanson. 7 Teletubbies. 8 The Verve. 9 East 17. 10 Dunblane. 11 You'll Never Walk Alone. 12 George Michael. 13 Take That. 14 Freddie Mercury. 15 Andre. 16 Mariah Carey. 17 The Waves. 18 Albarn. 19 Whitney Houston. 20 French. 21 Barbie. 22 Denver. 23 Madonna. 24 911. 25 Israel. 26 Manchester. 27 Republica. 28 Day. 29 Essex. 30 Titanic.

1 Which former leader went on trial in his own country in October 2005?
2 In which country were the Borgias a powerful family?
3 Benazir Bhutto was Prime Minister of which Muslim state?
4 Which Al was crime boss of Chicago during Prohibition?
5 Which South African shared the Nobel Peace Prize with FW de Klerk in 1993?
6 What was President John F. Kennedy's wife called?
7 Which Australian painter and TV presenter received a CBE in 2006?
8 In which country was Terry Waite imprisoned?
9 Roman Emperor Hadrian gave his name to what in Britain?
10 Which animals did Hannibal use to frighten the Romans?
11 Hirohito was Emperor of which country during WWII?
12 Which Russian word for Caesar was used by Russian monarchs?
13 What was T.E. Lawrence's sobriquet?
14 Which Russian revolutionary took his name from the River Lena?
15 In which century did Columbus discover America?
16 Which 11thC Scottish king was the subject of a Shakespeare play?
17 In which country of the UK was David Livingstone born?
18 Which British admiral Horatio was born in Norfolk?
19 Where is Botany Bay?
20 Which country put the first woman in space?
21 Which journalist John was imprisoned in Beirut with Brian Keenan?
22 What was Argentinean vice president Eva Duarte's married name?
23 Ho Chi Minh founded the Communist Party in which country?
24 Angela Merkel became leader in which country?
25 Which outspoken TV chef received an OBE in the 2006 New Year's Honours?
26 In which country was Joan of Arc born?
27 Where was the tomb of Tutankhamun discovered in 1922?
28 Which famous Indian monument was built by Shah Jahan?
29 Zulu leader Buthelezi became a government minister where?
30 Which nurse is famous for her work during the Crimean War?

Answers | Pot Luck 37 *(see Quiz 76)*

1 Arsenal. 2 Marzipan. 3 Rural England. 4 Two. 5 22. 6 Putty. 7 Roger Bannister. 8 Ballet. 9 Glasgow. 10 Eleven. 11 Right. 12 A skateboard. 13 Carrot. 14 Gymnasts. 15 Billy Butlin. 16 The sea. 17 A fiddle. 18 Cookery. 19 Canada. 20 19th. 21 Collar bone. 22 Victoria. 23 The service. 24 Forget. 25 Grass. 26 Kill You. 27 Val Kilmer. 28 1990s. 29 The knight. 30 Red and black.

1 Which English team made their first Champions League final appearance in 2006?

2 What name is given to the almond coating often on a Christmas cake?

3 C.P.R.E. is the Council for the Protection of what?

4 How many Bank Holidays are there in May?

5 How many yards are there between the wickets in cricket?

6 What sticky paste usually holds glass in a window?

7 Who was the first person to run a mile in under four minutes?

8 What is performed by the Russian Bolshoi company?

9 Which Scottish city has the biggest population?

10 How many players can a team have on the field in American football?

11 On a UK coin does Elizabeth II face left or right?

12 What has a kicktail and four wheels?

13 Which vegetable, high in vitamin A, is said to be good for the eyes?

14 What kind of athletes perform a flic-flac?

15 Who set up England's biggest chain of holiday camps?

16 Neptune was the god of what?

17 According to the saying, which instrument can you be as fit as?

18 What type of TV programmes are presented by Keith Floyd?

19 Which is biggest – the USA, Germany or Canada?

20 Was basketball developed in the 17th, 18th or 19th century?

21 What is the common name for the clavicle?

22 Africa's biggest lake is named after which British queen?

23 What Is the name given to the first hit in a game of tennis?

24 What do elephants never do according to the saying?

25 Bamboo is a very large variety of what?

26 What will too much love do, according to Brian May?

27 In the movies, which Val replaced Michael Keaton as Batman?

28 In which decade was "Hollyoaks" first broadcast?

29 Which chess piece is shaped like a horse's head?

30 What two colours are Dennis the Menace's sweater?

1 On which type of show is Ainsley Harriott most likely to appear?
2 Which Carol was the first presenter of "Changing Rooms"?
3 Which series looks at the love lives of Carrie, Charlotte and Samantha?
4 Which programme is often referred to simply as Corrie?
5 Which Zoe succeeded Gaby Roslin on "The Big Breakfast"?
6 Which impersonator Rory starred in "Who Else"?
7 Patrick Kielty and Fearne Cotton host which "Island"?
8 Do the Royle Family live in London, Manchester or Newcastle?
9 In which country was "Ballykissangel" set?
10 Scriptwriter Carla Lane is famous for campaigning on whose behalf?
11 Who was the BT housewife in the ads as played by Maureen Lipman?
12 In which show did David Jason call Nicholas Lyndhurst a plonker?
13 Which Rik was involved in a quad bike accident in 1998?
14 Which "Have I Got News for You?" star's real name is Paul Martin?
15 Which Helen appeared nude on the cover of Radio Times to celebrate her 50th birthday?
16 Who was the taller in the Peter Cook and Dudley Moore partnership?
17 Which comic Griff has been involved in restoring buildings?
18 Who is Paul O'Grady's blonde, cigarette-smoking alter ego?
19 What was the occupation of Bramwell in the TV series?
20 Was "Dragon's Den" about business plans or wildlife?
21 Who is Reeves' TV comedy partner?
22 In which show would you see the neighbour-from-hell Dorien Green?
23 Which TV cook went on tour on "The Rhodes Show"?
24 What is the first name of "Prime Suspect" writer La Plante?
25 Which morning show did Chris Evans and Gaby Roslin present?
26 Which TV astronomer was born Patrick Caldwell-Moore?
27 The game show "Boys and Girls" was introduced by which Vernon?
28 Who presented "The Full Wax"?
29 Which Victorian drama series has a hospital called The Thrift?
30 Laurence Llewelyn-Bowen is a TV expert on what?

Quiz 78 | Pot Luck 38

Answers – page 85

1 In 1959, what kind of vehicle crossed the Channel for the first time?
2 How many minutes are there per round in professional boxing?
3 Which animal built the hill that William III's horse stumbled on?
4 In "Ali", which actor Will played the great Muhammad Ali?
5 Which Channel Isle is famous for very creamy milk?
6 Which soccer boss left Arsenal following "bung" allegations?
7 Which animals do sailors say desert a sinking ship?
8 Which triangle are ships and planes said to disappear in?
9 What were used on illegally parked cars for the first time in 1983?
10 The leaf from which tree is a logo for Air Canada?
11 Who was the legendary King Arthur's wife?
12 Who was the one woman in the late Edward Heath's first cabinet?
13 Which Red Indian married Laughing Water?
14 What does a liquid turn into if it is heated up?
15 Which Gareth was the first runner-up on "Pop Idol"?
16 A muster is a collection of what type of birds?
17 Who wrote about Noddy and Big Ears?
18 What is the proper name for a mouth organ?
19 Who is Paul Daniels' wife?
20 What is the start of a hockey match called?
21 What colour was Bobby Shafto's hair in the nursery rhyme?
22 Which popular drink was invented by Dr John Pemberton?
23 Which sport did Sam Snead play?
24 In book and film, which musical instrument is linked with Captain Corelli?
25 In "Starlight Express" what do the performers wear on their feet?
26 Which sport is featured in the "Rocky" movies?
27 Which animal family do chipmunks belong to?
28 What colour is umber?
29 Which Arsenal keeper was Germany's No. 1 for the 2006 World Cup finals?
30 Which puppet show has two old men called Statler and Waldorf?

Answers | **TV Times 2** *(see Quiz 77)*

1 Cookery. 2 Smillie. 3 Sex and the City. 4 Coronation Street. 5 Ball. 6 Bremner. 7 Love Island. 8 Manchester. 9 Ireland. 10 Animals. 11 Beattie. 12 Only Fools and Horses. 13 Mayall. 14 Paul Merton. 15 Mirren. 16 Peter Cook. 17 Griff Rhys Jones. 18 Lily Savage. 19 Doctor. 20 Business plans. 21 Mortimer. 22 Birds of a Feather. 23 Gary Rhodes. 24 Lynda. 25 The Big Breakfast. 26 Patrick Moore. 27 Vernon Kaye. 28 Ruby Wax. 29 Bramwell. 30 Home decorating.

1 Which sport are the Lord's Taverners famous for playing?
2 Which Denise won European gold in the heptathlon in 1988?
3 Which Australian bowler was first to pass 700 Test wickets?
4 Sergey Bubka has set a world record in which field event over 30 times?
5 Which British tennis star reached the Wimbledon semi-finals in 1998?
6 Which summer sport did Kerry Packer revolutionise in the 70s?
7 Did Lance Armstrong dominate the Tour de France or Tour of Italy?
8 Chris Boardman suffered an accident riding what in summer 1998?
9 Which country staged the summer Olympics in 1984 and 1996?
10 Between 1990 and 1998 all Ladies Wimbledon Singles champions were born in which continent?
11 The summer Olympics are held every how many years?
12 In cricket, what must a ball not do to score six runs?
13 Jonathan Edwards specialises in what type of jump?
14 For which international side did Shane Warne play cricket?
15 Which golfer is known as the Great White Shark?
16 Which Martina did Martinez beat in the 1994 Wimbledon final?
17 Which Tour is the world's premier cycling event?
18 Which German tennis player's father Peter was jailed for tax fraud?
19 Sonia O'Sullivan races for which country?
20 How many runners are there in the 400m relay team?
21 Which Jana won Wimbledon in 1998 after her third final?
22 You would do a Fosbury flop in which athletics event?
23 Which cricket club is nicknamed the "Cradle of Cricket"?
24 How many balls an over are there in cricket?
25 Who told a Wimbledon umpire "You cannot be serious!"?
26 Which West Indian cricketer was called Vivian?
27 Who was top National Hunt jockey from 1999–2000 through to 2005?
28 Which Jimmy won Wimbledon doubles with Ilie Nastase?
29 What was the nationality of tennis pin-up Gabriela Sabatini?
30 Which team competes against America in the Ryder Cup?

Answers | Pot Luck 39 *(see Quiz 80)*

1 Sunderland. 2 Stirrups. 3 Dogger Bank. 4 Nine. 5 US President. 6 Perception. 7 Scandinavia. 8 One. 9 He was bald. 10 Animated cartoons. 11 A reservoir. 12 A spider. 13 The 1812 Overture. 14 14th February. 15 Tony Blackburn. 16 Victoria. 17 Four. 18 Moses. 19 The Pacific Ocean. 20 Teeth. 21 Elizabeth Hurley. 22 The maiden all forlorn. 23 Arms. 24 Helsinki. 25 Worms. 26 Four. 27 Jade. 28 Four. 29 A collage. 30 Sixpence.

1 What was the first soccer club to be managed by Roy Keane?
2 What are the metal loops that you place your feet in when horse riding?
3 Which bank is a dangerous sand bar in the North Sea?
4 How many players are there in a rounders team?
5 Whose official plane is Air Force One?
6 What does the letter P stand for in ESP?
7 Which group of countries did the Vikings come from?
8 How many Popes have been English – one, two or three?
9 What colour was Kojak's hair?
10 What kind of programmes are Hanna and Barbara famous for?
11 What is a man-made lake in which water is stored called?
12 What type of creature is a Black Widow?
13 Which overture has a date in its title and includes cannons and bells?
14 On what date did the St. Valentine's Day Massacre take place?
15 Which Tony won the first "I'm a Celebrity Get Me Out of Here"?
16 Melbourne is the capital of which Australian State?
17 How many walls surround a squash court?
18 In the Bible, who parted the sea?
19 Fiji is in which ocean?
20 Which part of your body has a coating of enamel?
21 In "Austin Powers International Man of Mystery" who was the leading actress?
22 Who milked the cow with the crumpled horn, in the rhyme?
23 Which parts of the Venus de Milo's body are missing?
24 In which city beginning with H was the 2005 World Athletics Championship held?
25 Would a vermicide be used to kill worms or mice?
26 How many presidents' faces are carved into Mount Rushmore?
27 Which green stone was buried by the Chinese with their dead?
28 How many New Testament Gospels are there?
29 What word describes a picture made from sticking scraps on to a background?
30 Which English coin was nicknamed the tanner?

Answers | Summer Sports *(see Quiz 79)*

1 Cricket. 2 Lewis. 3 Shane Warne. 4 Pole vault. 5 Tim Henman. 6 Cricket. 7 Tour de France. 8 Bicycle. 9 USA. 10 Europe. 11 Four. 12 Bounce. 13 Triple jump. 14 Australia. 15 Greg Norman. 16 Navratilova. 17 Tour de France. 18 Steffi Graf. 19 Ireland. 20 Four. 21 Novotna. 22 High jump. 23 Hambledon CC. 24 Six. 25 John McEnroe. 26 Viv Richards. 27 Mark McGwire. 28 Connors. 29 Argentinean. 30 Europe.

1 What force makes the Earth orbit the Sun?

2 What colour is the Great Spot on Jupiter?

3 Is Jupiter larger or smaller than Earth?

4 Which gas is present in the Earth's atmosphere which is not present on any other planet?

5 A solar eclipse occurs when the Moon gets between Earth and what?

6 Which is the seventh planet from the Sun?

7 What is the layer around the Earth called?

8 What is the name given to matter so dense that even light cannot escape its pull?

9 Which planet's name comes nearest the end of the alphabet?

10 Herschel planned to name Uranus after the King; which one?

11 What would you find on a celestial map?

12 Is the science of celestial bodies, astrology or astronomy?

13 Which colour in the rainbow has the shortest name?

14 Which TV programme called space The Final Frontier?

15 Were the first US Shuttle flights in the 1950s, 60s, or 80s?

16 Which show with Reeves & Mortimer shared its name with another term for meteors?

17 What is a group of stars which make a recognisable pattern called?

18 What does "S" stand for in NASA?

19 In which decade was the US's first satellite launched?

20 What is the English name for the lunar sea Mare Tranquillitas?

21 Castor and Pollux are two stars in which constellation?

22 John Young ate which item of fast food in space in 1968?

23 Was Apollo a US or USSR space programme?

24 Prior to being an astronaut was John Glenn in the Air Force or the Marines?

25 How long does it take the Earth to orbit the Sun?

26 Mishka, the 1980 Olympic mascot, was the first of which toy in space?

27 How is Ursa Major better known?

28 How many times did Gagarin orbit the Earth on his first space flight?

29 What travels at 186,272 miles per second?

30 Edward White was the first American to walk where?

---

1 In "Last of the Summer Wine", which part was played by Kathy Staff?
2 What colour is Dipsy in the "Teletubbies"?
3 An aftershock can sometimes follow what natural disaster?
4 For which sport was Sue Barker famous?
5 Which day's child is "fair of face" according to the traditional rhyme?
6 Which tradesman from Seville is featured in the title of an opera?
7 Which Scottish comic actor Robbie featured in the first Harry Potter movie?
8 In legend, who or what was Excalibur?
9 Which London club did soccer's Ian Wright join from Arsenal?
10 Which university is the oldest in England?
11 St Stephen's Day is generally known by what other name?
12 Did Sacha Baron Cohen's character Borat sport a moustache or a full beard?
13 What is a peregrine?
14 Who was Tony Blair's first Northern Ireland Minister?
15 What are the two main colours of the Argentinean flag?
16 Who had a No. 1 UK hit in September 1998 with "No Matter What"?
17 Which actor links "Play Misty for Me" and "Pale Rider"?
18 What type of fruit is a morello?
19 With which board game are Karpov and Kasparov associated?
20 Sizewell in Suffolk is associated with which form of power?
21 Which gas is the full name for marsh gas?
22 Alan Shearer beat which Newcastle star's goal-scoring record in season 2005–6?
23 In the Bible, who was Adam and Eve's firstborn son?
24 Keith Duffy joined "Coronation Street" from which Irish boy band?
25 Which character in "Coronation Street" was played by Violet Carson?
26 The song "Tomorrow" comes from which musical?
27 In which Italian city is the Rialto Bridge?
28 How many noughts are in the written number one hundred million?
29 What is the most lasting symbol of the French Exhibition of 1889?
30 Royal Sovereign is a type of which soft fruit?

Answers | Science & Nature: Space *(see Quiz 81)*

1 Gravity. 2 Red. 3 Larger. 4 Oxygen. 5 The Sun. 6 Uranus. 7 Atmosphere. 8 Black Hole. 9 Venus. 10 George. 11 Stars. 12 Astronomy. 13 Red. 14 Star Trek. 15 80s. 16 Shooting Stars. 17 Constellation. 18 Space. 19 1950s. 20 Sea of Tranquillity. 21 Gemini. 22 Burger. 23 USA. 24 Marines. 25 A year. 26 Teddy bear. 27 Great Bear. 28 Once. 29 Light. 30 Space.

1 Which Oscar winner became a Labour MP?

2 Which actress received an Oscar for "Erin Brokovich"?

3 Which actress Ms Berry won an Oscar for "Monster's Ball"?

4 Which Kevin won Best Director and starred in "Dances with Wolves"?

5 "Braveheart" was set in which country?

6 Who won Best Actor for "The Silence of the Lambs"?

7 Who directed "Schindler's List"?

8 Which British actor Jeremy was a winner with "Reversal of Fortune"?

9 Was it Tom Hanks or Tom Cruise who won in 1993 and again in '94?

10 Sonny's ex-wife won Best Actress in "Moonstruck"; who was she?

11 Which Susan won for "Dead Man Walking"?

12 Which foot is named in the title of the movie with Daniel Day-Lewis?

13 Was Clint Eastwood Best Actor or Best Director for "Unforgiven"?

14 How often are the Oscars presented?

15 Which keyboard instrument gave its name to a film with Holly Hunter?

16 Kathy Bates won with "Misery" based on which Stephen's novel?

17 Which Kate was Oscar-nominated for "Titanic"?

18 Did Madonna receive one, two or no nominations for "Evita"?

19 What was Best Picture when Tom Hanks won Best Actor for "Forrest Gump"?

20 Which Al was Best Actor for "Scent of a Woman"?

21 Which Shirley won an Oscar at the age of five?

22 For which film did James Cameron win a 1997 Oscar?

23 Which British movie about the 1924 Olympics was a 1980s winner?

24 Which Oscar winner based in India holds the record for most extras?

25 Which son of Kirk Douglas won for "Wall Street"?

26 "Platoon" was about which Asian war?

27 Which Ralph was an "English Patient" winner?

28 "Talk to the Animals" came from which movie about a Doctor?

29 For her role in "The Hours" actress Nicole Kidman wore a false what?

30 "Dances with Wolves" was the first film of what type to win Best Picture for 60 years?

Quiz 84 | Pot Luck 41

1 Which David directed the epic movie "Lawrence of Arabia"?
2 Which island is off the north-western tip of Wales?
3 The triple jump involves a run and then which three movements?
4 Which black boats sail along the canals of Venice?
5 Which bird was taken to work by miners to test for gas?
6 Mount Olympus is in which European country?
7 Who was England's skipper in the 2006 World Cup tournament?
8 Which super hero of comics and movies can spin a web?
9 For which sport was Gilles Villeneuve famous?
10 What colour did Dr Banner become when he got angry?
11 How many legs does a fully grown insect have?
12 What can be discovered by counting the rings in a tree trunk?
13 Who or what is Sweet William?
14 What kind of creature is an anchovy?
15 What game are you playing if you hold a bat in a penholder grip?
16 Which celebrity chef wrote an autobiography entitled "Humble Pie"?
17 Which word collectively describes all the stars and planets?
18 Which has the longer tail, a monkey or ape?
19 Myleene Klass was a member of which TV talent show winners?
20 Which country produces Valencia oranges?
21 Where in your body would you find marrow?
22 Which tree does mistletoe grow on?
23 Who live at 342 Greasepit Terrace, Bedrock?
24 In which Dickens novel does Jacob Marley's ghost appear?
25 Which islands were invaded in 1982 by the Argentineans?
26 What colour are the stars on the American flag?
27 Which country would you visit to kiss the Blarney Stone?
28 Which highwayman had a horse called Black Bess?
29 Was the 2006 Labour Party Conference held in Maidstone, Manchester or Margate?
30 How many strings are there on a Spanish guitar?

Answers | The Movies: The Oscars *(see Quiz 83)*

1 Glenda Jackson. 2 Julia Roberts. 3 Halle Berry. 4 Costner. 5 Scotland. 6 Anthony Hopkins. 7 Steven Spielberg. 8 Irons. 9 Hanks. 10 Cher. 11 Sarandon. 12 Left Foot. 13 Director. 14 Once a year. 15 The Piano. 16 King. 17 Winslet. 18 None. 19 Forrest Gump. 20 Pacino. 21 Temple. 22 Titanic. 23 Chariots of Fire. 24 Gandhi. 25 Michael. 26 Vietnam. 27 Fiennes. 28 Doolittle. 29 Nose. 30 Western.

1 Which language other than English is an official language of the Channel Islands?
2 In which country did Saddam Hussein's 2005–06 trial take place?
3 You would find Delphi on a map of which country?
4 Which is further North, Clacton or Brighton?
5 Which continent has an Ivory Coast?
6 On which island would you find the Giant's Causeway?
7 If you were on a French autoroute what type of road would you be on?
8 Which Gulf lies between Saudi Arabia and Iran?
9 Lake Superior is on the border of the USA and which other country?
10 Which tiny European landlocked state is a Grand Duchy?
11 Macedonia was formerly a part of which communist republic?
12 Which Himalayan kingdom has been called the world's highest rubbish dump because of waste left behind by climbers?
13 Which Australasian capital shares its name with a Duke and a boot?
14 Which river which flows through Germany is Europe's dirtiest?
15 Where would you be if you saw Nippon on the map?
16 Whose address is often referred to as Number Ten?
17 Which motorway goes past Stoke on Trent?
18 On which continent is the Basque country?
19 The Home Counties surround which city?
20 Malta is to the south of which island to the south of Italy?
21 The Ural Mountains mark the eastern frontier to which continent?
22 How is the London Orbital Motorway better known?
23 Is Moldova in Europe or Africa?
24 Which island republic lies to the north west of the UK?
25 Miami is a port in which US state?
26 Kew Gardens are next to which London river?
27 Which country has Lakes Garda, Maggiore and Como?
28 Is Madagascar an island or is it an African peninsula?
29 In which city is Red Square?
30 Which country's official languages are Hebrew and Arabic?

Answers | Pot Luck 42 *(see Quiz 86)*

1 Gaz. 2 Rosary. 3 Sewing Machine. 4 University. 5 Herod. 6 Jonathan Ross. 7 Five of a kind. 8 Cat. 9 M. 10 Salmon. 11 Arquette. 12 Finland. 13 Badminton. 14 Walking distance. 15 12. 16 Nigella Lawson. 17 100. 18 The Office. 19 Huit. 20 Notting Hill. 21 Blue. 22 Squirrel. 23 Five. 24 Germany. 25 Golf. 26 Deadly nightshade. 27 The Matrix. 28 Mars. 29 Supper. 30 Blue.

1 Actor Robert Carlyle led "The Full Monty" as which character?

2 What does a Catholic call the string of beads used when praying?

3 In 1851, what was invented by Isaac Singer?

4 In what type of educational establishment was "Educating Rita" set?

5 In the Bible, which King tried to get the baby Jesus put to death?

6 Which top-earning presenter replaced Barry Norman on BBC's Film programme?

7 What is the highest ranking hand in Poker Dice?

8 In cartoons, what type of animal is Sylvester?

9 Which letter represents 007's boss?

10 Which fish leap up river to get to their spawning grounds?

11 What name did Courteney Cox add to her name after marrying actor David?

12 In which country did saunas originate?

13 A shuttlecock is used in which game?

14 What is measured by a pedometer?

15 How many creatures give their names to Chinese years?

16 Who wrote the best-selling "How to be a Domestic Goddess"?

17 How many decades are there in a millennium?

18 Which comedy was set in the offices of the Wenham Hogg paper merchants?

19 What is the French word for the number eight?

20 In which part of London is there an annual famous carnival?

21 If put in an alkaline solution, what colour does litmus paper become?

22 Which animal lives in a drey?

23 If December 1 is a Tuesday, how many Wednesdays are in the month?

24 Did Beethoven come from Austria, Germany or Holland?

25 For which sport is Sam Torrance famous?

26 Belladonna is also known by which Deadly name?

27 "The Matrix Reloaded" was the first sequel to which movie?

28 The month March is named after which Roman god?

29 Leonardo da Vinci's religious painting featured The Last... what?

30 What colour is connected to neutral in modern three-core electric cable?

---

1 Which part of the body names a millennium feature on the London skyline?

2 Which sport would you watch at Aintree?

3 Are there more chairs at the start or end of a game of musical chairs?

4 What links a novice's ski slope and a garden centre?

5 What name is given to the promotional scheme to save points for cheaper plane travel?

6 In the year 2005 most Bank Holidays fell on which day of the week?

7 What colour would a Sloane Ranger's wellies be?

8 The initials RSVP come from a request in which language ?

9 What colour are most road signs on UK motorways?

10 In which UK county might you holiday on the Broads?

11 What is the name of the most famous theatre in London's Drury Lane?

12 In which city is the exhibition centre Olympia?

13 What would you hire at Moss Bros?

14 Butlin's was the first type of what?

15 What is the flower-shaped ribbon awarded at gymkhanas called?

16 What is a less formal name for a turf accountant?

17 Which magazine's title is the French word for "she"?

18 On which summer bank holiday is the Notting Hill Carnival held?

19 Which public track can be used for horses but not traffic?

20 On which date in May was May Day traditionally?

21 Does a busker entertain indoors or out of doors?

22 In which month would you celebrate Hogmanay?

23 In golf, what is usually meant by the nineteenth hole?

24 What is a horse chestnut called when it's used in a children's game?

25 Which card game has two forms called auction and contract?

26 What colour uniform do Guides wear?

27 Are seats in the circle of a theatre on the ground or first floor?

28 Where would a shopper be if they went to M&S?

29 If you wore jodhpurs you'd probably be about to do what?

30 On which ground in north west England do you watch Test cricket?

Answers | Pot Luck 43 *(see Quiz 88)*

1 Queen Elizabeth II. 2 Wales. 3 The species. 4 England. 5 Jailhouse Rock. 6 Hair. 7 Cleo Laine. 8 The Teletubbies. 9 Shaken but not stirred. 10 Hadlee. 11 (West) Germany. 12 Raspberry. 13 Oskar. 14 Brazil. 15 Sunday. 16 Scarlet. 17 Isle of Wight. 18 Pet Shop Boys. 19 Dean. 20 Cat. 21 Scotland. 22 Delia (Smith). 23 Skier. 24 Jackson. 25 Salt. 26 Medieval. 27 John Major's son James. 28 Barbie. 29 Gordon Strachan. 30 Rugby Union.

1 Who described 1992 as an "annus horribilis"?
2 In which country would you see the Great and Little Orme?
3 According to Rudyard Kipling the female of what is deadlier than the male?
4 Which country hosted soccer's 1966 World Cup?
5 Which "Jailhouse" song gave Elvis another No. 1 in 2005?
6 What falls out if you have alopecia?
7 Which singer is Mrs Johnny Dankworth?
8 Who live at Home Hill?
9 How does James Bond like his Martini served?
10 Which Richard was the first knighted New Zealand cricketer?
11 Europe's first motorway was built in which country?
12 What rude noise is the English equivalent of a Bronx Cheer?
13 What was Schindler's first name in the film "Schindler's List"?
14 In which South American country was Ayrton Senna born?
15 If January 1 was on a Thursday what day would February 1 be?
16 What colour was The Pimpernel created by Baroness Orczy?
17 Shanklin and Sandown are on which Isle?
18 Which Boys had a No. 1 in the 1980s with "Always On My Mind"?
19 Who was the male half of the Torvill and Dean partnership?
20 What kind of animal was Korky from the Dandy comic?
21 Does Ewan McGregor come from Ireland or Scotland?
22 IDEAL is an anagram of the first name of which famous cook?
23 Is Alberto Tomba a skier, a track athlete or an ice hockey player?
24 Which singer Michael had a No. 1 with "Earth Song"?
25 Sodium chloride is better known as which condiment?
26 Was Brother Cadfael a fictional medieval or Victorian detective?
27 Which Prime Minister's son did Emma Noble become engaged to?
28 Which doll has a boyfriend called Ken?
29 Which Gordon replaced Martin O'Neill as Celtic manager?
30 If Lions are playing Wallabies what sport are you watching?

---

1 Which day follows TFI on Chris Evans' show?
2 Who was the host of the variety show "Lenny Goes to Town"?
3 Which medical drama takes place in Holby's A & E department?
4 "The Jerry Springer Show" comes from which country?
5 What is the name of Catherine Tate's schoolgirl character?
6 What is presented to the 'victim' at the end of "This is Your Life"?
7 Whose comedy and chat show is called "The Bigger Picture"?
8 Steve Irwin was famous for hunting which creatures?
9 How many rooms are changed in "Changing Rooms"?
10 "Newsround" is aimed at which group of viewers?
11 In which series set in Ireland did barmaid Assumpta meet a sad end?
12 Which near silent walking disaster was created by Rowan Atkinson?
13 Who is Mel Smith's TV comedy partner?
14 Which Geoff gardened at Barnsdale?
15 Which series was dubbed "Barewatch" and "Boobwatch"?
16 Which charity campaign has Pudsey Bear as its mascot?
17 Which Michael's 70s chat show was revived in 1998?
18 In which Practice have doctors Kerruish, Glover and Attwood worked?
19 Which was broadcast later, "Newsnight" or "News at Ten"?
20 Who is the host of GMTV's "Lorraine Live"?
21 What is the profession of TV's Jo Frost?
22 What follows Police, Camera..., in the show about awful drivers?
23 In which city is "The Cosby Show" set?
24 Which drama series where Robson and Jerome found fame is about army life?
25 On which day of the week does the so-called God slot take place?
26 On TV, what is "The Royal"?
27 Which Cilla Black series made dreams come true?
28 Which motor magazine now with Jeremy Clarkson began in 1978?
29 Which "Torchwood" star was a "How Do You Solve a Problem Like Maria?" judge?
30 Which Files feature Mulder and Scully?

Answers   Pot Luck 44 *(see Quiz 90)*

1 Eagle. 2 Wales. 3 Stairway to Heaven. 4 Faraday. 5 Paint. 6 Lyon. 7 Yorkshire. 8 Bell shaped. 9 Hair salon. 10 Hood. 11 Water. 12 Les Battersby. 13 Metronome. 14 Before. 15 South Africa. 16 A3. 17 Slade. 18 Atmosphere. 19 Belgium. 20 Mars. 21 Alien. 22 Ear. 23 Medusa. 24 Cricket. 25 Dick. 26 1940s. 27 Normandy. 28 George Michael. 29 Zimbabwe. 30 Lisa Riley.

1 Which comic did Dan Dare first appear in?

2 Golfer Ian Woosnam comes from which country?

3 Which song links Rolf Harris and Led Zeppelin?

4 Which inventor Michael appeared on a £20 note?

5 Gouache is a type of what?

6 The notorious Klaus Barbie was the Butcher of where in France?

7 Which county do the Arctic Monkeys come from?

8 What shape is something if it is campanulate?

9 Was "Cutting It" set in a butcher's, a hair salon or a hospital?

10 Which Robin was the spoof film "Men in Tights" about?

11 Which word can go in front of BISCUIT, CLOSET and COLOUR?

12 As which character was "Coronation Street" actor Bruce Jones the neighbour from hell?

13 Which ticking instrument keeps perfect time for a musician?

14 Was the Automobile Association founded before or after World War I?

15 Which nation came back to international rugby in 1993?

16 Which is bigger, A3 or A4 paper?

17 Which band featured Noddy Holder and Dave Hill?

18 The mesosphere and the stratosphere are layers of what?

19 With which country are Walloons associated?

20 What links a chocolate bar, a planet and a god of war?

21 "Aliens" and "Alien Evolution" were sequels to which movie?

22 In which part of the body are the smallest bones?

23 In Greek legend, who had a bad hair day with snakes on her head?

24 Gubby Allen was linked with which sport?

25 What was the first name of Wacky Racer Mr Dastardly?

26 Was Chris Tarrant born in the 1940s or the 1960s?

27 Operation Overlord was the codename for the 1944 Allied invasion of where?

28 Who took a "Careless Whisper" to No. 1 in the 1980s?

29 Which country do golfers Nick Price and Mark McNulty come from?

30 Which Lisa presented the show "You've Been Framed"?

1 Who sang a "Barcelona" duet with Freddy Mercury?
2 Which composer wrote the "Four Seasons"?
3 Which branch of performing is Michael Flatley famous for?
4 In which country was the Halle Orchestra founded?
5 Which dancer Wayne toured in 1998 to mark his 50th birthday?
6 Who composed the incidental music for Ibsen's play "Peer Gynt"?
7 Which writers of comic opera are referred to as G&S?
8 Which playwright was known as the Bard of Avon?
9 Billy Smart was associated with what type of entertainment?
10 In which country is an eisteddfod held?
11 Which Circle is a professional association of conjurors?
12 Which charity gala with many different performers is held in November and attended by the Royal Family?
13 Which Lord Andrew wrote the musical "Whistle Down the Wind"?
14 In Rodgers and Hammerstein who wrote the music?
15 In which country was the Bolshoi Ballet founded?
16 Which famous Paul wrote the oratorio "Ecce Cor Meum"?
17 Which London theatre shared its name with a half human, half fish mythical creature?
18 At what time of year would you go and watch a nativity play?
19 Which Monty Python-based musical opened in the UK in the autumn of 2006?
20 The Last Night of the Proms takes place in which month?
21 A person playing a pantomime dame is usually which sex?
22 What type of singing made Maria Callas famous?
23 What was the surname of US musical composers George and Ira?
24 What is the final concert at the Promenade Concerts called?
25 Two out of the Three Tenors are which nationality?
26 Which Sir Noel wrote and starred in his plays and musicals?
27 What is the first name of Scarborough-based playwright Ayckbourn?
28 Opera singer Lesley Garrett is from which county?
29 Do you stand or sit for the Hallelujah Chorus from "The Messiah"?
30 In panto how do you respond to "Oh yes it is!"?

Answers | Pot Luck 45 *(see Quiz 92)*

1 50 Cent. 2 Arsenal. 3 Bill Wyman. 4 H.G. 5 Felicity. 6 Pub. 7 Pottery. 8 Long-haired. 9 James Bond. 10 Goldie Hawn. 11 Wok. 12 The Archers. 13 Beef. 14 Horse. 15 Spoons. 16 Hello. 17 Nigel. 18 King Edward. 19 Crawford. 20 Arkansas. 21 Canada. 22 Etna. 23 Smoking. 24 Deer. 25 Outside. 26 Two (South Australia & New South Wales). 27 Moonlight Serenade. 28 New Testament. 29 Jeroboam. 30 Bronx.

Quiz 92 | Pot Luck 45

Answers – page 99

LEVEL 1

1 Which rapper works with G-Unit?
2 England soccer star Ashley Cole began his career at which London club?
3 Who is older, Bill Wyman or the Prince of Wales?
4 What are the two initials of early 20th Century sci-fi writer Wells?
5 Which Kendall starred in the sitcom "Solo"?
6 Craig Cash's "Early Doors" was set in what type of establishment?
7 What did Clarice Cliff make?
8 Is an Afghan hound short-haired or long-haired?
9 Which secret agent was created by Ian Fleming?
10 Kate Hudson is the daughter of which actress Goldie?
11 What is a round-bottomed Chinese cooking pan called?
12 In which radio series is there a pub called The Bull?
13 What sort of meat is usually in a hamburger?
14 What type of animal is a palomino?
15 What is Uri Geller famous for bending?
16 Would you say Bonjour to a French person when you say hello or goodbye?
17 Violinist Kennedy chose to drop which first name professionally?
18 Which monarch gave his name to a type of potato?
19 Which Michael created the Phantom in Lloyd Webber's musical?
20 Is Bill Clinton's home state Arkansas or Arizona?
21 In which country is Hudson Bay?
22 Which Sicilian mountain is Europe's highest volcano?
23 ASH is a pressure group against what?
24 Which animal might be fallow or red?
25 Would you find a gazebo inside or outside your home?
26 How many Australian states have South in their names?
27 Was Glenn Miller's theme tune "Moonlight Sonata" or "Moonlight Serenade"?
28 Is the book of Jude in the Old or New Testament?
29 Which is larger, a magnum of champagne or a Jeroboam?
30 Which tough area of New York gives its name to a gin, vermouth and orange cocktail?

Answers | Leisure: Performing Arts *(see Quiz 91)*

1 Monserrat Caballe. 2 Vivaldi. 3 Dance. 4 UK. 5 Sleep. 6 Edvard Grieg. 7 Gilbert & Sullivan. 8 William Shakespeare. 9 Circus. 10 Wales. 11 Magic Circle. 12 Royal Variety Show. 13 Lloyd Webber. 14 Rodgers. 15 Russia. 16 Paul McCartney. 17 Mermaid. 18 Christmas. 19 Spamalot. 20 September. 21 Male. 22 Opera. 23 Gershwin. 24 Last Night of the Proms. 25 Spanish. 26 Coward. 27 Alan. 28 Yorkshire. 29 Stand. 30 "Oh no it isn't!".

1 How often is the World Cup held?
2 Did Jimmy Greaves ever play in a World Cup Final?
3 Who won the last World Cup of the 20th century?
4 What colour shirts were England wearing when they won in 1966?
5 Who became known sarcastically as The Hand of God?
6 Who was sent off in France 98 and fled to Posh Spice in New York?
7 Which side from Great Britain did not make France 98?
8 Which 1966 World Cup veteran resigned as Eire manager in 1995?
9 Which British side did Brazil play in the first match of France 98?
10 Which European country hosted the 2006 tournament?
11 Which country did Louis Saha play for in the 2006 World Cup?
12 Who were beaten finalists in the last World Cup of the 20th century?
13 In France 98 which Caribbean side were called the Reggae Boys?
14 Who was axed from the England side in '98 after reports of kebab binges?
15 Which former Man Utd keeper played in the 2006 Final?
16 Which German boss Jurgen resigned after the 2006 tournament?
17 In France 98 whom did Suker play for?
18 Who was the only Englishman to lift the World Cup before 2000?
19 Which central American country was the first to host the World Cup twice, in 1986?
20 Which ex-World Cup manager's autobiography is "An Englishman Abroad"?
21 What colour are Brazil's shirts?
22 Who were the only non-Europeans to win the World Cup in the 90s?
23 Who was England's youngest player in France 98?
24 What colour-coded hair was seen on the Nigerian team in France 98?
25 Which Gary was top scorer in the 1986 World Cup?
26 In which month did France 98 finish?
27 Which Scandinavian side was third in the 1994 US tournament?
28 Which South American side knocked England out of France 98?
29 In which city did France 98 begin and end?
30 Which country did Blackburn's Lucas Neill play for in the 2006 World Cup?

Answers	Pot Luck 46 *(see Quiz 94)*

1 Lancashire. 2 L.B. 3 Kent. 4 Rum. 5 Locum. 6 Argentina. 7 Dog. 8 Northamptonshire. 9 DH Lawrence. 10 Apple. 11 Germany. 12 Italy. 13 Alan Titchmarsh. 14 Gunnell. 15 Ernie Wise. 16 China. 17 Westlife. 18 Potter. 19 Holly. 20 Colin Farrell. 21 Cuckoo. 22 Tenor. 23 Bit. 24 Addams. 25 Chris de Burgh. 26 Tennis. 27 Alice (in Wonderland). 28 Sleeve. 29 Celine Dion. 30 Perambulator.

1 Mike Atherton played for which county cricket club?
2 Which were the initials of US President Johnson?
3 In which county is Ashford International station?
4 Does a Pina Colada contain rum or gin?
5 Which word for a duty doctor is a Latin name for place holder?
6 Which country's Rugby Union side are the Pumas?
7 Is a Dandie Dinmont, a dog, a cat or a horse?
8 In which county is the stately home of Althorp?
9 Which controversial author used the initials for his first names David Herbert?
10 What sort of fruit flavour does Calvados have?
11 In which country were BMWs first made?
12 St Francis of Assisi is patron saint of which country?
13 Which Alan presented the TV programme "How to be a Gardener"?
14 Which Sally was British women's team captain in the 1996 Olympics?
15 Which late comedian was the one with "short, fat hairy legs"?
16 Which country was once called Cathay?
17 Which boy band had a No. 1 with their version of Billy Joel's "Uptown Girl"?
18 Which Dennis created "The Singing Detective"?
19 Which Buddy did Alvin Stardust sing about?
20 Which Irishman Colin starred in the movie "Phone Booth"?
21 Which bird lays its eggs in the nests of other birds?
22 Was the singer Mario Lanza a bass, baritone or tenor?
23 What name is given to the part of the bridle in a horse's mouth?
24 Wednesday and Pugsley are part of which family?
25 Christopher Davidson found fame as a singer as which Chris?
26 Maria Bueno was famous for which sport?
27 In fiction, which girl swam in a pool of her own tears?
28 A raglan forms which part of a garment?
29 Who had a huge 1995 hit with "Think Twice"?
30 Pram is an abbreviation of which word?

Answers | Sport: World Cup Fever *(see Quiz 93)*

1 Every four years. 2 No. 3 France. 4 Red. 5 Diego Maradonna. 6 David Beckham. 7 Wales. 8 Jack Charlton. 9 Scotland. 10 Germany. 11 France. 12 Brazil. 13 Jamaica. 14 Paul Gascoigne. 15 Fabien Barthez. 16 Jurgen Klinsman. 17 Croatia. 18 Bobby Moore. 19 Mexico. 20 Bobby Robson. 21 Yellow. 22 Brazil. 23 Michael Owen. 24 Green. 25 Lineker. 26 July. 27 Sweden. 28 Argentina. 29 Paris. 30 Australia.

1 Which Yasser founded the PLO?
2 Which Kennedy announced he was running for President in 1960?
3 Nikita Krushchev was head of state of which Union?
4 In which Italian city were the 1960 summer Olympics held?
5 Whose Lover was the subject of a court case in book form?
6 The USSR sent its first man where in April 1960?
7 Which Russian dancer Rudolph defected to the West?
8 Across which former European capital was a Wall built?
9 Which drug taken by pregnant mothers caused abnormalities in babies?
10 Which Harold became Labour leader in 1963?
11 Of where did Neil Armstrong say, "The surface is like fine powder"?
12 What were mailbags containing over £1 million stolen from?
13 Caroline was the name of Britain's first offshore pirate what?
14 Which British WWII leader died in 1965?
15 What sort of champion was Arkle?
16 Which communist country had its famous Red Guards?
17 Which knighted soccer star retired aged 50?
18 Who launched the Queen Elizabeth II – QE2 – on Clydebank?
19 Which model Jean was called The Shrimp?
20 Which homeless charity was set up after TV's "Cathy Come Home"?
21 What product was banned from TV advertising on health grounds?
22 Which Rolling Stone singer was best man at David Bailey's wedding?
23 Which notorious East End gangland twins were jailed for murder?
24 Which rock star married Patricia Beaulieu?
25 Which capital was said to Swing in the 60s?
26 Which Martin famously gave his "I have a dream" speech?
27 If Mods rode scooters, who rode motorbikes?
28 LBJ was President of which country?
29 How were Ian Brady and Myra Hindley known?
30 Which actress Marilyn was found dead in her bungalow near Hollywood?

1 Which John married actress Sheila Hancock?

2 Which pre-decimal coin had the value of two shillings?

3 Which group revived a previous hit in the 90s with the help of Roy "Chubby" Brown?

4 Which TV presenter's shows have had Toothbrush and Breakfast in their titles?

5 Were the Olympic Games last held in Russia in 1960, 1980 or 1988?

6 Who is Popeye's rival?

7 Was Sir Walter Scott Scottish?

8 Which English soccer side was managed by the late Bob Paisley?

9 What is the main language in Brazil?

10 Which Macaulay starred in the cartoon and live action film "The Pagemaster"?

11 Which is greater in distance, a mile or a kilometre?

12 Which MP Harriet was axed in Tony Blair's first Cabinet reshuffle?

13 Who had a 2005 No. 1 single with "I'll be OK"?

14 How many red cards are there in a standard pack of cards?

15 Ray Davies was writer and singer with which band?

16 Adonis, Apollo and Poseidon were all what?

17 Tara and Willow featured in which occult-based series?

18 Which dog is larger – a borzoi or a corgi?

19 The Micra was made by which car company?

20 "Crossroads" was set near which major city?

21 A vixen is the female of which animal?

22 Which alphabet is used by Muscovites?

23 What links the names Chamberlain, Heath and Wilson?

24 Which jockey Bob fought back from cancer to win the Grand National?

25 Who is Simply Red's lead singer?

26 Which was the first antibiotic to be discovered?

27 Which Welsh actress won an Oscar for her role in "Chicago"?

28 For which sport is Sunningdale famous?

29 A Muscovy is what type of bird?

30 Which musical Paul got involved with frogs and Rupert Bear?

| **Answers** | Past Times: The 60s *(see Quiz 95)* |

1 Arafat. 2 John. 3 Soviet. 4 Rome. 5 Lady Chatterley's. 6 Space. 7 Nureyev. 8 Berlin. 9 Thalidomide. 10 Wilson. 11 The Moon. 12 Train. 13 Radio station. 14 Churchill. 15 Horse. 16 China. 17 Sir Stanley Matthews. 18 Queen Elizabeth II. 19 Jean Shrimpton. 20 Shelter. 21 Cigarettes. 22 Mick Jagger. 23 Kray twins. 24 Elvis Presley. 25 London. 26 Luther King. 27 Rockers. 28 USA. 29 Moors murderers. 30 Monroe.

Quiz 97

The Movies: Tough Guys

Answers – page 106

LEVEL 1

1 Which actor was nicknamed "Bogey"?
2 Which actor Marlon was paid $18 million for nine minutes in "Superman" in 1978?
3 Which western star John first acted as Duke Morrison?
4 Which Samuel starred as a gangster in "Pulp Fiction"?
5 Which Bruce starred in "The Jackal"?
6 Which Kiwi won an Oscar for his role in "Gladiator"?
7 Tough guy Robert de Niro sang about New York in which film?
8 Which lager did "Crocodile Dundee" star Paul Hogan advertise?
9 Which Vietnam veteran Oliver directed "Platoon"?
10 Which star of "The Godfather" bought an island called Tetiaroa?
11 Which Martin was assigned to assassinate Brando in "Apocalypse Now"?
12 What did George C. Scott refuse to do about his Oscar for "Patton"?
13 Gene Hackman played cop Popeye Doyle in which classic thriller?
14 Ray Liotta played a member of which criminal organisation in "Goodfellas"?
15 Which Bruce was the psychiatrist in "The Sixth Sense"?
16 Was Charles Bronson one of ten or fifteen children?
17 Is Bruce Willis a cop or a soldier in the "Die Hard" movies?
18 Which hell raiser Oliver released a single "Lonely for a Girl" in 1965?
19 Lee Marvin headed a Dirty cast of how many in the 1967 movie?
20 Which singer who died in 1998 was the tough guy captain in "Von Ryan's Express"?
21 How many gunfighters were hired in The Magnificent film of 1960?
22 On what vehicle did Steve McQueen try to flee in "The Great Escape"?
23 Which Sylvester starred in "Judge Dredd"?
24 What is the first name of "Reservoir Dogs" director Tarantino?
25 Which tough guy Arnold has appeared on a postage stamp of Mali?
26 Which Mel starred in the "Lethal Weapon" series of films?
27 Which bare-headed actor was in "The Magnificent Seven" and "The King and I"?
28 Which Clint got the part in "Dirty Harry" when Sinatra pulled out?
29 Which James Bond has an actor son called Jason?
30 Was "The Untouchables" with Kevin Costner set in the 20s, 40s or 60s?

Answers | Pot Luck 48 *(see Quiz 98)*

1 Tennis. 2 Heart. 3 Chris Tarrant. 4 Australia. 5 Frog. 6 Dingle. 7 Rot away. 8 Five. 9 Ten. 10 Aberdeen. 11 Boyzone. 12 Belgium. 13 Black Bess. 14 Purdy. 15 Eric Clapton. 16 Marylebone. 17 Bahamas. 18 The Taming of the Shrew. 19 Margaret Thatcher. 20 Hidden Agenda. 21 Violin. 22 Cornwall. 23 English. 24 British Prime Minister. 25 Susannah. 26 Vingt. 27 Aircraft. 28 Wizzard. 29 Blue. 30 France.

1 For which sport is Billie-Jean King famous?

2 According to the proverb, absence makes which organ grow fonder?

3 Who hosted ITV's "Who Wants to be a Millionaire"?

4 In which country is Ayer's Rock?

5 Which species of creature includes the most poisonous animal in the world?

6 Which soap family included Lisa, Marlon and Shadrach?

7 If something is biodegradable, what will it do?

8 How many noughts are in the written number two hundred thousand?

9 Every how many years is a National Census taken in Britain?

10 Where are you if you visit the Granite City?

11 Which group had a No. 1 album in 1998 with "Where We Belong"?

12 In which country is the town of Spa?

13 What was the name of Dick Turpin's horse?

14 In the "New Avengers", which character was played by Joanna Lumley?

15 Which guitarist is nicknamed "Slowhand"?

16 In cricket, what does the initial M stand for in MCC?

17 Nassau is the capital of which group of islands?

18 In which Shakespeare play does Kate marry Petruchio?

19 Who was Tory leader immediately before John Major?

20 What sort of "Agenda" was a 2003 hit for Craig David?

21 Which musical instrument does Tasmin Little play?

22 Which English county boasts the longest coastline?

23 What nationality was Bridget in "Bridget Jones's Diary"?

24 Eden, Heath and Macdonald have all held which important position?

25 Who is Trinny's partner giving advice on "What Not to Wear"?

26 What is the French word for the number twenty?

27 What are DC-10s and 747s?

28 "See My Baby Jive" was a 70s No. 1 for which magic-sounding group?

29 What colour is azure in heraldry?

30 Which country is immediately south of Belgium?

---

1 In which country did black activist Steve Biko die in 1977?
2 Which US President was brought down by the Watergate scandal?
3 What did a policeman use to hide a streaker's embarrassment in a famous incident at Twickenham in 1974?
4 Which London-born comic Charlie was knighted?
5 Which tree population was decimated by a Dutch disease?
6 Did Skytrain provide cut price tickets by air or rail?
7 Who succeeded John Paul I as Pope?
8 The New English version of which Book was published in 1970?
9 Which Czech tennis star Martina defected to the West?
10 In which country did Pol Pot conduct a reign of terror?
11 Which Sebastian was a record-breaking middle-distance runner?
12 Which father of twins was the husband of the British PM?
13 Which princess was sportswoman of the year in 1971?
14 The Queen celebrated how many years on the throne in her Jubilee?
15 Which Lord disappeared after his nanny was murdered?
16 Who beat four male candidates to become Tory leader in 1975?
17 Which war ended with the fall of Saigon in 1975?
18 Which country's athletes were murdered at the 1972 Olympics?
19 John Curry won Olympic gold on what surface?
20 In which county did a Ripper carry out horrific murders?
21 Which Lord and Royal uncle was murdered off Ireland?
22 Which Mother won a Nobel Peace Prize?
23 Charles de Gaulle died after being president of which country?
24 Were Sunderland in the first or second division when they won the FA Cup in 1973?
25 Where was the monarchy restored after the death of Franco?
26 In 1971 the first British soldier was killed in which British province?
27 Evonne Goolagong from which country won Wimbledon in 1971?
28 Which Chris was Jimmy Connors' fiancée when he first won Wimbledon?
29 Which James succeeded Harold Wilson as Prime Minister?
30 David Steel became leader of which political party in 1976?

Answers | Pot Luck 49 *(see Quiz 100)*

1 Orange. 2 Jennifer Saunders. 3 Madonna. 4 London & Birmingham. 5 Unchained Melody. 6 Goldcrest. 7 18. 8 Martin. 9 Cricket. 10 1940s. 11 Enya. 12 Red Indian tribes. 13 Take That. 14 White. 15 Four. 16 Mind. 17 Alfred Hitchcock. 18 Five. 19 Charles Dickens. 20 Hutch. 21 Accrington Stanley. 22 Northumberland. 23 MW. 24 Green. 25 A king. 26 Yorkshire. 27 Food. 28 Angostura Bitters. 29 Jennifer Aniston. 30 Queensland.

Quiz 100 | Pot Luck 49

Answers – page 107

LEVEL 1

1 In international soccer, what is the main colour of Holland's shirts?
2 Who is older – Ruby Wax or Jennifer Saunders?
3 "Into the Groove" gave a first UK No. 1 for which singer?
4 Which two cities were linked by the M1 when it first opened?
5 Which song was a British No. 1 for Jimmy Young, the Righteous Brothers, Robson & Jerome and Gareth Gates?
6 What is Britain's smallest songbird?
7 How many sides are there in a pair of nonagons?
8 Which George was the main producer of The Beatles' hits?
9 EW Swanton wrote about which sport?
10 Was Joanna Lumley born in the 1940s, 50s or 60s?
11 How is Eithne Ni Bhraonain better known in the music world?
12 Mohawk, Seminole and Sioux are all names of what?
13 Which star group was Jason Orange a member of?
14 Is Riesling a red or white wine?
15 How many Teletubbies are there?
16 Russell Crowe starred in the movie "A Beautiful" what?
17 Who links the films "Rebecca", "Psycho" and "Vertigo"?
18 What's the most number of Sundays that could occur in December?
19 Which author created the reclusive character Miss Havisham?
20 On TV, did David Soul play Starsky or Hutch?
21 Which founder members of the Football League returned to the League in 2006?
22 What is England's most north easterly county?
23 Is Radio 5 Live broadcast on MW or FM?
24 What colour is verdigris which appears on copper or brass?
25 Who is killed if regicide is committed?
26 Ridings used to divide which county?
27 Is Robert Carrier linked with food, theatre or sport?
28 Pink gin is gin flavoured with what?
29 Who played the character Rachel in "Friends"?
30 Brisbane is the capital of which Australian state?

| **Answers** | **Past Times: The 70s** *(see Quiz 99)* |

1 South Africa. **2** Nixon. **3** His helmet. **4** Chaplin. **5** Elm. **6** Air. **7** John Paul II. **8** Bible. **9** Navratilova. **10** Cambodia. **11** Coe. **12** Denis Thatcher. **13** Anne. **14** 25. **15** Lucan. **16** Margaret Thatcher. **17** Vietnam. **18** Israel. **19** Ice. **20** Yorkshire. **21** Mountbatten. **22** Teresa. **23** France. **24** Second. **25** Spain. **26** Northern Ireland. **27** Australia. **28** Evert. **29** Callaghan. **30** Liberal.

108

1 Which corporation developed the iPod?

2 What type of company can be found in Silicon Glen in Scotland?

3 In a car, what might be disc or drum?

4 Was the first modern cassette made in the 1940s, 60s or 70s?

5 Which type of transport has rubber skirts?

6 A rotor propels what type of aircraft?

7 Did early TV have 405 or 625 lines?

8 The Manhattan Project in the early 1940s was developing what?

9 Which substance, found to be dangerous, is called "woolly rock"?

10 What is the lowest number on the Beaufort Scale?

11 Apples and Apricots were what in the technological world?

12 Is coal obtained from decayed animal or plant matter?

13 What produces bubbles in the making of champagne?

14 Is the empennage of a plane at the front or the tail?

15 William Morris, Lord Nuffield was the first UK manufacturer of mass-produced what?

16 What does "P" stand for in DTP?

17 Which British bridge became the world's longest when completed in 1980?

18 What ill-fated personal transport was invented by Sir Clive Sinclair?

19 Which letter is farthest left on a computer keyboard?

20 Which country is the world's largest exporter of grain?

21 Which metal is used in thermometers?

22 Which colour identifies an ordinary diesel pump at a service station?

23 Nylon took its name from which two cities?

24 What device is indicated by a circle inside a square in clothing labels?

25 Which boom is produced by breaking the sound barrier?

26 C-Curity was the first type of which fastener?

27 What does "C" stand for in ASCII?

28 What sort of factory did Joseph Rowntree found?

29 What does a pluviometer measure?

30 Bournville was established for the workers of which company?

---

1 Had Theo Walcott played in the Premiership before his 2006 World Cup call-up?
2 Which duo had hits with "Mrs Robinson" and "America"?
3 What is the fear of enclosed spaces called?
4 Which Sunday comes before Easter Day?
5 On TV, which night featured a show from the London Palladium?
6 Alphabetically, which is the last of the calendar months?
7 What would a palaeontologist study?
8 Which Disney creature nickname was given to Tony Blair?
9 Which veteran comic Bob celebrated his 100th birthday on 29th May 2003?
10 When Eric Weiss escaped from his name he was known as who?
11 Which race course hosts the Ebor Handicap?
12 Which female presenter fronted the long-running "That's Life"?
13 Which metal has the chemical symbol Fe?
14 Which Terry writes the best-selling sci-fi "Discworld" novels?
15 Which English county did Brian Lara first play for?
16 What's the sport if the Chicago Bears take on the Miami Dolphins?
17 What does a contestant call in "The Weakest Link" to keep the accumulated cash?
18 In which country did golf originate?
19 Holly the computer appeared on which TV sci-fi comedy?
20 Which is Australia's largest lake?
21 Who composed the "New World Symphony"?
22 In "Coronation Sreet" was Roy's Rolls the name of a cafe or a car hire?
23 Which Harry Potter novel was the first with the word Blood in the title?
24 Vocalist Enya hails from which country?
25 In which city was the movie "Moulin Rouge" set?
26 "Sugar Sugar" was a one-off No. 1 for which group?
27 Which word can go in after BIRTHDAY, HEN, LABOUR and STAG?
28 Which Barrymore was in "E.T." and "Batman Forever"?
29 What does the I stand for in ITV?
30 Who had a No. 1 album with "Friday's Child"?

1 Who was head of the family in "Till Death Us Do Part"?
2 Which house was Revisited in the classic 1980s drama?
3 Where was the BBC's 1992 ill-fated soap set?
4 On which weekend evening was "Jim'll Fix It" broadcast?
5 In "Tenko" the women were imprisoned by whom?
6 What was Lovejoy's occupation?
7 Which series was about a Mobile Army Surgical Hospital in Korea?
8 Which Michael played the hapless Frank Spencer?
9 What was unusual about Hopkirk in the Randall and Hopkirk agency?
10 What institution was "Please Sir" set in?
11 What was the rank of Phil Silvers' "Bilko"?
12 Who were the US TV equivalent of The Beatles?
13 Which Leonard Rossiter sitcom sounds like a problem with old houses?
14 How was Arthur Fonzerelli known in "Happy Days"?
15 Which animals did Barbara Woodhouse work with?
16 Who was June in "Terry and June"?
17 What sort of animal was Grizzly Adams?
18 What was Torquay's most famous hotel run by Basil and Sybil?
19 "Jewel in the Crown" was set in wartime where?
20 In which county was "All Creatures Great and Small" set?
21 What sort of performers were in Spitting Image?
22 Which father of Paula Yates presented "Stars on Sunday"?
23 What was the profession of Albert Steptoe and son Harold?
24 Which hero was "Riding through the glen, With his band of Men"?
25 Which classic sci-fi series began in the 23rd century?
26 In which country was "Van der Valk" set?
27 What sort of statesman was Alan B'Stard?
28 Which Eric played Hattie Jacques' brother?
29 Was it Mork or Mindy who came from the planet Ork?
30 What sort of Men were Bill and Ben?

Quiz 104 | Past Times: The 80s | Answers – page 111

1 Which serving British PM survived an assassination attempt?
2 In which city did the SAS storm the Iranian embassy?
3 Edwina Currie resigned over what type of farm food?
4 Which Ben was disqualified from the Seoul Olympics for drug taking?
5 In which Sea did the oil rig Piper Alpha catch fire?
6 Which north London Tube station was gutted by fire in 1987?
7 Who was Labour leader when Thatcher had her third election victory?
8 Which late Duchess's jewels were auctioned for over £30 million?
9 The Herald of Free Enterprise sank off which Belgian port?
10 President Marcos was ousted in a rebellion in which island country?
11 Desmond Tutu became an Archbishop in which country?
12 Who was the second of the Queen's sons to marry in the 80s?
13 Was Zola Budd a swimmer, a runner or a gymnast?
14 At which UK stadium was the Live Aid concert held?
15 Which Eric, half of a classic comedy duo, died in 1984?
16 Which Tory minister Cecil resigned in a scandal in 1983?
17 In which Yorkshire city's football ground was there a fatal fire in '85?
18 What is the full name of the Lib Dems, formed in 1989?
19 Sally Ride became the USA's first woman where?
20 At which Common was there a camp against cruise missiles?
21 Outside which London store did a bomb explode in December 1983?
22 Which Swedish tennis star retired age 26?
23 In what type of accident was Princess Grace of Monaco killed?
24 Which soap asked the audience asked "Who shot JR?"
25 Which war in the south Atlantic was Britain involved in?
26 Which Mike became the youngest heavyweight boxing champion?
27 Which Bob rode Aldaniti to a Grand National win in 1981?
28 Which US president was the victim of an assassination attempt?
29 In which city was Beatle John Lennon murdered?
30 Where was Lady Diana Spencer working when photographed in a seemingly see-through skirt?

Answers | TV Gold (see Quiz 103)

1 Alf Garnett. 2 Brideshead. 3 Spain. 4 Saturday. 5 Japanese. 6 Antiques dealer. 7 M*A*S*H. 8 Crawford. 9 He was a ghost. 10 School. 11 Sergeant. 12 The Monkees. 13 Rising Damp. 14 The Fonz/Fonzie. 15 Dogs. 16 June Whitfield. 17 Human. 18 Fawlty Towers. 19 India. 20 Yorkshire. 21 Puppets. 22 Jess Yates. 23 Rag & bone merchants. 24 Robin Hood. 25 Star Trek. 26 Holland. 27 New Statesman. 28 Sykes. 29 Mork. 30 Flowerpot men.

1 Which BBC radio and TV service broadcasts abroad?
2 Which ex-newspaper editor Piers became a star presenter on American TV?
3 The Sporting Life devotes itself to which sport?
4 Which radio and TV listings magazine is published by the BBC?
5 Which independent radio station specialises in classical music?
6 Is "The Archers" on Radio 1 or Radio 4?
7 Where does Capital Radio broadcast to?
8 What is the Sunday version of Daily Sport called?
9 Which BBC Radio station has Live after its number?
10 In which north of England city is Granada TV based?
11 What sort of column tells of stories and rumours about celebrities?
12 What does M stand for in the pop paper NME?
13 Is GQ for men or women?
14 Which Rebekah was the first female to edit "The Sun" newspaper?
15 On which shelf would someone buy an "adult" magazine?
16 What does FT stand for in the name of the financial daily newspaper?
17 What is the Daily Mail's Sunday paper called?
18 On which day of the week is the News of the World published?
19 Which corporation is known as Auntie?
20 Which magazine about celebs is based on the Spanish mag Hola!?
21 Which Rupert founded Sky Television?
22 Which page in a newspaper is famous for its nude photos?
23 Which frothy beverage shares the name of a children's morning TV show on Five?
24 Which satirical magazine shares its name with the nickname for a detective?
25 Rupert Bear is linked with which newspaper?
26 Border TV serves the borders of which two countries?
27 What professional person would read The Lancet?
28 How often does the magazine Take A Break appear?
29 Which comic Ricky was a pioneer in podcasting?
30 Which Sir David co-founded LWT and TV-am?

Answers | Pop: Superstars *(see Quiz 107)*

1 Liverpool. 2 Pink Floyd. 3 Charles. 4 Bassey. 5 Stewart. 6 Sting. 7 Madonna. 8 Barry. 9 Madonna. 10 Michael Jackson. 11 Diana Ross. 12 Angels. 13 Phil Collins. 14 Mick Jagger. 15 Bee Gees. 16 David Bowie. 17 Neil Diamond. 18 Aretha Franklin. 19 U2. 20 Elvis Presley. 21 Beach Boys. 22 Bruce Springsteen. 23 Wonder. 24 Turner. 25 Elton John. 26 Motown. 27 Rod Stewart. 28 Orbison. 29 Streisand. 30 Manilow.

1 Sir Paul McCartney was awarded the freedom of which city?
2 Which legendary band released "The Wall"?
3 Which soul star Ray has the nickname The Genius?
4 Which Shirley was dubbed the Tigress from Tiger Bay?
5 Supermodel Rachel Hunter married which superstar Rod?
6 Which ex-Police singer founded the Rainforest Foundation in 1988?
7 Who does not use her surname Ciccone?
8 Which brother completed the Gibb trio with Maurice and Robin?
9 "Hung Up" gave a 12th No. 1 single for which superstar?
10 Which rock superstar was Lisa Marie Presley's second husband?
11 Which female sang on Westlife's "When You Tell Me that You Love Me"?
12 In 2005 which Robbie Wiliams song was voted best in 25 years of BRIT awards?
13 Which drummer's solo album "No Jacket Required" was a best-seller?
14 Which Rolling Stone did not normally play an instrument on stage?
15 Which group was heard on the soundtrack of "Saturday Night Fever"?
16 Whose hits range from "The Laughing Gnome" to "Space Oddity"?
17 Who sang "You Don't Bring Me Flowers" with Barbra Streisand?
18 Which Queen of Soul sang the best version of "Nessun Dorma" according to Pavarotti?
19 Which band would you find The Edge and Bono in?
20 Who lived in a mansion called Graceland?
21 Which boys liked "California Girls"?
22 Whose "Streets of Philadelphia" was his highest hit at the time in 1994?
23 Which Stevie dropped the tag Little and had hits well into adulthood?
24 Which Tina recorded Bond theme "Goldeneye"?
25 Which superstar founded the Rocket record label?
26 All Lionel Richie's early hits were on which record label?
27 Which Scottish football fan has the first names Roderick David?
28 Which Roy charted with "Crying" with kd lang four years after his death?
29 Which Barbra did actor James Brolin marry in 1998?
30 Which Barry's song "Copacabana" became a musical?

| **Answers** | **Leisure: The Media** *(see Quiz 108)* |

1 World Service. 2 Piers Morgan. 3 Horse racing. 4 Radio Times. 5 Classic FM. 6 Radio 4. 7 London. 8 Sunday Sport. 9 Five. 10 Manchester. 11 Gossip column. 12 Musical. 13 Men. 14 Rebekah Wade. 15 Top shelf. 16 Financial Times. 17 Mail on Sunday. 18 Sunday. 19 BBC. 20 Hello! 21 Murdoch. 22 Three. 23 Milkshake! 24 Private Eye. 25 Daily Express. 26 England & Scotland. 27 Doctor. 28 Weekly. 29 Ricky Gervais. 30 Frost.

1 Who became US President in 1992 when Governor of Arkansas?

2 Which playwright Arthur, an ex- of Marilyn Monroe, died in 2005?

3 Which scientist gave his name to the process of pasteurisation?

4 Who left $9 million to give prizes in five different fields?

5 Did Tony Blair have one, three or five children when he became Prime Minister?

6 Who lit the fuse for the 1605 Gunpowder Plot?

7 Was it John Ford or Henry Ford who manufactured cars?

8 During which war did Anne Frank write her diary?

9 Indira Gandhi was Prime Minister of which country?

10 John Paul Getty made his millions from which commodity?

11 Who was Labour leader Neil Kinnock's wife who became an MEP?

12 Who was the first 20th-century Prince of Wales to be divorced?

13 How was Argentinean Ernesto Guevara de la Serna better known?

14 William Gladstone was Prime Minister under which monarch?

15 What was suffragette leader Emmeline Goulden's married name?

16 Who became President of Iraq in 1979?

17 How many English kings have been called Stephen?

18 What was the nationality of the Duchess of Windsor?

19 Which legendary cricketer had the first names William Gilbert?

20 How old was Hitler when he died, 46, 56 or 66?

21 By which name was silent movie star Joseph Keaton better known?

22 Which Nelson was the first black President of South Africa?

23 Which Chinese leader instigated the Great Leap Forward in 1958?

24 Which Marx brother had a moustache, cigar and funny walk?

25 According to the Bible who was the mother of Jesus?

26 Which trombonist Glenn became a famous bandleader?

27 Who was Italian dictator between 1926 and 1943?

28 What was the nationality of inventor Marconi?

29 Whom did George W. Bush defeat standing as President for the second term?

30 Who was the youngest US President to die in office?

Answers | Pop: Charts *(see Quiz 105)*

1 Madonna. 2 Wannabe. 3 Elton John. 4 Don't Cry for Me Argentina. 5 My Way. 6 1950s. 7 Wet Wet Wet. 8 The White Cliffs of Dover. 9 Frank & Nancy Sinatra. 10 Arctic Monkeys. 11 Manchester United. 12 Engelbert Humperdinck. 13 Jennifer Rush's. 14 Spice Girls. 15 Craig David. 16 17 years. 17 Whistle Down the Wind. 18 Kylie Minogue. 19 USA. 20 The Pussycat Dolls. 21 The Simpsons. 22 Denmark. 23 The Wonder Stuff. 24 Prodigy. 25 Pet Shop. 26 Backstreet Boys. 27 Richard. 28 Madonna. 29 Boyzone. 30 Jimmy Nail.

1 Whose album "True Blue" was No. 1 in 28 countries?

2 What was The Spice Girls' first No. 1?

3 Whose charity hit included "Something About the Way You Look Tonight"?

4 Which of Madonna's two hits from "Evita" got higher in the charts?

5 Which Frank Sinatra hit has spent most weeks in the UK charts?

6 In which decade did the UK singles charts begin?

7 Who as well as The Troggs charted with "Love is All Around"?

8 Which wartime song charted with Robson & Jerome's "Unchained Melody"?

9 Which father and daughter had a No. 1 with "Somethin' Stupid"?

10 "I Bet You Look Good on the Dancefloor" was a 2005 No. 1 for which band?

11 Which soccer side charted with "Come On You Reds"?

12 Whose "Release Me" spent a record number of weeks in the charts?

13 Was Celine Dion's "Power of Love" the same as Jennifer Rush's or Frankie Goes to Hollywood's?

14 Who was the first all-female band to have three consecutive No. 1s?

15 Who was singing "All The Way" in the 2005 charts?

16 Was Gareth Gates aged 17, 20 or 27 when he first had a No. 1 single?

17 Which musical did Boyzone's No. 1 "No Matter What" come from?

18 Who is the most successful Australian female to have been in the UK singles charts?

19 Billboard is a list of best-selling records where?

20 "Stickwitu" was the second No. 1 for which girl group?

21 Which family were at No. 1 with "Do the Bartman"?

22 Which Scandinavian country do chart toppers Aqua come from?

23 Who accompanied Vic Reeves on his No. 1 hit "Dizzy"?

24 Whose '96 No. 1s were "Firestarter" and "Breathe"?

25 Which Boys' first No. 1 was "West End Girls"?

26 Which Boys had the 2005 hits "Incomplete" and "Just Want You to Know"?

27 Which solo Briton Cliff has spent most weeks in the UK singles charts?

28 Which female solo star has spent most weeks in the British charts?

29 "Love Me for a Reason" charted for The Osmonds and which band?

30 Who wrote the series "Crocodile Shoes" and its chart songs?

| **Answers** | Who was Who? *(see Quiz 106)* |

1 Bill Clinton. 2 Arthur Miller. 3 Louis Pasteur. 4 Nobel. 5 Three. 6 Guy Fawkes. 7 Henry Ford. 8 Second World War. 9 India. 10 Oil. 11 Glenys Kinnock. 12 Charles. 13 Che Guevara. 14 Queen Victoria. 15 Pankhurst. 16 Saddam Hussein. 17 One. 18 American. 19 W.G.Grace. 20 56. 21 Buster Keaton. 22 Mandela. 23 Mao Zedong. 24 Groucho. 25 Mary. 26 Miller. 27 Mussolini. 28 Italian. 29 John Kerry. 30 John F. Kennedy.

Quiz 109 | Pop: Who's Who?

Answers – page 119

LEVEL 1

1 Who is Julian Lennon's stepmother?
2 Which pop wife has Liam and a shamrock tattooed on her ankle?
3 Which George did not make a record for five years because of a dispute with Sony?
4 Which female released an album declaring she was "No Angel"?
5 Which Elaine changed her surname from Bickerstaff and went on to star in many West End musicals?
6 Which Stevie led the campaign to commemorate Martin Luther King's birthday in the US?
7 How is Katherine Dawn Lang better known?
8 Bernie Taupin collaborated with which performer for over 20 years?
9 Which Boys were famous for their surfing sound?
10 Whose real name is Charles Edward Anderson Berry?
11 In what type of tragic accident did John Denver meet his death?
12 Which composer of Boyzone's "No Matter What" appeared with them on "Top of the Pops"?
13 Andrew Ridgeley was the less famous half of which group?
14 Which band always comes last alphabetically?
15 Who was "Born to Do It" according to his No. 1 selling album?
16 The Spice Girls recorded their early hits on which label?
17 PJ and Duncan were also known as who?
18 Which soul star did Bryan Ferry name his son Otis after?
19 What are the first names of the Everly Brothers?
20 Was Bryan Adams born in Canada or the USA?
21 Who was left-handed, Lennon or McCartney?
22 Which ex-husband of Cher died in a skiing accident ?
23 Bjork hails from which country?
24 Who made the album "Let's Talk About Love"?
25 Which band released the album "Hail to the Thief"?
26 "That's My Goal" was a first No. 1 single for which Shayne?
27 Which Mark co-founded Dire Straits?
28 What name links Ant and Faith?
29 Which hit by D:Ream was used in the 1997 Labour election campaign?
30 Who changed his name to a symbol?

Answers	Celebs: The Royals *(see Quiz 110)*

1 Stark. 2 Brother-in-law. 3 Some of her dresses. 4 Anne. 5 Helen Mirren. 6 Princess Michael of Kent. 7 Margaret. 8 Panorama. 9 Eton. 10 Bulimia. 11 Sarah, Duchess of York. 12 Harry. 13 Andrew. 14 The Queen. 15 Britannia. 16 Miss. 17 Balmoral. 18 Laura. 19 Christmas. 20 Candle in the Wind. 21 Grace Kelly. 22 USA. 23 Westminster. 24 Monaco. 25 Photographer. 26 Paris. 27 Windsor. 28 Queen Victoria. 29 Navy. 30 Anne.

1 Which famous actress Koo was romantically linked to Prince Andrew?

2 What relation was Prince Philip to Princess Margaret?

3 What did the Princess of Wales sell at auction in 1997?

4 What is the Princess Royal's real first name?

5 Who played the Queen in a 2006 film about the death of Princess Diana?

6 What is the title of the wife of Prince Michael of Kent?

7 Which Princess was prevented from marrying divorced Peter Townsend in the 1950s?

8 On which programme did Princess Diana say her marriage had been "a bit crowded"?

9 Prince Harry followed Prince William to which school in 1998?

10 Which dietary illness did Princess Diana allegedly suffer from?

11 Who is the mother of Princesses Beatrice and Eugenie?

12 Which son of Prince Charles has red hair?

13 Who is older, Prince Andrew or Prince Edward?

14 Which Royal is always referred to as Her Majesty?

15 Which Royal yacht was decommissioned in 1997?

16 Is Princess Anne's daughter a Princess, or a Miss?

17 Where is the Queen's holiday home north of the border?

18 What is the first name of Princes William and Harry's step sister?

19 At which time of year does the Queen always make a TV broadcast?

20 What did Elton John sing at Princess Diana's funeral?

21 Which wife of Prince Rainier of Monaco was an Oscar winner?

22 Was Charles and Camilla's first overseas tour together to Russia or USA?

23 In which Abbey did Prince Andrew and Sarah Ferguson marry?

24 Prince Albert succeeded to which throne in 2005?

25 Which profession is shared by Lords Snowdon and Lichfield?

26 In which city was Princess Diana tragically killed?

27 Which castle was reopened in 1998 after being damaged by fire?

28 Who was the last British monarch of the 19th century?

29 Before his marriage was Prince Philip in the army or the navy?

30 Which Princess was married to Captain Mark Phillips?

Answers | Geography: World tour *(see Quiz 111)*

1 Nile. 2 Pope. 3 West. 4 Afghanistan. 5 Bombay. 6 Abominable. 7 Australia. 8 Southern. 9 India. 10 Peru. 11 Caribbean. 12 Zimbabwe. 13 Suez. 14 Coast. 15 Pacific. 16 South Africa. 17 Abraham Lincoln. 18 Arizona. 19 Australia. 20 Sahara. 21 Monarchy. 22 Africa. 23 Danube. 24 Atlantic. 25 Iran. 26 Arctic Circle. 27 Southern. 28 Hungary. 29 China. 30 Canada.

1 Which long river has White and Blue tributaries?
2 Which religious leader is head of state of the Vatican?
3 Is Perth on the west or east coast of Australia?
4 Which country was the centre of operations for the Taliban?
5 Does Bombay or Tokyo have the higher population?
6 What sort of Snowman is another name for the Himalayan yeti?
7 What is the world's smallest, flattest and driest continent?
8 Is Argentina in the northern or southern half of South America?
9 Pakistan and Bangladesh both border which country?
10 Which country's name is an anagram of PURE?
11 The West Indies lie in which Sea?
12 Zambia is a neighbour of which country which also begins with Z?
13 Which Egyptian canal links the Red Sea and the Mediterranean?
14 Is Ghana on the African coast or wholly inland?
15 Which ocean is the world's deepest?
16 In which country is the homeland of KwaZulu?
17 Who is commemorated at Washington's Lincoln Memorial?
18 Which US state has the zipcode (postcode) AZ?
19 New South Wales is in which country?
20 Which African desert is the world's largest?
21 Is Swaziland a monarchy or a republic?
22 Mount Kilimanjaro is the highest point of which continent?
23 Which river runs through Belgrade, Budapest and Vienna?
24 Which ocean lies to the east of South America?
25 Which Islamic Republic used to be called Persia?
26 Two thirds of Greenland lies in which Circle?
27 Is Namibia in northern or southern Africa?
28 In which country in Europe could you spend a forint?
29 Which People's Republic has the world's largest population?
30 Alberta is a province of which country?

Medium Questions

For the majority of pub quiz situations, these questions are going to be your primary line of attack. They're tricky enough to make people think about the answer, but they're not so mind-straining that your audience is going to walk off feeling humiliated. And that's important. The majority of folks in the pub are going to know roughly half of the answers to these questions, and where people fall down totally will be in subjects that they know nothing about. If you're setting a quiz for lone contestants, make good use of these questions.

If you're working with teams, you may find that this section is a little on the simple side still. Pick any four people from the bar, and you'll find that between them, they have at least some knowledge of most areas. That means that scores for teams on this sort of material should be around the 75% mark, which leaves plenty of room for doing well or doing badly, but still lets everyone feel good about themselves.

So, either way, use these questions wisely. Rely on their power to help you out of a sticky situation (although that might just be beer on the pub carpet), and you won't go far wrong. They will provide the backbone of your quiz.

Quiz 1 — Pot Luck 1

1 Stamp duty is normally paid on the sale of what?

2 In which country is Aceh province, scene of the 2004 tsunami?

3 What does a BACS system transfer?

4 Who wears a chasuble?

5 Who or what is your doppelganger?

6 Emphysema affects which part of the body?

7 Which term for school or university is from the Latin meaning "bounteous mother"?

8 Which salts are hydrated magnesium sulphate?

9 What was the last No. 1 single made by Steps?

10 What did Plaid Cymru add to its name in 1998?

11 Which punctuation mark would an American call a period?

12 For which film did George Clooney win Best Supporting Actor in 2006?

13 Where were the Elgin marbles from originally?

14 Which song starts, "Friday night and the lights are low"?

15 According to legend, what will happen to Gibraltar's ape population if the British leave?

16 Is BST before or behind GMT?

17 Which country does Man Utd's Nemanja Vidic represent?

18 How many valves does a bugle have?

19 What name is given to the compulsive eating disorder?

20 What is a Blenheim Orange?

21 Which childhood disease is also called varicella?

22 What do citronella candles smell of?

23 Which part of the anatomy shares its name with a punctuation mark?

24 Which tax did council tax immediately replace?

25 Which English archbishop signs his name Ebor?

26 Which saint was born in Lourdes?

27 Which proposal for a single currency shares its name with a bird?

28 Where is the auditory canal?

29 Where is a fresco painted?

30 How long must a person have had to be dead to qualify for a blue plaque?

Answers | Sport: Cricket *(see Quiz 2)*

1 Brisbane. 2 Chris Read. 3 Tony Lewis. 4 Trevor McDonald. 5 Terrence. 6 Kapil Dev. 7 Somerset. 8 Denis Compton. 9 Shakoor Rana. 10 Dennis Lillee. 11 Michael Atherton. 12 The Oval. 13 Graham Alan Gooch. 14 Langer & Hayden. 15 Headingley. 16 Muthiah Muralitharan. 17 William Gilbert. 18 David Gower. 19 Northants. 20 Lancashire. 21 Sunglasses. 22 Sunil Gavaskar. 23 Hansie Cronje. 24 Don Bradman. 25 Graeme Hick. 26 Imran Khan. 27 Antigua. 28 The Times. 29 Sri Lanka. 30 Left.

1 Where was the first Test played in the 2006–7 Ashes?
2 Who was Geraint Jones's main rival as keeper in the 2006–7 Ashes?
3 Which former test cricketer became President of the MCC in 1998?
4 Which newsreader has written biographies of Viv Richards and Clive Lloyd?
5 What is Ian Botham's middle name?
6 Which Indian was the second bowler to reach 400 Test wickets?
7 Which English county did Viv Richards play for?
8 Which cricketer was the first British sportsman to appear in a major advertising campaign?
9 Which umpire did Gatting publicly argue with in Faisalabad?
10 Which Australian was the first man to take 300 wickets in Test cricket?
11 Who played in the most tests as England captain?
12 Which is the most southerly of the six regular English Test grounds?
13 Which cricketer's initials are GAG?
14 In Aussie opening partnerships, who are Justin and Matthew?
15 At which ground did England beat South Africa to clinch the 1998 series?
16 David Lloyd was reprimanded for criticising which Sri Lankan bowler in 1998?
17 What were WG Grace's first two names?
18 Whose record did Graham Gooch pass when he became England's leading run scorer?
19 Which county does Monty Panesar play for?
20 Who won the 1998 Nat West Trophy?
21 In 1996 Darren Gough became the first England bowler to bowl wearing what?
22 Which Indian cricketer scored 10,122 runs in 125 matches between 1971 and 1987?
23 Who captained the South Africans on their 1998 England tour?
24 Which cricketer's bat was auctioned for £23,000 in 1997?
25 Which Rhodesian became Zimbabwe's youngest professional at the age of 17 in 1985?
26 Who captained Pakistan in the 1992 World Cup victory?
27 On which island did Brian Lara make his record-breaking 375?
28 In which newspaper was it announced that English cricket had died, leading to competition for the Ashes?
29 In which country is Khettarama Stadium?
30 Which hand does David Gower write with?

1 Which "EastEnders" funeral took place at Christmas 2005?
2 Why does a glow worm glow?
3 Which comedy actor swam the Channel for Sports Relief in 2006?
4 Who had hits with "Caught in a Moment" and "In The Middle"?
5 Cambodian leader Saloth Sar was better known by what name?
6 How many holes are most major golf tournaments played over?
7 In the song, what colour rose is linked with Texas?
8 Tokai wine comes from which country?
9 In which month did Samuel Pepys begin his famous diary?
10 Whom was Lord Lucan said to have murdered?
11 Mont Blanc stands in France as well as which other country?
12 William Wilkins designed which London gallery?
13 Which city has an American football team called the Cowboys?
14 Which is the world's oldest surviving republic?
15 Which Latin words did HM the Queen use to describe the year 1992?
16 Which cave is the most famous on the Scottish Isle of Staffa?
17 Cars with the international vehicle registration SF come from where?
18 Number 22 in bingo is represented by a pair of little what?
19 What is the core of an ear of maize called?
20 What was the title of the Eurovision winner for Bucks Fizz?
21 How many did Arsenal score to win the first FA Cup Final decided on penalties?
22 Which country's stamps show the word "Hellas"?
23 Who were the subject of the Cat and Mouse Act of 1913?
24 How many points are scored for a motor racing Grand Prix win?
25 What is the largest structure ever made by living creatures?
26 Papworth Hospital is in which county?
27 Who said, "Float like a butterfly, sting like a bee"?
28 Which magazine was first published in the 1840s and last in the 1990s?
29 Which road is crossed by the horses during the Grand National?
30 Which religious ceremony comes from the Greek word for "to dip"?

Answers | **The Movies: All Action** *(see Quiz 4)*

1 Goldeneye. 2 Platoon. 3 Jeremy Irons. 4 Ridley Scott. 5 Charles Bronson. 6 Jim Carrey. 7 Best Director. 8 Wesley Snipes. 9 Live and Let Die. 10 Faye Dunaway. 11 Donald Pleasence. 12 Die Hard with a Vengeance. 13 Harrison Ford. 14 Marseilles. 15 Apollo 13. 16 Bruce Willis. 17 Popeye Doyle. 18 James Caan. 19 Irish. 20 Brad Pitt. 21 Lost in Space. 22 Phil Collins. 23 Cabbie. 24 Paul & Linda McCartney. 25 JFK. 26 Sean Bean. 27 Jeremy Irons. 28 Arnold Schwarzenegger. 29 New York. 30 Leonardo DiCaprio.

Quiz 4 — The Movies: All Action

Answers – page 123

1 Which Bond film shares its name with Ian Fleming's Jamaican home?
2 What was the third of Oliver Stone's films about Vietnam?
3 Which English Oscar winner was the villain in "Die Hard III"?
4 Which Brit directed "Black Hawk Down" and "Hannibal"?
5 Who played Bernardo in "The Magnificent Seven" and Danny Velinski in "The Great Escape"?
6 Who was The Riddler in "Batman Forever"?
7 Which Oscar did Kevin Costner win for "Dances with Wolves"?
8 Who played the defrosted super-villain in "Demolition Man"?
9 What was Roger Moore's first Bond film in 1973?
10 Who had her first major starring role in "Bonnie & Clyde"?
11 Who plays the President in "Escape from New York"?
12 Which was the third Die Hard film?
13 Who played Indiana Jones?
14 Where was "French Connection II" set?
15 Astronaut Jim Lovell was portrayed by Tom Hanks in which film?
16 Who heads the crew which saves the world in "Armageddon"?
17 Whom did Gene Hackman play in "The French Connection"?
18 Who played Sonny Corleone in "The Godfather" and its sequel?
19 What nationality cop did Sean Connery play in "The Untouchables"?
20 Who co-starred with Morgan Freeman in "Seven"?
21 Which 1998 film of a 60s cult TV series starred Gary Oldman and William Hurt?
22 Who played the train robber of the title role in "Buster"?
23 What was Mel Gibson's job in the 1997 thriller "Conspiracy Theory"?
24 Which husband and wife were Oscar nominated for the song from "Live and Let Die"?
25 Which Oliver Stone movie with Kevin Costner was about events prior to Kennedy's assassination?
26 Which Yorkshireman played the IRA terrorist in "Patriot Games"?
27 Which British 90s Oscar winner featured in "The Man in the Iron Mask"?
28 Who was the construction worker who had flashbacks in "Total Recall"?
29 Where does the action of "Godzilla" take place?
30 Who played two roles in the 90s version of "The Man in the Iron Mask"?

Answers | Pot Luck 2 (see Quiz 3)

1 Nana Moon. 2 To attract mates. 3 David Walliams. 4 Sugababes. 5 Pol Pot. 6 72. 7 Yellow. 8 Hungary. 9 January. 10 Sandra Rivett. 11 Italy. 12 The National Gallery. 13 Dallas. 14 San Marino. 15 Annus horribilis. 16 Fingal's cave. 17 Finland. 18 Two little ducks. 19 A corncob. 20 Making Your Mind Up. 21 5 (in 2005). 22 Greece. 23 Suffragettes. 24 10. 25 The Great Barrier Reef. 26 Cambridgeshire. 27 Muhammad Ali. 28 Punch. 29 Melling Road. 30 Baptism.

Quiz 5 Pot Luck 3

Answers – page 126

1 Which Nigel went from "EastEnders" to the West End in "Guys and Dolls"?
2 Who was voted Beard of the Year 2006?
3 Spy-writer David J. Cornwell writes under which name?
4 What is the unit of measurement for the brightness of stars?
5 Which "-ology" is the study of birds' eggs?
6 Which Dire Straits album included "Money for Nothing"?
7 Who were Janet, Pam, Barbara, Jack, Peter, George and Colin?
8 In which country would you be to visit Agadir?
9 What name is given to a bell tower not attached to a church?
10 Van Pelt is the surname of which "Peanuts" character?
11 What is the best hand in a game of poker?
12 The Virgin record label was launched by which instrumental album?
13 Was Madonna's "Confessions on a Dance Floor" a No. 1 album in 5, 15 or 25 countries?
14 In the official conker rules, how many strikes per turn are allowed?
15 Which country celebrated its bicentenary in 1988?
16 What word commonly describes a spasm of the diaphragm?
17 Daniel Carroll found theatrical fame under which name?
18 In pop music, who looked into his father's eyes?
19 Who lit the funeral pyre of Mrs Indira Gandhi?
20 What was the name of Sports Relief's 2006 equine celebrity show?
21 Which comedian plays the role of Brian Potter in "Phoenix Nights"?
22 John Sentamu was Bishop of where, before becoming Archbishop of York?
23 Switzerland's Mont Cervin is better known by what name?
24 Who wrote the novel "Where Eagles Dare"?
25 Which England cricket captain had the middle name Dylan?
26 What do the initials CND stand for?
27 What is the collective name for a group of frogs?
28 Who was the first act to have seven consecutive US No. 1 singles?
29 Eton school is in which county?
30 Which country was first to host Summer and Winter Olympics in the same year?

Answers | Leisure: Food & Drink 1 *(see Quiz 6)*

1 Fish. 2 Kirschwasser. 3 Gin. 4 Sugar. 5 November. 6 Curry powder. 7 Greece. 8 Halal. 9 20. 10 Kiwi fruit. 11 Gelatine. 12 Marty Wilde. 13 Mrs Beeton. 14 Nut. 15 Coca Cola. 16 Guinness Red. 17 Clarified butter. 18 Carrot. 19 Bloody Mary. 20 Manchester United. 21 Nouvelle cuisine. 22 Aluminium. 23 Bergamot. 24 Rhodes to Home. 25 Black. 26 Tana. 27 Poisonous raw. 28 Mushroom. 29 Cherry. 30 Milk.

Quiz 6

Leisure: Food & Drink 1 | Answers – page 125 | **LEVEL 2**

1 What type of food is gravadlax?
2 Which type of brandy is made from cherries?
3 Which spirit is Pimm's No. 1 based on?
4 Aspartame is an alternative to what when added to food?
5 In which month does Beaujolais Nouveau arrive?
6 Which powder includes turmeric, fenugreek, chillies and cumin?
7 Which country produces more than 70% of the world's olive oil?
8 What name is given to food prepared according to Muslim law?
9 How many standard wine bottles make up a Nebuchadnezzar?
10 Which fruit is also called the Chinese gooseberry?
11 Agar agar is a vegetarian alternative to what?
12 Which 50s pop star's name is cockney rhyming slang for mild?
13 How is cook Isabella Mary Mayson better known?
14 What sort of food is a macadamia?
15 Atlanta is the headquarters of which drinks company?
16 In 2006 Guinness announced they were to launch which colour variety?
17 What is ghee?
18 Caraway is related to which family of vegetables?
19 Which queen's nickname is the name of a cocktail?
20 Which football team does Gary Rhodes support?
21 Which term coined in the 70s describes food which does not have rich sauces?
22 What are most beer and soft drinks cans made from?
23 Which flavour is traditionally used in Earl Grey tea?
24 What was Gary Rhodes' range of convenience foods called?
25 What colour are fully ripened olives?
26 What is TV chef Gordon Ramsay's wife called?
27 Why do cashew nuts have to be roasted to be eaten?
28 What is a morel?
29 What is a morello?
30 Which drink did Bob Geldof advertise?

| **Answers** | **Pot Luck 3** *(see Quiz 5)* |

1 Nigel Harman. 2 Monty Panesar. 3 John Le Carré. 4 Magnitude. 5 Oology. 6 Brothers in Arms. 7 The Secret Seven. 8 Morocco. 9 A campanile. 10 Lucy. 11 Royal flush. 12 Tubular Bells. 13 25. 14 Three. 15 Australia. 16 Hiccough. 17 Danny La Rue. 18 Eric Clapton. 19 Rajiv Gandhi. 20 Only Fools On Horses. 21 Peter Kay. 22 Birmingham. 23 The Matterhorn. 24 Alistair MacLean. 25 Bob Willis. 26 Campaign for Nuclear Disarmament. 27 An army (or colony). 28 Whitney Houston. 29 Berkshire. 30 France.

Answers – page 128

1 The illness pertussis is more commonly called what?
2 Who spent longer as Middlesbrough manager – Bryan Robson or Steve McClaren?
3 Which rock is the largest monolith in the world?
4 Which Spanish team were the first winners of the European Cup?
5 What type of animal can be Texel and Romney Marsh?
6 Where would you hurt if you were kicked on the tarsus?
7 The Bee Gees were born on which island?
8 What action does a dromophobic fear?
9 In which country is the world's second highest mountain, K2?
10 What nationality is Salman Rushdie?
11 Who made the top ten albums with "Then and Now – 1964–2004"??
12 Which tanker went down on the Seven Stones reef off Land's End?
13 Which large forest is the nearest to London's Liverpool Street Station?
14 Which hit by Judy Collins entered the UK charts on eight occasions?
15 Who played Lord Longford in the 2006 drama about his life?
16 In which decade did Constantinople become Istanbul?
17 How many bridesmaids attended Princess Diana?
18 Which poet gave his name to a Cape to the south of Brisbane?
19 Which Russian town produced deformed sheep after a 90s disaster?
20 What is Paul McCartney's first name?
21 Which drug took its name from the Greek god of dreams?
22 Which is the largest borough in the city of New York?
23 Which doll's name gave Aqua a No. 1 hit?
24 In 2005, why did Richard Griffiths ask a member of the audience to leave a West End show?
25 What is examined using an otoscope?
26 What is measured on the Mercalli Scale?
27 Along with Doric and Ionic, what is the third Greek order of architecture?
28 What is lowered by a Beta Blocker?
29 How many pieces does each backgammon player use?
30 A Blue Orpington is a type of what?

Answers | **Nature: Animal World** *(see Quiz 8)*

1 Suffocation. 2 Sett. 3 Velvet. 4 Black. 5 Dachshund. 6 It cannot bark. 7 Afrikaans. 8 Mauritius. 9 Antelope. 10 Snow leopard. 11 Fight. 12 Squirrel. 13 One. 14 Cattle. 15 Hearing. 16 32. 17 Fawn. 18 Hooves. 19 Blood of birds and mammals. 20 Sheep. 21 Pink. 22 White. 23 Japan. 24 Caribou. 25 Lemurs. 26 White / cream. 27 V shape. 28 Elk. 29 Sand. 30 Border collie.

1 How do the anaconda's victims die?

2 What is the badger's system of burrows called?

3 What is the skin on a deer's antlers called?

4 What colour face does a Suffolk sheep have?

5 Which small breed of dog has a German name meaning badger dog?

6 What is unusual about the sound of the dingo?

7 Aardvark means "earth pig" in which African language?

8 On which island was the dodo formerly found?

9 What is an impala?

10 What type of leopard is another name for the ounce?

11 Pit bull terriers were bred to do what?

12 To which family does the prairie dog belong?

13 Does the Indian rhinoceros have one or two horns?

14 Bovine Spongiform Encephalitis is a fatal disease of which animals?

15 Tinnitus affects which of the senses?

16 How many teeth do human adults have?

17 What is the most common colour of a Great Dane?

18 What does an ungulate animal have?

19 What do vampire bats feed on?

20 Lanolin is a by product of which domestic animal?

21 If a mammal has albinism what colour are its eyes?

22 What colour are dalmatians when they are born?

23 The tosa is a dog native to which country?

24 What is the reindeer of North America called?

25 Which group of primates are found only on Madagascar?

26 What colour is the coat of a samoyed?

27 What shaped mark does an adder have on its head?

28 What is another name for the wapiti?

29 What do alligators lay their eggs in?

30 Which dog do shepherds now most commonly use for herding sheep?

Answers	Pot Luck 4 *(see Quiz 7)*

1 Whooping cough. 2 Bryan Robson. 3 Ayers Rock. 4 Real Madrid. 5 Sheep. 6 Ankle. 7 Isle of Man. 8 Crossing the road. 9 Pakistan. 10 British. 11 The Who. 12 Torrey Canyon. 13 Epping Forest. 14 Amazing Grace. 15 Jim Broadbent. 16 1930s. 17 Five. 18 Byron. 19 Chernobyl. 20 James. 21 Morphine. 22 Queens. 23 Barbie. 24 Her mobile phone kept ringing. 25 Ear. 26 Earthquakes. 27 Corinthian. 28 Blood pressure. 29 15. 30 Chicken.

1 In which US state is Death Valley?

2 Which Sea does the River Jordan flow into?

3 Who was Speaker of the House after Bernard Weatherill?

4 What was the first Craig David hit to feature the word "Love" in the title?

5 Which BBC magazine was launched in 1929?

6 What did Captain Cook call the Islands of Tonga?

7 Which celebrity was murdered in 1980 outside New York's Dakota Building?

8 Who played Lennie Godber in the TV series "Porridge"?

9 Which naval base is situated in Hampshire?

10 Who featured on The Pussycat Dolls' No. 1 "Don't Cha"?

11 What is Marc Bolan's son's Christian name?

12 Which war is the first for which there are photographic records?

13 Writer Mary Westmacott is better known by what name?

14 Who or what was a ducat?

15 Which day is the last quarter day in a calendar year in England?

16 Which actor links "The Charmer" with "Dangerfield"?

17 In the Bible, who was Jacob's youngest son?

18 What was suffragette Mrs Pankhurst's Christian name?

19 In which sport is the Plunkett Shield competed for?

20 Which animal has breeds called Roscommon, Kerry Hill, Ryedale?

21 Which two countries was the Cod War of the 1970s between?

22 What colour are Rupert Bear's trousers?

23 Caboc, Dunlop and Morven are cheeses from which country?

24 Which animal can be red, arctic, bat-eared and fennec?

25 Newman Noggs appears in which Charles Dickens novel?

26 What name is given to the base of your spine?

27 Whom did Sandy Powell ask "Can You Hear Me, ..?"

28 Which actress links the films "Ghostbusters" and "Alien"?

29 Perth is the capital of which state?

30 Which word describes both a blunt sword and a very thin sheet of metal?

Answers | Geography: The UK (see Quiz 10)

1 Brighton. 2 Melinda Messenger. 3 South Kensington. 4 Stoke Mandeville. 5 Suffolk. 6 Severn Tunnel. 7 Newgate. 8 Canary Wharf (Isle of Dogs). 9 Salopian. 10 Army exercises. 11 Essex & Suffolk. 12 Bristol. 13 M6. 14 Glastonbury. 15 Big Ben. 16 Blackpool. 17 Windscale. 18 Horses. 19 Clyde. 20 Nottingham. 21 Wiltshire. 22 Edinburgh. 23 Petticoat Lane. 24 Papworth. 25 Hyde Park. 26 Aberdeen. 27 Bath. 28 Straits of Dover. 29 Castle. 30 Bristol.

1 Which seaside resort has Lanes and a nudist beach?
2 Which Page Three blonde is Swindon's most famous export?
3 In which part of London is the Natural History Museum?
4 Where is the National Spinal Injuries Unit?
5 In which county is Sizewell nuclear power station?
6 What is Britain's longest tunnel?
7 The Old Bailey is on the site of which former prison?
8 Where in London would a Canary sit on Dogs?
9 What is a native of Shropshire called?
10 What is Salisbury Plain primarily used for?
11 In which two counties is Constable Country?
12 Where is the Clifton Suspension Bridge?
13 Spaghetti Junction is on which road?
14 Which Somerset town is said to be the burial place of King Arthur?
15 Which bell was named after Benjamin Hall?
16 Which pleasure beach was the UK's top tourist attraction in 2005?
17 What was the former name of Sellafield?
18 Which animals are kept in the Royal Mews near Buckingham Palace?
19 Holy Loch is an inlet of which river?
20 Which city has an annual Goose Fair?
21 In which English county is Europe's largest stone circle?
22 Which castle is at the west end of the Royal Mile?
23 How is the Sunday market in London's Middlesex Street better known?
24 Which Cambridgeshire hospital is famous for its transplant surgery?
25 Speaker's Corner is on the corner of what?
26 Where is the administrative headquarters of the Grampian region?
27 Which city has a famous Royal Crescent?
28 The Goodwin Sands are at the entrance to which straits?
29 What type of historic structures can be found at Framlingham, Orford and Windsor?
30 Where is Temple Meads railway station?

Answers Pot Luck 5 (see Quiz 9)

1 California. 2 Dead Sea. 3 Betty Boothroyd. 4 World Filled with Love. 5 The Listener. 6 The Friendly Islands. 7 John Lennon. 8 Richard Beckinsale. 9 Gosport. 10 Busta Rhymes. 11 Roland Bolan. 12 Crimean. 13 Agatha Christie. 14 A coin. 15 Christmas Day. 16 Nigel Havers. 17 Benjamin. 18 Emmeline. 19 Cricket. 20 Sheep. 21 Iceland and Britain. 22 Yellow check. 23 Scotland. 24 Fox. 25 Nicholas Nickleby. 26 Coccyx. 27 Mother. 28 Sigourney Weaver. 29 Western Australia. 30 Foil.

1 How many other months have the same number of days as January?
2 December, January and February have the maximum of how many days?
3 In the carol "In the bleak midwinter…," what is the second line?
4 Prince Albert buying one in 1841 helped popularise which Xmas item?
5 In Islam Hajj Day is in which month?
6 Which word is used to mean flying away for the winter, as with many birds?
7 What name is given to the strike-filled winter of 1978–79?
8 In which winter month is Martin Luther Day?
9 Where in Italy were the 2006 Winter Olympics held?
10 December came where in sequence in the Roman calendar?
11 Thinking Day is celebrated in February by which female movement?
12 Which winter sport uses skates, stones and brooms?
13 What are the winter months in the southern hemisphere?
14 In which winter month was Elvis Presley's birthday?
15 What do frogs and bats do during the winter?
16 To ten years, when did Charles Dickens write "A Christmas Carol"?
17 Which winter month is named after the god of doorways and beginnings?
18 What is hit by sticks in ice hockey?
19 Who wrote "Winter" from the musical work "The Four Seasons"?
20 Which David Jason TV character's name is a personification of winter?
21 In the Christian calendar what are the four weeks before Christmas called?
22 In which Scandinavian country is December called joulukuu, meaning month of Christmas?
23 Whose birthday is celebrated on Burns Night?
24 In January 1901 oil was first discovered in which US state?
25 What is the French word for winter?
26 December begins in which star sign?
27 Waitangi Day is celebrated in February in which country?
28 In which country is Pearl Harbor Day celebrated?
29 December always begins with the same day as which autumnal month?
30 Which winter month's birthstone is the amethyst?

Answers | Pot Luck 6 *(see Quiz 12)*

1 Yellowstone National Park. 2 International Monetary Fund. 3 Volcanic gases. 4 Lentils. 5 Sheffield. 6 Barry Manilow. 7 Dean Kiely. 8 Hattie Jacques. 9 A will. 10 Thanksgiving. 11 Black. 12 The Wailers. 13 Fish soup. 14 National Exhibition Centre. 15 Boy George. 16 21. 17 Versailles. 18 30 minutes. 19 Scotland. 20 Belshazzar. 21 White rum. 22 Thunder & lightning. 23 Mick Hucknall. 24 The Andes. 25 The Derby. 26 An unborn baby. 27 Prunella Scales. 28 The peacock. 29 The Baltic. 30 Frogmore.

1 In which US National Park is the Old Faithful geyser?
2 What do the initials IMF stand for?
3 What is emitted from a fumarole?
4 What is the main ingredient in dhal, the Indian dish?
5 In which city is Bramall Lane?
6 Westlife had a No. 1 with "Mandy", but who had the original hit?
7 Who was in goal for the "great escape" run-in for Portsmouth 2006?
8 How is Josephina Jacques known in Carry On films?
9 To what would a codicil be added?
10 Which American annual celebration was first marked during 1789?
11 The first Girl Guides had to wear what colour stockings?
12 Which band claimed fifty per cent of Bob Marley's estate?
13 Cullen Skink is what kind of soup?
14 What does NEC stand for around Birmingham?
15 Who left Bow Wow Wow to form Culture Club?
16 What is the maximum score in blackjack?
17 Which building in France has a famous Hall of Mirrors?
18 Does one revolution of the London Eye take around 15, 30 or 70 minutes?
19 Which country did Arsenal keeper Bob Wilson play for?
20 In the Bible, which character saw the first writing on the wall?
21 A Daiquiri is made from fruit juice and which alcoholic drink?
22 Astraphobia is the fear of which meteorological event?
23 Which male pop superstar once played with the Frantic Elevators?
24 Machu Picchu is in which mountain range?
25 What is the English equivalent of the Melbourne Cup?
26 What is surrounded by amniotic fluid?
27 Who links "Fawlty Towers" and "After Henry"?
28 Which bird is India's national symbol?
29 Which sea is the least salty in the world?
30 Where was the Duke of Windsor buried in 1972?

1 Which No. 1 hit for the Archies was in the charts for twenty six weeks?
2 Which Park was a hit for the Small Faces in 1967?
3 Who was singing about "Sheila" in 1962 and "Dizzy" in 1969?
4 Which 60s hit for Kitty Lester was an 80s hit for Alison Moyet?
5 When did the Shirelles want to know "Will You Still Love Me..."?
6 Which crime busting organisation gave the Shadows a 1961 hit?
7 What was Petula Clark's first No. 1 UK hit in 1961?
8 Which three numbers gave Len Barry his No. 3 hit in 1965?
9 Who had consecutive hits with "Daydream" and "Summer in the City"?
10 What was over for the Seekers in their 1965 UK No. 1 hit?
11 Charting again for Elvis in 2005, what was the name of "His Latest Flame"?
12 What were Emile Ford and the Checkmates Counting in 1960?
13 What was the Searchers' first No. 1?
14 What was on the other side of Shirley Bassey's "Reach for the Stars"?
15 Whose first Top Ten hit was 5-4-3-2-1 in 1964?
16 Which country was in the title of a '63 hit by Matt Monro?
17 Who recorded the original of the song used in "Four Weddings and a Funeral"?
18 What Girl was Neil Sedaka singing about in 1961?
19 The song "Starry Eyed" was a No. 1 on 1 January 1960 for which Michael?
20 Which words of exclamation were a 1960 No. 4 hit for Peter Sellers?
21 Which "Opportunity Knocks" star had a hit with "Those were the Days"?
22 What did The Move say they could hear grow in a 1967 hit title?
23 Which 60s hit for Kenny Lynch was a No. 1 for Robson and Jerome in 1995?
24 Who were "Glad All Over" in their No. 1 hit from 1963?
25 What was "skipped" in the lyrics of "Whiter Shade of Pale"?
26 What type of Feelings did Tom Jones have in his 1967 hit?
27 Which Group had consecutive No. 1s with "Keep On Running" and "Somebody Help Me"?
28 To which religious building were the Dixie Cups going in 1964?
29 Which weather sounding group had hits with "Robot" and "Globetrotter"?
30 Known by another name, Yusuf had his first Top Ten hit with which 60s song?

Answers | Pot Luck 7 *(see Quiz 14)*

1 1950s. 2 The Undertones. 3 The Hobbit. 4 Jeanette MacDonald. 5 Excalibur. 6 Woody Allen. 7 Colchester. 8 Uncle Mac. 9 You walk. 10 Ariel Sharon. 11 Roy Wood. 12 Brookside. 13 Arthur Lucan. 14 Eric Idle. 15 Hairy. 16 My Love (2000). 17 George III. 18 A dog. 19 Alex Ferguson. 20 Red Square, Moscow. 21 Private Fraser. 22 Schools. 23 Sheep & goats. 24 Mumps. 25 Shirley Williams. 26 A bolt or quarrel. 27 Amsterdam. 28 Shirley Temple. 29 Pig. 30 George VI.

1 In which decade did Lester Piggott first win the Derby?
2 Who had hits with "My Perfect Cousin" and "Jimmy Jimmy"?
3 Which folklore fantasy tale is subtitled "There and Back Again"?
4 Who was Nelson Eddy's singing partner in many musical films?
5 Which famous sword is sometimes called Caliburn?
6 Which famous film director has a son called Satchel?
7 Which is further North, Chelmsford or Colchester?
8 Children's broadcaster Derek McCulloch was known on the radio as whom?
9 What is your mode of transport if you go by Walker's Bus?
10 Which Israeli leader suffered a severe stroke in January 2006?
11 Which Wizzard star formed ELO in 1971?
12 In which TV soap was Trevor Jordache buried under the patio?
13 Who played Old Mother Riley in films and on stage?
14 Which member of the Monty Python team was born on the same day as John Major?
15 What does the word piliferous mean?
16 What was the first Westlife No. 1 to feature the word "Love" in the title?
17 Which King George bought Buckingham Palace?
18 What kind of animal is a Schnauzer?
19 Which soccer boss was the first to win the English double twice?
20 In which famous Square is St Basil's cathedral?
21 In the series "Dad's Army" which soldier's daytime job was an undertaker?
22 Chris Woodhead and Mike Tomlinson have both been Chief Inspectors of what?
23 Which animals are attacked by a disease called Scrapie?
24 Which childhood disease affects the parotid salivary gland?
25 Which female MP was one of the founder members of the SDP?
26 What can be fired by a crossbow?
27 In which city was Anne Frank when she wrote her diary?
28 Which actress played lead In the films "Dimples" and "Curly Top"?
29 Lard is mainly produced from which animal?
30 Which king was the last Emperor of India?

1 Who succeeded Ossie Ardiles as Spurs manager?
2 Which football team plays its home matches at Love Street?
3 Which English international played for three Italian clubs before moving to Arsenal?
4 Who was fined £20,000 for making a video on how to foul players?
5 Whose 1996 penalty miss prompted Des Lynam to say "You can come out from behind your sofas now"?
6 Who was PFA Young Player of the Year in '95 and '96?
7 Who left Tottenham immediately before George Graham took over?
8 Which football manager is singer Louise's father-in-law?
9 Which club side was Alan Ball playing for during the 1966 World Cup?
10 What is Glenn Hoddle in the cockney rhyming slang dictionary?
11 Which was the first Lancashire side Kenny Dalglish managed?
12 How is Mrs Paul Peschilsolido better known?
13 Wayne Rooney was doubtful for Germany 2006 after an injury sustained in which match?
14 Who was Man Utd manager immediately prior to Alex Ferguson?
15 Which team did Arsenal beat in the 2006 Champions League semi-finals?
16 Who was the first UK manager to walk out on a contract and work abroad?
17 Who has managed Internazionale of Milan and Blackburn Rovers?
18 Which 1980s FA Cup winners came nearest the start of the alphabet?
19 Who was Blackburn's top scorer in 2005–06, his only season at the club?
20 Who stayed longer as Newcastle boss – Sir Bobby Robson or Graeme Souness?
21 Who became Everton's record signing in June 2006?
22 Who was made Northern Ireland manager in February 1998?
23 Which England player was seen on the town wearing a sarong prior to France 98?
24 Who should Scotland have been playing when they arrived for a World Cup qualifier with no opposition?
25 Which ex-international managed Burnley in the 1997–98 season?
26 Whom did Jack Charlton play all his League football with?
27 George Graham was accused of taking a "bung" in the transfer of which player?
28 Whom did David O'Leary take over from as Aston Villa boss?
29 In which season did evergreen Ryan Giggs make his Man Utd league debut?
30 Which team beat Middlesbrough in the 2006 UEFA Cup Final?

Quiz 16 Pot Luck 8

Answers – page 135

LEVEL 2

1 Canary Wharf is in which London development?
2 Which lady resigned as a Labour MP in 2006 vowing to remain as an independent?
3 Which superstar was a former member of the group the King Bees?
4 Which Florida national park has a highway called Alligator Alley?
5 What do Australians mean when they talk about a billabong?
6 How old was Billy the Kid when he died?
7 What was the former name of Turkey?
8 Julia Smith became the wife of which famous sportsman?
9 What on a mountainside is scree?
10 Who was Kate Winslet's co star in "All the King's Men"?
11 What killed Sir Francis Drake?
12 What type of hat took its name from a novel by George DuMaurier?
13 The Aegean Sea is linked to the Ionian Sea by which canal?
14 Florence Nightingale was given the Freedom of which city in 1908?
15 Who is the heroine in Jane Austen's "Pride and Prejudice"?
16 What game started the 1969 war between El Salvador and Honduras?
17 In the 80s two thousand people were killed by a gas leak in which Indian town?
18 Which Bay is the largest in the world?
19 What is the highest break in snooker with the advantage of a free black ball?
20 Which blind music star ran for Mayor of Detroit in 1989?
21 Tomas Rosicky joined Arsenal from which club?
22 Who was responsible for setting up the Girl Guides movement?
23 In what year was Nelson Mandela released from prison?
24 Which band's album title reasoned "You Gotta Go There To Come Back"?
25 Rhodes is the largest of which group of islands?
26 What is a sumo wrestling ring made from?
27 The film "Dick Tracy" was promoted by which Madonna single?
28 The Battle of Britain is remembered on which date?
29 Which year did John Lennon perform his final live concert?
30 The 1959 Royal Variety Performance was cancelled for what reason?

1 Which Ponchielli piece features in "Fantasia"?
2 Which US-born Australian was the voice of John Smith in "Pocahontas"?
3 In which year was the Best Animated Feature Oscar first awarded?
4 What was the sequel to "Aladdin" called?
5 What colour are Mickey Mouse's gloves?
6 Perdita and Pongo are what type of animals?
7 How many Oscars, in total, was Disney given for "Snow White and the Seven Dwarfs"?
8 Which 1991 animated film was later a musical in London and the US?
9 Who is the best-known rabbit in "Bambi"?
10 Featuring Elton John songs, what was the highest-grossing animation movie of the 1990s?
11 Which of the Gabor sisters was a voice in "The Aristocats"?
12 Who created Tom and Jerry at MGM in the 40s?
13 What did Dumbo do immediately before his ears grew so big?
14 Which film of a fairy tale features the song "Bibbidy Bobbidy Boo"?
15 Which part did Kathleen Turner voice in "Who Framed Roger Rabbit?"?
16 Which Disney film was the first with a synchronised soundtrack?
17 "Colours of the Wind" was a hit song from which movie?
18 Which film with an animated sequence featured Angela Lansbury using her magic powers against the Nazis?
19 Who sings "He's a tramp" in "Lady and the Tramp"?
20 Where did Kim Basinger star as a sexy animated doodle, Holly, brought over to the real world?
21 Who sang in "Aladdin" after making her name in "Miss Saigon"?
22 Which 1990 film was about pizza-loving, sewer dwelling reptiles?
23 Which was the first film to feature, appropriately enough, computer-animated sequences?
24 What type of orphaned creature featured in "The Land Before Time"?
25 Which was the first animated film in the 90s which Tim Rice won an Oscar for?
26 Which dancer commissioned Hanna and Barbera to do an animation sequence in "Anchors Aweigh" in 1945?
27 Which Tchaikovsky ballet piece features in "Fantasia"?
28 In which film does Shere Khan appear?
29 Which characters made their debut in "Puss Gets the Boot" in 1940?
30 Who was the voice of Stuart in "Stuart Little 2"?

Quiz 18 | Pot Luck 9

1 Cars with the international vehicle registration C come from where?
2 The Paul Getty Museum is in which American state?
3 What is the American equivalent of an English bilberry?
4 What is added to Galliano to make a Harvey Wallbanger?
5 Which country is nearest to where the Titanic was found?
6 An average man has twenty square feet of what about his person?
7 In which country were the last summer Olympics of the 20th century in Europe?
8 In which decade was Cassius Clay – later Muhammad Ali – born?
9 From which tree family is the basket-making osier a member?
10 Which sport other than rugby is played for the Currie Cup?
11 In which country is the Great Sandy Desert?
12 Who had "Sticky Moments on Tour"?
13 The Cheviot hills run along the boundary between which countries?
14 Which seeds are in the sweet, Halva?
15 What note does an orchestra tune to?
16 What featured on McFly's No. 1 single with "All About You"?
17 Which Shakespeare play was banned during George III's time of madness?
18 Before being used as a name for US soldiers, what did "GI" stand for?
19 What is the flowery name of the daughter of Jennifer Garner and Ben Affleck?
20 Which gas is produced by adding water to calcium carbide?
21 Which berries are used in a Cumberland sauce?
22 What is a wadi?
23 In which country is the Potomac River?
24 Which element has the highest melting point?
25 Which Adrian Mole creator wrote "Queen Camilla"?
26 Which part of a tree gives Angostura Bitters its taste?
27 What is the metric word for a million?
28 What is the southern American stew of rice and okra called?
29 Which famous pop guitarist performed with the Notting Hillbillies?
30 George Galloway was in which party for the 2005 Parliamentary election?

Answers	Movies: Animation *(see Quiz 17)*

1 Dance of the Hours. 2 Mel Gibson. 3 2002. 4 The Return of Jafar. 5 White. 6 Dalmatians. 7 Eight. 8 Beauty and the Beast. 9 Thumper. 10 The Lion King. 11 Eva. 12 Hanna & Barbera. 13 He sneezed. 14 Cinderella. 15 Jessica Rabbit. 16 Steamboat Willie. 17 Pocahontas. 18 Bedknobs & Broomsticks. 19 Peggy Lee. 20 Cool World. 21 Lea Salonga. 22 Teenage Mutant Ninja Turtles. 23 Tron. 24 Dinosaur. 25 Aladdin. 26 Gene Kelly. 27 Nutcracker Suite. 28 Jungle Book. 29 Tom & Jerry. 30 Michael J. Fox.

1 Where according to the Bible is the site of the final battle between nations which will end the world?

2 In which Dickens novel did Uriah Heep appear?

3 "Old Possum's Book of Practical Cats" is composed of what?

4 To £5,000 how much do you receive for winning the Booker Prize?

5 In which book did John Braine introduce Joe Lampton?

6 What type of book is the OED?

7 What is the subject of Desmond Morris's "The Naked Ape"?

8 What type of books did Patricia Highsmith write?

9 Which detective first appeared in "A Study in Scarlet" in 1887?

10 The sequel to "Peter Pan" was called "Peter Pan in" what?

11 Which Gothic horror story has the alternative title "The Modern Prometheus"?

12 For what types of book is Samuel Pepys famous for?

13 Who wrote "The Female Eunuch" in 1970?

14 In which county were Jane Austen and Charles Dickens born?

15 Which former politician narrated the diaries of his dog Buster?

16 In "Charlie and the Chocolate Factory", what is Charlie's surname?

17 Which ex-jockey wrote a book of short stories called "Field of Thirteen"?

18 Whose horror stories include "Carrie" and "The Shining"?

19 Which "Sex & the City" star wrote the teen advice book "Being a Girl"?

20 Who wrote "Das Kapital"?

21 What was the name of the Original Conjuring Cat in "Old Possum's Book of Practical Cats"?

22 Which writer and politician bought poet Rupert Brooke's house?

23 Which fictional barrister was created by John Mortimer?

24 Whose first novel, "A Woman of Substance" became a best-seller?

25 The "Dummies" advice books are coloured black and what other main colour?

26 "The Day of the Jackal" is about an assassination plot on whom?

27 For which Salman Rushdie book did the Ayatollah impose a fatwa?

28 Who wrote "It's All Over Now" after her brief marriage to Bill Wyman?

29 To five years, how old was Mary Wesley when her first best-seller was published?

30 Award-winning novelist Ben Okri hails from which country?

Quiz 20 | Pot Luck 10

Answers – page 139

LEVEL 2

1 What is the highest point of the Pennines?
2 2006 marked the 30th anniversary of the death of which crime writer?
3 How many years was Nelson Mandela held in prison?
4 Which British boxer was the first to win three Lonsdale belts outright?
5 Who, according to a NOP survey in 1998, do young men call most on their mobile phones?
6 In which London park is Rotten Row?
7 Defender Stephen Carr joined Newcastle from which club?
8 What will a green phone kiosk only take for payment?
9 Which snooker star was nicknamed "Interesting" by "Spitting Image"?
10 In 1988 who scored 405 not out at Taunton?
11 Who died first, Gilbert or Sullivan?
12 Which was the first London football club to win a European title?
13 In which century did Joan of Arc become a saint?
14 Which American state is called the "Gambling State"?
15 Did John Glenn's first spaceflight last five, ten or 24 hours?
16 Which dessert is named after a famous ballerina?
17 Which river flows from northern Moscow to the Caspian Sea?
18 A Bruxelloise sauce is flavoured with which vegetable?
19 Who was the leading actor in "Play Misty for Me" with Jessica Walker?
20 Who created the Keystone Kops?
21 Who was the Mayor of Casterbridge in the Thomas Hardy novel?
22 What does an alphabetarian study?
23 Who became US President in the year John Lennon died in New York?
24 In which Swiss resort are the Golden Rose TV accolades awarded?
25 Which island is the largest of the Dodecanese group?
26 Which singer's third album was called "Living the Dream"?
27 What characters were created by Roger Hargreaves?
28 To which flower family does garlic belong?
29 Which drink can be green, black and oolong?
30 In which decade was the first American Superbowl?

Answers | Leisure: Books 1 *(see Quiz 19)*

1 Armageddon. 2 David Copperfield. 3 Poems. 4 £20,000. 5 Room at the Top. 6 Dictionary. 7 Man. 8 Crime fiction. 9 Sherlock Holmes. 10 Scarlet. 11 Frankenstein. 12 Diary. 13 Germaine Greer. 14 Hampshire. 15 Roy Hattersley. 16 Buckett. 17 Dick Francis. 18 Stephen King. 19 Kim Cattrall. 20 Karl Marx. 21 Mr Mistoffelees. 22 Jeffrey Archer. 23 Rumpole. 24 Barbara Taylor Bradford. 25 Yellow. 26 Charles de Gaulle. 27 The Satanic Verses. 28 Mandy Smith. 29 70. 30 Nigeria.

1 What colour is the flesh of a cantaloupe melon?
2 Simnel cake was traditionally eaten on which Sunday?
3 What is the fishy ingredient in Scotch woodcock?
4 What is a champignon?
5 Which spirit is Russia famous for producing?
6 What alcoholic drink is made in Hakushu, Yoichi and Yamazaki?
7 What is added to pasta to make it green?
8 Which drink is grown in the Douro basin and exported from Oporto?
9 Which cooking pot boils food at a higher temperature than boiling point?
10 What is another name for dietary fibre?
11 Which sauce/salad shares its name with Latin big-band music?
12 Where did satsumas originate?
13 What are cornichons?
14 Puerto Rico and Jamaica are the main producers of which spirit?
15 What colour is cayenne pepper?
16 What type of pastry is used to make a steak and kidney pudding?
17 Which drink is served in a schooner?
18 What is a Laxton's Superb?
19 Which seafood, usually fried in breadcrumbs, is the Italian name for shrimps?
20 Tofu and TVP come from which bean?
21 Tartrazine colours food which colour?
22 What is added to whisky to make a whisky mac?
23 Where would you buy a pint of Shires?
24 What colour is Double Gloucester cheese?
25 Which Mexican drink is distilled from the agave plant?
26 Which black, gourmet fungus is a native of France's Perigord region?
27 Which expensive vinegar is aged in wooden barrels?
28 Which grain is whisky made from?
29 What is red wine made with that white wine is not?
30 Vermouth is wine flavoured with what?

Answers | Kylie *(see Quiz 22)*

1 Spinning Around. 2 The Magic Roundabout. 3 Showgirl. 4 Melbourne. 5 You.
6 Fever. 7 Parlophone. 8 Love at First Sight. 9 Gemini. 10 Little Eva. 11 Dancing
Queen. 12 Mushroom. 13 Breathe. 14 In Your Eyes. 15 Glastonbury. 16 Spinning
Around. 17 Green Fairy. 18 Red Blooded Woman (2004). 19 Kylie. 20 Deconstruction.
21 Princess. 22 Can't Get You Out of My Head. 23 Body Language. 24 Lingerie. 25
Jason Donovan. 26 Body Language. 27 1960s. 28 13. 29 Kath & Kim. 30 Kylie.

1 Which was Kylie's first UK No. 1 of the new millennium?
2 Kylie voiced Florence in which 2006 movie?
3 Which tour was postponed when Kylie was diagnosed with cancer?
4 Which city does Kylie come from?
5 Which word completes her hits, "I Believe In ..." and "Giving ... Up"?
6 In 2001 which release returned her to No. 1 in the album charts?
7 Kylie moved to which UK label that launched The Beatles?
8 What was Kylie's first single to contain the word "Love"?
9 What is Kylie's star sign?
10 Who had the original hit with "The Loco-Motion"?
11 Which Abba classic did Kylie cover when closing the Sydney Olympics?
12 Which fungus-linked word names her early Australian recording label?
13 Which Kylie hit has the same title as a 2005 hit by Erasure?
14 Which charted first, "Chocolate" or "In Your Eyes"?
15 Which major British festival did Kylie pull out of in 2005?
16 Which No. 1 was promoted with a video showing Kylie in gold hot pants?
17 She played what colour of fairy in the movie "Moulin Rouge"?
18 What was Kylie's first Top Ten single with a colour in the title?
19 "On a Night Like This" was the first hit single on which she used which billing?
20 Which label handled Kylie's records in the UK for most of the 1990s?
21 What word completes her children's book, "The Showgirl..."?
22 What was Kylie's first million seller single in the UK?
23 What kind of "Language" featured in the title of Kylie's 2003 hit album?
24 Love Kylie was the name of a range of what?
25 Kylie's first hit duet was with which artist?
26 Both "Chocolate" and "Slow" featured on which album?
27 In which decade of the twentieth century was Kylie born?
28 Kylie started off with how many consecutive Top Ten hits – 3, 9 or 13?
29 In which TV series did she play a cameo as Epponnee Rae?
30 What was the one-word title of Kylie's first album?

Answers | Leisure: Food & Drink 2 *(see Quiz 21)*

1 Orange. 2 Mothering Sunday. 3 Anchovies. 4 Mushroom. 5 Vodka. 6 Japanese Whisky. 7 Spinach. 8 Port. 9 Pressure cooker. 10 Roughage. 11 Salsa. 12 Japan. 13 Gherkins (pickled cucumbers). 14 Rum. 15 Red. 16 Suet pastry. 17 Sherry. 18 Apple. 19 Scampi. 20 Soya. 21 Yellow. 22 Ginger wine. 23 Ambridge. 24 Orange-red. 25 Tequila. 26 Truffle. 27 Balsamic. 28 Malted barley. 29 Skins of the grape. 30 Bitter herbs.

Quiz 23 | Pot Luck 11

Answers – page 144

1 Who supposedly brought about the downfall of Barings Bank?
2 Which country was the first to legalise abortion?
3 Which Eurovision-winning group formed the Polar Music Company?
4 Luis Saha joined Man Utd from which club?
5 Mount Elbert is the highest peak in which American mountain range?
6 Adam and Eve were the main characters in which work by John Milton?
7 The movie "Cinderella Man" is about which boxer?
8 Whose murder conviction was overturned after 45 years in 1998?
9 Which famous riding school is in Austria?
10 What colour traditionally is an Indian wedding sari?
11 Which county first won the Benson and Hedges Cricket Cup twice?
12 Which Copenhagen statue is a memorial to Hans Christian Andersen?
13 Which Derbyshire town is famous for the church with a crooked spire?
14 The Parthenon in Athens was built as a temple to whom?
15 Which actress links Jackie in "Footballers' Wives" and Nikki in "The Bill"?
16 Which glands produce white blood cells?
17 What sort of creature is a guillemot?
18 What was the first film Bogart and Bacall starred in together?
19 Which role did Billie Piper play in "Dr Who"?
20 Which girl's name gave the Damned their only top ten hit?
21 Which chess piece can only move diagonally?
22 Which female's Living Proof farewell tour ended in April 2005?
23 William "Fatty" Foulkes played which sport?
24 Which oil company was founded by John D. Rockefeller?
25 At which Southwark inn did Chaucer's Canterbury Pilgrims meet?
26 Joseph Marie Jacquard is most remembered for which invention?
27 Before Winston Churchill went bald, what colour was his hair?
28 The word micro is what fraction in the metric system?
29 Which county included WG Grace as a team member?
30 Which musical instrument was first developed by Bartolomeo Cristofori?

Answers | Past Law & Order *(see Quiz 24)*

1 Haiti. 2 Bluebeard. 3 20th (1941). 4 Ruth Ellis. 5 Dr Crippen. 6 Philip Lawrence. 7 Official Secrets Act. 8 Lester Piggott. 9 Slavery. 10 Director of Public Prosecutions. 11 Cape Town. 12 St Valentine's Day. 13 Nick Leeson. 14 Michael Howard. 15 Iceland. 16 Back to Basics. 17 Treason. 18 Colditz. 19 Ethiopia didn't have electricity. 20 Cromwell Street. 21 Richard I. 22 Jack Straw. 23 Louise Woodward. 24 Road rage attack. 25 Robert Maxwell. 26 Peter Sutcliffe. 27 The Butcher of Lyon. 28 The Ritz. 29 Monster. 30 The Clintons.

1 Which country had the private security force the Tontons Macoutes?
2 What was the nickname of mass murderer Gilles de Rais who killed six of his seven wives?
3 In which century was the last execution at the Tower of London?
4 Which woman was hanged in 1955 for murdering David Blakely?
5 Cora was the wife of which doctor who murdered her?
6 In the 1990s which London head teacher was killed outside his school?
7 Which Act bans the disclosure of confidential items from government sources by its employees?
8 Which world-famous jockey was jailed in 1987 for tax evasion?
9 What did abolitionism seek to abolish?
10 What is the DPP, a post created in 1985?
11 Robben Island was a prison near which city?
12 Which Day saw seven of Bugs Moran's gang murdered by members of Al Capone's, disguised as policemen?
13 Whose crime was recounted in the film "Rogue Trader"?
14 Which one-time Home Secretary led his party in the 2005 general election?
15 The Althing is the parliament of which country?
16 Which phrase used by John Major in 1993 was used as a slogan to return to traditional British values?
17 In 1965 capital punishment was abolished except for which crime?
18 How was the prison camp Oflag IVC near Leipzig better known?
19 In what way was Ethiopian Emperor Menelik III thwarted in bringing the electric chair to his country?
20 What was the Gloucester street where Rose & Frederick West lived?
21 Robin Hood is said to have lived in Sherwood Forest during the reign of which king?
22 Which Home Secretary took his son to the police after allegations of drug selling?
23 Which British nanny's US trial was televised after a baby died in her care?
24 Why was the death of Stephen Cameron in 1996 a tragic first?
25 Who fell from the Lady Ghislaine leaving debts behind him?
26 What is the real name of the criminal dubbed The Yorkshire Ripper?
27 What was the nickname of Nazi war criminal Klaus Barbie?
28 Jonathan Aitken's court case centred on a stay in which Paris hotel?
29 Which 2004 movie starred Charlize Theron playing a real-life serial killer?
30 In the US whose involvement in the Whitewater affair had lengthy repercussions?

Answers | Pot Luck 11 *(see Quiz 23)*

1 Nick Leeson. 2 Iceland. 3 Abba. 4 Fulham. 5 The Rockies. 6 Paradise Lost. 7 James J. Braddock. 8 Derek Bentley. 9 The Spanish Riding School. 10 Scarlet. 11 Leicestershire. 12 The Little Mermaid. 13 Chesterfield. 14 Athena. 15 Gillian Taylforth. 16 Lymph glands. 17 Bird. 18 To Have and Have Not. 19 Rose Tyler. 20 Eloise. 21 The Bishop. 22 Cher. 23 Football. 24 Standard Oil. 25 The Tabard Inn. 26 The Jacquard loom. 27 Red. 28 A millionth. 29 Gloucestershire. 30 The piano.

Quiz 25 Pot Luck 12

Answers – page 146

LEVEL 2

1 What nationality was the spy Mata Hari?
2 The Dickens work Edwin Drood is different for what reason?
3 Which Australian soap star had the biggest-selling UK single in 1988?
4 What were the Boston Tea Party protesters against?
5 What is a Wessex Saddleback?
6 Who succeeded Gerhard Schroeder as German Chancellor?
7 Lyncanthropy involves men changing into what?
8 Which city's American football team is known as the Vikings?
9 Queen Wilhelmina who died in 1962 was Queen of which country?
10 The pop band America were formed in which country?
11 In curling how many shots at the target is each player allowed?
12 What was Janet Street-Porter's beastly last name before marriage?
13 Which Band Aid No. 1 hit was written by Midge Ure and Bob Geldof?
14 Which late singer became the third biggest-selling singles act of 2005?
15 Which American symbol was famously painted by Jasper Johns?
16 In fencing how many hits must a male fencer score for a win?
17 In gin rummy how many cards are dealt per player?
18 What nationality was the inventor of the Geiger counter?
19 Before it moved to Wales on which London hill was the Royal Mint?
20 In which century was the first circumnavigation of the earth?
21 Which is further South, Cardiff or Oxford?
22 Which river rises in the Black Forest?
23 Which road vehicle takes its name from the Hindu God Jagganath?
24 In which South American country is the condor sacred?
25 The first modern Olympics were held in which city?
26 Whom did Michael Sheen play in "Fantabulosa"?
27 What have you on your mouth if you suffer from herpes labialis?
28 Prince Edward resigned from which part of the military in 1987?
29 Mike Burden is the sidekick to which TV detective?
30 It ended in 2006, but in which city was the first ever "Top of the Pops" recorded?

Answers Communications *(see Quiz 26)*

1 Stansted. 2 Leeds. 3 Philips. 4 Decibel. 5 Seattle. 6 Telephone handset. 7 Trans Siberian. 8 Paris. 9 999 service. 10 Nothing. 11 Service. 12 Acoustics. 13 The Speaking Clock. 14 You Got M@il. 15 Video Cassette Recorder. 16 USA. 17 FBI's. 18 Derbyshire. 19 A12. 20 ADA. 21 Dundee. 22 Grand Canal. 23 Alaska. 24 A. 25 M62. 26 Some insects. 27 8. 28 Moscow. 29 Madam Mayor. 30 Channel Tunnel.

145

Quiz 26 | Communications

1 What is Britain's third largest airport?
2 Which northern city has the dialling code 0113?
3 Which company launched the CD-i in 1992?
4 dB is the symbol for what?
5 Where in America was the on-line bookstore Amazon first based?
6 An acoustic coupler allows computer data to be transmitted through what?
7 Which railway links European Russia with the Pacific?
8 Which city linked up with London by phone in 1891?
9 Which vital communications link began in July 1937?
10 How much is the maximum charge for postage in Andorra?
11 What does S stand for in ISP?
12 What is the science of sound and its transmission called?
13 What is another name for Timeline?
14 Which Tom Hanks movie had an email symbol in its title?
15 What is a VCR?
16 Which country has the most telephone subscribers?
17 On whose website did Leslie Ibsen Rogge appear, leading to his arrest?
18 In which county is East Midlands airport?
19 Which A road links London with East Anglia?
20 Which computer language was named after Ada Augusta Byron?
21 Which is the nearest city to the Tay road bridge?
22 Which waterway does Venice's Rialto bridge span?
23 Which state is the northern terminus of the Pan American highway?
24 In France all motorways begin with which letter?
25 Which motorway links Hull and Leeds?
26 Which living creatures can you send through the post?
27 How many bits are there in a byte?
28 In which city is the TASS news agency based?
29 How would you verbally address a Mayor who is a woman?
30 Which tunnel goes from Cheriton to Sangatte?

Answers | Pot Luck 12 *(see Quiz 25)*

1 Dutch. 2 It is not finished. 3 Kylie Minogue. 4 Tea taxes. 5 Pig. 6 Angela Merkel. 7 Wolves. 8 Minnesota. 9 Holland. 10 England. 11 2. 12 Bull. 13 Do They Know It's Christmas. 14 Elvis Presley. 15 The stars & stripes. 16 Five. 17 10. 18 German. 19 Tower Hill. 20 16th. 21 Cardiff. 22 Danube. 23 Juggernaut. 24 Peru. 25 Athens. 26 Kenneth Williams. 27 Cold Sores. 28 The Marines. 29 Reg Wexford. 30 Manchester.

1 Who had a No. 1 UK hit with "The Reflex"?
2 In English what is the only anagram of the word ENGLISH?
3 Which rules are American football played to?
4 In which South African city was the 1995 Rugby Union World Cup Final?
5 Which musical was based on the play "Pygmalion"?
6 If you suffer from bulimia, what do you have a compulsive urge to do?
7 Which striker Paul rejoined Man City in 2006?
8 Which triangular-shaped Indian pastry contains meat or vegetables?
9 Which part of Spain is named after its many castles?
10 The range of the pH scale is zero to what?
11 Which everyday objects can be decorated with the King's Pattern?
12 Stage performer Boy Bruce the Mighty Atom became known as who?
13 Which Russian word means "speaking aloud"?
14 Which Top Ten "ride" was taken by the group Roxette?
15 What is the name of the world's largest Gulf?
16 At which UK oil depot was there a massive fire in December 2005?
17 Ouzo is what flavour?
18 What does a trishaw driver do with his legs?
19 Which hospital did TV Doctor Kildare work at?
20 Which is the slowest swimming stroke?
21 What is the best-selling single of all time?
22 What does E stand for in "E-numbers"?
23 In Peter Pan which part of Peter was kept in a drawer?
24 What word links an ice cream holder and a brass instrument?
25 Who performed "Sgt Pepper" to open Live 8 with Paul McCartney?
26 In which Dickensian drama did Gillian Anderson play Lady Dedlock?
27 What is the epicarp of an orange?
28 Who was George W. Bush's first Secretary of State?
29 Which three Time Travel films were directed by Robert Zemeckis?
30 Which European country has the only active volcanoes in Europe?

Answers	Pop Music: The 70s *(see Quiz 28)*

1 Love Me for a Reason. 2 Pigeon. 3 Cher. 4 Eddie Holman. 5 Dawn. 6 Ray Stevens. 7 Heart. 8 Squeeze. 9 January. 10 The Kinks. 11 10538. 12 Matthews Southern Comfort. 13 Leo Sayer. 14 Your Song. 15 The Floral Dance. 16 Minnie Riperton. 17 Sweet Sensation. 18 Paul Simon. 19 Nathan Jones. 20 B A Robertson. 21 Rainbow. 22 New York. 23 Samantha. 24 Summer Nights. 25 The Commodores. 26 Rivers of Babylon. 27 Midnight. 28 In the Summertime. 29 Donna Summer. 30 Eye Level.

1 Which 70s hit by the Osmonds gave Boyzone a hit in '94?

2 Which Lieutenant's only UK No. 1 hit was "Mouldy Old Dough"?

3 Who sang that she was "born in the wagon of a travelling show"?

4 "(Hey There) Lonely Girl" was the only UK hit for which vocalist?

5 Tony Orlando sang in which group that had a girl's name?

6 The craze for streaking gave a No. 1 to which Ray?

7 Which part of the body was mentioned in the title of a Blondie hit?

8 Who were "Up The Junction" in 1979?

9 Which month links Pilot and part of a song title for Barbara Dickson?

10 Whose hits from 1970 include "Victoria" and "Apeman"?

11 What was the number of ELO's Overture in their first hit?

12 The No. 1 UK hit "Woodstock" was a one-hit wonder for which group?

13 Who had a No. 1 single in 2006, but first charted with "The Show Must Go On"?

14 Which Elton John 70s hit with a two-word title returned to the Top Ten in 2002?

15 What links Terry Wogan and the Brighouse and Rastrick Brass Band?

16 "Loving You" was a high-pitched No. 2 UK hit for which female singer?

17 Which group had a No. 1 UK hit with "Sad Sweet Dreamer"?

18 Who wanted to be taken to the Mardi Gras?

19 Which 1971 Supremes hit was later a hit for Bananarama?

20 Who had hits with "Bang Bang" and "Knocked It Off" in 1979?

21 The 1979 No. 6 hit "Since You've Been Gone" was a hit for whom?

22 Which US city was named twice in a Gerard Kenny hit from 1978?

23 Whom did Cliff Richard say Hello to when he said Goodbye to Sam?

24 In which song do the chorus beg, "Tell me more, tell me more!"?

25 Which group had hits in the 70s with "Easy", "Still" and "Sail On"?

26 What was on the other side of Boney M's "Brown Girl in the Ring"?

27 What time was Gladys Knight's train leaving for Georgia?

28 Which Mungo Jerry hit was used in an anti drink-drive campaign?

29 Which disco-style singer had the word Love in the title of four of her first five Top Ten hits?

30 Which No. 1 from 1972 was the theme for the Van Der Valk series?

Answers | Pot Luck 13 *(see Quiz 27)*

1 Duran Duran. 2 Shingle. 3 The Harvard rules. 4 Johannesburg. 5 My Fair Lady. 6 Eat. 7 Paul Dickov. 8 Samosa. 9 Castile. 10 Fourteen. 11 Cutlery. 12 Bruce Forsyth. 13 Glasnost. 14 Joyride. 15 Gulf of Mexico. 16 Buncefield. 17 Aniseed. 18 Pedal. 19 Blair Hospital. 20 Breast stroke. 21 Candle in the Wind (1997). 22 European. 23 His shadow. 24 Cornet. 25 U2. 26 Bleak House. 27 The peel. 28 Colin Powell. 29 Back to the Future. 30 Italy.

Quiz 29 Pot Luck 14

Answers – page 150

LEVEL 2

1 If a bridge player has a Yarborough, what is the top scoring card?
2 Which "Strictly Come Dancing" judge has the longest name?
3 In the Grand National, how many times did Red Rum run?
4 Which was the first railway terminus in London?
5 Which term is used when a mortgage is more than the value of a house?
6 Whose hits include "Slave to Love" and "This is Tomorrow"?
7 What is a Clouded Yellow?
8 How was Agatha Miller better known?
9 El Paso is in which American state?
10 Which road leads from Westminster to Blackfriars along the north bank of the Thames?
11 The first player to score 100 Premier League goals played for which club?
12 In which board game is FIDE the governing body?
13 A BBC estimate said half the population had watched which live event in 2005?
14 In which year did TV soap "EastEnders" first appear?
15 What is the Mirror of Diana, located in Northern Italy?
16 Beta Vulgaris is the Latin name for which crop?
17 Which film featured the Joe Cocker hit "Up Where We Belong"?
18 Who wrote the opera from which Here Comes the Bride is taken?
19 Lime Street Station is in which English city?
20 Cars with the international vehicle registration IS come from where?
21 Which magazine, established in 1922, claims to be the most widely read in the world?
22 What happened to Ken Barlow's second wife in "Coronation Street"?
23 What type of fruit is a Laxton Superb?
24 Who plays grandma Kumar at No. 42?
25 A sericulturist breeds which creatures?
26 Robbie Elliott and Nobby Solano have both had two spells at which soccer club?
27 What term describes the fineness of yarns?
28 Where do mice live who are proverbially poor?
29 Joseph Grimaldi achieved everlasting fame as what?
30 Who made history in 1982 by going to an Anglican service in Canterbury Cathedral?

Answers | World Football *(see Quiz 30)*

1 Japan. 2 Lazio. 3 Ruud Gullit. 4 Gary Lineker. 5 Australia. 6 Croatia. 7 Barcelona. 8 Prague. 9 Graham Poll. 10 Mario Zagallo. 11 Benfica. 12 Germany. 13 Davor Suker. 14 Argentina. 15 Roger Milla. 16 Uruguay. 17 Gerard Houllier. 18 Edson Arrentes do Nascimento. 19 Italy. 20 Switzerland. 21 Emmanuel Petit. 22 Ronaldo's. 23 Zinedine Zidane. 24 Dennis Bergkamp. 25 Matthias Sammer. 26 St Denis. 27 Dunga. 28 Stanley Matthews. 29 Marco Materazzi. 30 Alexi Lalas.

Quiz 30 | World Football

Answers – page 149 | **LEVEL 2**

1 In which country is the club Grampus Eight?
2 Which Italian team did Gazza play for?
3 Who was Dutch captain when they won the European Championship in 1988?
4 Who was leading scorer in the 1986 World Cup finals?
5 Which international side did Venables manage after England?
6 Who won the third-place final in the 1998 World Cup?
7 Which side did Cruyff move to from Ajax in 1973?
8 Dukla and Sparta are from which European city?
9 In a 2006 game, which British ref. showed three yellow cards to the same player?
10 Which Brazilian football coach was sacked after France '98?
11 Which Portuguese side did Graeme Souness manage?
12 Which country ran a full-page "thank you" ad in The Times after Euro 96?
13 Who won the Golden Boot in the 1998 World Cup?
14 Cesar Menotti managed which victorious World Cup side?
15 Who is the oldest player ever to score in the World Cup finals?
16 Penarol is a club side in which country?
17 Which Frenchman moved to Liverpool when Ronnie Moran retired?
18 What is Pele's full name?
19 Who, with England and Holland, was eliminated from France 98 on penalties?
20 Which country does Arsenal's Philippe Senderos represent?
21 Who scored the last goal in France 98?
22 Whose much-seen girlfriend in France 98 was Suzana Werner?
23 Who received the Golden Ball as outstanding player of the 2006 World Cup?
24 Which overseas star won most Premiership Player of the Month awards in 1997–98?
25 Which German won European Player of the Year in 1996?
26 In which stadium was the opening match of France 98?
27 Who captained Brazil in the 1998 World Cup Finals?
28 Who was the first European Footballer of the Year?
29 Who scored Italy's open play goal in the 2006 World Cup Final?
30 Which US star of the 1994 World Cup became the first American player to take part in Italy's Serie A?

| **Answers** | Pot Luck 14 *(see Quiz 29)* |

1 Nine. **2** Craig Revel Horwood. **3** Five. **4** Euston Station. **5** Negative equity. **6** Bryan Ferry's. **7** A Butterfly. **8** Agatha Christie. **9** Texas. **10** The Embankment. **11** Blackburn (Alan Shearer). **12** Chess. **13** Live 8 concert. **14** 1985. **15** A lake. **16** Sugar beet. **17** An Officer and a Gentleman. **18** Wagner. **19** Liverpool. **20** Iceland. **21** Reader's Digest. **22** She committed suicide. **23** An apple. **24** Meera Syal. **25** Silkworms. **26** Newcastle United. **27** Denier. **28** Church. **29** A clown. **30** The Pope.

1 In 2005 Mahmoud Abbas triumphed in which elections?
2 Which Man Utd player signed in 2005 had played for Ajax and Juventus?
3 Which group had a No. 1 UK hit in 1992 with Ebenezer Goode?
4 In which sport were Jack Broughton and James Figg champions?
5 Which Aldous Huxley novel is set in the seventh century AF?
6 Which instrument was Jose Feliciano famous for playing?
7 Which Queen was played in films by Jean Simmons and Bette Davis?
8 US talent show "You're the One that I Want" chooses performers for which musical?
9 Which musical instruments represent Peter in "Peter and the Wolf"?
10 Who presented "Restoration Village" on TV?
11 A glaive was what kind of weapon?
12 In which century was the first Indianapolis 500 first held?
13 In which country do soldiers wear skirts called fustanella?
14 What can be done if an object is scissile?
15 Which film studios were founded by Harry, Sam, Albert and Jack?
16 Which word can describe a listening device, an illness and an insect?
17 Which famous actress starred in "Courage of Lassie" and "Lassie Come Home"?
18 Who was older when he died, Benny Hill or Richard Burton?
19 TV presenter Alison Holloway became which comic Jim's third wife?
20 What type of fruit is a jargonelle?
21 Which part of the head is studied by a phrenologist?
22 Whose ancestral home is Woburn Abbey?
23 Who wrote the poem "Four Quartets"?
24 Which children's game is played on the fingers with looped string?
25 Jane Harris and Nel Mangel appeared in which soap?
26 Brassica Rapa is the Latin name for which vegetable?
27 Which band's hits include "Infinite Dreams" and "Holy Smoke"?
28 Which two letters are in the internet code for Malta?
29 Excess bile pigment in the bloodstream causes which illness?
30 Whom was Dennis Bergkamp named after?

Answers	Blockbusters *(see Quiz 32)*

1 Five. 2 Chocolate. 3 The Robe. 4 Francis Ford Coppola. 5 Normandy. 6 M*A*S*H.
7 Hearst. 8 Crocodile Dundee. 9 James Caviezel. 10 Midnight Cowboy. 11 Dan
Aykroyd. 12 The English Patient. 13 Vito Corleone. 14 Pierce Brosnan. 15 Ron Kovic.
16 Gone with the Wind. 17 Wall Street. 18 Braveheart. 19 Dune. 20 John Huston.
21 Terminator II. 22 Austrian. 23 All About Eve. 24 1930s. 25 Goldblum. 26 Jim
Carrey. 27 Carrie Fisher. 28 Celine Dion. 29 The Last Samurai. 30 Cop.

1 How many crew members were there in the Nostromo in "Alien"?
2 What type of sauce was used in the shower scene in "Psycho"?
3 Which 1953 film was the first made in Cinemascope?
4 Who directed "The Godfather" and all its sequels?
5 "Saving Private Ryan" dealt with events in which part of France?
6 Which anti-war comedy did Robert Altman direct?
7 Which newspaper magnate was said to be the model for Orson Welles' Citizen Kane?
8 Which 80s film was the most profitable in Australian history?
9 Who played Christ in Mel Gibson's "The Passion of the Christ"?
10 What was John Schlesinger's first US film, made in 1969 with Dustin Hoffman and Jon Voight?
11 Who starred in, and co-wrote "Ghostbusters"?
12 Which film starred Juliette Binoche and Kristin Scott Thomas?
13 What was the name of Marlon Brando's character in "The Godfather"?
14 Which James Bond actor starred in "Dante's Peak"?
15 What was the name of Tom Cruise's character in "Born on the Fourth of July"?
16 In which classic did Olivia de Havilland play Melanie Wilkes?
17 In which film did Michael Douglas say "Greed is good"?
18 What was Mel Gibson's first film as actor, director and producer?
19 Which David Lynch space epic was based on the work of Frank Herbert?
20 Who was directing "The African Queen" when his daughter Anjelica was born?
21 Which sequel had the subtitle "Judgement Day"?
22 What is Schindler's nationality in "Schindler's List"?
23 What was the last film before Titanic to win 14 Oscar nominations?
24 In which decade was "Gone with the Wind" made?
25 Which Jeff was the mathematician in "Jurassic Park"?
26 Who became a human cartoon in "The Mask"?
27 Who played Princess Leia in the "Star Wars Trilogy"?
28 Who sang the theme song for "Titanic"?
29 In which movie did Tom Hanks play Captain Nathan Algren?
30 What was Michael Douglas' profession in "Basic Instinct"?

---

1 Which TV cop was christened Ilynea Lydia Mironoff?
2 In which crime drama did Tim Pigott-Smith play DCI Vickers?
3 Which show features DCI Michael Jardine?
4 What was Paul Nicholls' first major series after leaving "EastEnders"?
5 Who was Don Johnson's character in "Miami Vice"?
6 What was the name of law enforcer Michael Knight's computer buddy?
7 Which series featured Shell who gave birth to Ronan Beckham?
8 Which series featured the Wentworth Detention Centre?
9 Who played the TV "Avengers" role played by Uma Thurman on the big screen?
10 Which member of the Ruth Rendell Mysteries cast also scripted some of the shows?
11 In which series did the character Charlie Barlow first find fame?
12 Which "Blue Peter" presenter played Dangerfield's son in the police surgeon series?
13 In which 90s series did Neil Pearson star as Det. Sup. Tony Clark?
14 In which police station was Frank Farillo the chief?
15 What was Fitz's full name in "Cracker"?
16 Peter Falk played which offbeat TV cop?
17 Which real crime series was based on the German "File XY Unsolved"?
18 In which series did Rowan Atkinson appear as a police officer?
19 Who was the British half of "Dempsey and Makepeace"?
20 Which long-running show increased the length of episodes in 1998 to one hour in a bid to improve ratings?
21 Stacey Keach played which detective from Mickey Spillane's novels?
22 "The Body in the Library" was the first in an 80s series about which sleuth?
23 Which series began with an Armchair Theatre production "Regan"?
24 Loretta Swit from "M*A*S*H" was replaced by Sharon Gless in which US series?
25 Who played barrister Kavanagh in the TV series?
26 Which detective was based at Denton police station?
27 How long did the "Morse" episodes usually last?
28 In which series did Samantha Janus star as Isobel de Pauli?
29 In which series did Charlie Hungerford appear?
30 Which series was based on the Constable novels by Nicholas Rea?

Answers | Pot Luck 16 *(see Quiz 34)*

1 Hamlet. 2 Central Park Zoo, New York. 3 Take That. 4 Surrey. 5 Elizabeth I. 6 Tommy Steele. 7 Tutti Frutti. 8 A boat. 9 Rockall. 10 Portillo. 11 Fox. 12 Rudyard Kipling. 13 Van Gogh. 14 Trams. 15 George I. 16 Johnny Dankworth. 17 Chaka Khan. 18 Peter Davison. 19 Vertigo tour. 20 Michel Platini. 21 Scurvy. 22 Time. 23 Glucose. 24 Sheridan. 25 Texas. 26 Best Supporting Actress. 27 July, August. 28 Fairy tales. 29 Epiglottis. 30 Much.

Quiz 34 | Pot Luck 16

1 In which Shakespeare play does a ghost walk on the battlements?
2 In "Madagascar" where do the animals escape from?
3 Which group had No. 1 hits with "Babe" and "Pray" in 1993?
4 Charterhouse Public School is found in which county?
5 Miranda Richardson played whom in the second "Blackadder" series?
6 Whose autobiography was called "Bermondsey Boy"?
7 Which 1987 TV series featured the ageing rock band The Majestics?
8 What is a gallivat?
9 Which British island is 230 miles West of the Hebrides in the Atlantic?
10 Which Michael lost his Enfield seat in the 1997 general election?
11 A skulk is the collective name for a group of which animal?
12 Who wrote "How the Leopard Got His Spots"?
13 Who painted the picture called "Irises"?
14 On which forms of transport would you find knifeboards?
15 Handel's "Water Music" was composed for which English King?
16 Who is Cleo Laine's bandleader husband?
17 Who had UK hits with "Ain't Nobody" and "I'm Every Woman"?
18 Georgia Moffett is the daughter of which ex-"Dr Who"?
19 What was the name of U2's 2005 tour of America?
20 From 1983–85 which Frenchman was European Footballer of the Year?
21 What disease are you suffering if you are scorbutic?
22 Dr Steve Hawking wrote the best-selling a brief history of what?
23 What is the other name for grape-sugar?
24 Who wrote the play "The School for Scandal"?
25 Which band made the hit albums "White on Blonde" and "The Hush"?
26 The film "The Piano" received Oscars for Best Actress and Best what?
27 In a single calendar year which two consecutive months total most days?
28 What did Charles Perrault collect?
29 Which flap of cartilage prevents food from entering your windpipe?
30 Which member of Robin Hood's gang was the son of a miller?

Answers | TV: Cops & Robbers *(see Quiz 33)*

1 Helen Mirren. 2 The Vice. 3 Taggart. 4 City Central. 5 Sonny Crockett. 6 KITT. 7 Bad Girls. 8 Prisoner Cell Block H. 9 Diana Rigg. 10 George Baker. 11 Z Cars. 12 Tim Vincent. 13 Between the Lines. 14 Hill St. 15 Eddie Fitzgerald. 16 Columbo. 17 Crimewatch UK. 18 The Thin Blue Line. 19 Makepeace. 20 The Bill. 21 Mike Hammer. 22 Miss Marple. 23 The Sweeney. 24 Cagney & Lacey. 25 John Thaw. 26 Jack Frost. 27 Two hours. 28 Liverpool One. 29 Bergerac. 30 Heartbeat.

1 What are the three Baltic states?
2 In which country does the Douro reach the Atlantic?
3 What is the capital of Catalonia?
4 What is Northern Ireland's chief non-edible agricultural product?
5 What do the Germans call Bavaria?
6 Which European capital stands on the river Liffey?
7 What is the Eiffel Tower made from?
8 How is the Danish region of Jylland known in English?
9 In which forest does the Danube rise?
10 Which was the first country to legalise voluntary euthanasia?
11 What covers most of Finland?
12 In which country is the world's highest dam?
13 What is the capital of the Ukraine?
14 What is a remarkable feature of the caves at Lascaux in SW France?
15 What is Europe's highest capital city?
16 Where is France's Tomb of the Unknown Soldier?
17 Which area of the Rhone delta is famous for its nature reserve?
18 In which country would you find Kerkyra?
19 What are the two official European languages of Luxembourg?
20 The Magyars are the largest ethnic group of which country?
21 Where is Castilian an official language?
22 Abruzzi is a mountainous region of which country?
23 Which is the largest of the Balearic Islands?
24 On which island was the Mafia founded?
25 What is the UK's chief Atlantic port?
26 Tallinn is the capital of which Baltic state?
27 What is the main religion of Albania?
28 In which country would you meet Walloons?
29 In which country was the Millau Viaduct built?
30 Which country has Larisa and Volos amongst its chief towns?

Answers | Pot Luck 17 *(see Quiz 36)*

1 Texas. 2 Culture Club. 3 Keith. 4 Lola. 5 Midsummer Day. 6 Ronnie Biggs. 7 Elvis Presley. 8 Mary Quant. 9 Ice skating. 10 Henry Crabbe. 11 Hedges and shrubs. 12 Michael Caine. 13 Saint Swithin. 14 C & F. 15 Blackburn Rovers. 16 Cricket. 17 A fox. 18 Mother. 19 Isle of Man. 20 Correct English. 21 1,440. 22 Dr Hook. 23 Cluedo. 24 Hurdles. 25 Idaho. 26 Green Wing. 27 Brunel. 28 Griffith. 29 Spiders. 30 Paul Young.

1 Tony Christie tried to find it, but in which US State is Amarillo?
2 Whose hits include "Victims" and "Church of the Poison Mind"?
3 What is Rupert Murdoch's first name?
4 On CBeebies who is Charlie's younger sister?
5 In a calendar year what is the second quarter day in England?
6 Which robber on the run was in the film "The Great Rock and Roll Swindle"?
7 Who was older when he died, John Lennon or Elvis Presley?
8 Which fashion designer opened a shop in 1957 called Bazaar?
9 In which sport would you find a movement called a Salchow?
10 What is the name of the detective in "Pie in the Sky"?
11 What material does a topiarist work with?
12 Which actor was Rita's tutor in the film "Educating Rita"?
13 Which Saint has 15th July as his Feast Day?
14 Which two musical notes do not have flats on black keys?
15 Striker James Beattie made his league debut with which club?
16 Sabina Park is most famous for which sport?
17 Which animal can be described as vulpine?
18 "Atom Heart.....", what was the first Pink Floyd album to top the UK charts?
19 Where are Union Mills and Onchan Head in the British Isles?
20 Author HW Fowler produced a book in 1926 as a guide to what?
21 How many minutes are there in a day?
22 Who had a hit on the telephone in 1972 with "Sylvia's Mother"?
23 Moving through rooms to solve a murder involves which board game?
24 What can be 84cm, 91cm or 106cm in height in sport ?
25 The towns of Anaconda and Moscow are in which US State?
26 Which TV series features Dr Caroline Todd?
27 The university sited in Uxbridge is named after which engineer?
28 Which Melanie has been the partner of Antonio Banderas?
29 Which creatures mainly belong to the arachnidae family?
30 Who had hits with "Senza Una Donna" and "Come Back and Stay"?

Quiz 42 | Pot Luck 20

Answers – page 161

LEVEL 2

1 Which drink did American Indians call Firewater in the Wild West ?
2 Which former Corrie actress played Beverley Tull in "Bad Girls"?
3 Who sends encyclical letters?
4 The White Death was a name for which former common disease?
5 According to the song, where does everyone dance in Avignon?
6 Which musical and movie is based on the writing of Christopher Isherwood?
7 Who was the first permanent replacement for Michael Hutchence in INXS?
8 Which leaves taste of aniseed?
9 Which group had a Top Ten hit with "Black Knight"?
10 What is the fruit of a baobab tree called?
11 What was a bridewell?
12 Which model's childhood nickname was "Mosschops"?
13 Who is the voice of Rodney Copperbottom in "Robots"?
14 "A week is a long time in politics" was said by which politician?
15 Who or what is Futoshiki?
16 What is the official language of the Ivory Coast?
17 What are pruned in coppicing?
18 Which group featured in "The Great Rock 'n' Roll Swindle"?
19 Which Ava was one of Frank Sinatra's wives?
20 If a plant is a hydrophyte where does it live?
21 A papillon is a type of what?
22 What was Bing Crosby's first name?
23 Which two countries are separated by the Skagerrak?
24 Which royal film star appeared in "Dial M for Murder"?
25 What does the Blue Cross Charity, founded in 1897, provide aid to?
26 In which Scottish city are Salisbury Crags?
27 Which South American country has the sucre as the unit of currency?
28 Who composed the music for the musical "Strike Up the Band"?
29 What does the C stand for in ACAS?
30 Which song was sung in three different films by Doris Day?

Answers | **Pop Music: The 80s** *(see Quiz 41)*

1 When I Fall in Love. 2 Good Tradition. 3 Dreams. 4 Sheena Easton. 5 Love Don't Live Here Anymore. 6 Candy Girl. 7 Dead or Alive. 8 Swing Out Sister. 9 Pet Shop Boys. 10 Give It Up. 11 Thompson Twins. 12 Ghost Town. 13 Let's Go Dancin'. 14 Cambodia. 15 The Style Council. 16 Funky Town. 17 Down Under. 18 Linx. 19 Crocodile Dundee. 20 Stevie Wonder. 21 Lion. 22 Mony Mony. 23 Holding Back the Years. 24 Hey Little Girl. 25 One (You Win Again). 26 Through the Barricades. 27 Bananarama. 28 Monday. 29 David Bowie. 30 Christians.

162

Quiz 41 — Pop Music: The 80s

Answers – page 162

LEVEL 2

1 Which hit was No. 2 for Rick Astley and No. 4 for Nat King Cole in '87?
2 What was the first Top Ten hit for Tanita Tikaram?
3 What were "shattered" in the 1987 No. 5 hit for Johnny Hates Jazz?
4 Who joined Kenny Rogers on "We've Got Tonight"?
5 Which Jimmy Nail hit was a cover of a Rose Royce hit?
6 New Edition got to No. 1 in '83 with which Girl?
7 Who were spun around by their No. 1 "You Spin Me Round (like a record)"?
8 Which group had Top Ten hits with "Breakout" and "Surrender"?
9 Whose first UK No. 1 hit was "West End Girls"?
10 What was KC and the Sunshine Band's only UK No. 1 in the 80s?
11 Which twins had hits with "Love on Your Side" and "Doctor Doctor"?
12 Which town got The Specials to No. 1 in 1981?
13 What followed "Ooh La La La" in the 1982 hit for Kool and the Gang?
14 The name of which Asian country gave Kim Wilde an 80s hit?
15 Having left the Jam, Paul Weller charted regularly with which band?
16 Where did Lipps Inc. take us to in their No. 2 from 1980?
17 Which antipodean title was a No. 1 for Men at Work in 1983?
18 The song "Intuition" was the only UK Top Ten single for which duo?
19 Mental As Anything had a No. 3 with "Live It Up" from which film?
20 Who joined Julio Inglesias on his No. 5 success "My Love"?
21 Which animal was sleeping on the No. 1 hit by Tight Fit?
22 Which '87 Billy Idol hit was a cover of an earlier Tommy James hit?
23 What was Simply Red's first Top Ten UK hit?
24 Which Del Shannon hit became an 80s hit for Icehouse?
25 How many No. 1 singles did The Bee Gees have throughout the 1980s?
26 What in 1986 was Spandau Ballet's last UK Top Ten hit?
27 Who joined Fun Boy Three on "It Ain't What You Do" in 1982?
28 Which day links a No. 2 by the Bangles with a No. 3 by New Order?
29 Who had No. 1 singles working with Queen and then Mick Jagger?
30 Whose first Top Ten hit was "Harvest for the World" in 1988?

Answers | Pot Luck 20 *(see Quiz 42)*

1 Whiskey. 2 Amanda Barrie. 3 The Pope. 4 Tuberculosis. 5 On the bridge. 6 Cabaret. 7 JD Fortune. 8 Fennel. 9 Deep Purple. 10 Monkey bread. 11 A prison. 12 Kate Moss. 13 Ewan McGregor. 14 Harold Wilson. 15 Number game. 16 French. 17 Trees. 18 The Sex Pistols. 19 Gardner. 20 In water. 21 A dog. 22 Harry. 23 Denmark and Norway. 24 Grace Kelly. 25 Animals. 26 Edinburgh. 27 Ecuador. 28 George Gershwin. 29 Conciliation. 30 Que Sera Sera.

161

1 What is the area of the City of London?
2 What is the last word of Rule Britannia?
3 What does the Footsie show?
4 Which branch of the Royal Navy is concerned with aviation?
5 What name is given to the MP who has served in the House of Commons the longest?
6 A driving licence is issued until the driver reaches what age?
7 In which Lane is London's Dorchester Hotel?
8 In the Old Testament Aaron was the elder brother of which prophet?
9 Which shipping company operated the Queen Mary and the Queen Elizabeth?
10 Which dog's name comes from the Welsh for dwarf dog?
11 In which two English counties are the Cinque Ports?
12 What colour coats do Chelsea Pensioners wear in the summer?
13 Cranwell trains cadets for which of the armed forces?
14 Which river flows through Baghdad?
15 How many kilometres per hour is 30 miles an hour?
16 What is discrimination against the elderly called?
17 Which former child singing star presented a late-night chat show on Channel 4 in 2006?
18 In what type of vehicle was the 1918 World War armistice signed?
19 What is another name for hypertension?
20 What is another name for a Denver boot?
21 Which police department deals with illegal gambling and pornography?
22 James McFadden joined Everton from which club?
23 In religious terms what does absolution purify?
24 Who wrote the fantasy novel "The Silmarillion"?
25 Which condition will an antitussive help alleviate?
26 What is the principal Roman Catholic church in England?
27 What colour is a disabled driver's badge?
28 Who had hits with "Dear Prudence" and "Hong Kong Gardens"?
29 The permanent disappearance of a species is described by which word?
30 Which Simon replaced Mark Lamarr as host of "Never Mind the Buzzcocks"?

Answers	People & Places *(see Quiz 39)*

1 Kennedy. 2 France. 3 UK & Ireland. 4 The Romanovs. 5 Eton. 6 Crimean War. 7 Edmund Hillary. 8 Hitler. 9 17. 10 Ronald Reagan. 11 Mary Robinson. 12 Alabama. 13 Helmut Kohl. 14 Kofi Annan. 15 Flora's maid. 16 Donald Maclean. 17 Argentina. 18 Lord Mountbatten. 19 Axis. 20 Whitechapel. 21 The French. 22 Israel. 23 John F. Kennedy. 24 France. 25 Noriega. 26 Little St Bernard. 27 Mary McAleese. 28 My Lai. 29 Madeleine Albright. 30 Dublin.

1 Which US President's father was a former Ambassador in the UK?
2 Edith Cresson was which country's PM from 1991–92?
3 The Downing Street Declaration in 1993 involved the Prime Ministers of which two countries?
4 Which family died at Ekaterinburg in 1918?
5 Which school provided the UK with 19 Prime Ministers before 2000?
6 In which war did British soldiers first wear balaclava helmets?
7 Which mountaineer was the first person since Scott to reach the South Pole overland, in 1958?
8 The "Bomb Plot" of 1944 failed to assassinate whom?
9 What was the minimum age for joining the UK Home Guard in WWII?
10 Which former US President was a distant relative of Princess Diana?
11 Who was the first woman President of Ireland?
12 In which US state did Martin Luther King lead the 1955 bus boycott?
13 Who lost power in Germany in 1998 after 16 years?
14 Who became Secretary General of the UN in 1997?
15 Who was Bonnie Prince Charlie disguised as when he escaped to France with Flora MacDonald?
16 Who defected to the USSR with Guy Burgess in 1951?
17 Carlos Menem became President of which country in 1989?
18 Who was the first Governor General of India, until 1948?
19 What was the alliance between the Germans and the Italians in World War II called?
20 Where in the East End of London did Jack the Ripper operate?
21 As a double agent, Mata Hari was executed by whom?
22 Mrs Meir was the first woman PM in which country?
23 Who was the USA's first Roman Catholic President?
24 Which country has had Jospin and Raffarin as Prime Ministers?
25 Which Panamanian leader was nicknamed Pineapple Face?
26 Which Pass did Hannibal use to cross the Alps?
27 Who became President of Ireland in 1997?
28 In which Vietnamese village were 109 civilians massacred by US troops in 1968?
29 Who was the first woman US Secretary of State?
30 TV's "Murphy's Law" is set in which city?

Answers | Pot Luck 19 *(see Quiz 40)*

1 One square mile. 2 Slaves. 3 Stocks & share prices. 4 Fleet Air Arm. 5 Father of the House. 6 70. 7 Park Lane. 8 Moses. 9 Cunard. 10 Corgi. 11 Kent and Sussex. 12 Red. 13 RAF. 14 Tigris. 15 48. 16 Ageism. 17 Charlotte Church. 18 Railway carriage. 19 High blood pressure. 20 Wheel clamp. 21 Vice Squad. 22 Motherwell. 23 The soul. 24 JRR Tolkien. 25 A cough. 26 Westminster Cathedral. 27 Orange. 28 Siouxsie and the Banshees. 29 Extinction. 30 Simon Amstell.

1 Which animal can be described as ursine?
2 Who was older when he died, Graham Hill or James Hunt?
3 Which prize for fiction was instigated in 1969?
4 Which Jackie Wilson hit was No. 1 nearly thirty years after it was made?
5 A tarpon is a type of what?
6 In the pop charts in 2004, how was Yusuf Islam known when last in the charts?
7 If something is vernal, what is it connected with?
8 Where do Southend United football club play their home games?
9 How did both James I's mother and son die?
10 The sidewinder belongs to which group of snakes?
11 Which Radio 4 programme celebrated its 60th birthday in October 2006?
12 Which was the first commercial jet aircraft in the world?
13 Jazz musician John Coltrane played which instrument?
14 In March 2005, who became the first person to fly a plane solo, non-stop around the globe without refuelling?
15 Which part was played by Audrey Hepburn in the film "My Fair Lady"?
16 Wapentakes, hundreds and hides were all areas of what?
17 What is the collective name for a litter of piglets?
18 Who gave Pip his wealth in "Great Expectations"?
19 Who wrote the novel "Jurassic Park"?
20 How many squares have pieces on them at the start of a chess game?
21 In which London park are The Holme, The Broad Walk and Winfield House?
22 What does the differential on a car allow the driving wheels to do?
23 The abbreviation GDP stands for what?
24 The Gulf of Sidra is located off the coast of which continent?
25 Which day of the week is named after the Norse Goddess Freya?
26 Winnipeg is the capital of which Canadian province?
27 What type of creature is a flying fox?
28 Cristiano Ronaldo joined Man Utd from which club?
29 In which decade was the Guinness Book of Records first published?
30 In a calendar year what is the first quarter day in England?

Answers | Hobbies & Leisure 1 *(see Quiz 37)*

1 Battles of the English Civil War. 2 Ascot. 3 Hunt. 4 Red. 5 Beaulieu. 6 32. 7 Shakespeare's Globe. 8 July. 9 Field hockey. 10 Porgy and Bess. 11 Kensington. 12 Monopoly. 13 National Trust. 14 10 feet (3.05m). 15 Annual Percentage Rate. 16 Japan. 17 Raymond Blanc. 18 Tennis. 19 Oxford Street. 20 July and August. 21 Medals. 22 Second day. 23 Dolly Parton. 24 Rodeo. 25 Short tennis. 26 California. 27 Dramatic. 28 Polo. 29 Flags. 30 Pottery.

1 The Sealed Knot Society re-enacts what?
2 Which racecourse has a famous Royal Enclosure?
3 What is the Quorn in Leicestershire?
4 What colour are hotels in Monopoly?
5 Where is the National Motor Museum?
6 What is the maximum number of pieces on a chessboard at any one time?
7 Sam Wanamaker founded which London theatre?
8 In which month do the French celebrate Bastille Day?
9 If you played outdoor hockey in the US what would it be called?
10 In which opera is the song "Summertime"?
11 Where in London did Laura Ashley open her first shop?
12 What is the world's biggest-selling copyrighted game?
13 Which organisation is the largest private landowner in Britain?
14 How high is a netball post?
15 If you have a credit card what is an APR?
16 Where did karaoke singing originate?
17 Who opened a bistro called Le Petit Blanc in 1984?
18 David Mercer, Chris Bailey and John Barrett have commentated on which sport?
19 Where was the first Virgin record shop?
20 During which months was the museum to Diana, Princess of Wales open at Althorp in 1998?
21 What might a numismatist collect along with coins?
22 Which day at Royal Ascot is Ladies' Day?
23 Who founded a theme park called Dollywood?
24 Bronco busting and steer wrestling take place at what type of event?
25 Which form of tennis is played on a smaller court, usually by children?
26 In which US state did skateboarding begin as an alternative to surfing?
27 What does the D stand for in NODA?
28 Which game is played at Hurlingham?
29 In slalom skiing what must you turn between?
30 What would be your hobby if you used slip?

1 Which American was UK champion jockey in 1984, 1985 and 1987?

2 In which month does the Cheltenham Festival take place?

3 Which two races make up the autumn double?

4 How long is the Derby?

5 How many times did Willie Carson win the Derby?

6 Which late Cabinet Minister had been the Glasgow Herald's racing tipster?

7 Who had nine Derby wins and was champion jockey 11 times?

8 Which British racehorse owner sold Vernons Pools in 1988?

9 Who was Champion Jockey a record 26 times between 1925 and 1953?

10 Which Light was a Derby winner for Kieren Fallon?

11 Which Classic was the first to be run on a Sunday in England?

12 In 1995 which horse won the Derby, the King George VI and the Prix de l'Arc de Triomphe?

13 Alex Greaves was the first female jockey in which race?

14 Where is Valentine's Brook?

15 At which racecourse is the Steward's Cup competed for annually?

16 Who was riding Devon Loch when it so nearly won the National?

17 What is Frankie Dettori's real first name?

18 Which Jim was rider for Best Mate's Cheltenham Gold Cup triple triumphs?

19 Which horse won the Cheltenham Gold Cup in 1964, '65 and '66?

20 Who was the UK's first overseas champion jockey after Steve Cauthen?

21 Where is Tattenham Corner?

22 What is the highest jump in the Grand National?

23 Where did Walter Swinburn sustain severe injuries in February 1997?

24 Who won the Grand National in 1993?

25 Which auctioneers were founded in London in 1766 but now have annual sales in Newmarket?

26 Which racecourse is near Bognor Regis?

27 What was unusual about the status of Mr Frisk's winning rider in the 1990 National?

28 How old are horses who run in nursery stakes?

29 In which month is Royal Ascot?

30 What colour was in the name of 2001 Grand National winner Marauder?

Answers | TV: Sitcoms *(see Quiz 44)*

1 Dermot. **2** Gareth Blackstock. **3** Only Fools and Horses. **4** Drop the Dead Donkey. **5** Richard Wilson. **6** Jean Alexander. **7** Seinfeld. **8** A wheelchair. **9** Till Death Us Do Part. **10** Fawlty Towers. **11** Porridge. **12** Annie. **13** Cockerel. **14** Thelma. **15** Napoleon. **16** Bubble. **17** After Henry. **18** Are You Being Served?. **19** Gary Sparrow. **20** As Time Goes By. **21** Barker. **22** Cher. **23** They were witches. **24** Baldrick. **25** Allo Allo. **26** Green. **27** Christopher Biggins. **28** Geraldine Grainger. **29** Bottom. **30** Gordon.

1 What was the name of Harry Enfield's character in "Men Behaving Badly"?

2 What was the name of the Chef in "Chef!"?

3 What was the most successful sitcom of the 1980s?

4 Which series took place at the Globelink News Office?

5 Which sit com star worked in a hospital laboratory before becoming an actor?

6 Which former soap star plays Auntie Wainwright in "Last of the Summer Wine"?

7 Which US sitcom, which had 180 episodes, finished in May 1998?

8 In "Phoenix Nights" Peter Kay's character used what for mobility?

9 "All in the Family" was a US spin-off from which UK sitcom?

10 Where would you find guests Major Gowen, Miss Tibbs and Miss Gatsby?

11 "Going Straight" was the sequel to what?

12 What was the name of Jim Hacker's wife in "Yes Minister"?

13 In "The Good Life", who or what was Lenin?

14 In "The Likely Lads", whom did Bob marry?

15 In "Dad's Army" what did the air raid warden always call Mainwaring?

16 Who was Edina's PA in "Absolutely Fabulous"?

17 Which series with Prunella Scales as Sarah France had three years on radio before transferring to TV?

18 "Grace and Favour" was a sequel to which sitcom?

19 What is the name of the time traveller in "Goodnight Sweetheart"?

20 Which show's theme song begins, "You must remember this..."?

21 Which Ronnie's famous roles have included Arkwright and Fletcher?

22 Which star of "Mermaids" made a guest appearance on "Will & Grace"?

23 What was strange about Samantha Stephens and her mother Endora?

24 Who was Blackadder's servant?

25 Which sitcom was a send-up of "Secret Army"?

26 What was Dorien's surname in "Birds of a Feather"?

27 Who was the effeminate Lukewarm in "Porridge"?

28 What was the Vicar of Dibley's name?

29 In which series did Richie and Eddie first appear?

30 What was Brittas's first name in "The Brittas Empire"?

Quiz 45 | Pot Luck 21

Answers – page 166

LEVEL 2

1 If you nictitate at someone, what do you do?
2 Who offered Demi Moore a million dollars in "Indecent Proposal"?
3 Monument Valley is in which American state?
4 Which island off the north Devon coast is named after the Norse for puffin?
5 Who had 2005 hits with "Devil" and "Superman"?
6 On 14 April 1912, what occurred off Newfoundland?
7 Which "Strictly Come Dancing" star kept goal for both Man Utd and City?
8 Which instrument was played by David in the Bible?
9 Who is taller, Madonna or Dawn French?
10 Which organisation was founded in 1953 by Reverend Chad Varah?
11 In corned beef what are the corns?
12 Which people used knotted cords called quipu for calculation?
13 Which character was played by Maggie Smith in "Sister Act"?
14 Who wrote the novel "Journey to the Centre of the Earth"?
15 At which school was Thomas Arnold a famous headmaster?
16 Which "Cagney & Lacey" star appeared in the TV thriller "The State Within"?
17 How many squadrons make up a wing in the Royal Air Force?
18 Who followed U Thant as Secretary General of the United Nations?
19 Which high street chain was founded in 1961 by Selim Zilkha?
20 What does the book Glass's Guide contain?
21 What does B stand for in ASBO?
22 Who directed the epic action movie "Gladiator"?
23 What is an aspen?
24 The Battle of Pinkie of 1547 was fought in which country?
25 What nationality was Amy Johnson?
26 Which animal has the longest pregnancy?
27 Anything above scale 12 on the Beaufort Scale would describe what?
28 Which group were made up of Cass, Michelle, John and Denny?
29 Cars with the international vehicle registration PA come from where?
30 Whom did Shylock want to take his pound of flesh from?

Answers | **Musical Movies** *(see Quiz 46)*

1 Amos Hart. 2 Ursula Andress. 3 Cyd Charisse. 4 Maurice Chevalier. 5 The Philadelphia Story. 6 Martin Scorsese. 7 Dirty Dancing. 8 Whitney Houston. 9 Richard E. Grant. 10 Master of ceremonies. 11 Antonio Banderas. 12 The Nightmate Before Christmas. 13 Rex Harrison. 14 Moulin Rouge. 15 Marlon Brando. 16 Yul Brynner. 17 Baron Georg Von Trapp. 18 Freddie Eynsford-Hill. 19 Saturday Night Fever. 20 Autry. 21 1950s. 22 Albert Finney. 23 South Pacific. 24 Chim Chim Cheree. 25 Help! 26 Fiddler on the Roof. 27 Jonathan Pryce. 28 Sammy Davis Jr. 29 Cabaret. 30 Monroe.

Quiz 46 | Musical Movies

Answers – page 165

1 Which Chicago character calls himself Mr Cellophane?
2 Which Bond girl starred with Elvis Presley in "Fun in Acapulco"?
3 Who danced with Gene Kelly in the Broadway Ballet section of "Singin' in the Rain"?
4 Who sang "Thank Heaven for Little Girls" in "Gigi"?
5 "High Society" was a musical version of which classic?
6 Which controversial figure directed the musical "New York, New York"?
7 Josef Brown starred in the West End stage premiere of which hit movie?
8 Who sang most of the soundtrack of "The Bodyguard"?
9 Who had a managerial role in "Spiceworld"?
10 Joel Grey won an Oscar for which role in the 1970s classic "Cabaret"?
11 Who played Che in the film version of "Evita"?
12 Which Tim Burton film featured a hostile takeover of present delivery at Christmas?
13 Who played the Doctor in the musical film version of "Doctor Doolittle"?
14 "Children of the Revolution" and "The Red Room" are songs featured in which film?
15 Which tough guy actor played Sky Masterson in "Guys and Dolls"?
16 Which star of "The King and I" was born in Russia?
17 Who does Julie Andrews's character marry in "The Sound of Music"?
18 Which character sings "On the Street Where You Live" in "My Fair Lady"?
19 Which 1970s film became a stage musical in London in 1998?
20 Which Gene was the singing cowboy?
21 In which decade does the action of "Grease" take place?
22 Which English actor played the millionaire benefactor in "Annie"?
23 In which musical does Nurse Nellie Forbush appear?
24 Which of the many songs in "Mary Poppins" won the Oscar?
25 What was The Beatles' second film?
26 Which musical is the tale of a Jewish milkman in pre-revolutionary Russia?
27 Who played Eva's husband in "Evita"?
28 Who led "The Rhythm of Life" sequence in Sweet Charity?
29 Which 1970s musical film was set in pre-war Berlin?
30 Which Marylin sang "Diamonds are a Girl's Best Friend"?

Answers | Pot Luck 21 *(see Quiz 45)*

1 Wink. 2 Robert Redford. 3 Arizona. 4 Lundy. 5 Stereophonics. 6 The Titanic sank.
7 Peter Schmeichel. 8 Harp. 9 Madonna. 10 Samaritans. 11 Salt. 12 The Incas.
13 Mother Superior. 14 Jules Verne. 15 Rugby School. 16 Sharon Gless. 17 Three.
18 Kurt Waldheim. 19 Mothercare. 20 Vehicle prices. 21 Behaviour. 22 Ridley Scott.
23 A tree. 24 Scotland. 25 British. 26 Elephant. 27 Hurricane. 28 The Mamas and Papas. 29 Panama. 30 Antonio.

Quiz 47 | Pot Luck 22 | Answers – page 168 | LEVEL 2

1 What is a pickled gherkin made from?

2 Which keeper was a winner in the first FA Cup Final decided on penalties?

3 What is the name of Britney Spears' second son?

4 Pooh Bah appears in which Gilbert and Sullivan operetta?

5 Which Classic race is run over the longest distance?

6 Who was the brother of Flopsy, Mopsy and Cottontail?

7 What form did the head of the Sphinx take?

8 Which voice in singing is pitched between a tenor and a soprano?

9 Which birds collect in a covey?

10 Which now deposed leader led Iraq into the 1990s Gulf War?

11 Titian is what colour?

12 What part did Madonna play in the film "Shanghai Surprise"?

13 What does the M stand for in MIRAS?

14 Which almost eradicated disease was called Phthisis?

15 "The Moonstone" by Wilkie Collins is about a jewel from which country?

16 In which country is Lake Bala the largest natural lake?

17 Which "Pop Idol" sang at the Queen's Jubilee celebrations?

18 The US state of Maryland was named after the wife of which King?

19 What type of bars join places of equal atmospheric pressure on a chart?

20 Which tennis star was sued by Judy Nelson for palimony?

21 Who played Mark Antony opposite Liz Taylor in the film "Cleopatra"?

22 Which veteran presented "Old Dogs, New Tricks" with Lynn Faulds Wood?

23 Which European city hosted the 2004 summer Olympics?

24 What is the first name of PD James' detective Dalgleish?

25 Which part did Dustin Hoffman play in the film "Hook"?

26 What was the title of the 1994 East 17 Christmas No. 1 UK hit?

27 Who was British PM directly before Edward Heath?

28 Which Open win was Nick Faldo's first?

29 What can be solo boxing, a lush mineral or a round timber?

30 Which part did Gene Hackman play in the "Superman" films?

Answers | Living World *(see Quiz 48)*

1 Tidal wave. 2 On the skin. 3 CJD. 4 Worm. 5 Haematology. 6 Hermaphrodite. 7 Falcon. 8 Ear. 9 Marine snail. 10 Knee. 11 Pigeons. 12 Anaemia. 13 Orange. 14 Fungus. 15 Skin. 16 Abdomen. 17 Shoulder blade. 18 Fish. 19 Short-sighted. 20 12. 21 Idi Amin. 22 Acne. 23 The kiss of life. 24 Tuberculosis. 25 Base of the brain. 26 Achilles tendon. 27 Liver. 28 Green. 29 Kidney. 30 Herring.

1 Tsunami is another name for what type of wave?
2 Where would a melanoma appear?
3 Which disease in humans has been linked to the cattle disease BSE?
4 What sort of creature is a fluke?
5 Which branch of medicine is concerned with disorders of the blood?
6 What name is given to an organism which is both male and female?
7 What sort of bird is a Merlin?
8 Which part of the body might suffer from labyrinthitis?
9 What sort of creature is an abalone?
10 Where is a bird's patella?
11 Which racing creatures live in lofts?
12 What condition is caused by a shortage of haemoglobin?
13 What colour are the spots on a plaice?
14 What is a puffball?
15 Which part of the body does scabies affect?
16 Which digestive organ lies below the thorax in invertebrates?
17 Where is a human's scapula?
18 What do most sharks live on?
19 If a person has myopia what problem does he or she have?
20 How many pairs of ribs does a human have?
21 Which putative monarch was portrayed in the film "The Last King of Scotland"?
22 Which skin disorder is caused by inflammation of the sebaceous glands?
23 What is the popular name for mouth-to-mouth resuscitation?
24 A BCG is a vaccination against which disease?
25 Where is the pituitary gland?
26 Which tendon pins the calf muscle to the heel bone?
27 Hepatic refers to which organ of the body?
28 What colour head does a male mallard usually have?
29 The adrenal gland is above which organ?
30 The pilchard is a member of which fish family?

| **Answers** | Pot Luck 22 *(see Quiz 47)* |

1 A cucumber. 2 Jens Lehmann. 3 Sutton Pierce. 4 The Mikado. 5 St Leger. 6 Peter (Rabbit). 7 A Human. 8 An Alto. 9 Partridges. 10 Saddam Hussein. 11 Red. 12 A missionary. 13 Mortgage. 14 Tuberculosis. 15 India. 16 Wales. 17 Will Young. 18 Charles I. 19 Isobars. 20 Martina Navratilova. 21 Richard Burton. 22 Esther Rantzen. 23 Athens. 24 Adam. 25 Captain Hook. 26 Stay Another Day. 27 Harold Wilson. 28 British. 29 Spar. 30 Lex Luthor.

1 Was Craig David aged 18, 22 or 25 when he first had a No. 1 single?
2 The city of Philadelphia was founded by which religious group?
3 Where would you normally play shovel-board?
4 Which is further North, Blackburn or Blackpool?
5 Which husband of Demi Moore starred in "The Guardian"?
6 Which motor racing team is named after the sacred flower in India?
7 Donald McGill was particularly associated with what seaside art form?
8 Who wrote "Willie Wonka and the Chocolate Factory"?
9 Who narrates "Treasure Island" other than Jim Hawkins?
10 What is the New Zealand National Day called?
11 Paul Merson made his league debut with which club?
12 Which ship sent the first S.O.S.?
13 Which actress penned the autobiography "The Two of Us"?
14 Who wrote "The God Delusion"?
15 Which flower is on the badge of the Boy Scouts?
16 Which former Lebanese hostage wrote a book with Jill Morrell?
17 Maddy Magellan is the partner of which fictional detective?
18 Which Marlon Brando film is based on Conrad's "Heart of Darkness"?
19 In which group of islands is Panay?
20 Sandra Kim became the youngest winner of which contest?
21 The Sierra Nevada mountains are in which American state?
22 Who played Edward in TV's "Edward and Mrs Simpson"?
23 STASHING is an anagram of which famous battle?
24 The TV series "Rebus" was based on the novels of which writer?
25 Whose hits include "Kayleigh" and "Lavender"?
26 Was the Sopwith Camel designed by Sopwith or Camel?
27 Where in the UK is Compton Bay?
28 From 2003 to 2006 which Andy was at Blackburn, Fulham, Man City and Portsmouth?
29 Which word links a pastime, a small horse and a small falcon?
30 Which daily food includes the protein casein?

Answers	Famous Celebs *(see Quiz 50)*

1 Mohammed Al-Fayed. 2 Longleat. 3 Sarah. 4 Oprah Winfrey. 5 Alan Clark. 6 Antonia de Sancha. 7 Edwina Currie. 8 Countess Spencer. 9 Holloway Prison. 10 Beatrice. 11 Texas. 12 Michael Heseltine. 13 Everton. 14 Jemima Khan. 15 Max Clifford. 16 Loos. 17 Sir Cameron Mackintosh. 18 Demi Moore. 19 David Bailey. 20 Elizabeth Hurley. 21 Diana, Princess of Wales. 22 Lord Snowdon. 23 Spencer. 24 Peter Stringfellow. 25 French. 26 Vivienne Westwood. 27 Chef. 28 George Galloway. 29 Geri Halliwell. 30 Martine McCutcheon.

1 Who owns The Ritz in Paris?

2 Which stately home and safari park belongs to the Marquis of Bath?

3 What were two out of Andrew Lloyd-Webber's three wives called?

4 On which US chat show did Madonna first discuss the adoption of a baby from Malawi?

5 Which Tory MP philanderer said "Only domestic servants apologise" after his Diaries were published?

6 The story of whose affair with David Mellor broke in 1992?

7 Which outspoken ex-MP shares her birthday with Margaret Thatcher?

8 What was the previous title of Raine, Comtesse de Chambrun?

9 Where did Geri Halliwell have a meeting behind closed doors to launch 1998 Breast Cancer Awareness Week?

10 What is the name of the daughter of Paul McCartney and Heather Mills?

11 Jerry Hall is from which US state?

12 Whose heart attack in Venice prevented him from pursuing the Tory leadership?

13 Theatre impresario Bill Kenwright is a director of which soccer club?

14 Which late billionaire's daughter has a son called Sulaiman?

15 Which PR man acted for Mandy Allwood and Bienvenida Buck?

16 Lady Lucinda Lambton is an expert on which convenient necessity?

17 Which knighted impresario had a record six West End musicals running in 1996?

18 Which Hollywood star actress is Rumer Willis's mum?

19 Which photographer discovered Jean Shrimpton in the 60s?

20 Who became the face of Estee Lauder in the mid-1990s?

21 Who was Mrs Frances Shand Kydd's youngest daughter?

22 How was Anthony Armstrong-Jones known after his royal marriage?

23 Which future Earl did model Victoria Lockwood marry in 1990?

24 Which Sheffield-born nightclub owner's most famous club is named after him?

25 What is the nationality of designer Catherine Walker?

26 Which outrageous designer was once the partner of Sex Pistols' manager Malcolm McLaren?

27 In which profession did Marco Pierre White find fame?

28 Dr Amineh Abu-Zayyad married which Respect MP?

29 Which singing celeb's autobiography was called "Just for the Record"?

30 Which ex "EastEnders" star was a bridesmaid to Liza Minnelli in 2002?

---

1 Which England player was likened to Mary Poppins by a director of his own club?

2 What would you do with a saxhorn?

3 Who was singer Lorna Luft's famous actress mother?

4 "What Will the Neighbours Say?" was the second album from which group?

5 Which cartoon character is in the class with bully Nelson Muntz?

6 Who said, "4–5 isn't a football result, it's an ice hockey match"?

7 Which is the largest and oldest Australian city?

8 Whose autobiography was called "Mustn't Grumble"?

9 How is the wife of a Knight addressed?

10 Light, Home and Third used to be what?

11 What name is given to a person who eats no food of animal origin?

12 Who wrote the song "Moon River"?

13 Who led the Scottish troops at Bannockburn?

14 Which Palace is the official home of the French president?

15 What is a water moccasin?

16 In which group of islands are St Martin's, St Mary's and Tresco?

17 Which people made an idol in the form of a Golden Calf in the Bible?

18 Which actor starred in the film "North by Northwest"?

19 Which city is called the City of Brotherly Love?

20 In which sport were John Louis and Barry Briggs associated?

21 Whose biography was called "Neither Shaken nor Stirred"?

22 Which famous Falls are on the Zambezi river?

23 What kind of flower can be a goldilocks?

24 Philippa Braithwaite married which star of "Doc Martin" and "Losing It"?

25 If you are a member of the Q Guild, what is your profession?

26 Which creature's name can go in front of crab, plant, wasp and monkey?

27 How many cards are in a tarot pack?

28 In "Trading Places" who traded places with Dan Aykroyd?

29 Diluted acetic acid is the correct name for which foodstuff?

30 Whose hits include "The Bitch is Back" and "Kiss the Bride"?

Answers	Leisure 2 *(see Quiz 52)*

1 Role Playing. 2 Boules. 3 May. 4 British Museum. 5 22. 6 Sumo wrestling. 7 Lawn tennis. 8 Their hands. 9 Yin and Yang. 10 York. 11 Weightlifting. 12 Bonsai. 13 Plastic shuttlecocks. 14 Scotland. 15 Windsurfing. 16 Lego. 17 Horse racing, cards. 18 Michael Caine. 19 Phillip Schofield. 20 Rose. 21 Normandy. 22 One. 23 AA. 24 China. 25 MCC. 26 Hamley's Regent Street, London. 27 In its ear. 28 Ever After. 29 Swimming. 30 Four.

1 What imaginative type of Game is known by the initials RPG?
2 Which French game's name is the French word for balls?
3 In which month is Spring Bank Holiday?
4 Which London Museum was the most visited in 2005?
5 How many balls are needed to play a game of snooker?
6 What is the national sport of Japan?
7 What is lawn tennis called when played on shale or clay?
8 In volleyball what do players hit the ball with?
9 What is the Chinese for "dark" and "light" believed to maintain equilibrium?
10 Where is the Jorvik Viking Museum?
11 In which sport would you snatch and jerk?
12 The name of which type of tree cultivation comes from the Japanese for "bowl cultivation"?
13 Which major change was introduced in badminton in 1949?
14 In which country is the oldest angling club in the world?
15 What is another name for boardsailing?
16 Which toy was invented by Danes Ole and Godtfred Christiansen?
17 If you were at or playing Newmarket which leisure pursuits would you be following?
18 Which cockney actor was a part owner of Langan's Brasserie?
19 Who played Dr Doolittle when it first appeared on the London stage?
20 Bourbon and Gallica are types of what?
21 In which French region is the annual apple festival at Orne?
22 If you received cotton, how many wedding anniversaries would you be celebrating?
23 Which UK motoring association describes itself as the fourth emergency service?
24 Which is the largest country where membership of the Scouts is not allowed?
25 Which club founded in 1787 voted to allow women members in 1998?
26 Where is the world's oldest toyshop?
27 Where does a Steiff teddy bear have its tag of authenticity?
28 What was the 1998 movie based on Cinderella, and starring Drew Barrymore called?
29 If you joined the Wasps in Wigan what sport would you compete in?
30 How many tournaments make up the Grand Slam in golf?

Answers	Pot Luck 24 *(see Quiz 51)*

1 Alan Shearer. 2 Play it. 3 Judy Garland. 4 Girls Aloud. 5 Bart Simpson. 6 Jose Mourinho (about Spurs v. Arsenal). 7 Sydney. 8 Terry Wogan. 9 Lady. 10 Radio channels. 11 A vegan. 12 Henry Mancini. 13 Robert the Bruce. 14 Elysée. 15 Snake. 16 Scilly Isles. 17 The Israelites. 18 Cary Grant. 19 Philadelphia. 20 Speedway. 21 Sean Connery. 22 Victoria Falls. 23 A buttercup. 24 Martin Clunes. 25 A Butcher. 26 Spider. 27 78. 28 Eddie Murphy. 29 Vinegar. 30 Elton John.

Quiz 53 | Pot Luck 25

Answers – page 174

LEVEL 2

1 Which club joined the Football League in 1978 and made the Premiership in 2005?
2 Dove Cottage was home of which poet?
3 Which Pole was first reached in 1909?
4 Which Day replaced Empire Day in 1958?
5 Alfred the Great ruled which Kingdom?
6 Estoril is a resort north east of which major city?
7 Which No. 1 for Norman Greenbaum was reworked by Gareth Gates?
8 Who was the founder lead singer with Led Zeppelin in 1968?
9 Freddie Powell found fame as which crazy comic?
10 Which British surgeon was a pioneer in improving surgery hygiene?
11 Who was the female lead in "Singing in the Rain"?
12 Which common garden flower has the name Dianthus barbatus?
13 Where were the Spode pottery works established in the 1760s?
14 Cars with the international vehicle registration BG come from where?
15 Which Club included Mr Winkle and Mr Tupman as members?
16 Never Say Die was the first Derby winner for which famous jockey?
17 In which area of England is "Wire in the Blood" set?
18 Which castle is the largest in Britain?
19 Edwin Hubble was concerned with which branch of science?
20 Which part did Albert Finney play in the 1974 film "Murder on the Orient Express"?
21 Sir Alfred Munnings is famous for painting which animals?
22 Comic character Dan Dare was known as the pilot of what?
23 Colonel Thomas Blood tried to steal what in 1671?
24 In a famous 1990s case, Robert Hoskins was convicted of stalking which star?
25 What sort of creature was a brawn?
26 If you suffered a myocardial infarction, what would have happened?
27 Who partnered Annie Lennox in the Eurythmics?
28 The Peace River is in which country?
29 In 1957, in which US state were there race riots at Little Rock?
30 Who won a best supporting actor Oscar for a role in "Million Dollar Baby"?

Answers | **Pop Music: The 90s** *(see Quiz 54)*

1 I Believe. 2 Too Much. 3 Sting & Bryan Adams. 4 Saturday. 5 Gabrielle. 6 Boombastic. 7 Colchester. 8 Back to Black. 9 Without You. 10 Would I Lie to You. 11 Germany. 12 The Bodyguard. 13 Prodigy. 14 Fairground. 15 Boyz II Men. 16 Looking Up. 17 I Wonder Why. 18 Spice Girls. 19 Cecilia. 20 Peter Andre. 21 Too Young to Die. 22 Ebeneezer Goode. 23 James Brown. 24 Kylie Minogue. 25 Think Twice. 26 Shiny Happy People. 27 Doop. 28 Beverley Craven. 29 The Real Thing. 30 Lady Marmalade.

173

1 What was the other side of Robson and Jerome's "Up on the Roof"?
2 Which Spice Girl hit came first – "Goodbye" or "Too Much"?
3 Which two singers joined Rod Stewart on the 1994 hit "All for Love"?
4 What night links Whigfield, Alexander O'Neal and Omar?
5 Who featured on East 17's No. 2 "If You Ever" in 1996?
6 Which 1995 hit gave Shaggy his second No. 1?
7 Blur were formed in which East Anglian town?
8 What is the title of Amy Winehouse's second album?
9 Which song title links No. 1s for Mariah Carey and Nilsson?
10 Which title links the Eurythmics to a 1992 No. 1 for Charles and Eddy?
11 Which country did pop/dance act Sash! come from?
12 Which film featured the song that was Whitney Houston's fourth UK No. 1?
13 Which dance/rock act was fronted by Keith Flint?
14 What was Simply Red's first UK No. 1 in 1995?
15 Who partnered Mariah Carey on "One Sweet Day"?
16 What was "EastEnders'" Michelle Gayle's first hit?
17 What was Curtis Stigers' first UK Top Ten success?
18 Which group held the Christmas single and album top spots in 1996?
19 Which female name was a No. 4 hit for Suggs in 1996?
20 Whose first two UK No. 1s were "Flava" and "I Feel You"?
21 What was Jamiroquai's first UK Top Ten hit?
22 Which song title gave The Shamen their only No. 1 in 1992?
23 Who was the self-styled "Hardest Working Man in Show Business?"
24 "Better the Devil You Know" was a hit for Sonia and which soap star?
25 What was the first UK No. 1 for Celine Dion?
26 What kind of people did R.E.M. take to No. 6 in 1991?
27 What was the one-hit wonder of the Dutch duo Doop?
28 Whose highest chart position was No. 3 in 1991 with "Promise Me"?
29 Which Tony Di Bart No. 1 hit from 1994 is the name of a group?
30 Which All Saints No. 1 was a cover of a 70s hit for Labelle?

Answers | **Pot Luck 25** *(see Quiz 53)*

1 Wigan. 2 William Wordsworth. 3 North. 4 Commonwealth Day. 5 Wessex. 6 Lisbon. 7 Spirit in the Sky. 8 Robert Plant. 9 Freddie Starr. 10 Joseph Lister. 11 Debbie Reynolds. 12 Sweet William. 13 Stoke. 14 Bulgaria. 15 Pickwick Club. 16 Lester Piggott. 17 North east. 18 Windsor. 19 Astronomy. 20 Hercule Poirot. 21 Horses. 22 The Future. 23 Crown Jewels. 24 Madonna. 25 A wild pig. 26 A heart attack. 27 Dave Stewart. 28 Canada. 29 Arkansas. 30 Morgan Freeman.

1 Which soap features the unlikely named character Mercedes McQueen?
2 What was "Coronation Street" originally going to be called?
3 What was the name of Joan Collins' character in "Dynasty"?
4 The Hart family appeared in which daily soap?
5 Which ex-husband of Joan Collins appeared on "EastEnders"?
6 Who played mechanic Chris in "Coronation Street" and left to pursue a pop career?
7 Which "Corrie" star produced a fitness video called "Rapid Results"?
8 In "Coronation Street", what is Spider's real name?
9 In which soap were Shane and Angel an item?
10 How did Kathy Glover's husband die in "Emmerdale"?
11 In "Coronation Street" what was Fiona's baby called?
12 Where did Kathy Mitchell go when she left Albert Square?
13 Which badboy Billy was played by David Crellin?
14 Whom did Dannii Minogue play in "Home & Away"?
15 Which Kemp joined Ross Kemp on the "EastEnders" cast?
16 In "Corrie" which of the Battersby girls is Janice's daughter?
17 Which Kim disappeared from "Emmerdale" and was thought to have been murdered?
18 Which soap did "Silent Witness" star Amanda Burton appear in?
19 Which TV company first produced "Emmerdale Farm"?
20 Which role did Norman Bowler play in "Emmerdale"?
21 Which ex-"Corrie" actress toured in the controversial play "The Blue Room"?
22 Which member of Emmerdale's Dingle family went on to present "You've Been Framed"?
23 Who was buried under the patio in "Brookside"?
24 Emmerdale's Sheree Murphy is married to which famous footballer?
25 Whose son in "Corrie" was once played by his real son Linus?
26 Where did Mavis go when she left The Street?
27 Which one-time boy band member played Ciaran in "Corrie"?
28 "Damon & Debbie" was a short-lived spin-off from which soap?
29 Who links narrating "The Wombles" and playing Wally in a soap?
30 Which soap had a bar called the Waterhole?

1 Alan Shearer's league career finished with a game against which team?
2 Which Kenny Rogers hit starts, "On a bar in Toledo..."
3 In which sport is there a piste other than skiing?
4 Which member of Queen would have been 60 in September 2006?
5 Which Chancellor of the Exchequer introduced TESSA?
6 Which character was played by Dooley Wilson in "Casablanca"?
7 Who wrote the play "Private Lives"?
8 Who invented the bagless vacuum cleaner?
9 Whose hits include "Waterfront" and "Alive and Kicking"?
10 Voords, Krotons and Autons have all appeared on which TV series?
11 Which children's writer's real name was Mrs Heelis?
12 How many seconds are there in three hours?
13 What was the dog called in the Famous Five books?
14 If you were using Dutch or Diaper Bonds what would you be doing?
15 What was Herman's Hermits' only No. 1 UK hit?
16 In which country was Salman Rushdie born?
17 What are you doing if you are mendicanting?
18 Who wrote the novel "Murder in Mesopotamia" in 1936?
19 Which team from outside Glasgow won the Scottish FA Cup three times from 1982–84?
20 In Monopoly, what is the next property after the Old Kent Road?
21 Whose mountain retreat was at Berchtesgaden?
22 Which programme replaced "Home Truths" on Radio 4?
23 Which was the first British National Park?
24 Fred Perry was World Champion in 1929 in which sport?
25 Which TV agony aunt's autobiography was "Agony? Don't Get Me Going"?
26 The condor belongs to which family of birds?
27 In which country is Arnhem Land?
28 In 2006, who was the Chief Rabbi??
29 Which actor was Gandhi in the 1982 film?
30 Who was first to win four World Snooker Championships in a row?

Answers | TV: Soaps *(see Quiz 55)*

1 Hollyoaks. 2 Florizel Street. 3 Alexis Carrington. 4 Family Affairs. 5 Anthony Newley. 6 Matthew Marsden. 7 Beverley Callard. 8 Geoffrey. 9 Home and Away. 10 In a fire. 11 Morgan. 12 South Africa. 13 Billy Hopwood. 14 Emma. 15 Martin. 16 Toyah. 17 Tate. 18 Brookside. 19 Yorkshire TV. 20 Frank Tate. 21 Tracy Shaw. 22 Mandy. 23 Trevor Jordache. 24 Harry Kewell. 25 William Roache's. 26 Lake District. 27 Keith Duffy. 28 Brookside. 29 Bernard Cribbins. 30 Neighbours.

1 What does TT stand for in the Isle of Man races?
2 Who first had a record-breaking car and a boat called Bluebird?
3 Who was the youngest F1 world champion before Fernando Alonso?
4 Which team did Jim Clark spend all his racing career with?
5 How many people are in the car in drag racing?
6 Which Belgian cyclist was known as "The Cannibal"?
7 How many times did Stirling Moss win the world championship?
8 In which country was the first organised car race?
9 Speedway's world champion Tony Rickardsson comes from which country?
10 By 1993 which French driver had won 51 Grand Prix from 199 starts?
11 Which ex-world champion was killed at the San Marino Grand Prix in 1993?
12 Which motor racing Park is east of Chester?
13 What type of racing is known in the US as Demolition Derbies?
14 How frequently does the Tour de France take place?
15 Who was the first man to be world champion on two and four wheels?
16 What relation was Emerson to Christian Fittipaldi?
17 Which Japanese team won its first F1 Grand Prix in 1967?
18 Who was the first man to win a Grand Prix in a car he designed?
19 Which non-French city was the first to start the Tour de France this century?
20 In 1994 who was the first Austrian to win the German Grand Prix since Niki Lauda?
21 Which Briton was the first world driver's champion to win Le Mans, in 1972?
22 In which country did the first mountain bike world championship take place?
23 Which Briton did Alain Prost overtake for a record number of Grand Prix wins?
24 Which was the first manufacturer to have over 100 Grand Prix wins?
25 Which famous British car won the Monte Carlo rally in 1967?
26 Who was the first Briton to wear the Tour de France yellow jersey after Tommy Simpson?
27 Who was the first British F1 Champion after James Hunt?
28 Who was the first driver to be sacked by Benetton twice?
29 Who was the first Frenchman to win the World Grand Prix title in '85?
30 Where is the home of the French Grand Prix?

Answers | Pot Luck 27 *(see Quiz 58)*

1 Suspicious Minds. 2 I'm with Stupid. 3 Karl Marx. 4 An insect. 5 Skull. 6 Woody Guthrie. 7 Winston Graham. 8 A clock. 9 Russia. 10 Belfast. 11 Bruce Lee. 12 David Lloyd. 13 Flies. 14 First signatory. 15 Michaelmas Day. 16 A dress. 17 Volcanic eruption. 18 Oak. 19 Goldfinger. 20 Desert-dweller. 21 Remington. 22 Augustus. 23 Rod. 24 Bob Hoskins. 25 Steve Coogan. 26 David Seaman. 27 Messengers. 28 Una Stubbs. 29 Tomato. 30 Neneh Cherry.

1 Which Gareth Gates hit contains the words, "We're caught in a trap"?

2 In which series did Mark Benton play a tramp called Sheldon?

3 Who produced the Communist Manifesto with Friedrich Engels?

4 What is a firebrat?

5 Where are your fontanelles?

6 Which American protest singer is linked to the "dustbowl ballads"?

7 Who wrote the stories subsequently televised as "Poldark"?

8 In which time device would you find an escapement?

9 The port of Archangel is in which country?

10 The Titanic was launched in which city?

11 Film star Lee Yuen Kam achieved fame as which kung fu expert?

12 Which former tennis player sold Hull City in 1998?

13 Which dirty insects are members of the Diptera family?

14 John Hancock was first to do what at the American Declaration of Independence?

15 In a calendar year what is the third quarter day in England?

16 What is a dirndl?

17 What, in 1902, destroyed the Martinique village of St Pierre?

18 Cork is produced mainly from which species of tree?

19 In which Bond film does the character "Oddjob" appear?

20 What does the word 'Bedouin' mean?

21 Which family made typewriters and invented the breech loading rifle?

22 Who was the first Roman Emperor?

23 Which word can be a unit of measure, a stick or a fishing implement?

24 Which actor played a black prostitute's minder in the film "Mona Lisa"?

25 Which comedian wrote and performed in "Saxondale"?

26 Who was England's first-choice keeper in the 2002 World Cup?

27 Is St Gabriel the patron saint of messengers, millers or musicians?

28 Which actress played the daughter of Alf Garnett?

29 A love apple is an archaic term for what?

30 Whose hits include "Manchild" and "Buffalo Stance"?

| **Answers** | **Sport: Hot Wheels** *(see Quiz 57)* |

1 Tourist Trophy. 2 Malcolm Campbell. 3 Emerson Fittipaldi. 4 Lotus. 5 One. 6 Eddie Merckx. 7 Never. 8 France. 9 Sweden. 10 Alain Prost. 11 Ayrton Senna. 12 Oulton Park. 13 Stock car racing. 14 Annually. 15 John Surtees. 16 Uncle. 17 Honda. 18 Jack Brabham. 19 London. 20 Gerhard Berger. 21 Graham Hill. 22 France. 23 Jackie Stewart. 24 Ferrari. 25 Mini. 26 Chris Boardman. 27 Nigel Mansell. 28 Johnny Herbert. 29 Alain Prost. 30 Magny Cours.

1 Which actor/director started the trend for spaghetti westerns?

2 What was the nationality of Meryl Streep's character in "A Cry in the Dark"?

3 Who was shunned by Hollywood in the 1940s when she left her husband for Roberto Rossellini?

4 Which poet's name was the middle name of James Dean?

5 Who was Hollywood's first black superstar?

6 Which famous dancer played a straight role in "On the Beach"?

7 Which Burt appeared in "Bean – The Ultimate Disaster Movie"?

8 On the set of which film did the Richard Burton/Elizabeth Taylor affair begin?

9 What is the first name of Julia Roberts' character in "Closer"?

10 Who received her first Oscar nomination for "Silkwood"?

11 Whose roles vary from Cruella de Vil on film to Norma Desmond on stage?

12 How old was Macaulay Culkin when he was first married?

13 Which married superstars starred in "The Big Sleep" in 1946?

14 Which comedian co-founded United Artists in 1919?

15 Dietrich appeared in the German "The Blue Angel"; who appeared in the US version?

16 Which actor's last film was "The Misfits" in 1960?

17 Who was voted No. 1 pin-up by US soldiers in WWII?

18 How many parts did Alec Guinness play in "Kind Hearts and Coronets"?

19 What is the profession of Nicole Kidman's father?

20 In which country did Charlie Chaplin spend the final years of his life?

21 Who was Truman in "The Truman Show"?

22 Which superstar did Tony Curtis parody in "Some Like It Hot"?

23 Who portrayed Frankie Dunn in a sport-related movie?

24 Who is the physician in the 1990s remake of "Doctor Doolittle"?

25 How many Road films did Crosby, Hope and Lamour make?

26 Who was the psychotic cabbie in Scorsese's "Taxi Driver"?

27 Who announced her retirement when she married Ted Turner in 1991?

28 Who was Jodie Foster's character in "The Silence of the Lambs"?

29 Who directed "The Horse Whisperer"?

30 Who played Margo Channing in "All About Eve"?

Answers | Pot Luck 28 *(see Quiz 60)*

1 Three. 2 A Helicopter. 3 MI5. 4 M People. 5 Labrador. 6 Gabrielle. 7 The Old Curiosity Shop. 8 Greece. 9 On the seabed. 10 Kent. 11 Shoes. 12 Melvyn Hayes. 13 Sistine. 14 Music of Black Origin. 15 Bismarck. 16 Le Mans. 17 Sap. 18 Peru. 19 The World War. 20 Pregnant. 21 Jackie Rae. 22 Aston Villa. 23 Bits and pieces. 24 Guildford. 25 Isle of Wight. 26 The Lion King. 27 Nkima. 28 Pearl Harbor. 29 Commissioner Dreyfus. 30 Whitewater.

1 How many times did Joe Frasier fight Muhammad Ali?
2 What was designed and made in a viable form by Sikorsky in 1941?
3 The TV series "Spooks" is about which organisation?
4 Who had hits with "One Night in Heaven" and "Moving On Up"?
5 Which "dog like" peninsula formed Canada's tenth province in 1949?
6 What was Coco Chanel's Christian name?
7 Quilp appears in a book about what kind of Shop?
8 In which European country are the Pindus Mountains?
9 If a creature is demersal, where does it live?
10 In which county was the first Youth Custody Centre set up in 1908?
11 Espadrilles are a type of what?
12 Who played the part of "Gloria" in "It Ain't Half Hot, Mum"?
13 Michelangelo painted the ceiling of which famous Chapel?
14 In the music world what does MOBO mean?
15 Who was called the "Iron Chancellor"?
16 Where is motor racing's Grand Prix d'Endurance staged?
17 If a creature is succivorous what does it feed on?
18 The source of the Amazon is in which South American country?
19 Al Capone said he was accused of every death except the casualty list of what?
20 If something or someone is gravid what does it mean?
21 Who was the first presenter of the TV series "The Golden Shot"?
22 At which club did Gareth Southgate play most league games?
23 What does "Chop Suey" literally mean?
24 In which city is the University of Surrey?
25 Carisbrooke Castle is on which Isle?
26 In which Disney film is a young lion called Simba?
27 What was the name of Tarzan's monkey friend in the Tarzan stories?
28 Which 2001 film was about real-life events in the Pacific 60 years ago?
29 Which part was played by Herbert Lom in the Pink Panther films?
30 The Clintons were implicated in which 1990s US property scandal?

Quiz 61 | On the Map

1 Which South American city has a famous Copacabana beach?
2 The Bass Strait divides which two islands?
3 Which Middle East capital is known locally as El Qahira?
4 Where is the official country home of US Presidents?
5 Whose Vineyard is an island off Cape Cod?
6 Where was Checkpoint Charlie?
7 Which US state has a 'pan handle' separating the Atlantic from the Gulf of Mexico?
8 In which two countries is the Dead Sea?
9 The site of ancient Babylon is now in which country?
10 On which river is the Aswan Dam?
11 The Trump International Hotel & Tower was built where in the USA?
12 The Fens were formerly a bay of which Sea?
13 What is Japan's highest peak?
14 To which country do the Galapagos Islands belong?
15 Aconcagua is an extinct volcano in which mountain range?
16 Where in California is the lowest point of the western hemisphere?
17 In which London Square is the US Embassy?
18 Ellis Island is in which harbour?
19 Which city is known to Afrikaners as Kaapstad?
20 On which Sea is the Gaza Strip?
21 What are the three divisions of Glamorgan?
22 Which river cuts through the Grand Canyon?
23 Where in India are Anjuna beach and Morjim beach?
24 Which continents are separated by the Dardanelles?
25 Which US state capital means "sheltered bay" in Hawaiian?
26 Hampstead is part of which London borough?
27 Which country owns the southernmost part of South America?
28 Where is the seat of the UN International Court of Justice?
29 The Golan Heights are on the border of which two countries?
30 Which is the saltiest of the main oceans?

Answers	Pot Luck 29 *(see Quiz 62)*

1 West Side Story. 2 Tom and Jerry. 3 Love. 4 John Hunt. 5 Backstreet Boys. 6 The Real Thing. 7 Rugby League. 8 Potato famine. 9 Language sounds. 10 Joe Louis. 11 Tom Cruise. 12 Robert Mugabe. 13 Calcium. 14 40. 15 Honeysuckle. 16 Shoe. 17 Clerestory. 18 Nine. 19 Rock Hudson. 20 Fred Astaire. 21 Trampolining. 22 Niagara Falls. 23 Bournemouth. 24 Ole Gunnar Solskjaer. 25 Mariah Carey. 26 A Nelson. 27 Britain. 28 Freddie Laker. 29 Cameron Diaz. 30 15th.

Quiz 62 | Pot Luck 29

Answers – page 181

1 The song "America" comes from which musical?
2 Which cartoon duo starred in the Oscar-winning film "Quiet Please"?
3 Kate Bush had an album called The Hounds Of ... what?
4 In 1953 who was leader of the British expedition which conquered Everest?
5 Which group had a huge hit with "Millennium"?
6 Who had a UK Top Ten hit with "Can You Feel the Force"?
7 Which sport was founded in Britain on 28 August 1895?
8 Black Forty Seven in Ireland in the 19th century related to what?
9 What is phonetics the study of?
10 Who was World Heavyweight boxing champion in WWII?
11 Which actor links "Risky Business", "Cocktail" and "Top Gun"?
12 Who was the first president of Zimbabwe?
13 Which element is found in shells, bones and teeth?
14 How old are you if you are a quadragenarian?
15 Which flower is also called the Woodbine?
16 Which item of clothing features on the poster for the movie "The Devil Wears Prada"?
17 A row of windows in the upper wall of a church is known by what name?
18 What is the most times a day of the week can occur in two months?
19 Who was older when he died, Humphrey Bogart or Rock Hudson?
20 Who starred opposite Judy Garland in the film "Easter Parade"?
21 In which sport are there moves called Triffus, Rudolf and Miller?
22 The Horseshoe and American combine to form which famous falls?
23 Which is further West, Bognor or Bournemouth?
24 Who completed ten seasons at Old Trafford in 2006 after playing for Molde?
25 Who has had hits with "Hero" and "Anytime You Need a Friend"?
26 What name is given to a score of 111 in cricket?
27 In Orwell's 1984 what is called Airstrip One?
28 Whose cheap transatlantic air service in 1977 was called "Skytrain"?
29 Who was the third of "Charlie's Angels" with Drew Barrymore and Lucy Liu?
30 In which century was the Battle of Agincourt?

Answers | On the Map (see Quiz 61)

1 Rio de Janeiro. 2 Australia & Tasmania. 3 Cairo. 4 Camp David. 5 Martha's Vineyard. 6 Between East and West Berlin. 7 Florida. 8 Israel & Jordan. 9 Iraq. 10 Nile. 11 Chicago. 12 North Sea. 13 Mount Fujiyama. 14 Ecuador. 15 Andes. 16 Death Valley. 17 Grosvenor. 18 New York. 19 Cape Town. 20 Mediterranean. 21 Mid, South, West. 22 Colorado. 23 Goa. 24 Europe & Asia. 25 Honolulu. 26 Camden. 27 Chile. 28 The Hague. 29 Israel & Syria. 30 Atlantic.

1 Which cereal can survive in the widest range of climatic conditions?
2 The hellebore is known as what type of rose?
3 What colour are edelweiss flowers?
4 Which plant is St Patrick said to have used to illustrate the Holy Trinity?
5 Succulents live in areas lacking in what?
6 How many points does a sycamore leaf have?
7 What is the ornamental shaping of trees and shrubs called?
8 What is an alternative name for the narcotic and analgesic aconite?
9 What colour are laburnum flowers?
10 What is another name for a yam?
11 What shape are flowers which include the name campanula?
12 What is a frond on a plant?
13 Which climbing plant is also called hedera helix?
14 Agronomy is the study of what?
15 What is a Sturmer?
16 Which fruit is called "earth berry" in German from where the plant grows?
17 What is another name for belladonna?
18 What is the effect on the nervous system of taking hemlock?
19 Are the male, female or either hop plants used to make beer?
20 What is the most common plant grown in Assam in India?
21 Aspen is what type of tree?
22 Which flowering plant is named after the sixteenth-century German botanist Leonhart Fuchs?
23 The ground powder form turmeric dyes food which colour?
24 The pineapple plant is native to which continent?
25 What is the purpose of a plant's petals?
26 Which type of pesticide is used to kill weeds?
27 What colour are the leaves of a poinsettia?
28 What name is given to the wild yellow iris?
29 Which plant is famous for having a "clock"?
30 What colour are borage flowers?

1 Which former First Lady was nicknamed "The Smiling Mamba"?

2 Who had hits with "Joanna" and "Celebration"?

3 Where would you see a facula?

4 Who played the title character in "The Life and Death of Peter Sellers"?

5 Which country has a unit of currency called the Leone?

6 The seaside town of Westward Ho is in which county?

7 Oloroso is a type of which drink?

8 Back in the charts in 2005, in what year was Bananarama's first hit?

9 Which Wonder of the World statue was at Olympia?

10 In which century did William Caxton establish the first English printing press?

11 Cocoa is prepared from the seeds of which tree?

12 Who joined John Torode as a judge on "Celebrity Masterchef"?

13 What is driven by a mahout?

14 What does the cooking expression al dente mean?

15 Which Oliver was Lord Protector of Britain?

16 Which label is distinguished as fashion designed by Armani?

17 Which celeb's childhood nickname was Liver Lips?

18 Who would use a jacquard?

19 In "The Wizard of Oz", which animal was seeking courage?

20 Who captained the US Ryder Cup team in 1997?

21 Who was the Bond girl in "Die Another Day"?

22 Pumpkin Pie is the traditional dessert on which special American day?

23 Who played Eleanor Bramwell in the TV series of the same name?

24 Who painted "The Starry Night"?

25 Which word can be a swan, a horse, a bread roll and a basket?

26 What was Diana Ross's first solo No. 1 in the UK?

27 What are progeny?

28 Who had hits with "I Can't Dance" and "Invisible Touch"?

29 In which part of East London was David Beckham born?

30 If you heard a John Gabel Entertainer, what would be playing?

Answers | **Nature: Plant World (see Quiz 63)**

1 Barley. 2 Christmas rose. 3 White. 4 Shamrock. 5 Water. 6 Five. 7 Topiary. 8 Monkshood. 9 Yellow. 10 Sweet potato. 11 Bell-shaped. 12 Leaf. 13 Ivy. 14 Crops and soils. 15 Apple. 16 Strawberry. 17 Deadly nightshade. 18 Paralysis. 19 Female. 20 Tea. 21 Poplar. 22 Fuchsia. 23 Yellow. 24 South America. 25 Attract pollinators. 26 Herbicide. 27 Red. 28 Flag. 29 Dandelion. 30 Blue.

1 Germany's Red Army Faction was popularly called what after its two founders?

2 The Equal Opportunities Commission was set up to implement which act?

3 Who became US Vice President after Spiro Agnew resigned?

4 Where did the Gang of Four seize power in 1976?

5 Which natural disaster did Guatemala City suffer in 1976?

6 In the Vietnam War who or what was Agent Orange?

7 Who was Nixon's White House Chief of Staff at the height of the Watergate scandal?

8 On which Pennsylvania Island was there a nuclear leak in 1979?

9 In 1978 Mujaheddin resistance began in which country?

10 Who made a precocious speech aged 16 at the 1977 Tory Party conference?

11 Who opened her first Body Shop in 1976?

12 Where was Obote replaced by Amin in 1971?

13 The Pahlavi Dynasty was overthrown by the Islamic revolution in which country?

14 Which Argentine leader died in 1974 and was succeeded by his third wife?

15 Which woman MP did Jack Straw replace as MP for Blackburn?

16 In films, which actor played the comic book character with an S on his chest?

17 Which dictator was deposed in Cambodia in 1979?

18 Which "King" died in 1977 aged 42?

19 What was Harare called until the end of the 1970s?

20 What was inside US incendiary bombs during the Vietnam War?

21 Which title did Quintin Hogg take when made Lord Chancellor in '70?

22 SALT negotiations took place between which two countries?

23 Which future Labour leader became Trade & Industry Secretary in '78?

24 Who first charted in the 1970s and had a 2005 No. 1 with "Ghetto Gospel"?

25 In which country was a monarchy restored in 1975?

26 The Sandinistas overthrew which government in 1979?

27 Who succeeded Heath as Tory leader?

28 Sapporo was the centre of the 1972 winter Olympics in which country?

29 Which country did the USSR invade in 1979?

30 In which department was Thatcher a Minister before leading the Party?

Answers | TV: TV Times 1 *(see Quiz 66)*

1 Anne Charleston. 2 Nephew. 3 Warrior. 4 Miss America. 5 New Faces. 6 Helicopters. 7 Kel. 8 Grant Bovey. 9 Elton John. 10 Ulrika Jonsson. 11 Assumpta. 12 Michael Jackson. 13 Shoplifting. 14 Snowball Merriman. 15 Basildon. 16 Trevor McDonald. 17 Bingo. 18 Jennifer Patterson. 19 Tony Slattery. 20 Torvill & Dean. 21 Delia Smith. 22 Televangelism. 23 Girls Aloud. 24 Sian Lloyd. 25 Sam Malone. 26 The Bee Gees. 27 Les Dennis. 28 Ricki Lake. 29 John Virgo. 30 On a bed.

1 Which actress moved from Madge in "Neighbours" to Millie in "Emmerdale"?

2 What relation is "ER"'s George Clooney to US singer Rosemary?

3 Which Gladiator was jailed in 1998 for corruption?

4 Superwoman Lynda Carter held which beauty queen title?

5 On which TV show was Jim Davidson "discovered"?

6 Outside TV what type of transport business does Noel Edmonds run?

7 What is the name of Kath's husband in Australian comedy "Kath & Kim"?

8 In the celeb boxing's "The Fight", Ricky Gervais took on which Grant?

9 The TV profile "Tantrums and Tiaras" was about which pop superstar?

10 Which TV presenter's relationship with Stan Collymore ended violently in Paris during the 1998 World Cup?

11 Who was the first landlady of Fitzgerald's in "Ballykissangel"?

12 Martin Bashir's 2003 UK TV interview led to involvement in a court trial of which celeb?

13 What was Richard Madeley arrested for in 1990?

14 Which character did Nicole Faraday play in "Bad Girls"?

15 In which town was Essex girl Denise Van Outen born?

16 Which "News at Ten" presenter had the first British TV interview with Nelson Mandela after his release?

17 Which game was "Bob's Full House" based on?

18 Which TV cook wears a diamond-studded crash helmet?

19 Who presented the C5 medical quiz show "Tibs and Fibs"?

20 Who were the first couple to be BBC Sports Personality of the Year?

21 Which cook founded Sainsbury's The Magazine with her husband?

22 In the US Jim Bakker and Jimmy Swaggart are famous for what type of show?

23 Which girl band won the first "Popstars: The Rivals"?

24 Which weather girl went to the same university as Glenys Kinnock?

25 Which character did Ted Danson play in "Cheers"?

26 Which pop group walked out on Clive Anderson on his "All Talk" show?

27 Which comedian's marriage foundered after he appeared in "Celebrity Big Brother"?

28 Which talk show hostess appeared in the film "Hairspray" with Divine?

29 Who was the resident snooker player on "Big Break"?

30 Where did Paula Yates conduct her "Big Breakfast" interviews?

Answers | Past Times: The 70s *(see Quiz 65)*

1 Baader-Meinhof Gang. 2 Sex Discrimination Act. 3 Gerald Ford. 4 China. 5 Earthquake. 6 Weedkiller. 7 Alexander Haig. 8 Three Mile Island. 9 Afghanistan. 10 William Hague. 11 Anita Roddick. 12 Uganda. 13 Iran. 14 Peron. 15 Barbara Castle. 16 Christopher Reeve (Superman). 17 Pol Pot. 18 Elvis Presley. 19 Salisbury. 20 Napalm. 21 Lord Hailsham. 22 USA & USSR. 23 John Smith. 24 Elton John. 25 Spain. 26 Nicaragua. 27 Thatcher. 28 Japan. 29 Afghanistan. 30 Education.

1 Mica Paris and who replaced Trinny & Susannah on "What not to Wear"?
2 Which famous survey started in 1086?
3 From which musical does the song "One" come?
4 Ronald Reagan was in which political party?
5 Which Stephen directed the movie "Billy Elliot"?
6 In the Bible, what was the prophet Elijah carried up to heaven in?
7 What nationality was Casanova?
8 What was Al Jolson's most famous line?
9 If a substance is oleaginous what does it mainly contain?
10 Which General led the junta in the 1982 seizure of the Falklands?
11 Which famous Castle is on the River Dee?
12 What did the Owl and the Pussycat dine on?
13 Vera Welch sang under what name?
14 What was presenter Gabby Logan's surname before she married?
15 Which outlandish musician's real name was Simon Ritchie?
16 Which handicapped physicist has appeared in adverts for BT?
17 Who is buried at the Arc de Triomphe?
18 During exercise which acid builds up in the muscles?
19 Which Kevin has played for WBA, Sunderland, Everton and Wigan?
20 Which singer had a backing group called the Checkmates?
21 What is added to egg yolks and vanilla to make advocaat?
22 Who played "Blanco" in the TV series "Porridge"?
23 What nationality was Rachmaninov the composer?
24 What is xerography?
25 Which 1956 hit links The Platters with a 1987 Freddie Mercury hit?
26 Which Dutch town is particularly famous for its blue pottery?
27 Where would you find an apse?
28 What was abolished on 18 December 1969 in Britain?
29 Which tycoon started the newspaper called Today?
30 Who was the first golfer to lose play-offs in all four majors?

Answers	Pop Music: Albums *(see Quiz 68)*

1 Chris Rea. 2 Chicago XIII. 3 Eternal. 4 George Michael. 5 News of the World. 6 The Revolution. 7 Pet Shop Boys. 8 Frank Sinatra. 9 OK Computer. 10 Sting. 11 No Parlez. 12 River Deep – Mountain High. 13 Wannabe. 14 Definitely/Maybe. 15 Pulp. 16 Alanis Morisette. 17 Be Here Now. 18 Blue. 19 Physical. 20 Slippery When Wet. 21 The Rolling Stones. 22 Sex. 23 Nigel Kennedy. 24 Gasoline Alley. 25 Goat. 26 The Wall. 27 Enya. 28 Waterloo. 29 Ten. 30 Diva.

1 Who released the album "Auberge"?

2 What was the thirteenth album released by Chicago?

3 Which group's debut album, "Always & Forever", shadowed their name?

4 Whose debut solo album was called "Faith"?

5 Which Queen album shares its name with a newspaper?

6 On the 80s album "Purple Rain" who backed Prince?

7 Which duo released albums called "Introspective" and "Very"?

8 Which US superstar has had over 70 chart albums in his career?

9 What was Radiohead's first album to make No. 1 in the British charts?

10 Who guested with Dire Straits on the "Money For Nothing" track?

11 Which phrase with a French flavour was the title of Paul Young's debut album?

12 What was the title of Ike and Tina Turner's only album?

13 What is the first track on "Spice"?

14 A picture of Burt Bacharach appeared on the cover of which best-selling 90s album?

15 Whose debut album was called "Different Class"?

16 "Supposed Former Infatuation Junkie" was whose follow-up to a 30 million-selling album?

17 Which Oasis album came out first – "Be Here Now" or "The Masterplan"?

18 On the Beautiful South's 1996 album what is the "Colour"?

19 Which Olivia Newton-John 1981 album could describe some exercise?

20 Which Bon Jovi album was best kept dry?

21 What was the title of the first album released by The Rolling Stones?

22 What were Madonna's book and 1992 album called?

23 Which musician took Vivaldi's "The Four Seasons" into the charts?

24 Rod Stewart's first album was called after which alley?

25 What animal is on the cover of the Beach Boys' album "Pet Sounds"?

26 Which construction has given its name to a Pink Floyd album?

27 Which Irish singer got to No. 1 with "Shepherd Moons"?

28 Which battle was the title of the first Abba album?

29 How many Good Reasons had Jason Donovan on his first No. 1?

30 Which Annie Lennox album topped the charts in 1993?

---

1 Who played Eddie to claim a Best Supporting Actor Oscar in a boxing movie?

2 Which World War II film would have been called Dar el-Beida had it been titled in the local language?

3 Which Michael Cimino film about Vietnam won five Oscars in the 70s?

4 Whom did Daniel-Day Lewis portray in "My Left Foot"?

5 Which veteran won an Oscar in 1981 two years after his daughter?

6 For which movie did Helen Hunt win in 1997?

7 For which film did Tom Hanks win playing a lawyer dying from AIDS?

8 Who overcame deafness to win for "Children of a Lesser God"?

9 Who won the Best Director award for "Titanic"?

10 For which films did Tom Hanks win in successive years?

11 Who won the Best Actor Oscar for "High Noon"?

12 What type of worker did John Gielgud play when he won his Oscar for "Arthur"?

13 In which decade did Katharine Hepburn win her first Oscar?

14 Who won three Oscars for "Annie Hall"?

15 For which film did Brando win his second Oscar?

16 Who won his first best actor Oscar for "Kramer vs. Kramer"?

17 Which singer won an Oscar for "From Here to Eternity"?

18 For which film did Steven Spielberg win his first award?

19 What was unusual about Holly Hunter's performance in "The Piano"?

20 Which father and son actor and director won for "The Treasure of the Sierra Madre"?

21 In the year "Gandhi" won almost everything who was Best Actress for "Sophie's Choice"?

22 Who won Oscars for "Dangerous", "Jezebel" and "All About Eve"?

23 Who won as Dan Aykroyd's mother in "Driving Miss Daisy"?

24 How many times between 1990 and 1997 did Best Picture and Best Director Oscars go to the same film?

25 Who played the psychotic nurse in "Misery" and won Best Actress?

26 What did Anthony Hopkins win first, a knighthood or an Oscar?

27 Who won for her role as Blanch in "A Streetcar Named Desire"?

28 Who won Best Director for "The English Patient?"

29 Who won for her first film "Paper Moon"?

30 Which actress was nominated for "The Wings of the Dove"?

Quiz 73 — Pot Luck 34

1 Where is fibrin found in your body?
2 What is the vegetable common to the Indian dishes of Aloo Gobi and Aloo Palak?
3 Which group had hits including "Homely Girl" and "Kingston Town"?
4 The word "ketchup" comes which language?
5 Who presented "The Secret Life of the Manic Depressive"?
6 Who first took the much-covered song "Light My Fire" to No. 1?
7 With 7 goals, Lua-Lua was top scorer for which Premiership side?
8 Woburn Abbey is the home of which family?
9 What is a durian?
10 Which film starred John Cleese as an under-pressure headmaster?
11 The composer Bela Bartok came from which country?
12 What can be an animal enclosure or a unit of weight?
13 What does the abbreviation BHP stand for?
14 Which poetic names lend themselves to an expression for a devoted, elderly couple?
15 How does a judge hear a case when it is heard In Camera?
16 From 1968 to 1970 which actor was Mr Universe?
17 What does the word 'biscuit' literally mean?
18 The Lent Lily is sometimes used as another name for which flower?
19 What is a Tree Ear?
20 What was Little Lord Fauntleroy's name?
21 Toad of Toad Hall was a dramatised version of which Kenneth Grahame tale?
22 Which sport is Clare Francis famous for?
23 In the film "Look Who's Talking" whose voice was the baby's thoughts?
24 Which tree usually provides the wood for the Highland Games caber?
25 Whose hits include "Wishing Well" and "All Right Now"?
26 What colour is the tongue of a giraffe?
27 Which sport featured in the movie "A League of Their Own"?
28 Californian, Yellow Horned and Opium are all types of which flower?
29 Where is the Sea of Vapours?
30 What is the wading bird the bittern's cry called?

Answers	The Oscars *(see Quiz 74)*

1 Morgan Freeman. 2 Casablanca. 3 The Deer Hunter. 4 Christy Brown. 5 Henry Fonda. 6 As Good as It Gets. 7 Philadelphia. 8 Marlee Matlin. 9 James Cameron. 10 Philadelphia, Forrest Gump. 11 Gary Cooper. 12 Butler. 13 1930s. 14 Woody Allen. 15 The Godfather. 16 Dustin Hoffman. 17 Frank Sinatra. 18 Schindler's List. 19 She never spoke. 20 Walter & John Huston. 21 Meryl Streep. 22 Bette Davis. 23 Jessica Tandy. 24 Eight (all of them). 25 Kathy Bates. 26 Oscar. 27 Vivien Leigh. 28 Anthony Minghella. 29 Tatum O'Neal. 30 Helena Bonham-Carter.

Quiz 72 | Record Breakers | Answers – page 191 | LEVEL 2

1 Which American was the first to win the Men's Singles Grand Slam?
2 Who in 1979 became the youngest player to complete the double of 1,000 runs and 100 wickets?
3 Which Swede, in 1987, was the first man for 40 years to win a match at Wimbledon without losing a game?
4 Who was the first woman tennis player to win $1 million?
5 Who was the first Briton after 1950 to win the British Open golf three years in succession?
6 Which lady claimed three fastest winning times in the London Marathon?
7 Which woman won 20 Wimbledon titles between 1961 and 1979?
8 Franz Klammer was a record breaker in which sport?
9 Which woman became the youngest Wimbledon semi-finalist for 99 years in 1986?
10 Who broke the world record for an individual innings of 501 in 1994?
11 How many world records did Mark Spitz break when he won his seven gold medals?
12 Who, in 1987, was the first British golfer to win the World Match-Play Championship?
13 Whose 1500m world record did Steve Cram break in 1985?
14 Who was the first British woman swimmer to win a world title?
15 Who is the elder of the motor racing Schumacher's – Michael or Ralf?
16 Which Namibian was the first to break the 200m indoors 20-second barrier?
17 Who was the first British winner of the US Masters in 1988?
18 In 1988 who became the first boxer to win world titles at five official weights?
19 What was the first major to be claimed by Tiger Woods?
20 Who was the first Thai snooker player to win a major tournament?
21 In 1972 Mark Spitz broke Olympic records doing which two strokes?
22 Who holds the record for most goals scored in FA Cup Finals?
23 Who broke Bob Beaman's long jump record set at the 1968 Olympics?
24 Who was the then youngest ever winner of the US Masters in 1980?
25 Who was the first British soccer player to earn £100 per week?
26 Which US hurdler was undefeated in 122 races?
27 Which British shot putter was world No. 1 in 1975?
28 Which Liz won the fastest ever debut marathon when she won in New York in 1991?
29 Which Town did Man Utd beat by a record nine goals in 1995?
30 Who in 1968 became the oldest Briton to win a Grand Prix?

| **Answers** | Pot Luck 33 *(see Quiz 71)* |

1 Abseiling. 2 Dallas. 3 Connie Fisher. 4 Horses. 5 Nik Kershaw. 6 Charlotte. 7 Lloyds of London. 8 Southampton. 9 Babe Ruth. 10 Paddington. 11 Spencer. 12 Porto. 13 A dance. 14 Penguins. 15 Quoits. 16 Happy Talk. 17 Whales. 18 Moulin Rouge. 19 A herb. 20 Capri. 21 Holby City. 22 Syd Little. 23 Princess Beatrice. 24 Grosvenor Square. 25 A snake. 26 South. 27 Richard III. 28 Peter Sellers. 29 A Parish. 30 Mr Darcy.

1 What describes descending a sheer face by sliding down a rope?
2 Donna Reed replaced Barbara Bel Geddes in which TV series?
3 Who won TV's "How Do You Solve a Problem Like Maria?"
4 Which animal is feared by a hippophobe?
5 Whose hits include "Wide Boy" and "Wouldn't It be Good"?
6 The novel "Shirley" was written by which of the Bronte sisters?
7 In which London building does the Lutine Bell hang?
8 Which is further South, Folkestone or Southampton?
9 Which American sportsman was said to be earning more than the US president in 1925?
10 Which famous bear came from Peru?
11 What did the S stand for in Charlie Chaplin's middle name?
12 Nuno Valente joined Everton from which club?
13 What is a passepied?
14 Which species can be Fairy, Black-footed and Crested?
15 Which game uses flattened iron rings thrown at a hob?
16 What was the title of Captain Sensible's No. 1 UK hit in 1982?
17 Which mammals will expire when stranded on dry land?
18 In which movie did Ewan McGregor sing Elton John's "Your Song"?
19 What is tansy?
20 Which island is in the Bay of Naples?
21 In which series did Amanda Mealing play Connie Beauchamp?
22 Cyril Mead became known as which comic?
23 In the order of accession to the British throne who is the first female?
24 In which London Square is the American Embassy?
25 What is a taipan?
26 Is Coventry North or South of Leicester?
27 Which English King was the last to die in battle?
28 Who was older when he died, Peter Sellers or Tony Hancock?
29 What is the smallest administrative unit in the Church of England?
30 In "Pride and Prejudice" whom does Elizabeth Bennet finally marry?

Answers | Record Breakers (see Quiz 72)

1 Donald Budge. 2 Kapil Dev. 3 Stefan Edberg. 4 Chris Evert. 5 Nick Faldo. 6 Paula Radcliffe. 7 Billie Jean King. 8 Skiing. 9 Gabriela Sabatini. 10 Brian Lara. 11 Seven. 12 Ian Woosnam. 13 Steve Ovett's. 14 Karen Pickering. 15 Michael. 16 Frankie Fredericks. 17 Sandy Lyle. 18 Sugar Ray Leonard. 19 US Masters. 20 James Wattana. 21 Freestyle & butterfly. 22 Ian Rush. 23 Mike Powell. 24 Seve Ballesteros. 25 Johnny Haynes. 26 Ed Moses. 27 Geoff Capes. 28 McColgan. 29 Ipswich. 30 Graham Hill.

1 After what sort of activity might you suffer from the bends?
2 What would you buy from Stanley Gibbons?
3 What colour are houses in Monopoly?
4 What shape is a sumo wrestling ring?
5 Which Hindu system of philosophy is used as a means of exercise and meditation in the west?
6 In which game do you score "one for his knob"?
7 The Fastnet race is part of the contest for which Cup?
8 Which game's name comes from a piece of its equipment looking like a bishop's crosier?
9 At which station do you arrive in Paris if you have travelled from the UK by Eurostar?
10 The YOC is the junior branch of which organisation?
11 If you were a collector of Clarice Cliff what would you collect?
12 A Monopoly game based on which Sci-fi film was released in 1997?
13 What is a grand slam in Bridge?
14 Camogie is the women's equivalent of which sport?
15 What sort of swimming takes place with musical accompaniment?
16 Which three Quaker families made most of Britain's chocolate?
17 In which country is De Efteling Theme Park?
18 Which sport is played at London's Queen's Club?
19 Which pizza restaurant was the first of a chain founded in London?
20 What sort of club is the Royal and Ancient?
21 Which organisation's anthem is "Jerusalem"?
22 What was the Worldwide Fund for Nature formerly called?
23 Which open-air zoo is near Dunstable in Bedfordshire?
24 Which boy reporter was created by Belgian artist Herge?
25 What colour carrier bag do you get when you shop at Laura Ashley?
26 In athletics, what is attached to a chain and a handle and thrown?
27 Which sport has Greco-Roman and Freestyle, as two distinct styles?
28 The annual Round the Isle race goes round which Isle?
29 La Defence and Les Halles are Christmas markets in which city?
30 Where were Walker's Crisps first made?

Answers | Pot Luck 32 *(see Quiz 69)*

1 Margaret Kelly. **2** Etta James. **3** Sleep on it. **4** The Passion Play. **5** Mahogany. **6** Chelsea. **7** Jones. **8** Die Hard 2. **9** Clean & pollution free. **10** Pectin. **11** Distemper. **12** A rope. **13** Prime Minister. **14** God. **15** Rouen. **16** Tony. **17** Partridge. **18** Axis. **19** Marlene Dietrich. **20** Lowestoft. **21** Rain. **22** Taboo. **23** White. **24** Aegean Sea. **25** Egyptian. **26** Green. **27** The Kinks. **28** Her right hand. **29** Plexiglass. **30** Sugababes.

1 Who formed the famous dance troupe the Bluebell Girls?
2 Whose CDs include "Seven Year Itch" and "Stickin' to My Guns"?
3 What would you do with a futon?
4 Which play is performed every ten years at Oberammagau?
5 Which wood was mainly used by Thomas Chippendale?
6 In which London area is The Royal Hospital?
7 In Nov. 2006, a Cardiff get together was organised for people with which surname?
8 Bruce Willis destroyed a plane with his cigarette lighter in which film?
9 What does a blue flag at a beach mean?
10 Which carbohydrate causes jam to gel?
11 If a dog is suffering from "hard pad" what form of disease has it got?
12 What is a hawser?
13 In "The Amazing Mrs Pritchard" what did Mrs P become?
14 Theophobia is a fear of what?
15 In which French town was Joan of Arc burnt at the stake?
16 What was the name of cowboy Tom Mix's horse ?
17 The quail is the smallest member of which bird species?
18 What is the singular of axes in mathematics?
19 Which actress's real name was Maria Magdalena von Losch?
20 Which port is the most easterly in Britain?
21 What is the common weather in a pluvial region?
22 Which Polynesian word means prohibited or forbidden?
23 What colour is the egg of a kingfisher?
24 The Dodecanese Islands are in which sea?
25 What nationality was Secretary General of the UN Boutros Boutros Ghali?
26 In board games, what colour is the Reverend in Cluedo?
27 Whose hits include "Sunny Afternoon" and "Tired of Waiting for You"?
28 What is on top of the Mona Lisa's left hand?
29 What do Americans call Perspex?
30 In which girl group did Amelle Berrabah replace Mutya Buena?

Quiz 75 | Pot Luck 35

Answers – page 196

1 What are Spode, Bow and Chelsea all types of?
2 Whick rock star teamed up with Sir Patrick Moore and Phil Lintott to write a book on astronomy?
3 Which Italian area produces Chianti?
4 Which scale measures the level of alkalinity and acidity?
5 TV's "Death of a President" was about the fictional assassination of which world leader?
6 Where will you return to if you throw a coin into the Trevi Fountain?
7 What in your body are affected by phlebitis?
8 Who was caretaker manager of Spurs after the departure of Glenn Hoddle in 2003?
9 Whose hits include "Again" and "That's the Way Love Goes"?
10 Which TV character lived on Scatterbrook Farm?
11 Which High Street travel agents devised the holiday package tour?
12 In finance what is a PEP?
13 How did Curtis Jackson, born 1976, become known in the music world?
14 What does the Greek odeon mean?
15 If you were using a tambour, what needlecraft would you be doing?
16 What is the currency of Greece?
17 Which actor co-starred with Juliette Binoche in "Breaking & Entering"?
18 In which century was cockfighting banned?
19 Which supermarket chain paid for the new National Gallery wing opened in 1991?
20 Cars with the international vehicle registration ET come from where?
21 Who started the Habitat chain of shops in 1964?
22 Who is smaller, Janet Street Porter or Naomi Campbell?
23 Edmonton is the capital of which Canadian province?
24 Who played Shirley Valentine in the film?
25 What is the white of an egg called as an alternative to albumen?
26 Which 007 actor was also TV's Remington Steele?
27 The Ashanti tribe live in which African country?
28 Which lady took over as Secretary of State for Education from David Blunkett?
29 What is held annually in London in Ranelagh Gardens?
30 Where was tennis star Monica Seles playing when she was stabbed?

Answers	Famous Names *(see Quiz 76)*

1 Gianni Versace. 2 Pierre Cardin. 3 Queen Mother. 4 Ffion. 5 Getty. 6 Madonna. 7 Elizabeth. 8 Kevin Pietersen. 9 Mao Zedong. 10 Monica Lewinsky. 11 Diego Velázquez. 12 Vivienne Westwood. 13 Reese Witherspoon. 14 Emma Forbes. 15 Both vicars. 16 Tony Blair. 17 Jack Rosenthal. 18 Brian Jones. 19 Ridley Scott. 20 Carol. 21 Football. 22 Hans Holbein. 23 MTV. 24 Gloria Hunniford. 25 Imelda Marcos. 26 Step daughter. 27 Michael. 28 Lord of the Dance. 29 Magic Johnson. 30 Jack Ryder.

1 Whose funeral in Milan in 1997 was attended by Elton John and Naomi Campbell?

2 Which Frenchman was the first to launch menswear and ready to wear collections?

3 How was the former Lady Elizabeth Bowes-Lyon better known?

4 What is the first name of Mrs William Hague?

5 Which oil billionaire founded the world's highest-funded art gallery?

6 Which famous American enrolled her baby daughter for Cheltenham Ladies' College in September 1998?

7 What is John and Norma Major's daughter called?

8 Which England cricketer was linked with Liberty X singer Jessica Taylor?

9 Chiang Ching was the third wife of which political leader?

10 Linda Tripp was the confidante of which famous name?

11 Who painted "The Rokeby Venus" in 1647–51?

12 Which fashion designer launched a perfume called Boudoir?

13 Which actress topped Julia Roberts's record fee for a single movie?

14 Who is Nanette Newman's famous TV presenter daughter?

15 What did David Frost's and Virginia Wade's father have in common?

16 Whose first names are Anthony Charles Lynton?

17 Which playwright won a BAFTA award for the "Bar Mitzvah Boy"?

18 Which Rolling Stone bought, and died at AA Milne's house?

19 Which director was knighted in the year his movie "Matchstick Men" came out?

20 What is Margaret Thatcher's journalist daughter called?

21 At which sport did Pope John Paul II excel in his youth?

22 Who painted "The Ambassadors" in 1533?

23 Which TV awards did the Beckams present in late spring 2003?

24 Who married millionaire hairdresser Stephen Way in 1998?

25 Who was the wife of Ferdinand Marcos at the time of his death?

26 What relation was Cherie Blair to Pat Phoenix, who played Elsie Tanner in "Coronation Street"?

27 What was the first name of Marks of Marks & Spencer?

28 What links Nataraja in Hinduism and performer Michael Flatley?

29 Who was the first basketball player to declare he was HIV positive?

30 Which former "EastEnders" actor did Hear'Say's Kym Marsh marry?

Answers | Pot Luck 35 *(see Quiz 75)*

1 Porcelain. 2 Brian May. 3 Tuscany. 4 pH scale. 5 George W. Bush. 6 Rome. 7 Veins. 8 David Pleat. 9 Janet Jackson. 10 Worzel Gummidge. 11 Thomas Cook. 12 Personal Equity Plan. 13 50 Cent. 14 Theatre. 15 Embroidery. 16 Drachma. 17 Jude Law. 18 19th century. 19 Sainsbury's. 20 Egypt. 21 Terence Conran. 22 Naomi Campbell. 23 Alberta. 24 Pauline Collins. 25 Glair. 26 Pierce Brosnan. 27 Ghana. 28 Estelle Morris. 29 Chelsea Flower Show. 30 Hamburg.

1 Which show provided BBC sales with a third of their 1997 profits?

2 Which woman writer created the character Jane Tennison?

3 Which ex-Tory leader was born the same day as ex-Goodie Bill Oddie?

4 What is Dr Ross's first name in "ER"?

5 In which decade was Parliament first televised?

6 Best known as Kat Slater of "EastEnders", what is actress Jessie Wallace's real name?

7 Which rugby player joined Ulrika Jonsson as a "Gladiators" presenter?

8 Who played Owen Springer in "Reckless"?

9 Which priest replaced Father Peter in "Ballykissangel"?

10 Which ex-"Gladiators" presenter became an "I'm a Celebrity" contestant?

11 On GMTV where did Mark Freden regularly report from?

12 Which superstar did Matthew Corbett abandon finally in 1998?

13 Which role did Denise Robertson have on "This Morning"?

14 Which one-time Spice Girl advertised Walkers crisps with Gary Lineker?

15 Who was the blonde captain on "Shooting Stars"?

16 How is TV presenter Leslie Heseltine better known?

17 How many letters make up the conundrum in "Countdown"?

18 Which night was the dreaded eviction night on "Big Brother Four"?

19 Who contracted amoebic dysentery while making a Holiday show with her daughter?

20 "Frasier" was a spin-off from which series?

21 Who plays Ally McBeal?

22 How many points do you get for a starter in University Challenge?

23 In which soap did Darius from "Pop Idol" make his acting debut?

24 On which show did Tommy Walsh and Charlie Dimmock find fame?

25 For which sport did Frank Bough win an Oxbridge blue?

26 Whom did David Dimbleby replace on "Question Time"?

27 Who wrote the acclaimed series of monologues "Talking Heads"?

28 Who played Darcy in "Pride and Prejudice"?

29 Which fivesome helped launch Channel 5?

30 Jimmy Savile received an honorary doctorate from which university?

Answers | Pot Luck 36 *(see Quiz 78)*

1 Bev. 2 Leprosy. 3 Danny Murphy. 4 Mustard. 5 Tam O'Shanter. 6 On the Moon.
7 Peach & plum. 8 Stereophonics. 9 The bones. 10 An oak tree. 11 Aspirin. 12
Your Eminence. 13 1983. 14 Nelson Mandela. 15 Blackcurrant. 16 Belisha Beacon.
17 Arizona. 18 Daphne du Maurier. 19 Leo Sayer. 20 The Netherlands. 21 1/10th.
22 Aestivation. 23 88. 24 Niamh Kavanagh. 25 A flower. 26 Wakefield. 27 The
brain. 28 Cannon. 29 Bathsheba. 30 JB Priestley.

1 Who was Corrie's Fred preparing to marry when he suffered a fatal heart attack?
2 What did Robert the Bruce die of?
3 Who has played for Crewe, Liverpool, Charlton and Spurs?
4 Dijon is famous for which condiment?
5 Which Robbie Burns hero gave his name to a flat cap?
6 Where is the Bay of Rainbows?
7 A nectarine is a cross between which two fruits?
8 Which top-selling band featured Stuart Cable on drums?
9 What is affected by osteomyelitis?
10 What is Charles II said to have hidden in after the Battle of Worcester?
11 What is the common name for the medication acetylsalicylic acid?
12 How is a Cardinal addressed?
13 When was the wearing of seat belts in the front of a car made compulsory?
14 Thabo Mbeki succeeded which President of South Africa?
15 Which fruit is in creme de cassis?
16 Which beacon was named after a 1930s Minister of Transport?
17 The Painted Desert is in which American state?
18 Who wrote "My Cousin Rachel" and "Frenchman's Creek"?
19 Whose hits include "Moonlighting" and "More than I Can Say"?
20 Queen Juliana abdicated from which country's throne in 1980?
21 What fraction is a cable of a nautical mile?
22 What is the opposite of hibernation?
23 How many keys does a normal piano have?
24 Which female Irish singer won the Eurovision Song Contest with "In Your Eyes"?
25 What is a corn-cockle?
26 What town is the "capital" of West Yorkshire's Rhubarb Triangle?
27 Which part of the body uses forty per cent of the oxygen in blood?
28 Which corpulent TV detective was played by William Conrad?
29 Who was the mother of King Solomon?
30 Who wrote "The Good Companions"?

Answers | TV: TV Times 2 (see Quiz 77)

1 The Teletubbies. 2 Lynda La Plante. 3 Michael Howard. 4 Doug. 5 1980s. 6 Karen Slater. 7 Jeremy Guscott. 8 Robson Green. 9 Father Aidan. 10 John Fashanu. 11 Hollywood. 12 Sooty. 13 Agony aunt. 14 Victoria Beckham. 15 Ulrika Jonsson. 16 Les Dennis. 17 Nine. 18 Friday. 19 Esther Rantzen. 20 Cheers. 21 Calista Flockhart. 22 10. 23 Hollyoaks. 24 Ground Force. 25 Soccer. 26 Peter Sissons. 27 Alan Bennett. 28 Colin Firth. 29 The Spice Girls. 30 Leeds.

1 In 2004, the Large Binocular Telescope was built on Mt Graham in which US state?

2 Which word describes a body in free fall in space?

3 Which planet has the satellite Europa?

4 Which space station is named after the Russian word for "peace"?

5 Ranger and Surveyor probes preceded exploration of where?

6 What name is given to a site for watching astronomical phenomena?

7 In which decade was Sputnik 1 launched?

8 Saturn rockets were developed for which moon programme?

9 Who was Soyuz TM-12's British passenger in 1991?

10 The first non-stop transatlantic flight was between which two countries?

11 What does a space shuttle land on when it returns to Earth?

12 What is the Oort cloud made out of?

13 Which Space Agency built Ariane?

14 Which communications satellite was the first to relay live TV transmissions?

15 Which rockets shared their name with the giant children of Uranus and Gaia in Greek myth ?

16 Which part of the moon did Armstrong first walk on?

17 Which of our planets is nearest the end of the alphabet?

18 Claudie Andre-Deshays was the first woman in space from which country?

19 Whose spacecraft was Vostok 1?

20 After retiring as an astronaut John Glenn followed a career in what?

21 Which clouds are formed highest above the ground?

22 How was Michael Collins a pioneer of lunar flight?

23 What is the largest planet in the solar system?

24 Phobos is a moon of which planet?

25 What was Skylab?

26 Which pioneering spacecraft was first launched in April 1981?

27 What is Jupiter's red spot made from?

28 Which country launched the first space probe in 1959?

29 Which constellation is known as The Hunter?

30 Which is larger, Mars or Earth?

Answers | Pot Luck 37 *(see Quiz 80)*

1 Cockerel. 2 George V. 3 A Will. 4 Nixon. 5 Daphne du Maurier. 6 Rioja. 7 Clot. 8 1959. 9 Craig David. 10 Steven Spielberg. 11 17th. 12 Shallot. 13 The Grampians. 14 Optician's. 15 Blind. 16 Grounds called The Stadium Of Light. 17 St Mark. 18 The Great Pyramids of Giza. 19 Sausage. 20 Joseph Priestley. 21 Chantelle Houghton. 22 B2. 23 British Prime Ministers. 24 Zacharias. 25 Sunderland. 26 WH Smiths. 27 Sinn Fein. 28 Legs. 29 Danube. 30 Yoghurt.

1 Which creature do French sports fans traditionally let loose before the start of a big match?

2 Which king unveiled the Victoria memorial?

3 What is made by a testator?

4 Who telephoned Neil Armstrong during his first moon walk?

5 Which novelist had three novels adapted by Alfred Hitchcock to films?

6 Which wine-growing region is divided into Baja, Alta and Alavesa?

7 What does fibrin cause to happen to blood?

8 Did Buddy Holly die in 1956, 1959 or 1961?

9 Which top-selling writer/singer was born May 5, 1981, in Southampton?

10 Which director appeared in "The Blues Brothers"?

11 In which century was the Taj Mahal constructed?

12 A Bordelaise sauce is flavoured by which vegetable?

13 Ben Nevis is in which mountain range?

14 Where would you probably be looking at a Snellen Chart?

15 In Bingo, what are numbers ending in zero called?

16 What do Sunderland and Benfica soccer clubs share?

17 Who is the Patron Saint of Venice?

18 What are Mycerinus and Cheprun the second two greatest of?

19 What would you be eating if you ate a Spanish chorizo?

20 Which scientist first discovered the composition of air?

21 Which "Celebrity Big Brother" winner wrote "Living the Dream: My Story"?

22 Which letter and number represent the vitamin riboflavin?

23 Derby, Pelham and Russell have all been what?

24 Who was John the Baptist's father?

25 Alan Stubbs broke his two spells at Everton by playing for which club?

26 Euston became Britain's first railway station to have what in 1848?

27 In 1921 which political party burnt down Dublin's Custom House?

28 Which part of your body is protected by puttees?

29 Which river flows through six different European countries?

30 What is the main ingredient in an Indian raita?

---

1 Which opera venue is near Lewes?
2 Sir John Barbirolli was conductor of which orchestra at the time of his death?
3 If a sonata is for instruments what is a cantata written for?
4 Which London theatre was the home of Gilbert & Sullivan operas?
5 Sadler's Wells theatre is famous for which performing arts?
6 Equity in the USA deals only with performers where?
7 Wayne Sleep was principal dancer with which ballet company?
8 What do you press with the right hand on an accordion?
9 Which of the Three Tenors played the title role in the film version of "Otello" in 1986?
10 How many strings are there on a double bass?
11 Richard Eyre replaced Peter Hall as artistic director at which London theatre?
12 What were all Joseph Grimaldi's clowns called?
13 What shape is the sound box on a balalaika?
14 Which male voice is between bass and tenor?
15 Where is an annual Fringe Festival held?
16 In which US city was the Actors Studio founded?
17 What is the official name of London's Drury Lane theatre?
18 Miles Davis is famous for playing which musical instrument?
19 Which king did Handel write The Water Music for?
20 Whose 1986 recording of Vivaldi's "The Four Seasons" sold over a million copies?
21 What was Paul McCartney's first classical oratorio?
22 An anthem is usually accompanied by which musical instrument?
23 Which mime artist created the clown-harlequin Bip?
24 In 2004 the Webber Douglas Academy formed a partnership with which drama school?
25 Which theatre near Blackfriars was London's first new theatre in 300 years when opened in 1959?
26 What was the slogan of London's Windmill Theatre?
27 Which musical instruments did Leo Fender create?
28 What was the first black-owned record company in the USA?
29 Who has written more plays, Shakespeare or Ayckbourn?
30 Which Camden theatre re-opened in 2006?

Answers | Pot Luck 38 *(see Quiz 82)*

1 Hertfordshire. 2 A miller. 3 Frank Morgan. 4 Andy. 5 Rome. 6 Canada. 7 Michael Bentine. 8 Nijinsky. 9 Grass. 10 As a tomato. 11 Star fish. 12 Quaver. 13 Vicarage. 14 Southampton. 15 Trollope. 16 Borneo. 17 The Trunk. 18 Maggie Smith. 19 Lactose. 20 Fluke. 21 Vera Lynn. 22 Little Women. 23 Mick Jagger. 24 LA Galaxy. 25 Judaea. 26 Prince Edward. 27 Rowan Williams. 28 Alan Milburn. 29 A barrister. 30 Shell-shaped.

1 Hemel Hempstead and St Albans are in which county?
2 Who would use a quern?
3 Who played the title role in the film "The Wizard of Oz"?
4 Whom did Ricky Gervais play in "Extras"?
5 The Spanish Steps are in which European city?
6 Cars with the international vehicle registration CDN come from where?
7 Which zany comedian devised the TV show "It's a Square World"?
8 Which Russian-sounding horse won the 2000 Guineas, St Leger and the Derby in 1970?
9 What kind of a plant is fescue?
10 When Judi Dench was dressed as a lobster for Film Four, how was Ewan McGregor dressed?
11 What type of sea creature is a brittle star?
12 Musically which note is half the value of a crotchet?
13 "Murder at the..." where was Miss Marple's first appearance?
14 Antmi Niemi joined Fulham from which club?
15 Which writer Anthony created the county of Barsetshire?
16 What is the largest island in Asia?
17 Which part of an elephant has 40,000 muscles?
18 Who played the lead role in the film "The Prime Of Miss Jean Brodie"?
19 Which type of sugar is found in milk?
20 What word can describe a lucky chance and the hook of an anchor?
21 Which female vocalist was known as 'The Forces Sweetheart'?
22 Which novel preceded "Good Wives"?
23 Which pop star married Bianca de Macias in May 1971?
24 Which football team did David Beckham sign for in January 2007?
25 Herod the Great ruled which kingdom?
26 Which Prince's childhood nickname was JAWS?
27 Who succeeded George Carey as Archbishop of Canterbury?
28 Which Blair-ite Alan became Secretary of State for Health?
29 What is the English equivalent of a Scottish Advocate?
30 What shape is a dish called a coquille?

---

1 Who had a hit in 1972 with "A Thing Called Love"?

2 Which hit in letters followed "Stand by Your Man" for Tammy Wynette?

3 Which group had a No. 1 hit in 1976 with "Mississippi"?

4 Which best-selling country and pop star married Mutt Lange?

5 Whose song was a No. 1 for John Denver in 1974?

6 Which Patsy Cline hit was covered by Julio Iglesias in 1994?

7 In which year was "Achey Breaky Heart" a hit for Billy Ray Cyrus?

8 Who had a No. 11 UK hit with "Talking in Your Sleep" in 1978?

9 Hiram Williams is the real name of which singer?

10 Which opera singer joined John Denver to record "Perhaps Love"?

11 Who duetted with Ronan Keating on the chart hit "Last Thing on My Mind"?

12 Which Kris wrote "Help Me Make It Through the Night"?

13 Who had a hit in the summer of 1998 with "How Do I"?

14 Who wrote the autobiography "Coal Miner's Daughter"?

15 Who joined Kenny Rogers on the No. 7 hit "Islands in the Stream"?

16 What is Reba McEntire's real name?

17 Which specialist type of singing links Frank Ifield and Slim Whitman?

18 Who duetted with Mark Knopfler on the album "Neck and Neck"?

19 In the No. 1, which drums were heard by Jim Reeves?

20 Who sang "All I Have to do Is Dream" with Bobbie Gentry in 1969?

21 Who had a backing band called the Waylors?

22 What is the name of the theme park owned by Dolly Parton?

23 George Jones' 1975 hit "The Battle" told of the split from his wife. Who was she?

24 Which Banks were a hit in 1971 for Olivia Newton-John?

25 Which song was a No. 2 UK hit for Tammy Wynette and KLF in 1991?

26 Who wrote the classic song "Crazy"?

27 Who formed the Trio with Dolly Parton and Linda Ronstadt?

28 Who took "Cotton Eye Joe" to No. 1 in 1994?

29 Which No. 9 for Elvis was a No. 10 for Carl Perkins in 1956?

30 Which "modern girl" joined Kenny Rogers on "We've Got Tonight"?

---

1 What was the name of Kate Winslet's character in Titanic?
2 Who was Culture Secretary when the UK won the staging of the 2012 Olympics?
3 Which top-selling band featured Kian Egan on vocals?
4 What is kelp?
5 Who had hits with "Fox on the Run" and "Wig-Wam Bam"?
6 What name is an African lake, a station and a former Queen?
7 What type of vessel was the Torrey Canyon?
8 Which brewing company produces London Pride?
9 What is the more common name for toxaemia?
10 Which members of the big cat family collect in a leap?
11 Who preceded Harold Macmillan as Prime Minister?
12 In the Shakespeare play who killed Macbeth?
13 Which heavy character was missing from the 2006 Robin Hood TV series?
14 Newmarket and Ipswich are both in which county?
15 Reflexology treats your body through what?
16 What can be a short jacket and a dance?
17 What are auctioned at Tattersalls?
18 Who was Phileas Fogg's companion in "Around the World in 80 Days"?
19 Which French-Canadian became Canadian Prime Minister in 1968?
20 Archibald Leach, born in Bristol, became which Hollywood star?
21 In which decade did John Wayne die?
22 Which English club has had Velimir Zajec and Alain Perrin as managers?
23 Which part of your body would interest a rhinologist?
24 In 1926 what was held for the first time at Brooklands?
25 Mesopotamia was the ancient name for which modern-day country?
26 Which female singer made the album "Day without Rain"?
27 Whose report in the 1940s was vital in setting up the welfare state?
28 Which Stevie Wonder No. 1 was in the film "The Woman in Red"?
29 What type of animal is a Lippizaner?
30 Which digit is your pollex?

1 Which Australian was the first to score 60 tries in international rugby?

2 Who was the first Englishman to reach 750 points in major internationals?

3 Who was the first English player to play in 50 internationals?

4 Which country in 1995 asked to increase the number of teams in the Five Nations Cup?

5 Which colours do Bath play in?

6 Which Welsh Union player was a regular captain on "A Question of Sport"?

7 In which part of London did the London Broncos start out?

8 Who won the Man of Steel in 1996 and 2004?

9 For which side did Brian Bevan score 740 tries in 620 matches?

10 What were Bradford before they were Bulls?

11 Who retired as Scottish captain after the 1995 World Cup?

12 Who was Wigan's leading try scorer in the 1994/95 season?

13 Where would you watch Rhinos playing rugby?

14 Paul Sackey was at which club when he first won a cap, aged 27?

15 Which international side has the shortest name?

16 Who are the two sides in the Varsity Match?

17 Which rugby team plays its home games at Welford Road?

18 Who was leading try scorer in the 1995 rugby union World Cup?

19 In 1998 what colour cards were substituted for yellow ones?

20 Who joined Leeds in 1991 after playing on the other side of the Pennines since 1984?

21 What did Bath Football Club change its name to in the mid-90s?

22 Who was the first non-white Springbok, before the end of apartheid?

23 Which rugby side added Warriors to its name?

24 In which decade was Rugby Union last played in the Olympics?

25 How old was Will Carling when he was first made England Captain?

26 Who played a record-breaking 69 times at fly half for England between 1985 and 1995?

27 In 1980 who led England to their first Grand Slam in 23 years?

28 Where is the annual Varsity match played?

29 How many years had Wigan's unbeaten run in the FA Challenge Cup lasted when it ended in 1996?

30 Whom did Martin Offiah play for in his first years as a League player?

Quiz 86 | Pot Luck 40

Answers – page 205

LEVEL 2

1 Where in your body is your scapula?
2 Canterbury stands on which river?
3 Who had hits with "God Save the Queen" and "C'Mon Everybody"?
4 Sebastian Coe became MP for which constituency in 1992?
5 Which former colony was called the jewel in Queen Victoria's crown?
6 What was the sport of Karen Briggs and Nicola Fairbrother?
7 Which Henry became King of England in 1100?
8 In the film "Mary Poppins", Mary said she would stay until what changed?
9 Which Treaty on European Union was signed in December 1991?
10 Which surname links No. 1 hit singers Jimmy, Paul and Will?
11 What was the former name of Belize?
12 Which actor married Melanie Griffith twice?
13 What was Ffion Hague's maiden name?
14 Which river does Leicester stand on?
15 What is decathlon champion Daley Thompson's first name?
16 Which Vera Lynn song was a No. 1 UK hit in 1954?
17 Which German violinist was married to André Previn?
18 Who was given Blenheim Palace as a reward for his military service?
19 In the Bible, who denied Jesus three times before the cock crowed twice?
20 A Turk's Head is a type of what?
21 Alphabetically which chemical element is the last?
22 Which European capital was considered cleanest in a 1995 survey?
23 What is a frigatoon?
24 "The Garden of the Gods" is in which American state?
25 Ariel Sharon belonged to which political party in Israel?
26 Which manager Phil took Colchester into the Championship for the first time?
27 Which TV series has characters called Gracie, Sicknote and George?
28 What was King Charles II's nickname?
29 Kings Lynn and Norwich are both in which county?
30 Who was the presenter of "Countdown" when it was first televised?

Answers | Sport: Rugby *(see Quiz 85)*

1 David Campese. 2 Jonny Wilkinson. 3 Rory Underwood. 4 Italy. 5 Blue, black and white. 6 Gareth Edwards. 7 Fulham. 8 Andy Farrell. 9 Warrington. 10 Northern. 11 Gavin Hastings. 12 Martin Offiah. 13 Leeds. 14 Wasps. 15 Fiji. 16 Oxford University and Cambridge University. 17 Leicester. 18 Jonah Lomu. 19 White. 20 Ellery Hanley. 21 Bath Rugby Club. 22 Errol Tobias. 23 Wigan. 24 1920s. 25 22. 26 Rob Andrew. 27 Bill Beaumont. 28 Twickenham. 29 Eight. 30 Widnes.

Quiz 87 | Movies: Westerns | Answers – page 208

LEVEL 2

1 What was the first film in which Clint Eastwood starred as "The man with no name"?
2 Who played the sadistic sheriff in Eastwood's "Unforgiven"?
3 Which actor's films include "Big Jim McLain", "McLintock" and "McQ"?
4 Which star of "Maverick" played Brett Maverick in the TV series?
5 Which Oscar did Kevin Costner win for "Dances with Wolves"?
6 What is the name of the original tale that the "Magificent Seven" is based on?
7 What weather feature was in the title of the song from Butch Cassidy won an Oscar?
8 Who was the star of "Jeremiah Johnson"?
9 Which comedy actor starred in the comedy western "The Paleface"?
10 Who starred with brother Charlie Sheen in "Young Guns"?
11 Which Oscar winner for "Fargo", married director Joel Coen?
12 Who played the woman poker player in "Maverick"?
13 Which actor was "The Bad"?
14 Which "Back to the Future" film returns to the Wild West?
15 In which musical western does the song "Wandrin' Star" appear?
16 Which Hollywood legend was the narrator in "How the West was Won"?
17 Which film was originally called "Per un Pugno di Dollari"?
18 Which country singer was in "True Grit"?
19 Which son of a "M*A*S*H" star appeared in "Young Guns II"?
20 Whom did John Wayne play in "The Alamo"?
21 Clint Eastwood became mayor of which town?
22 Which 1985 film was a revised remake of the classic "Shane"?
23 Where is the village where the action of "The Magnificent Seven" centres?
24 Where was "The Good, the Bad and the Ugly" made?
25 What was the name of Mel Brooks' spoof western?
26 Which English comic appeared in "Desperado"?
27 Which 80s teenage western starred actors known as the Brat Pack?
28 What was Tonto's horse called?
29 Who was Gene Autry's most famous horse?
30 Traditionally, what colour is the western hero's hat?

Answers | TV: TV Times 3 *(see Quiz 88)*

1 Andrew. 2 William G. Stewart. 3 Watchdog. 4 Coronation Street. 5 Helen Baxendale. 6 Anna. 7 Downtown. 8 Des O'Connor. 9 Geoff Hamilton. 10 Liverpool. 11 Mel Smith & Griff Rhys-Jones. 12 Los Angeles. 13 Sandi Toksvig. 14 Sex therapist. 15 The contestants. 16 Jools Holland. 17 Rockit. 18 Blockbusters. 19 Spencer Tracy. 20 Shauna Lowry. 21 Kevin. 22 Gymnastics. 23 All Creatures Great and Small. 24 Hugh Scully. 25 Michael Palin. 26 Monica Lewinsky. 27 Footballers' Wives. 28 Julia Sawahla. 29 One True Voice. 30 Midsomer Murders.

1 "Men Behaving Badly"'s Leslie Ash was born the same day as which Prince?
2 Who first presented Channel 4's "Fifteen To One"?
3 Alice Beer first found fame on which show?
4 Which show was first broadcast on Friday 9 December 1960?
5 Which "Cardiac Arrest" star also starred in "Friends"?
6 What was the lawyer played by Daniela Nardini in "This Life" called?
7 Which song did Emma Bunton record for the BBC's "Children in Need" 2006?
8 Who was chosen to succeed Des Lynam on "Countdown"?
9 Whose last series was "Paradise Gardens"?
10 In which city did the docu soap "Hotel" take place?
11 Which comedy duo are famous for their head-to-head discussions?
12 In which city did lifeguard Mitch Buchanan work?
13 Who was the female team captain in the 90s "Call My Bluff"?
14 What was the occupation of Linda in "Strictly Confidential"?
15 Who decides who leaves the competition in the "Weakest Link"?
16 Which musician's name completes the title "Later...with..."?
17 Who is the bouncing frog of Fimble Valley?
18 In which show might a contestant ask "Could I have a P please, Bob?"
19 Whom is Robbie Coltrane's son Spencer named after?
20 Which redhead assists Rolf Harris at the "Animal Hospital"?
21 What was the name of the spotty teenager played by Harry Enfield?
22 Presenter Suzanne Dando represented Great Britain at which sport?
23 Which series centred on Skeldale House?
24 Who has hosted "Antiques Roadshow" through most of the 90s?
25 Who tried to emulate Phileas Fogg in a 1989 documentary?
26 Who did Roseanne offer a million dollars to appear on her talk show in October 1998?
27 Gary Lucy came to fame on which show?
28 Which "Ab Fab" star took Caroline Quentin's place as Jonathan Creek's sidekick?
29 Which boy band won the first series of "Popstars: The Rivals"?
30 In which series did mum Joyce have a daughter called Cully?

Quiz 89 | Pot Luck 41

Answers – page 210

LEVEL 2

1 Which Queen wrote the Casket Letters?
2 Which former Take That star had "Child" at No. 3 in 1996?
3 What can be metric royal, metric demy and metric crown?
4 In which TV series was the character "Boss Hogg"?
5 Who succeeded Charles Clarke as Home Secretary?
6 Which almond cake is traditionally made for Mothering Sunday?
7 Who had hits with "We are Glass" and "Cars"?
8 David Bentley joined Blackburn from which London club?
9 Which actress had lead roles in the films "Out of Africa" and "Silkwood"?
10 Which two European languages are spoken in Madagascar?
11 Which gallery hosted Pet Shop Boys Portraits from Oct. 2006 to Feb. 2007?
12 What were the giant insects in the science fiction film "Them"?
13 Which famous TV cook took his show "Around Britain"?
14 During which war does Norman Mailer's "The Naked and the Dead" take place?
15 Aylesbury and Milton Keynes are both in which county?
16 Which film director based "Tea with Mussolini" on his own experiences in 1930s Florence?
17 Which animal was used by Jenner to develop the vaccine against smallpox?
18 What is a davenport?
19 Which singer starred alongside Kyle McLachlan in "Dune"?
20 Who composed the music for "The Good, the Bad and the Ugly"?
21 Who had hits with "Blue Monday" and "World in Motion"?
22 What kind of musical instrument was a kit?
23 Which country did Charles and Camilla visit in October 2006?
24 Which John Carpenter film set in the Antarctic starred Kurt Russell?
25 Name the first yacht to win the America's Cup?
26 Which singing sisters were called Patti, Laverne and Maxine?
27 In which country are the guerrilla group the Tamil Tigers?
28 What name is given to the principal female singer in an opera?
29 The dish Eggs Florentine contains which vegetable?
30 Which town was Barbara Castle's parliamentary constituency?

Answers	World Tour *(see Quiz 90)*

1 Atlantic. 2 Las Vegas. 3 Broadway. 4 Inuit (Eskimos). 5 Cape of Good Hope. 6 Wind. 7 Honshu. 8 Australia. 9 China. 10 K2. 11 Okovango. 12 Indian. 13 Hawaii. 14 China. 15 Namibia. 16 Gobi. 17 Dow Jones. 18 Eskimo. 19 Michigan. 20 Zambia and Zimbabwe. 21 Trinidad. 22 French. 23 Canaries. 24 North coast of Africa. 25 Manhattan. 26 Tip of South America. 27 Greenland. 28 Kilimanjaro. 29 Israel. 30 Pakistan & Afghanistan.

1 The Sargasso Sea is part of which ocean?
2 Which US city's name means "The Fields"?
3 How is New York's "Great White Way" also known?
4 Which Canadians speak Inuktitut?
5 Which Cape was originally called the Cape of Storms?
6 In America what type of natural phenomenon is a Chinook?
7 What is the principal island of Japan?
8 Where is the town of Kurri Kurri?
9 The Guangzhou TV & Sightseeing Tower was constructed in which country?
10 By which abbreviation is the mountain Chogori known?
11 What is the only permanent river in the Kalahari desert?
12 Which Ocean's deepest point is the Java Trench?
13 Where would you be if someone put a lei round your neck?
14 Where is the world's longest canal?
15 Afrikaans is the official language of which country in addition to South Africa?
16 In which desert is the Bactrian camel found?
17 What is the name of the index on the New York Stock Exchange?
18 Which group of people have a name meaning "eater of raw meat"?
19 Which is the only Great Lake wholly in the USA?
20 The Kariba Dam is on the border of which two countries?
21 Calypso is the traditional song form of which Caribbean island?
22 Which European language is spoken in Chad?
23 Las Palmas is in which island group?
24 Approximately where was Carthage to be found?
25 Wall Street and Broadway lie on which island?
26 Where is the Magellan Strait?
27 What is the largest island between the North Atlantic and the Arctic?
28 What is Africa's highest volcano?
29 Where is there a Parliament called the Knesset?
30 Which two countries does the Khyber Pass separate?

Answers | Pot Luck 41 *(see Quiz 89)*

1 Mary, Queen of Scots. 2 Mark Owen. 3 Sizes of paper. 4 The Dukes of Hazzard. 5 John Reid. 6 Simnel Cake. 7 Gary Numan. 8 Arsenal. 9 Meryl Streep. 10 French & English. 11 National Portrait Gallery. 12 Ants. 13 Gary Rhodes. 14 WWII. 15 Buckinghamshire. 16 Franco Zeffirelli. 17 Cow. 18 A sofa or desk. 19 Sting. 20 Ennio Morricone. 21 New Order. 22 A small violin. 23 Pakistan 24 The Thing. 25 America. 26 The Andrews Sisters. 27 Sri Lanka. 28 Prima Donna. 29 Spinach. 30 Blackburn.

1 What is saxifrage?
2 In "EastEnders" which character killed Dirty Den in February 2006?
3 Who hoisted himself on to Sinbad the Sailor's shoulders?
4 How much are you paid if you hold an honorary post?
5 Which UK act first scored the dreaded "nul points" in the Eurovision Song Contest?
6 What can be a five-card game, a smooth, woolly surface or a sleep?
7 Which club did Will Carling play for?
8 Which Australian movie director links "Romeo and Juliet" and "Strictly Ballroom"?
9 Whose music albums have included "An Innocent Man"?
10 'Englander' is an anagram of which country?
11 Which actress played Michael Douglas's wife in "Fatal Attraction"?
12 What is a melodeon?
13 Which animal family are impala, eland and dik-dik all from?
14 Which famous stepson wrote "The Year of Eating Dangerously"?
15 In TV's "Upstairs Downstairs" what was the name of the cook?
16 Whose hits include "Dancin' on the Ceiling" and "Do It to Me"?
17 Which stone is inscribed "Cormac McCarthy fortis me fieri fecit AD 1446"?
18 Which actor played the leading role in the TV drama "Shogun"?
19 What name is given to withered apples used to make rough cider?
20 Who composed the music for the musical "Lady be Good"?
21 What is a grackle?
22 Which building was erected in 1851 for the Great Exhibition?
23 Which children's TV series has included Tucker Jenkins and Zammo?
24 Which "Corrie" character died with Gilbert and Sullivan playing in his car?
25 Which branch would you hold out to seek peace?
26 Arthur Hastings was the sidekick of which fictional sleuth?
27 Whose hits include "Detroit City" and "Love Me Tonight"?
28 The leader of an orchestra plays which instrument?
29 What was Mab's job in fairy folklore?
30 Anderson, Kiely and Myhre played for which Premiership side in 2005–06?

| **Answers** | Past Times: The 80s *(see Quiz 92)* |

1 UK and Eire. 2 Chernobyl. 3 FW de Klerk. 4 Dubcek. 5 Salman Rushdie. 6 Michael Foot. 7 Mitterrand. 8 Galtieri. 9 Kim Wilde. 10 Jamaica. 11 Greenpeace. 12 Iceland. 13 Twice. 14 Dirty Dancing. 15 Ken Livingstone. 16 Monday. 17 The Labour Party. 18 Grand Hotel. 19 Slobodan Milosevic. 20 Montserrat. 21 Mubarak. 22 Irangate. 23 David Blunkett. 24 Jimmy Carter. 25 Peter Mandelson. 26 Local authority. 27 Benazir Bhutto. 28 Zimbabwe. 29 South Africa. 30 Mikhail Gorbachev.

1 The Hillsborough Agreement was between which two countries?
2 Where was there a major nuclear leak in the USSR in 1986?
3 Who was the last white President of South Africa, elected in 1989?
4 Which former liberal leader was made speaker of the national assembly of Czechoslovakia in 1989?
5 A fatwa calling for the death of which writer was made by Iran in '89?
6 Who succeeded Callaghan as Labour leader?
7 Who became France's first socialist president in 1981?
8 Who was Argentine President during the Falklands Conflict?
9 Which 80s female hit maker is a celebrity gardener this century?
10 Michael Manley became leader of where in 1989?
11 Who owned Rainbow Warrior, sunk by the French in 1985?
12 Vigdis Finnbogadottir became head of state in which country?
13 How many times was Margaret Thatcher elected PM in the 80s?
14 Which film featured "(I've Had) The Time of My Life" in its soundtrack?
15 Who was leader of the GLC from 1981–86?
16 What was the Black day of the week of the 1987 stockmarket crash?
17 Who moved from Transport House to Walworth Road in 1980?
18 In which hotel was the Brighton bomb in 1984?
19 Who became President of Serbia in 1986?
20 Most of which Caribbean island's buildings were destroyed by hurricane Hugo in 1989?
21 Who became Egyptian President after Sadat's assassination?
22 What was the name of the scandal over arms for hostages in which Oliver North was implicated?
23 Which one-time member of Tony Blair's cabinet was leader of Sheffield City Council?
24 Whom did Ronald Reagan defeat to become US President in 1980?
25 Which spin doctor did Neil Kinnock engage to run the 1987 election campaign?
26 In 1989 state schools were allowed to opt out of whose control?
27 Which woman became PM of Pakistan after the death of Zia in a plane crash?
28 Where did the parties of ZANU and ZAPU merge in 1987?
29 In 1986 the pass laws, concerning the carrying of identity documents, were repealed in which country?
30 Which Russian leader introduced the policy of perestroika?

| **Answers** | Pot Luck 42 *(see Quiz 91)* |

1 A small rock plant. 2 Chrissie Watts. 3 The Old Man of the Sea. 4 Nothing. 5 Jemini. 6 A nap. 7 Harlequins. 8 Baz Luhrmann. 9 Billy Joel. 10 Greenland. 11 Anne Archer. 12 A musical instrument. 13 Antelope. 14 Tom Parker Bowles. 15 Mrs Bridges. 16 Lionel Richie. 17 The Blarney Stone. 18 Richard Chamberlain. 19 Scrumps. 20 George Gershwin. 21 A bird. 22 Crystal Palace. 23 Grange Hill. 24 Derek Wilton. 25 Olive. 26 Hercule Poirot. 27 Tom Jones. 28 Violin. 29 A midwife. 30 Charlton Athletic.

1 What type of animal is a Sooty Mangabey?
2 Which team lost the first FA Cup Final decided on penalties?
3 Whom did William III defeat in 1690 at the Battle of the Boyne?
4 Who won "X Factor 2"?
5 In Old English which word meant a field?
6 What were the eldest sons of French kings called from the 14th century?
7 Ely stands on which river?
8 Which 60s singer married the designer Jeff Banks?
9 In 1945, who became British Prime Minister?
10 In which month in 2006 was "Top of the Pops" aired for the last time?
11 Who had hits with "The Streak" and "Misty" in the 70s?
12 Who was President of the Philippines from 1965 to 1986?
13 Which Gate is a memorial for British Soldiers who fell at Ypres?
14 Who played Fred Kite in the film "I'm Alright, Jack"?
15 In "Bringing Down the House" Steve Martin starred with which rapper?
16 Which complaint was the Jacuzzi originally developed to help?
17 What did Anna Karenina throw herself under in the Tolstoy novel?
18 Who wrote "Dr Zhivago"?
19 In which soap does the Cat & Fiddle rival The Bull?
20 Which comedian was Connie Booth married to?
21 The sons of Max and Mira Weinstein founded which film company?
22 Who preceded Edward VI as Monarch?
23 In the film "The Tommy Steele Story" who played Tommy Steele?
24 Who finished his radio show with "B.F.N. Bye for now"?
25 Who had hits with "The Logical Song" and "Dreamer"?
26 In which year was Lord Mountbatten murdered?
27 What is the start of Psalm 23?
28 Which shaggy horned wild cattle live in the Tibetan mountains?
29 What was a gulag in Russia?
30 In the 1953 film "Houdini" who played the title role?

Answers	Leisure: Books 2 *(see Quiz 94)*

1 Oxford. 2 The Da Vinci Code. 3 Slavery. 4 Dictionary. 5 Jeeves. 6 The Greatest. 7 Lord Peter Wimsey. 8 Black Beauty. 9 Spycatcher. 10 Childcare. 11 Joan Collins. 12 Nigel Lawson. 13 Maeve Binchy. 14 Oranges. 15 Ruth Rendell. 16 Bill Bryson. 17 Agatha Christie. 18 The Godfather. 19 The English Patient. 20 John Le Carré. 21 Schindler's Ark. 22 Marie Stopes. 23 The Odessa File. 24 Alan Titchmarsh. 25 Detective novel. 26 Jeffrey Archer. 27 Wales. 28 A Tale of Two Cities. 29 Exodus. 30 Simenon.

Quiz 94 | Leisure: Books 2

1 In which university city is the Bodleian Library?

2 In which book does Bishop Aringarosa visit Castle Gandolfo?

3 "Uncle Tom's Cabin" was a novel which argued against what?

4 In the US what type of book is Webster famous for?

5 Who is the most famous manservant created by PG Wodehouse?

6 What was Muhammad Ali's autobiography called?

7 Which Dorothy L Sayers' creation was Harriet Vane's husband?

8 Which children's classic was written to encourage adults to be kinder to horses?

9 Which book by ex-intelligence agent Peter Wright, did the British government try to have banned?

10 What was the subject of Benjamin Spock's most famous books?

11 Which soap star wrote "Prime Time"?

12 Which ex-Chancellor of the Exchequer wrote a diet book?

13 Whose first successful novel was "Light a Penny Candle"?

14 What "Are not the Only Fruit" according to Jeanette Winterson?

15 Who wrote the detective novel "Road Rage"?

16 Who wrote "A Walk in the Woods"?

17 "The Murder of Roger Ackroyd" was an early novel by whom?

18 Which is Mario Puzo's most famous novel, first published in 1969?

19 Which Michael Ondaatje book was made into an Oscar-winning film with Ralph Fiennes?

20 Who created George Smiley?

21 Which was the first Thomas Keneally book to win the Booker Prize?

22 Which birth control campaigner wrote the book "Married Love"?

23 What was Frederick Forsyth's follow-up to "The Day of the Jackal"?

24 Which gardening expert wrote "Nobbut a Lad"?

25 "The Woman in White" is the first novel of what type in English?

26 Whose "Not a Penny More, not a Penny Less" was written to clear bankruptcy debts?

27 In Colin Dexter's books where does Lewis come from?

28 Which Dickens novel is about the French Revolution?

29 What is the second book of the Old Testament?

30 Which Georges wrote over a hundred novels featuring Jules Maigret?

Answers | Pot Luck 43 *(see Quiz 93)*

1 Monkey. 2 Man Utd. 3 James II. 4 Shayne Ward. 5 An acre. 6 Dauphin. 7 The Ouse. 8 Sandie Shaw. 9 Clement Attlee. 10 July. 11 Ray Stevens. 12 Ferdinand Marcos. 13 Menin Gate. 14 Peter Sellers. 15 Queen Latifah. 16 Arthritis. 17 A train. 18 Boris Pasternak. 19 The Archers. 20 John Cleese. 21 Miramax. 22 Henry VIII. 23 Tommy Steele. 24 Jimmy Young. 25 Supertramp. 26 1979. 27 The Lord is my shepherd. 28 Yaks. 29 A prison camp. 30 Tony Curtis.

1 What did MGM stand for?
2 What colour is puce?
3 Which "Pop Idol" winner appeared on "You are What You Eat"?
4 Who was the first presenter of the TV series "Tomorrow's World"?
5 Which cartoon character was the "fastest mouse in Mexico"?
6 Who had 90s No. 1 hits with "The Power" and "Rhythm is a Dancer"?
7 Which US state is the second smallest?
8 According to the saying, who rush in where angels fear to tread?
9 What is Blue Vinney?
10 Who wrote "Five Children and It" and "Wet Magic"?
11 Which terrier is the largest of the breed?
12 Who was the head of the German SS?
13 What is studied by a haematologist?
14 Which county is Morganwg Ganol in Welsh?
15 What type of creature is a turnstone?
16 Which country from 1867–1914 had a governor called The Khedive?
17 In the film "The Great Escape" which actor played the Forger?
18 Which Egyptian President was assassinated in 1981?
19 In the TV series "To the Manor Born" what was the name of the butler?
20 Which 'N Sync star launched the design label William Rast?
21 Who had hits with "Kiss from a Rose" and "Crazy"?
22 The town of Newcastle is in which Australian state?
23 What was Marc Bolan's real name?
24 What type of food is a bullace?
25 What is a snake's cast-off skin called?
26 The holiday camp Maplins featured in which TV series?
27 Stelios Giannakopoulos joined Bolton from which club?
28 What is mineral water mixed with quinine called?
29 Whose painting was reported to have been sold for $140 million in 2006?
30 What was sought by Jason and the Argonauts?

| **Answers** | Pop Music: Groups *(see Quiz 96)* |

1 The Blue Flames. 2 Swedish. 3 Red Hot Chilli Peppers. 4 Summer Love. 5 The News. 6 Chairmen of the Board. 7 Our eyes. 8 In Perfect Harmony. 9 Vic Reeves. 10 Def Leppard. 11 Live Forever. 12 Good Vibrations. 13 Simply Red. 14 Three Lions. 15 Cream. 16 1994. 17 California. 18 All Day and All of the Night. 19 Computer Love/The Model. 20 To Trancentral. 21 Bread. 22 Jake. 23 The Bangles. 24 Clannad. 25 Moving On Up. 26 My Perfect Cousin. 27 Elkie Brooks. 28 This millennium. 29 Cosmic Girl. 30 Las Vegas.

1 What was the name of Georgie Fame's backing group?
2 What nationality were "All That She Wants" group Ace of Base?
3 Whose "Live in Hyde Park" album celebrated the success of the 2004 concerts?
4 What "Sensation" were the Bay City Rollers singing about in 1974?
5 Huey Lewis was vocalist for which group?
6 Which Company band had a hit with "Give Me Just a Little More Time"?
7 What did Go West close in their No. 5 from 1985?
8 What followed in brackets on "I'd Like To Teach the World to Sing"?
9 Who did the Wonder Stuff serve as backing group for?
10 Which heavy band took "When Love and Hate Collide" to No. 2?
11 What was Oasis' first UK Top Ten single?
12 What was The Beach Boys' first UK No. 1?
13 Which band made the hit album "Home"?
14 Which Lightning Seeds No. 1 was the official song of the England Football
Team in 1996?
15 Ginger, Jack and Eric formed which trio?
16 In which year did Oasis first have a No. 1-selling album?
17 Which "Hotel" was visited by the Eagles in 1977?
18 What part of the day took the Stranglers to No. 7 in 1988?
19 In 1982, what was the name of the first UK No. 1 by a German group?
20 Which Last Train did KLF catch in their No. 2 UK hit in 1991?
21 Singer/ songwriter David Gates led which group?
22 Who was the brother in the title of a track by Free from 1970?
23 Which girl band had hits with "Manic Monday" and "Walk Like an Egyptian"?
24 Which Irish group had a No. 5 hit with the "Theme from Harry's Game"?
25 What action were M People doing in their No. 2 UK hit from 1993?
26 What relative was "Perfect" according to the hit by the Undertones?
27 Who was the female artist in Vinegar Joe?
28 Have U2 had more No. 1s in the last century or this millennium?
29 What sort of girl took Jamiroquai to No. 6 in 1996?
30 Where was ZZ Top on the No. 10 hit Viva?

1 Who was the first Briton to hold a world javelin record?
2 Hidetoshi Nakata of Japan made his Premiership debut with which club?
3 How many players are there in a Canadian football team?
4 Chester Whites, Durocs and Hampshire are all types of what animal?
5 What is killed by an analgesic?
6 The Dufourspitze is the highest mountain where?
7 When do ducks always lay their eggs?
8 What was the first Top Ten hit for the Sugababes?
9 Who preceded Corazon Aquino as President of the Philippines?
10 Which test would you be taking if you underwent a polygraph test?
11 Which American city's football team is called the Bears?
12 Which vitamin deficiency causes rickets?
13 Which suspension bridge crosses the River Avon?
14 Which volcano erupted in 1883 and lies between Java and Sumatra?
15 What is the vocal tinkling sound made by a deer called?
16 Which sea surrounds Heligoland?
17 Which famous TV duo starred in the sci-fi comedy "Alien Autopsy"?
18 The pituitary gland controls the production of what in the body?
19 Which prefix is a tenth in the metric system?
20 How many pounds does the Olympic hammer weigh?
21 Which museum hosted Kylie: The Exhibition from February to June 2007?
22 What was a Minster originally attached to?
23 What is the popular name for the wood-hyacinth?
24 Where is Britain's National Horseracing Museum?
25 Whom did James Earl Ray assassinate?
26 Which city hosted the final game in the 2006/07 Ashes in Australia?
27 Which fault line is San Francisco on?
28 Who won 100m gold at the 1988 Olympics after Ben Johnson's disqualification?
29 Where was the terrorist group ETA mainly active?
30 Who was called the Father of Medicine?

Answers | Sport: Who's Who *(see Quiz 98)*

1 Sonny Liston. **2** Natalie Tauziat. **3** Rocky Marciano. **4** Al Joyner. **5** Joe DiMaggio. **6** Jake La Motta. **7** Silver. **8** Ray Reardon. **9** Raymond van Barnevald. **10** Mary Decker Slaney. **11** Italy. **12** Ernie Els. **13** Nick Faldo. **14** Steve Davis. **15** Cook book. **16** Paul Azinger. **17** Chris Evert. **18** Davis. **19** Squash. **20** Denise Lewis. **21** Graeme Smith. **22** Rocket. **23** John Conteh. **24** Judo. **25** Mike Tyson. **26** Conchita Martinez. **27** Bernard Gallacher. **28** Snooker. **29** Peter Fleming. **30** Nigel Benn.

1 Whom did Muhammad Ali beat when he first became World Champion?

2 Who was runner up to Jana Novotna in the Wimbledon final in 1998?

3 Who was the first heavyweight boxing champion to retire undefeated?

4 Who was the late Flo Jo's husband?

5 Which husband of Marilyn Monroe was elected to the Baseball Hall of Fame?

6 Whose life was recorded on film in "Raging Bull"?

7 What colour individual medal did Sharron Davies win at the Moscow Olympics?

8 Which snooker champion was unkindly nicknamed Dracula?

9 Who beat Phil Taylor in the 2007 World Professional Darts Championship Final?

10 Whom did Zola Budd trip up at the Los Angeles Olympics in 1984?

11 British-born long jumper Fiona May represents which country in international athletics?

12 Which South African golfer's real first name is Theodore?

13 Which golfer split with his coach and his girlfriend in September '98?

14 Whom did Stephen Hendry replace as world No. 1 in the 1989–90 season?

15 Away from cricket, what sort of book did Aussie Matthew Hayden write?

16 Who was appointed USA captain for the 2008 Ryder Cup?

17 Who lost most Ladies Singles finals at Wimbledon in the 80s?

18 Which surname has been shared by three world snooker champions?

19 Peter Nicol won Commonwealth gold for Scotland in which sport?

20 Who successfully defended her heptathlon title at the 1998 Commonwealth Games?

21 Which cricketer with a very English surname was made South Africa captain in 2003?

22 Which Gladiator competed in the heptathlon in the 1998 Commonwealth Games?

23 Which Liverpudlian won the WBC Light Heavyweight Title in 1974?

24 Sharron Davies' one time fiancé Neil Adams was an international in which sport?

25 Who replaced Leon Spinks as Heavyweight Champion in 1987?

26 Who defeated Navratilova in the final at her last Wimbledon?

27 Who captained Europe to Ryder Cup success in 1995?

28 Allison Fisher is a former world champion in which sport?

29 Whom did John McEnroe win five Wimbledon Doubles titles with?

30 Which boxer is nicknamed "The Dark Destroyer"?

Answers | Pot Luck 45 *(see Quiz 97)*

1 Ray Parker, Jr. 2 Bolton. 3 Twelve. 4 Pigs. 5 Pain. 6 Switzerland. 7 In the morning. 8 Overload. 9 President Marcos. 10 A lie detector. 11 Chicago. 12 D. 13 The Clifton. 14 Krakatoa. 15 A bell. 16 The North Sea. 17 Ant & Dec. 18 Hormones. 19 Deci. 20 16. 21 V & A. 22 Monastery. 23 The bluebell. 24 Newmarket. 25 Martin Luther King. 26 Sydney. 27 San Andreas. 28 Carl Lewis. 29 Spain. 30 Hippocrates.

1 Which "Game for a Laugh" presenters had the same surname?
2 Who was the subject of "The Naked Civil Servant" with John Hurt?
3 Which sitcom told of Tooting revolutionary Wolfie?
4 Who found fame as "The Saint"?
5 Who played Louie de Palma in "Taxi"?
6 Which spaghetti western star played in "Rawhide" for six years?
7 Who conducted Eric Morecambe playing Grieg's Piano Concerto?
8 Which reporter found fame during her reporting of the Iranian Embassy siege in 1980?
9 In which weekly drama slot was "Cathy Come Home" first shown?
10 Which star of "The Likely Lads" starred in "New Tricks" with Alun Armstrong?
11 Who was the main character on "The Phil Silvers Show"?
12 Who became Mrs Clayton Farlow in "Dallas"?
13 Which series looked back at film clips 25 years old?
14 How were Bruce Wayne and Dick Grayson better known?
15 Which "Carry On" regular was the star of "Bless This House"?
16 Who was "lower class" on "The Frost Report" after John Cleese and Ronnie Barker?
17 Which soap was originally called "The Midland Road"?
18 Which famous singer/actor's daughter shot JR?
19 Which TV veteran narrated "Planet Earth"?
20 What was the surname of Morticia and Gomez?
21 Which area of the country received TV after the area London in 1949?
22 In which sitcom did Richard Beckinsale play Alan Moore?
23 Which series told of the bizarre life of the Clampett family?
24 Which comedian played Colin in "Colin's Sandwich"?
25 Which show has numbered David Jacobs, Noel Edmonds and Rosemarie Ford among its presenters?
26 What was the BBC's first soap of the 60s?
27 Which actor played the part of Uncle Albert in "Only Fools and Horses"?
28 The controversial "Death of a Princess" caused a rift with which country in 1980?
29 Who had a long-running TV show before starring in "Mary Poppins"?
30 Who is the only "Corrie" star remaining from the original cast?

---

1 In Cuba what is a habanera?
2 Which black powder is the oldest known explosive?
3 Who condemned Shadrach, Meshach and Abednego to the Fiery Furnace?
4 Which tribe did Sitting Bull belong to?
5 Sam Snead found fame in which sport?
6 Who was king at the time of the Gunpowder Plot?
7 Which musical instrument did Jack Benny play?
8 Which Latin phrase means "in place of a parent"?
9 Dun Laoghaire is a port and suburb of where?
10 Gerald Durrell was a director of which zoo?
11 Michael Balcon was head of which influential studios?
12 Who wrote "A Shropshire Lad"?
13 What is the oldest university in the USA?
14 Who was the volt named after?
15 What is the lower house of the US Congress called?
16 Genocide is the destruction of what?
17 In Scandinavian myth what is Gotterdammerung?
18 Which animals' legs did the Griffin have?
19 "The Duke – What a Bobby Dazzler" was the autobiography of which celeb?
20 Which director made "Blackmail", Britain's first successful talkie?
21 How many tournaments make up tennis's Grand Slam?
22 With which woman aviator did Frederick Noonan perish?
23 In which country was Hitler born?
24 What is a puck made from in ice hockey?
25 Which 50 Cent album topped both the UK and US charts in 2005?
26 Which double Oscar winner appeared in the movie "Stranger than Fiction"?
27 What is the Great Australian Bight?
28 Where in London was the Great Exhibition of 1851?
29 What is HRT?
30 Park Ji-Sung joined Man Utd from which club?

Answers | TV: TV Gold (see Quiz 99)

1 Matthew & Henry Kelly. 2 Quentin Crisp. 3 Citizen Smith. 4 Roger Moore. 5 Danny De Vito. 6 Clint Eastwood. 7 André Previn. 8 Kate Adie. 9 The Wednesday Play. 10 James Bolam. 11 Bilko. 12 Miss Ellie. 13 All Our Yesterdays. 14 Batman and Robin. 15 Sid James. 16 Ronnie Corbett. 17 Crossroads. 18 Bing Crosby's (Mary). 19 David Attenborough. 20 Addams. 21 Midlands. 22 Rising Damp. 23 The Beverly Hillbillies. 24 Mel Smith. 25 Come Dancing. 26 Compact. 27 Buster Merryfield. 28 Saudi Arabia. 29 Dick Van Dyke. 30 William Roache.

1 Which actor is the son of a Poet Laureate?

2 Which "Chinese Western" actor's real name was Lee Yuen Kam?

3 Which singer and actress was in "Dick Tracy"?

4 Kenneth Branagh cast which toothy comedian as Yorick in "Hamlet"?

5 Who played the adult Damien in "The Omen" films?

6 Which pop wife appeared with Robert Redford, aged four, in "The Great Gatsby"?

7 Which early screen comedian's real name was Louis Cristillo?

8 Who played Cruella de Vil's sidekick Jasper in "101 Dalmatians"?

9 Who beat Meryl Streep for the lead role in "The Horse Whisperer"?

10 Which Glaswegian played a gangster in "Goldeneye"?

11 Which serious actress played comedy opposite Schwarzenegger in "Junior"?

12 Who directed, scripted, composed and starred in "Yentl"?

13 Which ex-child star was US Ambassador to Czechoslovakia in 1989?

14 How were producers Harry, Albert, Sam and Jack known collectively?

15 What was Groucho Marx's real first name?

16 Which Cockney actor married the former Miss Guyana in 1973?

17 Which horror writer directed the film "Maximum Overdrive"?

18 Who played Mary Jane in "Spider-Man 2"?

19 Which star of "Look Who's Talking Too" was a regular on TV's "Cheers"?

20 Which Fonda starred in the remake of "Nikita"?

21 Who is Joely Richardson's famous mother?

22 Which comedies was Michael Balcon responsible for?

23 Which actress wrote "Postcards from the Edge"?

24 Who was the first Bond girl?

25 Which conductor is Woody Allen's father-in-law?

26 Which surname was shared by John, Lionel, Ethel and Drew?

27 "Hitch" was the first romantic comedy lead for which actor?

28 What was Ex-Python Terry Gilliam's futuristic nightmare film, surreally named for a South American country?

29 Who bought the screen rights to "Dick Tracy" and made a film from it?

30 Which blonde actress is Mrs Alec Baldwin?

Answers | Pot Luck 47 *(see Quiz 102)*

1 The Pope. 2 Estate car. 3 The deaf. 4 Dakota. 5 Thomas Sorensen. 6 Tibet. 7 Tax. 8 Munich. 9 Two. 10 SAS. 11 France (de Nimes). 12 Operation Desert Storm. 13 Franz Beckenbauer. 14 Leek. 15 Kite-shaped. 16 Election. 17 Teeth or bone. 18 Variety Club. 19 Friday's Child. 20 Houses of Parliament. 21 Mel Gibson. 22 Hospital. 23 American Revolution. 24 Sleeping policeman. 25 Nurse. 26 Merchant Navy. 27 Third degree. 28 Richard Harris. 29 Lutine Bell. 30 Red.

Quiz 102 Pot Luck 47

Answers – page 221

LEVEL 2

1 Who would deliver an edict called a bull?
2 What is a shooting brake?
3 Who does the RNID provide help for?
4 What was the first No. 1 single for Stereophonics?
5 Which Danish keeper played for Sunderland and Aston Villa?
6 The Dalai Lama is the spiritual leader of where?
7 In English history what was danegeld?
8 What is the capital of Bavaria?
9 How many days does a decathlon event last?
10 The US Delta Force is based on which British anti-terrorist force?
11 In which country did denim originate?
12 What was the codename for the operation to eject the Iraqis from Kuwait in 1991?
13 Who was the first person to manage and captain a World Cup-winning soccer side?
14 David was responsible for the adoption of what as a Welsh emblem?
15 What shape is the approved mark of the British Standards Institution?
16 At what occasion do you see a returning officer?
17 Caries is the decay and deterioration of what?
18 Which Club's President is the Chief Barker?
19 Which day of the week first appeared in a Will Young title hit?
20 Where in London is the Strangers' Gallery?
21 Which Mel read Helen Hunt's thoughts in the movie "What Women Want"?
22 What sort of institution is UCH?
23 The Battle of Bunker Hill was the first major engagement of what?
24 What name is given to a bump in the road to slow down traffic?
25 What is the profession of an RGN?
26 Whose flag is the red ensign?
27 Which degree of burns is life-threatening?
28 The biography of which late hell-raising actor was called "Behaving Badly"?
29 Which bell is found in the building of Lloyd's of London?
30 What colour is the ceremonial dress of a Yeoman of the Guard?

Answers | Movies: People *(see Quiz 101)*

1 Daniel Day-Lewis. 2 Bruce Lee. 3 Madonna. 4 Ken Dodd. 5 Sam Neill. 6 Patsy Kensit. 7 Lou Costello. 8 Hugh Laurie. 9 Kristin Scott Thomas. 10 Robbie Coltrane. 11 Emma Thompson. 12 Barbra Streisand. 13 Shirley Temple. 14 Warner Brothers. 15 Julius. 16 Michael Caine. 17 Stephen King. 18 Kirsten Dunst. 19 Kirstie Alley. 20 Bridget. 21 Vanessa Redgrave. 22 Ealing. 23 Carrie Fisher. 24 Ursula Andress. 25 André Previn. 26 Barrymore. 27 Will Smith. 28 Brazil. 29 Warren Beatty. 30 Kim Basinger.

Quiz 106 Pot Luck 49

1 What are the metal discs in the rim of a tambourine called?
2 Which word can be a pole with a foot rest or a wading bird?
3 What annual event is the Cumbrian town of Appleby noted for?
4 On what date does the pheasant shooting season legally start?
5 Who or what is Cader Idris?
6 Mr Birdseye – of frozen food fame – came from which country?
7 Who was the voice of "It" in the 2004 movie "Five Children and It"?
8 Which 1950s pop star had the first names Charles Hardin?
9 Which animals can be affected by a disease called vives?
10 Which Brigadier appeared in "Dr Who"?
11 Who played Mr Brown in the film "Mrs Brown"?
12 What is the official language of Haiti?
13 What was the name of Geoff Hamilton's garden?
14 What was Craig David's first album to sell over a million in the UK?
15 Barajas airport is in which city?
16 Ivan Compo joined Bolton from which Spanish side?
17 What is the oldest daily newspaper in England?
18 Demetria Guynes is better known as which actress?
19 Which country surrounds San Marino?
20 Which Order is the highest in the Order of Chivalry in Britain?
21 Who played the leading role in the TV series "Sorry"?
22 What was the name of AA Milne's son?
23 How many hours are there in a dog watch at sea?
24 Which small triangular bone is located at the base of the spinal column in man and some apes?
25 Fox and Dana are the first names of which pair?
26 Who co-starred with Halle Berry in the hit movie "Monster's Ball"?
27 What are osselets and ossicles?
28 Alton Towers Leisure Park is in which county?
29 Steve Backley held the world record in which sports event?
30 In "The Merchant of Venice" the suitors pick one of three what?

Answers | Freddie Flintoff *(see Quiz 105)*

1 1977. 2 Andrew. 3 One. 4 India. 5 Preston. 6 Trent Bridge. 7 Holly. 8 Lancashire. 9 Sagittarius. 10 400 (402). 11 A cricket bat. 12 New Zealand. 13 Boxer. 14 Right. 15 His honeymoon. 16 South Africa. 17 Michael Vaughan. 18 24. 19 India. 20 Jacques Kallis. 21 Third Test. 22 St Annes. 23 Pakistan. 24 Neil Fairbrother. 25 Dark glasses. 26 Sixes. 27 Australia. 28 South Africa. 29 Trafalgar Square. 30 Michael Atherton.

1 Was Freddie born in 1975, 1977 or 1980?

2 He isn't a Freddie, but what's his real name?

3 How many centuries did he make in the 2005 Ashes series?

4 Freddie first captained England in which country?

5 In Jan. 2006 he was awarded the freedom of which city?

6 At which ground did he make his Test debut?

7 Is his first daughter named Carol, Holly or Ivy?

8 Aged 17 he first appeared for which county?

9 What is Freddie's star sign?

10 In the 2005 Ashes did he score just over 400, 450 or 500 runs?

11 Who or what is a Woodworm Flame?

12 Against which country did he make his maiden Test century?

13 What breed were his dogs Red and Arnold?

14 Freddie's a right-handed batsman, but which is his bowling arm?

15 Trying to regain fitness, which major event did he postpone in March 2005?

16 His Test debut was against which country?

17 Who was the scheduled series Test skipper when Freddie took over?

18 In the 2005 Ashes how many wickets did Freddie take?

19 He was in which country when his second child was born in 2006?

20 Who shared the ICC joint player of the year award with Freddie in 2005?

21 Which Test was on his home county ground in the 2005 Ashes?

22 Aged 14, was he playing Northern League for St Annes or St Austel?

23 Against which country did he make his one-day England debut?

24 Which famous Lancashire cricketer Neil became Freddie's agent?

25 What did Freddie wear on his face for the official 2005 Ashes celebrations?

26 In March 2006 Freddie became the England player to hit most what in Tests?

27 Which team won the first Test in the 2005 Ashes?

28 Against which country did he first have a series batting average of 50 plus?

29 In which London square did the main 2005 Ashes celebrations take place?

30 Which Lancashire skipper Michael watched Freddie break into county cricket?

1 In the music world what did NKOTB stand for?
2 Hartley was the fictional town setting for which TV police serial?
3 Variola is the proper name for which killer disease?
4 Who competed against Messala in a literary chariot race?
5 Where did Laika, the first dog in space, die?
6 In which musical did "Pop Idol's" Darius Danesh win a coveted role?
7 Which sheriff killed Billy the Kid?
8 What was the first Madonna hit to mention an item of food?
9 Which Liverpool top scorer in 2004–05 was rewarded with a transfer?
10 Is a piri-piri sauce sweet, or hot and spicy?
11 Which Swiss resident won a Grammy for singing "Downtown"?
12 Which Richard died at the Battle of Bosworth Field?
13 Which is larger, the Isle of Wight or Anglesey?
14 Buster Bloodvessel was a member of which Ska-revival band?
15 Which holiday island saw the worst ever air crash with 582 deaths?
16 Which former world boxing champion has the Christian name Finbar?
17 What does the "C" stand for in the musical initials "CBS"?
18 Which motorway joins with the M25 at Heathrow Airport?
19 What is controlled by an Emir?
20 In World War II which German city suffered the most civilian deaths?
21 In which US state did the first Wal-Mart store open?
22 What name is given to the most westerly time zone in America?
23 What is an American football pitch also called?
24 Thomas Hardy wrote what type of material for the last twelve years of his life?
25 Which is further East, Cambridge or Peterborough?
26 Which movie veteran starred with Adam Sandler in "Anger Management"?
27 Which is the slowest-moving fish?
28 What did the "M" stand for in the name of the band OMD?
29 Cordwainers mainly worked with which material?
30 Which Elton John hit was the first name of Russian leader Khrushchev?

1 What is Portland Place's most famous House?
2 What does CNN stand for?
3 Which listings magazine celebrated its 75th birthday in 1998?
4 What is Britain's principal world news agency?
5 Which magazine is supposedly edited by Lord Gnome?
6 Where is Grampian TV based?
7 What does the ASA control?
8 What is the magazine of the Consumers' Association?
9 Who is the Daily Mail's most famous cartoon dog?
10 Where is The People's Daily a top-selling papers?
11 Which long-running futuristic comic featured Judge Dredd and Rogue Trooper?
12 Country Life was once edited by which royal photographer?
13 Red and yellow were the colours of which comic strip Rovers?
14 What is the full official title of GQ?
15 Which organisation had a magazine called "Expression!"?
16 Which daily paper founded in 1859 is devoted to horse racing?
17 In which part of the Commonwealth might you tune in to Penguin Radio?
18 Which Times Supplement is aimed at teachers?
19 How is the New Musical Express better known?
20 How does Dennis the Menace's mother always address her husband?
21 Which US-based magazine was the world's best seller until the 80s?
22 How is the journalists' trade union commonly known?
23 Which famous magazine was founded by Hugh Hefner?
24 Where is Yorkshire TV based?
25 In which part of London are Richard Murdoch's newspapers based?
26 Which was the ill-fated satellite TV company that competed with Sky?
27 Which major UK daily newspaper, still in circulation, did Robert Maxwell own?
28 Which left-wing faction had a newspaper called Militant?
29 Which major Murdoch UK paper has the longest name?
30 Which women's magazine did Cherie Blair guest edit?

1 What was Diana's official title at the time of her death?
2 Who is the oldest in line to the throne after Prince Charles?
3 Which Prince was a guest on the "Des O'Connor Show" in 1998?
4 On which island was Princess Margaret when she suffered a stroke?
5 Who was older, Princess Diana's mother or her stepmother?
6 In which country did the former Edward VIII marry Mrs Simpson?
7 Albert succeeded Baudouin in which country?
8 In which country did Fergie's mother spend the latter part of her life?
9 What does the Queen's only nephew do for a living?
10 At which sport did Harry excel in his first few weeks at Eton?
11 Who is the only child of the Queen not to have been divorced?
12 Who is third in line to the throne?
13 Who survived the crash in which Princess Diana died?
14 In which London residence did Charles & Camilla live after their marriage?
15 Seven kings of which country have been called Haakon?
16 Which Princess is the mother of Viscount Linley?
17 Which Princess is known by her husband's name?
18 Which former Royal residence was damaged by fire in 1986?
19 "Tiggy" Legge-Bourke was PA to which Prince for three years?
20 Which Princess is the mother of Marina Mowatt?
21 Who was Princess Diana's chauffeur on her final fatal car journey?
22 Which of Prince Charles' sons began his military training first?
23 Which grandchild of the Queen had her tongue pierced?
24 Which Royal in-law was dubbed "Fog" because he was thick and wet?
25 Who took the official engagement photos of Charles and Diana?
26 Who is Lady Sarah Chatto's aunt on her mother's side?
27 Which Princess married the son of a director of Walls sausages?
28 In which royal castle is St George's Chapel?
29 Which musical instrument did the late Princess Margaret play?
30 In 1994 Diana took an advisory role for which organisation?

Quiz 108 Pot Luck 50

Answers – page 227

1 Deva was a Roman city now known as what?
2 Spanning 30 years on the charts, how is Tony Fitzgerald better known?
3 What does a kleptomaniac do?
4 What is the popular name for the anaesthetic nitrous oxide?
5 Who was the first woman to be awarded the Order of Merit?
6 The doomed ship Titanic was registered in which English city?
7 In which year did Marc Bolan die?
8 What is made up of the minor arcana and the major arcana?
9 The Romanian dictator Ceausescu was executed on which day in 1989?
10 In "The Life and Death of Peter Sellers", who played his wife Britt Ekland?
11 Dame Eliza Manningham Buller was head of which organisation in 2006?
12 Which Lou was vocalist with the Velvet Underground?
13 Which shipping forecast area is due north of Rockall?
14 Which pier featured in a George Orwell book title?
15 If you are an angler why are you pleased if your monkey starts to climb?
16 In which city was painter LS Lowry born?
17 Where was King Arthur taken after his last battle?
18 Did "Dead Ringers" begin on radio or TV?
19 Which all-male bastion allowed women members for the first time in September 1998?
20 Who made the first televised 147 in snooker, in 1982?
21 Which Prince's childhood nickname was "The Sniggerer"?
22 Who wrote the "Emperor Concerto"?
23 For which medical breakthrough did Roentgen win the Nobel Prize in 1901?
24 How many Inns of Court are there in London?
25 Which TV and radio producer was nicknamed Dr Wally by Sir Terry Wogan?
26 Whose codename was "Pink" before she was surprised on "This is Your Life"?
27 What is a pommel a part of?
28 Cars with the international vehicle registration Z come from where?
29 In which century was the Battle of Naseby?
30 How many pecks are there in a bushel?

Answers | The Royals *(see Quiz 107)*

1 Diana, Princess of Wales. 2 Prince Andrew. 3 Edward. 4 Mustique. 5 Stepmother. 6 France. 7 Belgium. 8 Argentina. 9 Make furniture. 10 Football. 11 Prince Edward. 12 Prince Harry. 13 Trevor Reece Jones. 14 Clarence House. 15 Norway. 16 Margaret. 17 Michael of Kent. 18 Hampton Court. 19 Charles. 20 Alexandra. 21 Henri Paul. 22 Prince Harry. 23 Zara Phillips. 24 Mark Phillips. 25 Lord Snowdon. 26 The Queen. 27 Anne. 28 Windsor. 29 Piano. 30 International Red Cross.

228

1 Who was Chancellor, Foreign Secretary and PM between 1964 and 1979?
2 Artist Peter Blake found fame designing which world-famous Beatles album sleeve?
3 Which American was known as Ike?
4 Which future President organised the Free French Forces in WWII?
5 What was Indira Gandhi's maiden name?
6 Who became US Vice President in 1993?
7 Which title did Hitler take as Nazi leader?
8 Who was the last Tsarina of Russia?
9 Who was Soviet Foreign Minister from 1957 to 1985?
10 Whose resignation on 1 November 1990 began Thatcher's downfall?
11 Whose 1963 Report led to the closure of many railway stations?
12 Who was famous for his pictures of Campbell's Soup cans?
13 Who was British Prime Minister during the abdication crisis?
14 For how long were Hitler and Eva Braun married?
15 Who was the first singer to record two 007 theme tunes?
16 Which athlete became MP for Falmouth and Cambourne in 1992?
17 Which world leader celebrated his 80th birthday in July 1998?
18 Who was the first Archbishop of Canterbury?
19 Which US President publicly pardoned ex-President Nixon?
20 Who had the title Il Duce?
21 Which US evangelist asked his flock to make a "decision for Christ"?
22 In 1990 which ex-PM went to Iraq to try to secure the release of British hostages?
23 Who was the youngest queen of Henry VIII to be beheaded?
24 Which Prime Minister introduced the Citizens' Charter?
25 Who became Defence Secretary in May 1997?
26 What was the name of Horatio Nelson's daughter by Emma Hamilton?
27 Who said her boss Michael Howard had "something of the night about him"?
28 What was the religion of a French Huguenot?
29 Which Communist leader was named Josip Broz at birth?
30 In which category did Einstein win his Nobel prize in 1921?

Answers | Pop: Who's Who? *(see Quiz 110)*

1 Bay City Rollers. 2 Barbra Streisand. 3 Bill Tarmey. 4 Shakin' Stevens 5 Kate Bush. 6 Chris De Burgh. 7 Bruce Springsteen. 8 The Spice Girls. 9 Bono. 10 Richard Clayderman. 11 George Michael. 12 Emerson, Lake & Palmer. 13 Judith Durham. 14 Meatloaf. 15 Celine Dion. 16 Michael Caine. 17 Bill Medley. 18 Ken Hutchinson – Hutch. 19 Right Said Fred. 20 David Bowie. 21 Lily the Pink. 22 George Michael. 23 Rod Stewart. 24 Shirley Bassey. 25 Morgen. 26 Coco Hernandez. 27 Jarvis Cocker. 28 The Kemp Brothers. 29 Victoria "Posh". 30 Nick Berry.

Quiz 110 Pop: Who's Who?

1 The Longmuir brothers were in which 70s teeny bop group?
2 Who partnered Don Johnson on the Goya theme "Till I Loved You"?
3 Which "Coronation Street" star had a hit in 1994 with "Wind Beneath My Wings"?
4 Which UK male vocalist's real name is Michael Barratt?
5 Who duetted with Peter Gabriel on "Don't Give Up"?
6 Christopher John Davidson is the real name of which Irish vocalist?
7 Who had a No. 1 on both sides of the Atlantic with "Devils & Dust"?
8 Who launched the British Legion Poppy Appeal with Dame Vera Lynn in 1997?
9 Who featured on the 1986 Clannad hit "In a Lifetime"?
10 Which pianist and instrumentalist's real name is Philippe Pages?
11 Who was the younger of the two Wham! members?
12 Keith, Greg and Carl were the Christian names of which 70s trio?
13 Who was lead female singer with 60s group The Seekers?
14 Marvin Lee Aday is better known as which dead ringer vocalist?
15 Who had a No. 5 UK hit with the theme song "Because You Loved Me"?
16 Which actor shares his name with a 1984 hit by Madness?
17 Who sang the theme tune to "Dirty Dancing" with Jennifer Warnes?
18 Which TV detective had a No. 1 hit with "Don't Give Up on Us" in 1976?
19 Which group share their name with a Bernard Cribbins 1962 hit?
20 Who joined with Queen in the 1981 No. 1 hit "Under Pressure"?
21 Who invented Medicinal Compound according to the 1968 No. 1?
22 Which superstar has an autobiography called "Bare"?
23 Which pop legend said, "I really wanted to be a soccer star"?
24 Who partnered Chris Rea on the 1996 hit "Disco La Passione"?
25 Complete the A-ha trio – Pal, Mags and ....?
26 Which character was played by Irene Cara in "Fame"?
27 Who interrupted Michael Jackson's "Earth Song" at the 1996 Brit Awards?
28 Which brothers were members of Spandau Ballet?
29 Who was the first Spice Girl to get engaged?
30 Who links the '86 hit "Every Loser Wins" and the 1992 hit "Heartbeat"?

1 Which comedian wrote "Blackadder" with Richard Curtis?
2 Who hosted the talent-spotting show "My Kind of People"?
3 Who hosted the first series of "Guess Who's Coming to Dinner?"?
4 David Dimbleby's first wife wrote what type of books?
5 Which comedian created the character Stavros?
6 Who has the car number plate COM 1C?
7 Which star of "The Grand" is President of the Dyslexia Institute?
8 Which first name is shared by subsequent stars of "Dangerfield"?
9 Which ex-party leader chaired "Have I Got News for You" after Angus Deayton's departure?
10 Which radio name replaced Richard Baker presenting The Proms?
11 Which blonde first presented "Big Breakfast" with Chris Evans?
12 Julie Walters hails from which city?
13 Who replaced Carol Drinkwater as Helen in "All Creatures Great and Small"?
14 Whom did Hillary Clinton give her first ever UK TV interview to?
15 In which docu soap did Jeremy Spake find fame?
16 In "EastEnders" what was Dennis Rickman's relation to Vicki?
17 How is Derrick Evans better known?
18 Who became Jim Davidson's regular assistant on "The Generation Game"?
19 Which ex-Radio 2 presenter moved to "Open House" on Channel 5?
20 Whom could you regularly have Breakfast With... on Sunday mornings?
21 Who replaced Vanessa on ITV's morning talk show?
22 What did Trude Mostue train to be on TV?
23 Who first presented "Changing Rooms"?
24 In which drama series did the character Dr Beth Glover appear?
25 Who was the first woman tennis player to be BBC Sports Personality of the Year?
26 Who was the interviewer on C4's "The Last Resort"?
27 Who presented this century's revived "Treasure Hunt" with Dermot Murnaghan?
28 Whom did Fergie play in "Friends"?
29 Which Major seemed to be influenced by coughing on "Who Wants to be a Millionaire?"?
30 Who moved from "Newsnight" to "Tomorrow's World"?

Hard Questions

Ah yes, the hard questions. Cackle fiendishly, and take just a moment to stroke your white, diamond-collared cat before rubbing your hands together gleefully, because these questions are the real McCoy. The posers in this selection will sort the men out from the boys, and no mistake. If you do find any boys in the public bar by the way, be sure to let the landlord know, so he can give them a packet of crisps and a bottle of coke and send them outside. The quizzes in this section will make even the most dedicated trivia hound quake with fear. No one is going to get many of them correct, so if someone turns out an incredible score on these questions, search their coat for a copy of this book.

When you're selling a quiz, use these questions sparingly, like hot chilli powder. Even for teams, they're going to be decidedly tricky. You'll need to allow plenty of time for people to think about each question. What you don't want to do is make an entire night's quizzing out of this section, because you'll only make people feel stupid, and everyone hates a smart aleck who makes them look dumb. A few of these questions, strategically placed, can go a long way.

1 Asuncion is the capital of which country?
2 Which "Pop Idol" star was born Jan 20, 1979, in Berkshire?
3 Who had hits with "Take Your Time" and "Got to Have Your Love"?
4 What is a paravane used for?
5 Dr James Naismith devised which game?
6 In which decade was Jeremy Paxman born?
7 Which worldwide magazine was conceived by DeWitt Wallace?
8 To within two years, when were postcodes introduced to the UK?
9 Waterways Airways operates from which country?
10 Who is the elder – Rowan Atkinson or Clive Anderson?
11 What is prase?
12 Who, in 1890, composed the music for the opera "Ivanhoe"?
13 A poniard is a type of what?
14 Who led the Expedition of the Thousand in 1860?
15 Which 1960s No. 1 was written by Madden and Morse in 1903?
16 Which part of the body is affected by thlipsis?
17 Who was found dead in the first episode of "EastEnders"?
18 Which Mel Brooks film was a spoof of Hitchcock movies?
19 Which TV cookery series set out to create a menu for the Queen's 80th birthday?
20 Gabriel Heinze joined Man Utd from which club?
21 Antonio Salazar was dictator for many years in which country?
22 Which US anti-terrorist force is based at Fort Bragg?
23 William Benting was an English pioneer of what?
24 By volume, what makes up about 21% of our atmosphere?
25 Who starred with his wife in the film "Mr and Mrs Bridge"?
26 Whose one and only hit was "I've Never Been to Me" in 1982?
27 Which two political parties aligned to form the Ministry of All-the-Talents in 1806?
28 To which Court are US Ambassadors to Britain officially credited?
29 Which US poet had the middle names Weston Loomir?
30 Which was the first African team to compete in the Cricket World Cup?

Answers	**TV Detectives** *(see Quiz 2)*

1 Tom Barnaby (Midsomer Murders). 2 Prime Suspect – The Final Act. 3 Liverpool One. 4 Adrian Kershaw. 5 Reginald Hill. 6 Eddie Shoestring. 7 Charlie's Angels. 8 RD Wingfield. 9 CIB. 10 The Remorseful Day. 11 Rupert Davies. 12 Reilly – Ace of Spies. 13 The Rockford Files. 14 Crime Traveller. 15 Denise Welch. 16 Cadfael. 17 Imogen Stubbs. 18 Barbara Havers. 19 Taggart. 20 Stanton. 21 Van der Valk. 22 Sexton Blake. 23 Gideon's Way. 24 Cordelia Gray. 25 Chief Inspector Haskins. 26 Hercule Poirot. 27 The Body in the Library. 28 Reginald Hill (Dalziel & Pascoe).. 29 Henry Crabbe. 30 Simon Templar.

1 Which DCI was first seen in episodes called "The Killings at Badger's Drift" and "Written in Blood"?

2 What was the final drama featuring Det. Supt Jane Tennison called?

3 In which series was Samantha Janus transferred from the Met to Merseyside?

4 Who was Morse's sidekick in "The Wench is Dead"?

5 Which novelist created the characters of Dalziel and Pascoe?

6 Which detective worked for Radio West?

7 Which series centred on Townsend Investigations?

8 Which novelist created Jack Frost?

9 Which acronymic part of the Met did Tony Clark work for in "Between the Lines"?

10 What was the episode called in which Inspector Morse died?

11 Who introduced the very first series of "Detective"?

12 In which series did Inspector Tsientsin appear?

13 Which famous series was introduced with a message on an answering machine?

14 In which series was Slade assisted by Holly?

15 Who played Frances Spender in the Jimmy Nail series?

16 Whose investigations are based in Shrewsbury but often filmed in central Europe?

17 Who played mini-skirted detective Anna Lee?

18 In the 2003 series, who was Inspector Lynley's Detective Sergeant?

19 Which long running series began with a pilot called "Killer" in 1983?

20 Where did "The Cops" take place?

21 What was the full name of TV's most famous Dutch detective?

22 Who had a Rolls Royce called "The Grey Panther"?

23 Which 60s series had Chief Inspector Keen aiding his Commander?

24 Who is the detective in "An Unsuitable Job for a Woman"?

25 Who was Regan's boss in "The Sweeney"?

26 Which detective lived at Whitehaven Mansions?

27 Which was the first Miss Marple adaptation to star Joan Hickson on TV?

28 Who created the detectives played on TV by actors Clarke and Buchanan?

29 Who had retired from Barstock CID?

30 Claude Eustace Teal was invariably beaten in his dealings with whom?

Answers | Pot Luck 1 *(see Quiz 1)*

1 Paraguay. 2 Will Young. 3 Mantronix. 4 Mine-sweeping. 5 Basketball. 6 1950s. 7 Reader's Digest. 8 1968. 9 New Zealand. 10 Clive Anderson. 11 A type of quartz. 12 Sir Arthur Sullivan. 13 Dagger. 14 Garibaldi. 15 Two Little Boys. 16 The blood vessels. 17 Reg Cox. 18 High Anxiety. 19 Great British Menu. 20 Paris St Germain. 21 Portugal. 22 Delta Force. 23 Slimming diet. 24 Oxygen. 25 Paul Newman. 26 Charlene. 27 Whigs and Tories. 28 St James. 29 Ezra Pound. 30 East Africa (in 1975).

1 Phil Read won several World Championships in which sport?
2 What did an alchemist use an alembic for?
3 What was Eternal's first UK Top Ten hit?
4 In Hindu mythology who was goddess of destruction and death?
5 In which country is the Mackenzie River?
6 Which instrument did Lionel Hampton play?
7 How many Top Five hits did Elvis Presley have in 2005?
8 What was President Carter's wife's first name?
9 Who won the first squash World Open Championship?
10 Where is England's national hockey stadium?
11 Where was the constituency of former Home Secretary Charles Clarke?
12 Who wrote the novel "Rodney Stone"?
13 How many times is Annie mentioned in the lyrics of "Annie's Song"?
14 In Swift's novel what was Gulliver's first name?
15 To which part of the body does the adjective "cutaneous" refer?
16 In which sport were Hildon and Black Bears British Champions?
17 Whose first Top Ten hit was "What a Waste" in 1978?
18 Who was James I of England's father?
19 Which record label did Geri Halliwell sign up with when she left the Spice Girls?
20 What was the old name for stamp collecting?
21 Which "Countdown" regular wrote "The Language Report"?
22 Alfredo di Stefano of Real Madrid fame was born in which country?
23 What is the name of the police officer in "West Side Story"?
24 Which language's name means "one who hopes"?
25 Which public figure resigned over dealings concerning prostitute Monica Coghlan?
26 In the Old Testament which two books are named after women?
27 The Prix Goncourt is awarded for what?
28 Who joined Patrick Macnee on the 1990 No. 5 UK hit "Kinky Boots"?
29 Who or what is a dourousouli?
30 What was Steve McClaren's best finishing position as a club manager?

Answers | Books 1 *(see Quiz 4)*

1 John Cleese. 2 Full Disclosure. 3 Diana Rigg. 4 Martin Amis. 5 Dame Barbara Cartland. 6 Ronnie Spector. 7 Six. 8 Pat Conroy. 9 Clare Francis. 10 Madonna. 11 Isaac Asimov. 12 Darren Gough. 13 Pig. 14 Sussex. 15 Richard Noble. 16 Torvill & Dean. 17 South Africa. 18 Her Majesty's Stationery Office. 19 Stephen Hawking. 20 A Boy from Bolton. 21 Octaves. 22 Noah Webster. 23 Styles. 24 The Rainbow. 25 The Highway Code. 26 John Humphrys. 27 Bertie Ahern, father of Cecelia. 28 Guinness Book of Records. 29 Bridget Jones's. 30 Agatha Christie.

Quiz 4 | Books 1 | Answers – page 235 | LEVEL 3

1 Which comedian wrote "Families and How to Survive Them" with psychiatrist Robin Skynner?
2 What was Andrew Neil's autobiography called?
3 Who wrote an anthology of critics' anecdotes called "No Turn Unstoned"?
4 Whose first novel was "The Rachel Papers" in 1974?
5 Which novelist recorded an "Album of Love Songs" in 1978?
6 Which pop celebrity wrote "Be My Baby"?
7 How many Barchester Chronicles are there?
8 Who wrote the novel on which the movie "Prince of Tides" was based?
9 Who went from "Deceit and Betrayal" to "A Dark Devotion"?
10 Whose book "Sex", coincided with a dance album "Erotica"?
11 Which science fiction writer wrote the Foundation Trilogy?
12 Which cricketer wrote "Dazzler on the Dance Floor"?
13 Who or what was PG Wodehouse's Empress of Blandings?
14 The founder of Wisden played for which English county?
15 Whose quest for speed is recorded in his book "Thrust"?
16 Which sports stars' autobiography was called "Facing the Music?"
17 Rider Haggard's colonial service where influenced his books?
18 Who publishes Hansard?
19 Whose 1998 best seller argued that our universe is a part of a super universe?
20 What was boxer Amir Khan's autobiography called?
21 What did Compton Mackenzie refer to each individual volume of his autobiography as?
22 Whose 19th-century dictionary standardised US English?
23 Where was the Mysterious Affair in the first Agatha Christie in Penguin paperback?
24 Which colourful DH Lawrence book was banned because of its sexual content along with "Lady Chatterley" and "Women in Love"?
25 First appearing in 1931, what sold out of its new edition in three months in 1996?
26 Which journalist wrote "Beyond Words"?
27 Who is the father of the author of "A Place Called Here"?
28 What is the best-selling copyright book of all time?
29 Whose Diary was written by Helen Fielding?
30 Who wrote romantic novels as Mary Westmacott?

| **Answers** | Pot Luck 2 *(see Quiz 3)* |

1 Motor Cycling. 2 To distil liquids. 3 Stay. 4 Kali. 5 Canada. 6 Vibraphone. 7 17. 8 Rosalyn. 9 Geoff Hunt. 10 Milton Keynes. 11 Norwich South. 12 Sir Arthur Conan Doyle. 13 Never. 14 Lemuel. 15 Skin. 16 Polo. 17 Ian Dury & The Blockheads. 18 Lord Darnley. 19 Chrysalis. 20 Timbrology. 21 Susie Dent. 22 Argentina. 23 Officer Krupke. 24 Esperanto. 25 Jeffrey Archer. 26 Ruth and Esther. 27 Literature (in France). 28 Honor Blackman. 29 A monkey. 30 Seventh (Premiership).

Quiz 5 | Pot Luck 3

Answers – page 238

1 Who designed the tapestry behind the altar in Coventry Cathedral?
2 An odalisque is a female what?
3 Who founded the record label Maverick Records?
4 Both Clive Woodward and Andy Robinson are linked with which university?
5 Which English poet had the middle name Chawner?
6 The Russian Revolution began in which year?
7 Which notorious serial killer was found hanged in prison in January 2004?
8 Who is the elder – Zoe Ball or Gary Barlow?
9 In the 1980s Greg Lemond became the first American to do what?
10 Whose one and only hit was "Little Things Mean a Lot"?
11 Who created the Statue of Zeus about 430 BC?
12 Which Jackson Pollock painting reputedly sold for $140 million in 2006?
13 What was film star Edward G. Robinson's real name?
14 Who was the husband of cellist Jacqueline du Pre?
15 What is the drink kumiss made from?
16 Who came up with "The Book of Heroic Failures"?
17 What was discovered in 1930 by Clyde Tombaugh?
18 In the Bible, who was King David's father?
19 In 1865, where did the Confederates surrender?
20 Wellesley is the family name of which Dukes?
21 What is a dhole?
22 Norman Parkinson made his name in which field of art?
23 How many times did Steve Donoghue win the Derby?
24 Who created the Detective Inspector Anna Travis?
25 Lynn Ripley shone under which name as a pop singer?
26 Which theory was formulated by the German physicist Max Planck?
27 Which poet wrote, "She was a phantom of delight"?
28 Which England soccer manager was born in Burnley, Lancashire?
29 The Haber Process manufactures which gas?
30 Who was Banquo's son in Macbeth?

Answers | Albums *(see Quiz 6)*

1 Simon & Garfunkel. 2 If U Can't Dance. 3 Mystery Girl. 4 Vertigo. 5 Innuendo. 6 Alison Moyet (Essex). 7 American Pie. 8 Frank Sinatra. 9 All Things Must Pass. 10 Help! – The Beatles. 11 Sheer Heart Attack. 12 A black dog. 13 Face Value. 14 Tony Christie. 15 Blue. 16 Mark Coyle. 17 The Police. 18 The Sound of Music. 19 Goodbye Yellow Brick Road. 20 As a soloist, with Style Council and the Jam. 21 Chris De Burgh. 22 Fleetwood Mac. 23 Saturday Night Fever. 24 A postal strike. 25 Postcard. 26 On. 27 WEA. 28 Transformer. 29 Never for Ever. 30 Queen.

Quiz 6 | Albums

Answers – page 237

1 Who released the biggest-selling album in Britain in the 70s?
2 What was the final track on "Spice"?
3 Which 1988 album confirmed a comeback by Roy Orbison?
4 Dire Straits first albums came out on which label?
5 Which 6.5-minute hit was the title track of Queen's 7th No. 1 album?
6 Who charted with an album named after an English county?
7 Don McLean's "Vincent" came from which album?
8 Which superstar first charted with "Come Fly with Me"?
9 What was George Harrison's first solo album after the Beatles?
10 What was the first album to make its debut into the UK chart at No. 1?
11 Which album contains the line, "My kingdom for a horse"?
12 Who is not on the front cover of "Urban Hymns", but features on an inside cover shot?
13 What was Phil Collins' first solo No. 1 album?
14 Who had a No. 1 album in 2005, nearly 30 years after his previous album success?
15 What was the main colour on the cover of Enya's "Shepherd Moons"?
16 Who along with Oasis gets production credits on "Definitely Maybe"?
17 Which group had five consecutive No. 1 albums from 1979 to 1986?
18 Which original film soundtrack was on the charts for a staggering 382 weeks?
19 Which album first featured "Candle in the Wind"?
20 Paul Weller has topped the charts in which three guises?
21 Who was the first artist to enter the Swiss album charts at No. 1?
22 What was the last Fleetwood Mac album released before the world smash "Rumours"?
23 Which double-album film soundtrack was a 30 million seller in 1978?
24 Why weren't the album charts published in 1971 for eight weeks?
25 What was the name of Mary Hopkin's debut album?
26 Which word appeared in the titles of Will Young's first and third albums?
27 Tubular Bells launched the Virgin label, but which label put out Tubular Bells II?
28 Which album originally featured "Perfect Day"?
29 Which Kate Bush album featured a song about Delius?
30 In 2005 which group took over as having most weeks on the UK album charts?

Answers | Pot Luck 3 *(see Quiz 5)*

1 Graham Sutherland. 2 Slave. 3 Madonna. 4 Loughborough. 5 Rupert Brooke. 6 1917. 7 Dr Harold Shipman. 8 Zoe Ball. 9 Win the Tour de France. 10 Kitty Kallen. 11 Phidias. 12 Number 5, 1948. 13 Emmanuel Goldenberg. 14 Daniel Barenboim. 15 Milk. 16 Stephen Pile. 17 Pluto. 18 Jesse. 19 Appomattox. 20 Wellington. 21 An Asian wild dog. 22 Photography. 23 Six. 24 Lynda La Plante. 25 Twinkle. 26 Quantum theory. 27 Wordsworth. 28 Ron Greenwood. 29 Ammonia. 30 Fleance.

Quiz 7

Pot Luck 4

Answers – page 240

LEVEL 3

1 Who were the first group since The Beatles to have 14 consecutive Top Five singles?
2 What was Golden Earring's first UK Top Ten hit?
3 Started in 1850, what were Children's Temperance Societies called?
4 How long had David Cameron been an MP when he became Tory leader?
5 Gravure is a term connected with which industry?
6 What did Thomas Wheildon make?
7 To the nearest hundred how many islands make up the Maldives?
8 Who was Prime Minister during the General Strike?
9 Once of Newcastle, which country did Hugo Viana play for?
10 Mycology is the study of what?
11 What was the Carla Rosa, existing from 1875 to 1958?
12 Who was the last King of Troy according to legend?
13 What was George Burns' real name?
14 The word Ombudsman comes from which language?
15 Who played the barrel organ in "The Magic Roundabout"?
16 Who wrote the play "The Homecoming"?
17 Who was writer and producer for New Kids on the Block?
18 In which American state were Bonnie and Clyde killed in an ambush?
19 The Statue of Liberty's 100th birthday was celebrated in which year?
20 Which Christmas fruits have the Latin name *vaccinium macrocarpon*?
21 What is studied by a pedologist?
22 Spencer Gore was the first winner of what?
23 George Galvin performed in music-hall under what name?
24 Placido Domingo studied music at which National Conservatory?
25 Who was the last Prime Minister during the reign of Queen Victoria?
26 The star Betelgeuse is in which constellation?
27 Which major pop singer/songwriter was born 13 June 1968, in Manchester?
28 Who was the first woman to be Canadian Prime Minister?
29 What do a tinchel of men do?
30 Who is in the portrait auctioned in Nov. 2006, to set a record for an Andy Warhol work?

Answers | Cricket *(see Quiz 8)*

1 Vengsarkar. 2 Mark Taylor. 3 Leeward Islands. 4 Swansea, Glamorgan. 5 Old Trafford. 6 West Indies. 7 Geoff Boycott. 8 Old Trafford. 9 Cigarettes & Alcohol by Oasis. 10 James Andersen. 11 Imperial. 12 Australia. 13 Shell Shield. 14 59. 15 New Zealand & India. 16 Charlton Athletic. 17 Steve Bucknor. 18 Ivon. 19 India v. New Zealand. 20 India & Pakistan. 21 Bob Taylor. 22 Ricky Ponting. 23 Mike Gatting. 24 Wayne Larkins. 25 Mike Atherton. 26 Durham and Lancashire. 27 Alec Stewart. 28 Victoria. 29 Craig McDermott. 30 Surrey.

1 Who was the first overseas batsman to score three Test centuries at Lord's?
2 Which Aussie equalled Don Bradman's batting record in October 1998 but declared rather than beat it?
3 Which West Indian islands did Viv Richards play for?
4 Where did Sobers hit his 36 runs in one over and against whom?
5 Where did Dennis Amiss score the first century in a one-day international?
6 Against whom did Mike Atherton make his first international one-day century?
7 Who deputised for Mike Brearley as England skipper four times in 1977–8?
8 Where did Lance Gibbs take most of his wickets in England?
9 Which song did Phil Tufnell choose to escort him on to the field in the New Zealand test tour?
10 Alphabetically who came first in England's 2006/07 Ashes squad?
11 Until 1965 what did "I" stand for in ICC?
12 Which was the first women's side to win the World Cup in successive occasions?
13 Which competition in the West Indies was replaced by the Red Stripe Cup?
14 How many did Ashley Giles score in his final Ashes 2005 innings?
15 Graham Gooch became the first player to score 1,000 Test runs in an English summer against which sides?
16 Which football team did Alec Stewart's father play for?
17 Who was the first overseas umpire to umpire a Test Match in England?
18 What is David Gower's middle name?
19 Who was playing when the first hat trick by a bowler was scored in a World Cup?
20 Where was the first World Cup outside England played?
21 In 1995 Jack Russell broke whose record for dismissals in a Test match?
22 Who was born in Launceston, Tasmania, Dec. 19, 1974?
23 Whose autobiography was called "Leading from the Front"?
24 Who was the first batsman to score centuries against all the counties?
25 Who was the youngest Lancastrian to score a Test century, in 1990?
26 Which two counties had three players in England's 2006/07 Ashes squad?
27 Who was the first Englishman to score a century in each innings against the West Indies in 1994?
28 Which Australian state did Ben Hollioake's father play for?
29 Who was Australia's leading wicket taker on the 1994–5 Ashes tour?
30 Who won the first ever county championship?

Answers | Pot Luck 4 *(see Quiz 7)*

1 Steps. 2 Radar Love. 3 Bands of Hope. 4 Four years. 5 Printing (platemaking). 6 Pottery. 7 1200 (1196). 8 Stanley Baldwin. 9 Portugal. 10 Fungi. 11 An Opera Company. 12 Priam. 13 Nathan Birnbaum. 14 Swedish. 15 Mr Rusty. 16 Harold Pinter. 17 Maurice Starr. 18 Louisiana. 19 1986. 20 Cranberries. 21 Soils. 22 Men's singles, Wimbledon. 23 Dan Leno. 24 Mexico. 25 Marquis of Salisbury. 26 Orion. 27 David Gray. 28 Kim Campbell. 29 Hunt. 30 Chairman Mao.

Quiz 9 | Pot Luck 5 | Answers – page 242 | LEVEL 3

1 Who was the letter which revealed the Gunpowder Plot addressed to?
2 Which lecturer in philosophy wrote "The Second Sex"?
3 Which non-metallic element has the atomic number 6?
4 What was Marc Almond's first solo UK Top Ten hit?
5 Made in 1975 with George Segal, "The Black Bird" was a spoof of which screen classic?
6 In surveying, how long is a Gunter's Chain in feet?
7 Susan Godfrey was the first victim of which atrocity?
8 In which city was the infamous Gatting and Rana Test Match flare up?
9 Who was older when he died, Jimi Hendrix or Marc Bolan?
10 In which film did Chaplin first tackle dialogue?
11 Luke Concannon and John Parker were known as which musical duo?
12 What was a lamia in ancient mythology?
13 What date was the Stock Market's Black Monday of the 1980s?
14 Which saint was shot dead in 288 AD by arrows?
15 Which campaign group flour bombed the House of Commons in May 2004?
16 The European Economic Community was established in which year?
17 In poetry what was hung around the neck of the Ancient Mariner?
18 Turner, Campbell and Chrétien have all held which post?
19 What was the name of the Vicar of Dibley's betrothed?
20 Whose one and only hit was "Turtle Power" in 1990?
21 The sword is the symbol of which of the twelve apostles?
22 Which artist painted "Bubbles" used by Pears to advertise their soap?
23 What can be a unit of length or a small island in Scotland?
24 Who is the elder – Kenneth Branagh or Rory Bremner?
25 What is the name of America's National Cemetery?
26 In which country could you visit Umm?
27 Robert, Grattan and Emmett were which famous Wild West outlaw gang?
28 Who scripted the first series of "Blackadder" with Rowan Atkinson?
29 In 1941 which American defined the Four Freedoms?
30 Which team did England play in Sven-Goran Eriksson's last game as boss?

Answers | Battle Stations (see Quiz 10)

1 Auchinleck. 2 Panmunjom. 3 Madras. 4 Mohne & Eder. 5 Vidkun Quisling. 6 Right arm. 7 MacArthur. 8 Reims. 9 Richthofen's Flying Circus. 10 Gavrilo Princip. 11 Treaty of Sevres. 12 Switzerland & Luxembourg. 13 Anzio. 14 Second Battle of the Somme. 15 Major Johnny Paul Koroma. 16 29. 17 Contras. 18 Dien Bien Phu. 19 American. 20 Ardennes. 21 Japanese. 22 Tobruk. 23 Near Kiev, Ukraine. 24 Spanish Civil War. 25 Michel Aoun. 26 Boer War. 27 Tutsi v. Hutu. 28 Passchendaele. 29 Von Moltke. 30 Vichy France.

Quiz 10 | Battle Stations

Answers – page 241

1 Who led the British forces in the First Battle of El Alamein?
2 Where was the peace treaty signed after the Korean War?
3 What was the only place in India attacked by foreign forces in WWI?
4 Which dams were destroyed by bouncing bombs in 1943?
5 Which Norwegian leader aided the 1940 invasion of his country through non-resistance?
6 Which part of his body did Lord Raglan lose at Waterloo?
7 Who was commander of the US forces in the Pacific from March '42?
8 In which city did the German High Command formally surrender to General Eisenhower?
9 What was the German 11th Chasing Squadron known as in WWI?
10 Who assassinated Archduke Franz Ferdinand in 1914 thus precipitating WWI?
11 What was the last of the treaties which ended WWI?
12 Which countries were on either end of the Maginot Line?
13 Which birthplace of Nero was the site of an Allied beachhead invasion in WWII?
14 How is the battle at St Quentin in 1918 also known?
15 Who led the military coup in Sierra Leone's Civil War in 1997?
16 How many countries made up the coalition v. Iraq in the Gulf War?
17 In the Nicaraguan Civil War which faction had US support?
18 Where was France's defeat which brought about the division of Vietnam along the 17th parallel?
19 Hitler's plan "Watch on the Rhine" was aimed at which troops?
20 In which area of Belgium/Luxembourg was the Battle of the Bulge?
21 Which navy was defeated at the Battle of Midway Island in 1942?
22 The retreat by the British from which port brought about the replacement of Auchinleck by Montgomery?
23 Where is Babi Yar, where 100,000 people were slaughtered in 1941?
24 In which war did the Battle of Ebro take place?
25 Which General declared a "war of liberation" against Syrian occupation of Lebanon in 1989?
26 Which war was ended with the Peace of Vereeniging?
27 Who were the two opposing factions in the Rwandan Civil War in the mid-1990s?
28 How is the third battle of Ypres in WWI also known?
29 Who was in charge of the German troops in the First Battle of the Marne?
30 What name was given to that part of France not occupied by the Germans until 1942?

Answers | Pot Luck 5 *(see Quiz 9)*

1 Lord Monteagle. 2 Simone de Beauvoir. 3 Carbon. 4 The Days of Pearly Spencer.
5 The Maltese Falcon. 6 66. 7 Hungerford Massacre. 8 Lahore. 9 Marc Bolan.
10 The Great Dictator. 11 Nizlopi. 12 A snake-bodied female demon. 13 October
19th. 14 Sebastian. 15 Fathers 4 Justice. 16 1957. 17 An albatross. 18 Canadian
PM. 19 Harry Kennedy. 20 Partners in Kryme. 21 St Paul. 22 Millais. 23 Inch. 24
Kenneth Branagh. 25 Arlington. 26 Qatar. 27 The Daltons. 28 Richard Curtis. 29 FD
Roosevelt. 30 Portugal.

1 Which denomination of Ulster banknote featured George Best?
2 What was the middle name of Wallis Simpson, later Duchess of Windsor?
3 Which greedy giant was created by Rabelais?
4 Who is the elder – Tony Blair or Pierce Brosnan?
5 What is sorghum?
6 From what is the writing material true vellum made?
7 What is separated by the oval window and the round window?
8 Whose presidential hopes were ended by model Donna Rice?
9 What fraction of a gold object is a carat as a proportional measure?
10 What is a killick?
11 The Cassini-Huygens probe took pictures of which planet?
12 Which team featured in "Footballers' Wives"?
13 What name is given to an animal that may be slaughtered to provide food under Muslim law?
14 In which county did the Tolpuddle Martyrs form a trade union?
15 What is a bowyang ?
16 Which politician said that northerners die of "ignorance and crisps"?
17 In which decade was actress Kristin Scott Thomas born?
18 In Feb. 2005 a Class 47 diesel locomotive was named after which musician?
19 Which country without a D or a Z in its name has the internet code .dz?
20 What relation was Queen Victoria to George IV?
21 Who won the first WBC cruiserweight title in boxing?
22 Why were the Piccard brothers famous in the 1930s?
23 Which Roman god was the god of beginnings and doors?
24 What is gneiss?
25 What was Florence Nightingale the first woman to receive in 1907?
26 What was a "quod" in old slang?
27 Who preceded David II as King of the Scots?
28 How is Julie Anne Smith better known in movies?
29 "The Purple Rose of Cairo" was written and directed by which actor?
30 Which title did Saddam Hussein take first – President or Prime Minister?

Answers | Quiz and Games *(see Quiz 12)*

1 Zoe Tyler. 2 The Moment of Truth. 3 Patrick Kielty. 4 Alan Coren. 5 Kenny Everett. 6 David Sneddon. 7 Child's Play. 8 Vincent Price. 9 Countdown (OED). 10 Ally McCoist. 11 Richard Wilson. 12 Blockbusters. 13 Steve Brookstein. 14 Pass the Buck. 15 Max Robertson. 16 John Leslie. 17 Edwina Currie. 18 Newspaper – day of birth. 19 Matthew Kelly. 20 Princess Diana. 21 Blind Date. 22 Max Bygraves. 23 Armand Jammot. 24 Ed Tudor-Pole. 25 Double Your Money. 26 Paul Daniels. 27 British Museum. 28 Leslie Crowther. 29 The Great Garden Game. 30 Anthea Redfern.

1 Who was the voice coach on "How Do You Solve a Problem Like Maria?"?
2 Which show had a "Dream Directory"?
3 Who joined Anthea Turner on "The National Lottery's Big Ticket"?
4 Who opposed Sandi Toksvig in the 90s "Call My Bluff"?
5 Who was the first male team captain in "That's Showbusiness"?
6 Who was the first winner of "Fame Academy"?
7 In which quiz did Ronnie Corbett replace Michael Aspel as host?
8 Which horror movie actor was on the first "Celebrity Squares"?
9 In which show might Mark Nyman adjudicate?
10 Who was the footballing "A Question of Sport" team captain when Sue Barker took over on a regular basis?
11 Who was the Reverend Green in the second series of "Cluedo"?
12 In which show were you pleased to be on the "Hot Spot"?
13 Who was the 2004 winner of "X Factor"?
14 Which weekday elimination quiz was hosted by Fred Dinenage?
15 Who presented the original "Going for a Song"?
16 Which "Blue Peter" presenter took over "Wheel of Fortune"?
17 In "Celebrity Wife Swap" which ex-MP changed places with Mrs John McCririck?
18 What did contestants receive at the end of "Today's the Day"?
19 Who hosted "You Bet" before Darren Day?
20 Who was the subject of an entire show of "100%" in August 1998?
21 Sue Middleton and Alex Tatham famously followed a TV win on which show with marriage?
22 Who presented "Family Fortunes" immediately prior to Les Dennis?
23 Who created Countdown?
24 Who replaced Richard O'Brien on "The Crystal Maze"?
25 "The Sky's the Limit" was a variation of which show?
26 Whom did Bob Monkhouse replace on "Wipeout"?
27 Which building was central to Tony Robinson's "Codex" challenge?
28 Who first asked contestants to "Come on down"?
29 What was Channel 5's first gardening quiz called?
30 Who was the female half of the first husband-and-wife team to present "The Generation Game"?

Answers | Pot Luck 6 *(see Quiz 11)*

1 £5 2 Warfield. 3 Gargantua. 4 Tony Blair. 5 A cereal crop. 6 Calf skin. 7 Middle ear and inner ear. 8 Gary Hart. 9 1/24th. 10 A small anchor. 11 Saturn. 12 Earls Park. 13 Halal. 14 Dorset. 15 String tied to the knee to hitch trousers up. 16 Edwina Currie. 17 1960s. 18 Joe Strummer. 19 Algeria. 20 Niece. 21 Marvin Camel. 22 Balloonists. 23 Janus. 24 A type of rock. 25 The Order of Merit. 26 A prison. 27 Robert the Bruce. 28 Julianne Moore. 29 Woody Allen. 30 President (1979).

1 Who led the British force in 1898 at Omdurman?

2 What was Adam Ant's first UK Top Ten hit?

3 How many cubic centimetres in a cubic metre?

4 In which country was Fatos Nano returned to power as PM in 2002?

5 Which real island, famed in fiction, is some 25 miles south of Elba?

6 Who would use a fyke?

7 Who was the first Irish cyclist to win the Tour de France?

8 What first did Bernard Harris achieve when he did his space walk?

9 Who or what is Katherine Gorge?

10 Which two countries are separated by the Kattegat?

11 In which decade did Picasso die?

12 Houses in Sherwood Crescent were destroyed in which disaster?

13 Which classic film was billed as "The Eighth Wonder of the World"?

14 Which Royal House ruled from 1461 to 1485 in England?

15 What is a gribble?

16 How many books are there in the New Testament?

17 How many FA Cup Finals did Roy Keane play in?

18 Which city is the capital of Tibet?

19 "In No Way to Treat a Lady" what did the killer leave on the brow?

20 What is bohea?

21 The Greek goddess Nyx was the personification of what?

22 Ion Iliescu has twice been President of which country?

23 What form did the Yahoos have in Gulliver's Travels ?

24 "I Didn't Get Where I am Today" was which comedy writer's autobiography?

25 In which country is the national drink called pisco?

26 Whose one and only hit was "First Time" in 1988?

27 Which place is in Berkshire in England and Pennsylvania in America?

28 Unlucky for some, what was Westlife's 13th No. 1 single?

29 When George Bush Snr was elected president who was his Democrat opponent?

30 Which rock star has children called Rufus Tiger and Tiger Lily?

Answers   50s Films *(see Quiz 14)*

1 Giant. 2 St Swithin's. 3 Robert Morley. 4 Kim Novak. 5 Darby O'Gill and the Little People. 6 Richard Burton. 7 George Cole. 8 Danny Kaye. 9 Mount Rushmore. 10 Carry On Nurse. 11 Operation Petticoat. 12 Dorothy Dandridge. 13 George Sanders. 14 High Noon. 15 Mike Todd. 16 Viva Zapata!. 17 Jack Lemmon. 18 Anastasia. 19 The Trouble with Harry. 20 The Swan. 21 Yul Brynner. 22 No Way Out. 23 1915. 24 The Long Hot Summer. 25 Bewitched Bothered and Bewildered. 26 Green Grow the Rushes. 27 William Wyler. 28 Yves Montand. 29 Larry Adler. 30 Judy Garland.

1 James Dean died during the filming of which film in 1955?
2 In which hospital would you find Sir Lancelot Spratt?
3 Who played George III in "Beau Brummell"?
4 Who played the blonde that James Stewart was hired to follow in Vertigo?
5 In which 50s film did Sean Connery sing?
6 Which actor wins Christ's robe in a dice game in "The Robe"?
7 Who played the younger Scrooge in the classic with Alistair Sim?
8 Who replaced Astaire for the "Holiday Inn" remake "White Christmas"?
9 Where does the climax of "North by Northwest" take place?
10 What was the second "Carry On" film?
11 What was the only film where Tony Curtis and Cary Grant starred together?
12 Whose voice was dubbed by Marilyn Horne in "Carmen Jones"?
13 Who won Best Supporting Actor for "All About Eve"?
14 Which film was based on "The Tin Star" by John W. Cunningham?
15 Which one-time husband of Elizabeth Taylor produced "Around the World in 80 Days"?
16 What was the second of Brando's four consecutive Oscar nominations for between 1951 and 1954?
17 Who contributed a song for his 1957 film "Fire Down Below"?
18 Ingrid Bergman won a second Oscar for which film, marking her return from Hollywood exile?
19 What was Shirley Maclaine's debut film in 1955?
20 What was the last film Grace Kelly made before becoming a princess?
21 Who played the Pharaoh in "The Ten Commandments"?
22 What was Sidney Poitier's first film, in 1950?
23 "The African Queen", made in 1951, is about events in which year?
24 What was the first film in which Paul Newman and Joanne Woodward appeared together?
25 Which song did Rita Hayworth famously sing in "Pal Joey"?
26 What was Richard Burton's last UK film before turning to Hollywood?
27 Who won his third Best Director for his third Best Picture in 1959?
28 Which French superstar was the husband of the 1959 Oscar-winning Best Supporting Actress?
29 Who composed and played the music for "Genevieve"?
30 Who was replaced by Betty Hutton in "Annie Get Your Gun"?

Answers | Pot Luck 7 *(see Quiz 13)*

1 Lord Kitchener. 2 Dog Eat Dog. 3 One million. 4 Albania. 5 Monte Cristo. 6 A fisherman. 7 Stephen Roche. 8 First black man to walk in space. 9 National Park in Australia. 10 Denmark and Sweden. 11 1970s. 12 Jumbo jet crash, Lockerbie. 13 King Kong. 14 York. 15 A crustacean. 16 27. 17 Seven. 18 Lhasa. 19 A lipstick kiss. 20 Tea. 21 Night. 22 Romania. 23 Human. 24 David Nobbs. 25 Peru. 26 Robin Beck. 27 Reading. 28 You Raise Me Up. 29 Michael Dukakis. 30 Roger Taylor.

1 The Euroroute E24 is from Birmingham to which county town?
2 Which Scottish university was named after a jeweller and an inventor?
3 Which polo ground is in the park of a burnt-down former country house?
4 What is the smallest theatre at the Barbican in London called?
5 Where is Grimsetter Airport?
6 Which inlet of the Clyde was used as a US submarine base from the early 60s?
7 In which part of London is Kenwood?
8 Which shipping area is due north of Trafalgar?
9 In which county was the Open University founded?
10 John Peel lived in which county for the latter part of his life?
11 How many national parks does the Pennine Way pass through?
12 Which wall runs from the river Forth in the east to Clyde in the west?
13 What is the real name of "Petticoat Lane"?
14 Which county is due north of Buckinghamshire?
15 Where is the Post Office's main sorting office?
16 What name is given to someone born east of the Medway?
17 Which county is due South of Tyne and Wear?
18 Which colloquial name of the main church in Boston serves as a landmark for ships?
19 Who or what was London's Liverpool Street station named after?
20 Where is the official London residence of the Foreign Secretary?
21 What is the administration centre of Wiltshire?
22 How is London's Collegiate Church of St Peter better known?
23 Which House has an Egyptian Hall for banqueting?
24 Which important collection was given to the city of Glasgow in 1944?
25 Which World Heritage Site was built for the Duke of Marlborough?
26 Which house is headquarters and home to the BBC World Service?
27 What is MOMI on London's South Bank?
28 Which famous House is the only surviving part of Whitehall Palace?
29 Where is Scatsa Airport?
30 Which county is due south of Shropshire?

Answers | Pot Luck 8 *(see Quiz 16)*

1 Groove between nose and lip. 2 1940s. 3 Architecture. 4 Joseph Black. 5 Benjamin Britten. 6 Ian Woosnam. 7 Russia. 8 Family Plot. 9 Sri Lanka. 10 Flushing Meadow, New York. 11 Madonna. 12 John Gielgud. 13 Winston. 14 Real Sociedad. 15 Lynn Anderson. 16 Marsh Marigold. 17 100-30. 18 Henry Miller. 19 Rudolf Nureyev. 20 The Road to Hell (Part 2). 21 Wood. 22 Arthur. 23 TS Eliot. 24 Licence to Kill. 25 Corpuscles. 26 Stewart Copeland. 27 Edwin Land. 28 Neil Simon. 29 Communism. 30 Thomas Edison.

Quiz 16 Pot Luck 8

Answers – page 247

LEVEL 3

1 Where on your body is your philtrum?
2 In which decade was Delia Smith born?
3 Inigo Jones was famous in which profession?
4 Who discovered carbon dioxide in 1754 and called it "fixed air"?
5 Who was the first musician to be made a life peer?
6 Who won golf's World Matchplay Championship in 1987, 1990 and 2001?
7 Who defeated Sweden's forces at Poltava in 1709?
8 What was the last film directed by Alfred Hitchcock?
9 Which country known by two words since 1970 was long ago known as Serendip?
10 Where is the Louis Armstrong Stadium?
11 Who wrote Gary Barlow's second solo No. 1?
12 In "Brideshead Revisited" which actor played the father of Jeremy Irons?
13 What was John Lennon's middle name?
14 Mikel Arteta joined Everton from which club?
15 Whose only UK Top Ten hit from 1971 was called "Rose Garden"?
16 What is the more common name for the flower called the Kingcup?
17 What odds is a horse if it is "Burlington Bertie" in rhyming slang?
18 Who wrote "Tropic of Cancer" and "Tropic of Capricorn"?
19 Which ballet dancer died on the same day as Dizzy Gillespie?
20 What was Chris Rea's first UK Top Ten hit?
21 Amboyna is a richly coloured type of what?
22 What was Sir John Gielgud's first name?
23 Which poet wrote, "I have measured out my life with coffee spoons"?
24 What was Timothy Dalton's last film as James Bond?
25 Plasma in blood consists of platelets and red and white what?
26 Who was the drummer in the group Police?
27 Who invented the Polaroid camera in 1947?
28 "Barefoot in the Park" was written by which US playwright?
29 What is opposed by the John Birch Society in the USA?
30 Which famous inventor had the middle name Alva?

Answers | Around the UK *(see Quiz 15)*

1 Ipswich. 2 Heriot-Watt. 3 Cowdray Park. 4 The Pit. 5 Orkney. 6 Holy Loch. 7 Hampstead. 8 Finisterre. 9 Buckinghamshire. 10 Suffolk. 11 Three. 12 Antonine Wall. 13 Middlesex Street. 14 Northamptonshire. 15 Mount Pleasant. 16 Man of Kent. 17 Durham. 18 The Boston Stump. 19 PM Earl of Liverpool. 20 Carlton House Terrace. 21 Trowbridge. 22 Westminster Abbey. 23 Mansion House. 24 The Burrell Collection. 25 Blenheim Palace. 26 Bush House. 27 Museum of the Moving Image. 28 Banqueting House. 29 Shetlands. 30 Hereford and Worcester.

Quiz 17 Books 2

1 Which TV presenter published his "Unreliable Memoirs" in 1980?

2 Whose novel "A Time to Dance" was adapted into a controversial TV drama?

3 In "From One Charlie to Another", whom did Charlie Watts write about?

4 Which singer wrote the book "Tarantula"?

5 What was the colour of the first Penguin paperback?

6 Which blonde wrote "The Constant Sinner"?

7 Which John Grisham book set a record initial print run of 2.8 million?

8 To be considered for the Booker Prize a book has to be published where first?

9 What according to Dickens was "the best of times, the worst of times"?

10 Whose only novel won the Pullitzer Prize in 1937?

11 Which PM wrote "Sybil"?

12 For which novel did Tom Clancy receive an advance of $14 million?

13 Which joint 1992 Booker Prize winner had his book made into an Oscar-winning film?

14 Which Ian Fleming novel has the shortest title?

15 What was Hercule Poirot's last case called?

16 What did JM Barrie give the royalties from Peter Pan to?

17 Which former "EastEnders" actress wrote "The Other Side of Nowhere"?

18 What was the sequel to DH Lawrence's "The Rainbow"?

19 Who created Pomeroy's wine bar for his hero?

20 Whose early thrillers include "The Eye of the Needle"?

21 Who wrote "The House of Stairs" under a pseudonym?

22 Which detective novelist wrote the screenplay for "Strangers on a Train"?

23 What was Charles Dickens' second novel, after "Pickwick Papers"?

24 Who wrote "The Exorcist" which was made into a successful film?

25 How are Patrick Dannay and Manfred B. Lee better known?

26 Who produced "The Truth That Leads to Eternal Life"?

27 Who wrote the historical romance "Micah Clarke"?

28 Which novelist once owned a Rolls registration number ANY 1?

29 Whose early novels were "Bella", "Harriet" and "Prudence"?

30 Bob Skinner is the creation of which crime/thriller writer?

Answers	Pot Luck 9 (see Quiz 18)

1 The Zulus. 2 Phyllis Nelson. 3 Jose Maria Olazabal. 4 Aldeburgh. 5 Tracy-Ann Oberman. 6 Varicella. 7 Stereophonics. 8 Robbie Coltrane. 9 National Theatre. 10 Alan Alda (of M*A*S*H fame). 11 Soot. 12 The tennis Grand Slam. 13 Betty Driver and Elizabeth Dawn. 14 1970. 15 A hangman. 16 Paul Gauguin. 17 Hero. 18 Wear it. 19 Picture Post. 20 The Tube. 21 Jennifer Lopez. 22 Battle of Naseby. 23 1860. 24 New Zealand. 25 A hoofed mammal. 26 Chelsea. 27 Love in Bloom. 28 Kim Appleby. 29 Margaret Atwood. 30 Land's End.

Quiz 18 | Pot Luck 9

Answers – page 249

1 Cetewayo, Dingaan and Chaka have all led which people?

2 Whose one and only hit was "Move Closer" in 1985?

3 Which injured player did Ian Woosnam replace in the 1995 European Ryder Cup team?

4 Which Suffolk town was the first in Britain to have a woman mayor?

5 Who played Yvonne Hartman, head of the Torchwood Institute in "Doctor Who"?

6 What is the correct name for chickenpox?

7 Which top-selling band featured Richard Jones on bass?

8 Who is the elder – Phil Collins or Robbie Coltrane?

9 In the 80s which building did Prince Charles compare to a "nuclear power station"?

10 Which US actor's autobiography was titled "Never Have Your Dog Stuffed"?

11 The brown pigment bistre is prepared from what?

12 Maureen Connolly was the first female to perform what?

13 Which two "Corrie" actresses were awarded the MBE in millennium year?

14 In which FIFA World Cup were red and yellow cards first used?

15 What did Jack Ketch do for a living?

16 Van Gogh's "Sunflowers" used to hang in the bedroom of which other famous artist?

17 In mythology, whom did Leander swim the Hellespont nightly to see?

18 What would you do with a filibeg?

19 Bert Hardy was a staff photojournalist for which periodical?

20 Madonna's first British TV appearance was on which show?

21 Who was George Clooney's co-star in the movie "Out of Sight"?

22 Which battle was the decisive one in the English Civil War?

23 To ten years, when was the National Rifle Association of Great Britain formed?

24 In which country are the Sutherland Falls?

25 What is an alpaca?

26 Who were Wigan's opponents in their first ever Premiership game?

27 What was American comedian Jack Benny's signature tune?

28 Who had UK Top Ten hits in the 90s with "Don't Worry" and "G.L.A.D."?

29 Who wrote "The Handmaid's Tale"?

30 What did businessman Peter de Savray buy for £6.7 million in 1987?

Answers | Books 2 *(see Quiz 17)*

1 Clive James. 2 Melvyn Bragg. 3 Charlie Parker. 4 Bob Dylan. 5 Blue. 6 Mae West. 7 The Rainmaker. 8 Britain. 9 French Revolution (Tale of Two Cities). 10 Margaret Mitchell. 11 Disraeli. 12 Without Remorse. 13 Michael Ondaatje. 14 Dr No. 15 Curtain. 16 Children's Hospital. 17 Daniella Westbrook. 18 Women in Love. 19 John Mortimer (Rumpole). 20 Ken Follett. 21 Ruth Rendell as Barbara Vine. 22 Raymond Chandler. 23 Oliver Twist. 24 William Blatty. 25 Ellery Queen. 26 Jehovah's Witnesses. 27 Conan Doyle. 28 Jeffrey Archer. 29 Jilly Cooper. 30 Quintin Jardine.

1 Which Pete Ham and Tom Evans song has been at No. 1 with two different artists?

2 The Isley Brothers and which other Motown act recorded "Grapevine" before Marvin Gaye?

3 To the nearest year, how long was there between Sinatra's first and second UK No. 1s?

4 Where is the singer's home in the lyrics of "On the Dock of the Bay"?

5 What was the first song to be Christmas No. 1 in two different versions?

6 Which group wrote the song that was Will Young's second No. 1?

7 Which 1970 seven-week No. 1 was best selling UK single of the year?

8 Whom did Billy Joel dedicate his 1983 version of "Uptown Girl" to?

9 What was Elvis Presley's closing number in his Las Vegas stage act?

10 What was Cliff Richard's first self-produced No. 1?

11 What was the chief of the Diddymen's only UK No. 1?

12 Which standard has the line, "I see friends shaking hands saying how do you do"?

13 Which Beatles hit stayed in the UK Top 50 for 33 weeks in 1963?

14 Who had the first UK No. 1 with "Unchained Melody"?

15 Which film theme was the biggest-selling single of 1979?

16 Who took Led Zeppelin's "Stairway To Heaven" into the singles charts before Rolf Harris?

17 Who wrote "You'll Never Walk Alone"?

18 Which heavenly body is mentioned in the title of the song that gave George Michael his 4th solo and Elton John his 3rd No. 1?

19 Who played Buddy Holly in the 1978 movie "The Buddy Holly Story"?

20 Who wrote Aretha Franklin's first UK hit "Respect"?

21 What was Yusuf Islam's, once known as Cat Stevens, last Top Ten hit before "Father and Son"?

22 Which 1967 No. 1 recorded the longest-ever stay in the UK Top 50?

23 Which 1960s star, who died in 1988, charted with "Love Songs" album in 2001?

24 How many weeks in total did Whitney Houston top the US and UK charts with "I Will Always Love You"?

25 Which hit was the first No. 1 for writers Gerry Goffin and Carole King?

26 Which song includes the line, "nothing to kill or die for"?

27 What was the colour mentioned in the title of Tom Jones' final No. 1 in the 1960s?

28 What is the biggest international hit from Eurovision Song Contest?

29 What was Sam Cooke's real name?

30 What was the Beatles' first No. 1 in America?

Answers | Pot Luck 10 *(see Quiz 20)*

1 Richard. 2 Five. 3 Alexander Selkirk. 4 US President. 5 The Strand Magazine. 6 The Verve. 7 Chamonix, France. 8 Albert Reynolds. 9 A fusil. 10 Once. 11 Have a Go. 12 Room at the Top. 13 Liquids. 14 Shiny Happy People. 15 Gliders. 16 Foot or feet. 17 Royal Flying Corps. 18 Morgan. 19 Grasmere. 20 The skin that separates the nostrils. 21 Sandy Cummings. 22 Ian Woosnam. 23 A seal. 24 Prince Andrew of Greece. 25 Portugal. 26 Debussy. 27 Steps. 28 Paul Channon. 29 Average White Band. 30 St Dominic.

1 Which christian name derives from the Germanic for "strong ruler"?
2 Between 1963 and 2006, how many Bond films featured the Aston Martin DB5?
3 The novel "Robinson Crusoe" was based on whose experiences?
4 What important post did Millard Fillmore hold?
5 Which magazine serialised "The Adventures of Sherlock Holmes" in the 1890s?
6 Which group features Peter Salisbury on drums and Simon Jones on bass?
7 Where were the first Winter Olympics held in 1924?
8 Who preceded John Bruton as Prime Minister of Ireland?
9 What can be a type of musket or a type of rhomboid?
10 How many seasons in the top flight did Alan Curbishley's Charlton win more than they lost?
11 Which long-running radio quiz show was hosted by Wilfred Pickles?
12 In which John Braine book is Joe Lampton the central character ?
13 What does a manometer measure the pressure of?
14 What was R.E.M.'s first UK Top Ten hit?
15 Otto Lilienthal was associated with what form of transport?
16 In furniture, what can be bracket, bun and stile on a chest?
17 What amalgamated in 1918 with the Royal Naval Air Service to form the RAF?
18 What did the M stand for in EM Forster's middle name?
19 Where is the poet Wordsworth buried?
20 What is your columella?
21 In "Big Brother 3" who made a memorable escape by climbing over a roof?
22 Who was the first UK golfer to win the World Match-Play Championship?
23 In folktales a silkie was half man and half what?
24 Who was Prince Philip's father?
25 Jose Barroso took over as Prime Minister of which European country in 2002?
26 Who composed "Clair de Lune"?
27 Which pop quintet announced they were splitting up on Boxing Day 2001?
28 Who was Transport Secretary at the time of the King's Cross tube fire disaster?
29 Whose only UK Top Ten hit was "Pick Up the Pieces" in 1975?
30 Black Friars are members of the religious order established by whom?

Answers | **Musical Greats** (see Quiz 19)

1 Without You. 2 The Miracles. 3 12 years. 4 Georgia. 5 Mary's Boy Child. 6 The Doors. 7 In the Summertime. 8 Christie Brinkley. 9 Can't Help Falling in Love. 10 Mistletoe and Wine. 11 Tears. 12 What a Wonderful World. 13 She Loves You. 14 Jimmy Young. 15 Bright Eyes. 16 Far Corporation. 17 Rodgers and Hammerstein. 18 Sun. 19 Gary Busey. 20 Otis Redding. 21 Morning Has Broken. 22 Release Me. 23 Roy Orbison. 24 24 weeks. 25 I'm Into Something Good. 26 Imagine. 27 Green. 28 Waterloo by Abba. 29 Cook without an "e". 30 I Wanna Hold Your Hand.

Quiz 24 | Pot Luck 12 | Answers – page 255

1 Who crossed Niagara Falls in 1859 on a tightrope?
2 What did the Romans call the Isle of Wight?
3 Who is the voice of a 1951 Hudson Hornet in the Pixar movie "Cars"?
4 What are gar, wrasse, alewife and blenny?
5 What was Jim Reeves' first UK Top Ten hit?
6 Who is the actress daughter of actress Phillida Law?
7 Who composed the music for "Jaws" and "Star Wars"?
8 What was the capital of the ancient empire of Assyria?
9 On what date in 1986 did Prince Andrew marry Fergie?
10 Which part did Prunella Scales play in "A Question of Attribution"?
11 Which David was FA executive director during the Faria Alam affair?
12 Which presenter of "That's Life" was famous for his odd odes?
13 What is a futtock?
14 Which film star married Robyn Smith in 1980?
15 Which alloy contains 2% antimony, 8% copper and 90% tin?
16 Liane Carroll is famous for which type of music?
17 In which month did the 2004 Olympics open?
18 Which son of Henry VII married Catherine of Aragon in 1501?
19 In what year did Classic FM begin?
20 What are Lambda, Omicron and Tau all found in?
21 Charing, as in Charing Cross, comes from an Old English word meaning what?
22 What can be a trump at cards or a type of sandpiper?
23 The major town of Herat is in which war-torn country?
24 Where is English actor David Garrick buried?
25 Who followed up a No. 1 with "Find My Love"?
26 Walter Gropius was famous in what field?
27 What is the natural water form which the Chinese call Huang Ho?
28 Famed as Alfie Moon, what part did this actor play in "Grease" in the West End?
29 Which celebrated novelist lived at Greenaway house?
30 Who directed the film "You Can't Take It with You"?

Answers | TV Sitcoms (see Quiz 23)

1 Its star's John Challis (Boycie). 2 Philadelphia. 3 Hilary. 4 Dolly & Cissy. 5 Eddie Brown's. 6 Darrin Stephens (Bewitched). 7 North Tanton. 8 Paul Shane. 9 Mrs Polouvicka. 10 Bernard Hedges. 11 Seinfeld. 12 Roseanne & Dan Conner. 13 Harvey Bains. 14 Alf Garnett. 15 Who's the Boss?. 16 17 Railway Terrace. 17 The Gillies Hospital. 18 The Phil Silvers Show. 19 Stan Butler. 20 Chambers. 21 The Sunshine Cab Company. 22 Police detective. 23 Albert Kitchenere. 24 The butler Benson. 25 Marks & Gran. 26 Kathy Staff. 27 Mim. 28 Mike. 29 Eric Idle. 30 Dear John.

Quiz 23 | TV Sitcoms

1 In whose home is "The Green Green Grass" set?
2 "Thirtysomething" was set in which US state?
3 Who did "Casualty's" George play in "May to December"?
4 What were Private Godfrey's sisters called in "Dad's Army"?
5 Which bookie did Vince Pinner work for?
6 Who had a wife, daughter and mother-in-law who were witches?
7 In which real-life town was "Jam and Jerusalem" filmed?
8 Who sang the theme music for "You Rang M'Lord" with Bob Monkhouse?
9 What was Richard's mother called in "To the Manor Born"?
10 Which lead character had the nickname Privet?
11 In which series did George, Kramer and Elaine appear?
12 Which TV husband and wife lived in Lanford Illinois?
13 Who was the first manager of the Bayview Retirement Home?
14 Who in his later years had a black home help called Winston?
15 What was the US series on which "The Upper Hand" was based?
16 Which property was left to Jim Davidson in "Up the Elephant and Round the Castle"?
17 In which hospital did Sheila Sabatini work?
18 Which sitcom was first called "You'll Never Get Rich" in the US?
19 What was Reg Varney's character called in "On the Buses"?
20 What was Thelma's surname before she married Likely Lad Bob?
21 Elaine Nardo was the only female cabbie in which company?
22 What job did Michael Douglas do when he guested on "Will and Grace"?
23 What were Harold Steptoe's middle names?
24 Which character in "Soap" was later given his own series?
25 Who wrote the original series of "Shine on Harvey Moon"?
26 Which sit com star played Vera Hopkins in "Coronation Street"?
27 Who was Roger's wife in "Outside Edge"?
28 Who was the barman of the Nag's Head as frequented by the Trotters?
29 Who created the theme music for "One Foot in the Grave"?
30 Which show centred round the 1-2-1 Club?

Answers	Pot Luck 12 *(see Quiz 24)*

1 Charles Blondin. 2 Vectis. 3 Paul Newman. 4 Fish. 5 Welcome to My World. 6 Emma Thompson. 7 John Williams. 8 Nineveh. 9 July 23rd. 10 The Queen. 11 David Davies. 12 Cyril Fletcher. 13 A ship's timber. 14 Fred Astaire. 15 Pewter. 16 Jazz. 17 August. 18 Arthur. 19 1992. 20 The Greek alphabet. 21 Bend. 22 Ruff. 23 Afghanistan. 24 Westminster Abbey. 25 Fairground Attraction. 26 Architecture. 27 Yellow River. 28 Danny Zuko. 29 Agatha Christie. 30 Frank Capra.

1 What was the first Gareth Gates single not to make No. 1 in the UK?
2 Which creature is represented in the year the Chinese call hou?
3 A fear of cats is known as what?
4 Which country ruled Greece until 1830?
5 Who wrote the line: "The female of the species is more deadly than the male"?
6 How many species of ostrich are there?
7 Dakar is the capital of which country?
8 Which theme gave Clannad their first UK Top Ten hit?
9 Who is the elder – John Prescott or Trevor McDonald?
10 The spice allspice is made from which part of a plant?
11 Which "E" number is used to represent Tartrazine in products?
12 What is the main language of Andorra?
13 Which elderly couple were immortalised in a poem by Henry Woodfall?
14 Where on Dartmoor is Dartmoor prison?
15 Which jazz festival is held annually in Rhode Island?
16 What does the Latin ab initio mean?
17 Which Prime Minister was offered a dukedom when he retired in 1955?
18 The constellation Aquila has which name in English?
19 In which country is the city of Baku?
20 What does the musical term "con fuoco" mean?
21 Which bird appears with two heads on the Albanian flag?
22 Which letter in Braille comprises a single raised dot?
23 Which Noel Edmonds show featured the ill-fated Whirly Wheeler?
24 Subtitled "The Time-Torn Man", Claire Tomalin's book was about which writer?
25 What are separated by the Cook Straits?
26 In which year did the UK become a member of the UN?
27 Which country has the internet code .pi?
28 Which country's team dominated World Fly Fishing at the start of this century?
29 Prime Minister Wilfried Martens was leader of which country?
30 How would the letter E be formed in Morse Code?

Answers | Football (see Quiz 21)

1 Wilf McGuinness. 2 First woman ref of men's soccer. 3 Italy (1990). 4 Man City. 5 Richard Branson. 6 Liverpool. 7 Everton. 8 Wigan Athletic. 9 67 games. 10 Morocco. 11 Torino. 12 Brazil. 13 Peter Schmeichel. 14 Thomas Ravelli. 15 Diego Maradona. 16 Bari. 17 Chesterfield. 18 Bulgaria. 19 Inter Milan. 20 Gillespie Road. 21 Arnold Muhren. 22 West Brom. 23 Spurs v. Wolves. 24 Ajax. 25 90. 26 Ivar Ingimarsson. 27 Boston, USA. 28 Santos. 29 Ugo Ehiogu. 30 Rangers and Hearts.

1 Who preceded Frank O'Farrell as Man Utd manager?
2 How did Joan Bazely make history in 1976?
3 Who were the opponents in Peter Shilton's last game for England?
4 Which Premiership side lost nine of its last ten games in 2006 and stayed up?
5 Who offered the England and Scotland squads a week on his Caribbean island if they won the World Cup in 1998?
6 Roy Keane played his last Premiership game for Man Utd against which team?
7 Which club's motto is "Nil Satis Nisi Optimum"?
8 John Benson, Bruce Rioch and Steve Bruce have all managed which club?
9 To three, for how many games was Sven-Goran Eriksson in charge of England?
10 Ray Wilkins was sent off while playing for England against which country?
11 Who did Denis Law play for immediately before Man Utd?
12 Who was the only side to beat England over 90 minutes when Venables was manager?
13 Who appeared in a TV ad for bacon before the 1998 World Cup?
14 Who is Sweden's most capped player of all time?
15 Who led Naples to their first ever Italian championship?
16 Which of the Italian sides David Platt played for had the shortest name?
17 Bolton's Kevin Davies has played over 100 games for three clubs – which was first?
18 Who was fourth in the 1994 World Cup?
19 Roy Hodgson joined Blackburn Rovers from which club?
20 What was Arsenal tube station called before it was called Arsenal?
21 Who was the first Dutchman to play in an FA Cup Final?
22 Whom were Man Utd playing when George Best made his debut?
23 Which sides competed in the first all-British UEFA Cup Final?
24 Who were the first winners of the Inter Toto Cup?
25 How many times did Bobby Moore captain England in 108 internationals?
26 Who was Reading's only ever-present in their 2005–06 Championship win?
27 Where did Paul Ince captain England for the first time?
28 Which club side were the first to win the South American Cup?
29 Which defender scored his only England goal in Sven-Goran Eriksson's first game?
30 Which two Scottish sides did Antti Niemi play for prior to moving to England?

Quiz 25 | Animal World

Answers – page 258

LEVEL 3

1 What is the only mammal to live as a parasite?
2 How is a Sibbald's rorqual also known?
3 For how many hours in a period of 24 does a giraffe sleep?
4 What is the world's largest rodent?
5 What gives the sloth its greenish appearance?
6 Which mammal lives at the highest altitude?
7 Which animals are famously sold at Bampton Fair?
8 The mammal which can live at the greatest depth is a species of what?
9 From which part of a sperm whale is ambergris obtained?
10 Where does a cane toad squirt poison from?
11 What is the longest type of worm?
12 Where would you find a shark's denticles?
13 What does the male mouse deer have that no other deer has?
14 Where does a browser find food?
15 What is the Latin name for the Blue Whale?
16 A Clydesdale was originally a cross between a Scottish draught horse and a what?
17 What colour is a mandrill's beard?
18 The wisent is native to where?
19 Lemurs are only found in their natural habitat where?
20 What is the oldest indigenous breed of cat in the US?
21 What is a koikoi?
22 What is the average life expectancy of the mayfly?
23 Which protein is cartilage made up of?
24 The term monkey refers to all primates except apes, humans and what?
25 Why were Samoyeds originally bred?
26 Falabellas are native to where?
27 What is another name for the aye-aye?
28 Which animal has the longest tail?
29 What name is given to the smaller of a rhino's horns?
30 What does it mean if an animal is homoiothermic?

Answers | Pot Luck 13 *(see Quiz 26)*

1 Reading (2005–06). 2 Plumber. 3 Vladimir and Estragon. 4 Syphilis. 5 Scotland.
6 1950s. 7 JJ Barrie. 8 Rocks. 9 Mozambique. 10 Comet. 11 The Agricultural Hall.
12 Scottish Euro 96 single. 13 A diesel engine. 14 Goat Island. 15 Richard Bacon. 16 Painting. 17 Mexico. 18 Bronze. 19 Gail Platt. 20 He was a horse. 21 Irving Berlin.
22 Belgium. 23 After childbirth. 24 By Jack Rosenthal. 25 Enemy Coast Ahead. 26 Michael Crawford. 27 James and John. 28 30 million. 29 Sean Kelly. 30 TLC.

1 Which English soccer club were the first to clock up 105 points in a season?

2 What was the trade of John Galliano's dad?

3 In the Beckett play which characters were Waiting for Godot?

4 Which disease is diagnosed by the Wasserman Test?

5 The King of Alba ruled in which country?

6 In which decade was Sting born?

7 Whose one and only hit was "No Charge" in 1976?

8 What does a petrologist study?

9 Which African country lies between the sea and Zimbabwe?

10 What are Temple-Tuttle and Kohoutek both types of?

11 In which London hall was England's first official showjumping event held in 1869?

12 Rod Stewart donated the royalties from which single to the Dunblane fund?

13 The ship Petit Pierre was the first to be driven by what in 1902?

14 Which island is in the middle of Niagara Falls?

15 Who was the first "Blue Peter" presenter to be sacked?

16 For what did John Singer Sargent achieve fame?

17 In which country is the majority of the Yucatan Peninsula?

18 The statue of Albert opposite the Albert Hall is made from what?

19 In "Corrie" who was Leanne Battersby's first mother-in-law?

20 Why was the Roman consul Incitatus unusual?

21 Who composed "God Bless America"?

22 Violinist Arthur Grumiaux came from which country?

23 When can a woman suffer puerperal fever?

24 What was Jack Rosenthal's autobiography called?

25 "The Dambusters" film was based on which book?

26 Who is the elder – Michael Crawford or Eric Clapton?

27 Which of Jesus' disciples were sons of Zebedee?

28 In a 2001 census what was Canada's population to the nearest million?

29 Who won the first cycling World Cup?

30 Rozonda Thomas was part of which top-selling girl group?

Answers	**Animal World** *(see Quiz 25)*

1 Vampire bat. 2 Blue whale. 3 One. 4 Capybara. 5 Algae which grow on it. 6 Mount Everest pika. 7 Exmoor ponies. 8 Bat. 9 Intestine. 10 Behind its eyes. 11 Bootlace worm. 12 On its skin. 13 Canine teeth. 14 Anywhere above ground. 15 Balaenoptera musculus. 16 Flemish horse. 17 Yellow. 18 Europe (bison). 19 Madagascar. 20 Maine coon. 21 Poisonous frog. 22 Couple of hours. 23 Collagen. 24 Tarsiers. 25 Herd reindeer. 26 Argentina. 27 Lemur. 28 Asian elephant. 29 Forehead horn. 30 Warm-blooded.

1 In which 60s film did Richard Attenborough sing?
2 Who became head of production at EMI in 1969?
3 Between which two cities is "The Great Race" set?
4 Who directed the Civil War sequences of "How the West was Won"?
5 Who was Camembert in "Carry On – Don't Lose Your Head"?
6 Who inspired the David Hemmings role in Antonioni's "Blow Up"?
7 What is unusual about Christopher Lee's terrifying role in "Dracula – Prince of Darkness"?
8 What was the sequel to "A Million Years BC"?
9 Who devised the dance routines in "Half a Sixpence"?
10 Who is the only American in "King Rat"?
11 Who was the Doctor in the big screen "Doctor Who and the Daleks"?
12 Which film classic inspired Billy Wilder to make "The Apartment"?
13 Who played Princess Dala in "The Pink Panther"?
14 Who took over directing "Cleopatra" mid way through production?
15 Who was the singing voice of Tony in "West Side Story"?
16 Who wrote the music for "Lawrence of Arabia"?
17 In which film of her father's did Anjelica Huston make her screen debut?
18 Which golf course featured in "Goldfinger"?
19 What was Tracy and Hepburn's final movie together?
20 Which pop star starred in "Rag Doll" in 1960?
21 Which '62 Best Actor studied medicine at the University of California?
22 Who was Oscar-nominated for Pasha in "Doctor Zhivago"?
23 Which 60s Oscar winner was narrated by Michael MacLiammoir?
24 Who killed Ronald Reagan in his last film "The Killers"?
25 Whom did John Wayne play in "North to Alaska"?
26 For which film did Elizabeth Taylor win her second Oscar?
27 For which role was Dustin Hoffman nominated in 1969?
28 Which of the Redgrave clan appeared in "A Man for All Seasons"?
29 Who played opposite then wife Claire Bloom in "The Illustrated Man"?
30 Who was the older winner of the shared Best Actress Oscar in 1968?

1 Which wine comes from Worms?
2 How is sake usually drunk?
3 In which Berkshire village is Heston Blumenthal's Fat Duck restaurant to be found?
4 What were angostura bitters originally used for?
5 In the US if a dessert is served "à la mode" what is served with it?
6 Which vegetable is a passata made from?
7 What shape is a rugelach?
8 What is chenin blanc wine known as in South Africa?
9 Which term describes the fermented grape juice added to wine that has lost its strength to perk it up?
10 If a wine is madeirised what has happened to it?
11 Where is Marsala, famed for its fortified wine?
12 In wine terms what is the difference between frizzante and spumante?
13 Which folded pizza dough dish takes its name from the Italian for trouser leg?
14 Which cereal is polenta made from?
15 How does Malaga wine achieve its dark colour?
16 In which London borough did Jamie Oliver's healthy school dinner campaign begin?
17 Where does Dao wine come from?
18 In addition to Sauternes itself which four communes can call their wine Sauternes?
19 Where did balti cooking originate?
20 Who was the winner of "Masterchef Goes Large" in the early part of 2006?
21 Other than Spain and Portugal where does sack come from?
22 What is a red biddy?
23 Which food is also called the vegetable oyster?
24 In wine making which term describes turning the bottles so the sediment collects at the cork end?
25 In which district of Bordeaux is Chateau Petrus produced?
26 What is pradikat?
27 Which classic French sauce was named after a courtier of Louis XIV?
28 What is the study of wine called?
29 Which chef created the Bombe Nero and the peche melba?
30 Which sweet rice wine is used in Japanese cookery?

Quiz 29 | Pot Luck 14

Answers – page 262

1 A zinfandel is used for making what?
2 What separates Alaska from the other 48 US states?
3 How many times is "Um" sung in the chorus of 60s hit "Um Um Um Um Um Um"?
4 Who was the conductor of the Berlin Philharmonic at the 2006 Proms?
5 On which island which is also a country is Adam's Peak?
6 In which year did London Underground's Bakerloo Line open?
7 Who won Best Actor Oscar for his part in the musical film "Amadeus"?
8 If you have comedos, what are you suffering from?
9 What is the third largest city in Britain?
10 Who is the elder – David Bowie or Edwina Currie?
11 What is Warwickshire's county motif?
12 Which former PM became President of the Czech Republic in 2003?
13 What kind of weapon was an arbalest?
14 Which Austrian physicist gave his name to perceived frequency variations under certain conditions?
15 Imran Khan played cricket for which two English counties?
16 What is the meaning of the legal expression "caveat emptor"?
17 Which optical aid was invented by Benjamin Franklin?
18 What was the Bay City Rollers' first UK Top Ten hit?
19 Where are the ethmoid, vomer and zygomatic bones in your body?
20 Who was Severus Snape when Robbie Coltrane was Rubeus Hagrid?
21 The capital of Japan is an anagram of which former capital?
22 Who rode both Toulon and Moonax to St Leger triumphs?
23 Who wrote "All Quiet on the Western Front"?
24 Where did John McGregor found the first Canoe Club in 1866?
25 What is the main colour on the cover of Celine Dion's album "Let's Talk About Love"?
26 Michael Jackson, Billie and Alicia Keyes have had different singles with which same title?
27 Which European country lost the battle of Ulm in 1805?
28 On TV, who was the victim in the first series of "The Murder Game"?
29 Which country has Guyana to the east and Colombia to the west?
30 How did Emiliano Zapata, the Mexican revolutionary, die in 1919?

Answers | Kings & Queens (see Quiz 30)

1 17 Bruton St, London. 2 King George V and Queen Mary. 3 Edward VII. 4 Adelaide. 5 George I. 6 Hit with a cricket ball. 7 George V. 8 Henry II's wife Eleanor of Aquitaine. 9 Edward I (19). 10 It was his second. 11 The Pope. 12 Dunfermline. 13 Square, she was so obese. 14 Richard II. 15 River Soar. 16 Tax collectors. 17 Charles II. 18 St Stephen's Abbey Caen. 19 Henry I. 20 Edward VIII. 21 George I. 22 William IV. 23 Edward VII. 24 Christian IX of Denmark. 25 William II. 26 Four. 27 Norfolk. 28 Two. 29 Jane Seymour & Catherine Parr. 30 Gloucester Cathedral.

1 At which address was Elizabeth II born?
2 Who were the parents of the subject of "The Lost Prince" by Stephen Poliakoff?
3 Who was the only British monarch from the House of Wettin?
4 Who was William IV's queen?
5 Which monarch's mother was Sophia of Bohemia?
6 How did George II's eldest son die?
7 Who was the first British monarch to make a Christmas Day broadcast?
8 Which English king's wife was a former wife of Louis VII of France?
9 Which British monarch produced the most legitimate children?
10 What was notable about Henry VI's coronation in 1470?
11 Who made Henry VIII Fidei Defensor?
12 Where was Charles I born?
13 What shape was Queen Anne's coffin and why?
14 Which English king is reputed to have invented the handkerchief?
15 Where were Richard III's bones thrown when his grave was desecrated?
16 Why was Henry VIII's execution of Richard Empson and Edmund Dudley a popular move?
17 Who was threatened by the Rye House Plot?
18 Where is William the Conqueror buried?
19 Which king founded the first English zoo?
20 Who was the penultimate Emperor of India?
21 The Duchess of Kendal was mistress of which king?
22 Who was the first monarch born in Buckingham Palace?
23 Who was the first Emperor of India?
24 Who was Edward VII's father-in-law?
25 Which English king was killed by Walter Tyrel?
26 How many English kings reigned in the first half of the twentieth century?
27 In which county did George V die?
28 How many shirts did Charles I wear for his execution?
29 Who were Henry VIII's two oldest wives?
30 Where was Henry III crowned?

Answers | Pot Luck 14 (see Quiz 29)

1 Wine. 2 British Columbia. 3 24. 4 Simon Rattle. 5 Sri Lanka. 6 1906. 7 F. Murray Abraham. 8 Blackheads. 9 Glasgow. 10 Edwina Currie. 11 A standing bear next to a ragged staff. 12 Vaclav Klaus. 13 A giant crossbow. 14 Christian Doppler. 15 Worcestershire and Sussex. 16 Let the buyer beware. 17 Bifocal lenses. 18 Keep On Dancing. 19 Skull. 20 Alan Rickman. 21 Kyoto. 22 Pat Eddery. 23 Erich Remarque. 24 Richmond, Surrey. 25 Black. 26 Girlfriend. 27 Austria. 28 Catherine Prior. 29 Venezuela. 30 Assassinated.

Quiz 31 | Pot Luck 15

1 Who directed the1930s film "Mr Deeds Goes to Town"?
2 Who was the first Spaniard to win the French Open in tennis this century?
3 Shogi is a Japanese form of which game?
4 Which ex-"EastEnders" actress tried to revive her career in "Reborn in the USA"?
5 Which bird would you find in a squab pie?
6 Who played the lead character in the film "The Loneliness of the Long Distance Runner"?
7 Whose fourth volume of memoirs was called "North Face of Soho"?
8 What was Rolf Harris' first UK Top Ten hit?
9 Which famous actor played Philo Beddoe in two films?
10 Whom did Australia beat when they first won cricket's World Cup?
11 What is the legendary ship The Flying Dutchman doomed to do?
12 Which queen of England had most fingers?
13 Who wrote the novel "Fair Stood the Wind for France"?
14 Who is the elder – Joan Collins or Michael Caine?
15 Whose one and only hit was "Eye Level" in 1973?
16 To three years, when did the M1 motorway open?
17 What was found in 1939 at Sutton Hoo, in Suffolk?
18 What is of interest to a thanatologist?
19 Where would you find calderas?
20 Who wrote the novel "The Lost World"?
21 If something is napiform which vegetable shape is it?
22 What part of the body is studied by a myologist?
23 Which song features the words, "Here am I floating round my tin can"?
24 What was the Triangular Trade mainly concerned with?
25 What, in America, is a cayuse?
26 How many strokes underwater may a competitive breast-stroke swimmer make at the start and turn?
27 The town of Carrara in Italy is famous for what?
28 Who wrote humour books naming Mussolini and Hitler in the titles?
29 McBride, Pemberton and Radzinski all played for Fulham and which other club?
30 The Battle of Antietam was in which war?

Quiz 32 | Classic No. 1s

1 Who were the first Scottish group to have three No. 1s?
2 Which 1955 American movie had "Unchained Melody" as theme tune?
3 Which No. 1 was the first solo single by George Harrison?
4 Which Elvis hit made him the first artist with three consecutive British No. 1s?
5 Which Rod Stewart hit was originally the B-side of "Reason to Believe"?
6 Who was on top of the charts the week Everest was first climbed?
7 Who featured on the first No. 1 for Michael Andrews?
8 What was the first No. 1 from the Beatles' second film "Help!"?
9 Who wrote Chicago's No. 1 classic "If You Leave Me Now"?
10 Which lyricist of Aznavour's "She" was a writer on "Les Mis"?
11 What was on the other side of the double A No. 1 "Mull of Kintyre"?
12 Who co-wrote a No. 1 duet song under the pseudonym Ann Orson?
13 What finally knocked "(Everything I Do) I Do It for You" off the No. 1 spot?
14 Which film did Frank Ifield's "I Remember You" originally come from?
15 What was the third UK No. 1 single for the Sugababes?
16 What became the all-time best-UK selling single by a female duo?
17 Which Doris Day Oscar-winning song was from "The Man Who Knew Too Much" in 1956?
18 What was the first Westlife No. 1 single with a one-word title?
19 Which No. 1 hit by the Beatles equalled 7 weeks at the top with "From Me to You"?
20 What is the only George Michael song for which Andrew Ridgeley takes equal writing credit?
21 Which album title track gave Simon and Garfunkel their biggest hit?
22 Which 1920s standard gave Concetta Franconero a 6-week No. 1 hit?
23 Which Commodores classic became Motown's best UK seller?
24 Who is the male half of the duo that have spent most weeks at No. 1?
25 Which single marked Madonna's 20-year span of having UK No. 1s?
26 Apart from "Cathy's Clown", which other No. 1 for the Everly Brothers had a girl's name in the title?
27 In 2000, who became the youngest male to write and perform a UK No. 1 single?
28 Which single was the first by a UK performer to top the US charts in the 1960s?
29 Which 1975 megahit remained at No. 1 for 9 weeks?
30 Which No. 1 hit was Cliff Richard's first million-seller?

1 What is Kyzyl Kum in Russia?
2 Neville Cardus was associated with which sport?
3 Who played Paul Henreid's wife in the film "Casablanca"?
4 Which "Simpsons" catchphrase was first to make the on-line version of Oxford English Dictionary?
5 Where did the Dryad nymphs live in Greek mythology?
6 What sort of creature is a killdeer?
7 What type of music is Ira D. Sankey particularly noted for composing?
8 How old was Louis Braille when he invented his reading system for the blind?
9 Which actor starred in the silent films "Robin Hood", "The Three Musketeers" and "The Black Pirate"?
10 What was Five Star's first UK Top Ten hit?
11 Ficus Elastica is the Latin name for which plant?
12 In which sport is there a bonspiel?
13 Arch, loop and whorl are all parts of what?
14 What is pishogue a form of?
15 Permission was given to whom in 1988 to rebuild London's Globe Theatre?
16 Which country has the internet code .at?
17 A fylfot is better known as a what?
18 Alton Byrd was famous in which sport?
19 Who played the magical Supergran in the 1985 TV series?
20 Which 1990s Oscar Best Film did Colin Firth appear in as well as "Shakespeare in Love"?
21 Which actor was "The Virginian" on TV?
22 Which band's albums include "Load" and "Reload"?
23 Richard Meade won Olympic gold in which sport?
24 What is the main difference between squash and rackets?
25 In which year was the CBI set up?
26 Whose first Top Ten hit was "House of Love"?
27 In what unusual type of location was the late, great Jack Lemmon born?
28 In which country did the UK first score a Eurovision Song Contest no points?
29 Who would use a trochee?
30 Who wrote the play called "A Taste of Honey"?

| **Answers** | Tony Blair *(see Quiz 34)* |

1 Lynton. 2 Durham. 3 Barrister. 4 Energy. 5 2005. 6 Thanet North. 7 Taurus. 8 179. 9 The Queen & Prince Philip. 10 On the Record. 11 Deirdre Rachid (Coronation Street). 12 Trade & Industry. 13 European monetary union. 14 30. 15 Lord Liverpool. 16 Respect. 17 Hazel. 18 Derry Irvine. 19 Islington. 20 Home Secretary. 21 1998. 22 Grp Capt. Al Lockwood. 23 Tuesday & Thursday. 24 Alastair Campbell. 25 Michael Sheen. 26 Roy Hattersley. 27 Margaret Beckett. 28 Gerhard Schröder. 29 St John's. 30 Edinburgh.

1 What is Tony Blair's third Christian name?
2 In which city was he brought up?
3 What was his father's profession?
4 What was his first Shadow Cabinet post?
5 In which year was Tony and Cherie's Silver Wedding anniversary?
6 Which constituency did Cherie contest in 1983?
7 Tony Blair was born under which star sign?
8 To five, how big was his Labour majority in the Commons in 1997?
9 In 1997 Blair hosted a "people's banquet" for which Golden Wedding couple?
10 On which TV programme did he say "I'm a pretty straight sort of guy"?
11 He appealed to the Home Secretary to help which soap character?
12 Which first Cabinet post did he give to Peter Mandelson?
13 In 1998 "The Sun" withdrew its support for Blair over which issue?
14 How old was he when he won his first Parliamentary seat?
15 In 1997 he became the youngest Prime Minister since whom?
16 Which R-word did he say would be an important part of his third term as PM?
17 What was his mother's first name?
18 Who was the head of Chambers where he met his future wife Cherie?
19 Where in London were the Blairs living when Tony became PM?
20 What was Blair's first shadow Cabinet post under John Smith?
21 In which year was the Belfast (or Good Friday) agreement signed?
22 Who finished second at Sedgefield in 2003?
23 When was Prime Minister's Question Time before Blair's changes?
24 Which Blair loyalist resigned in August 2003?
25 Who portrayed Tony Blair in the films "The Deal" and "The Queen"?
26 Who preceded him as Shadow Home Secretary?
27 Who was the leader of the Labour Party immediately before Blair?
28 Who succeeded him after his first term as chair of G8?
29 Which Oxford college did he attend?
30 In which city was he born?

Answers | Pot Luck 16 *(see Quiz 33)*

1 A desert. 2 Cricket. 3 Ingrid Bergman. 4 D'oh. 5 In trees. 6 A bird (type of plover). 7 Hymns. 8 15. 9 Douglas Fairbanks. 10 System Addict. 11 Rubber plant. 12 Curling. 13 Fingerprints. 14 Sorcery. 15 Sam Wanamaker. 16 Austria. 17 Swastika. 18 Basketball. 19 Gudrun Ure. 20 The English Patient. 21 James Drury. 22 Metallica. 23 3 Day Eventing. 24 Squash uses a softer ball. 25 1965. 26 East 17. 27 In a lift. 28 Latvia. 29 A poet. 30 Shelagh Delaney.

1 With which police identification system is Francis Galton associated?
2 Which trees mainly produced the fossilised resin which becomes amber?
3 In spring 2003, which actor celebrated 25 years in "Emmerdale"?
4 If a ship is careened, what has happened to it?
5 What did Henry Segrave break at Daytona in 1927 and 1929?
6 What was the Beautiful South's first UK Top Ten hit?
7 Which event is the first in a Decathlon?
8 Which US President died on the same day as Aldous Huxley?
9 When is Haley's Comet predicted to make its next visit in Earth's vicinity?
10 Who wrote the "Gormenghast Trilogy"?
11 In which county is Chequers?
12 The King of which country was the "Prisoner of Zenda"?
13 Who was the first jockey to record three consecutive Derby wins?
14 What relation to King Arthur was Mordred?
15 Who designed the first lightning conductor?
16 Iraq's prime minister Nuri al-Maliki is a member of which party?
17 What is matzo?
18 Which actor played Captain Bligh, Quasimodo and Henry VIII in films?
19 Which Archbishop of Canterbury was burnt at the stake in 1556?
20 Darren Huckerby made his soccer league debut with which club?
21 Which "Men Behaving Badly" star was in the original "Les Mis" chorus in the West End?
22 Who played King Arthur in "First Knight"?
23 Whose one and only hit was "Michelle" in 1966?
24 What can be grapnel, sheet and bower?
25 A trudgen is used in which sport?
26 Which river was first explored by Mungo Park, a Scottish surgeon?
27 To five years, when were Nobel Prizes first awarded?
28 In the poem "Beowulf", what kills Beowulf?
29 What would you do with a gigot?
30 The sitcom in which Warren Mitchell made his name took its title from which book?

| **Answers** | Golf *(see Quiz 36)* |

1 South Africa. 2 Gene Sarazen. 3 Gentleman Golfers of Edinburgh. 4 1967. 5 1989 PGA. 6 Nick Price. 7 John Jacobs. 8 Nick Faldo. 9 Greg Norman. 10 Japan. 11 Carnoustie. 12 Royal Lytham. 13 John Daly in 1991. 14 Worcester, Massachusetts. 15 Willie Park. 16 Bobby Jones (in perpetuity). 17 David Leadbetter. 18 Mark Calcavecchio. 19 Nick Faldo. 20 Walter Hagen. 21 20. 22 Troon. 23 The Walrus. 24 Seven. 25 British Open. 26 K-Club. 27 Twice. 28 Fred Couples. 29 Two shots. 30 Royal Portrush.

Quiz 36 | Golf

Answers – page 267

1 Who retained golf's Dunhill Cup in 1998?
2 Who was the first man to win the US PGA and the US Open in the same year?
3 What was the world's first golf club called?
4 In which year was the previous Hoylake Open before 2006?
5 What was Payne Stewart's first victory in a major?
6 In 1986 Greg Norman equalled whose record low score of 63 in the US Masters?
7 Whom did Tony Jacklin replace as Ryder Cup captain?
8 Who was only the second person after Jack Nicklaus to win two successive US Opens?
9 Who did Nick Faldo sensationally beat to win his third US Masters?
10 Padraig Harrington won the 2006 Dunlop Phoenix tournament in which country?
11 In 1968 what became the longest course ever used for the British Open?
12 Where did Tom Lehman win his first major?
13 When Steve Jones first won the US Open he was the first qualifier to win a Major since whom?
14 Where did the very first Ryder Cup take place?
15 Who won the first ever British Open?
16 Who is the President of Augusta National Golf Club?
17 Whom did Nick Faldo sack as his coach at the same time as divorcing wife number two?
18 Who was the last American to win the British Open before John Daly in 1995?
19 Who was the first European to win the US Masters in the 90s?
20 Who was the first US-born winner of the British Open?
21 How old was Nick Faldo when he was first in a Ryder Cup team?
22 Which golf course boasts a Postage Stamp?
23 What was Craig Stadler's nickname?
24 By how many strokes did Tony Jacklin win his first US Open?
25 Gary Player won all the Majors but which did he win first?
26 At which golf course was the 2006 Ryder Cup played?
27 How many times did Jack Nicklaus win the US Amateur title before turning pro?
28 Who was the first American to win the US Masters in the 90s?
29 Chris Di Marco finished how many shots behind the winner of the British Open 2006?
30 What is the only Irish course to have staged the British Open?

Answers	Pot Luck 17 *(see Quiz 35)*

1 Fingerprints. 2 Coniferous trees. 3 Stan Richards (Seth Armstrong). 4 Turned on one side for cleaning. 5 Land Speed record. 6 Song for Whoever. 7 100 metres. 8 JF Kennedy. 9 2061. 10 Mervyn Peake. 11 Buckinghamshire. 12 Ruritania. 13 Steve Donoghue. 14 Nephew. 15 Benjamin Franklin. 16 Dawa party. 17 Unleavened bread. 18 Charles Laughton. 19 Thomas Cranmer. 20 Lincoln City. 21 Caroline Quentin. 22 Sean Connery. 23 Overlanders. 24 Anchors. 25 Swimming. 26 River Niger. 27 1901. 28 A dragon. 29 Eat it. 30 The Book of Common Prayer.

1 What was discovered by Garcia Lopez de Cardenas in 1540?
2 Whose first Top Ten hit was titled "September"?
3 In the Seven Years War who were Britain's two allies?
4 On which label did Gorillaz first have a No. 1 album?
5 Who was the first player to score 100 points in a NBA basketball game?
6 Rose Louise Hovick achieved fame under what name?
7 Who is the father of Marsha Hunt's daughter Karis?
8 What is the final line in the film "Gone with the Wind"?
9 Which newspaper was featured in the TV series "Hot Metal"?
10 The gemstone ruby is associated with which month?
11 What is the name of Phil and Jill Archer's farm?
12 In 2003, was Taiwan's population estimated at around 23, 27 or 30 million?
13 Which comic actor's father was the deputy speaker of the Irish Parliament?
14 Where on your body are the Mounts of the Sun, Mercury and Venus?
15 Which fungal disease has the name Ceratostomella Ulmi?
16 Who created the cartoon character Colonel Blimp?
17 Where is the village of Skara Brae?
18 Who won the 1989 Best Actor Oscar for the film "My Left Foot"?
19 Who is the elder – Ian Botham or Jim Davidson?
20 Which actor played the title role in the TV series "Dear John"?
21 Whose theme was a No. 4 UK hit in 1959 for Elmer Bernstein?
22 If you are an encratic person, what do you possess?
23 Who said, "There never was a good war, nor a bad peace"?
24 David Beckham made his league debut on loan at which club?
25 Who wrote "The White Company"?
26 Which general was the youngest in the American Civil War?
27 Who was top scorer for Man Utd in 1997–98 and Man City in 2005–06?
28 With which profession is the organisation RIBA associated?
29 Who founded the record label Respond?
30 Who in 1632 painted "The Anatomy Lesson of Dr Tulip"?

Quiz 38 | Famous Celebs

Answers – page 269

1 Whose first husband was John Dunbar when she was 18?
2 In which year did Freddie Flintoff make his Test debut?
3 Who announced her engagement to Riccardo Mazzucchelli in 1995?
4 What did Tara Palmer Tomkinson use to hide her modesty when posing nude with three friends?
5 What relation is Camilla Parker Bowles to Edward VII's mistress Mrs Keppel?
6 Who was Mandy Smith's second husband?
7 Who owns the private zoos, Howletts and Port Lympne?
8 Which Tory MP did Maria-Bienvenida Perez Blanco marry?
9 Former deb Henrietta Tiarks became which Marchioness?
10 Which restaurant chain did Nigella Lawson's great great grandfather found?
11 Who was Duchess of York before Fergie?
12 Which star actor is dad to Dylan and Paris?
13 Heller Toren is the mother of which blonde celeb?
14 Which title did Raine have before she married the late Earl Spencer?
15 Whose Regency home is Ray Mill House in Wiltshire?
16 In 2001 who refused to take a book to his desert island on "Desert Island Discs"?
17 Who is famous for his "wifelets"?
18 Who is Watford Grammar School's most famous old girl?
19 Who was Mick Jagger's best man when he married Bianca?
20 What is Tiggy Legge-Bourke's real first name?
21 Whose debut album was titled "On the 6"?
22 Who wrote an autobiography entitled "Living the Dream"?
23 Who discovered Jean Shrimpton in the 60s?
24 Queen Noor of Jordan studied for what profession before her marriage?
25 Who was the first wife of the ninth Earl Spencer?
26 Whose husbands were Alexander McCorquodale then his cousin Hugh?
27 Who was the most famous daughter of Major Bruce Shand?
28 Who replaced Claudia Schiffer as the face of Chanel?
29 Who became Dior's chief designer in 1996?
30 Which model Hamilton co-founded the elephant charity Tusk Force?

Answers | Pot Luck 18 *(see Quiz 37)*

1 The Grand Canyon. 2 Earth, Wind & Fire. 3 Hanover and Prussia. 4 Parlophone. 5 Wilt Chamberlain. 6 Gypsy Rose Lee. 7 Mick Jagger. 8 "Tomorrow is another day." 9 Daily Crucible. 10 July. 11 Brookfield. 12 23 million. 13 Ardal O'Hanlon. 14 Your hand. 15 Dutch Elm Disease. 16 David Low. 17 The Orkneys. 18 Daniel Day-Lewis. 19 Jim Davidson. 20 Ralph Bates. 21 Staccato's Theme. 22 Self-control. 23 Benjamin Franklin. 24 Preston. 25 Sir Arthur Conan Doyle. 26 George A. Custer. 27 Andy Cole. 28 Architects. 29 Paul Weller. 30 Rembrandt.

1 Who died in the avalanche in Klosters in 1988 involving Prince Charles' party?

2 Who was chairman of the Joint Chiefs of Staff during the Gulf War?

3 How many hours are there in a fortnight?

4 Which modern-day explorer has Twisleton-Wykeham as part of his name?

5 What was S Club 7's first hit single with a one-word title?

6 Who was Elizabeth I's State Secretary from 1573 to 1590?

7 Edward Whymper is associated with which leisure activity?

8 What did alchemists call the imaginary object that would turn base metals to gold?

9 Nicanor Duarte Frutos became President of which South American country?

10 Who designed and built the world's first iron bridge?

11 Who took her "Toot Toot" into the pop charts in the 80s?

12 Who is the elder – Sean Bean or Daniel Day-Lewis?

13 What was Michel Platini's club when he was three times European Footballer of the Year?

14 On the Chinese calendar, what is the only bird?

15 Where are the Padang Highlands?

16 What are you if you are described as being an ectomorph?

17 Where did Indian ink originally come from?

18 Which Premiership keeper was ever-present during the period from 2001 to 2004?

19 Who was the first female to present the main news on BBC and ITV?

20 What bird was the symbol of Persia's monarchy from 1739 to 1979?

21 What is the metal zinc extracted from?

22 Which game uses the expression "J'adoube"?

23 In London what was the Tyburn?

24 Who attempted the programme of social reform called Fair Deal?

25 Where in England might you do a Furry Dance?

26 What are measured in hadal, abyssal and bathyl zones?

27 Which country has the internet code .lk?

28 The word Eskimo means the eaters of what?

29 If you were banting, what would you be doing?

30 What was the Michael Bolton's first UK Top Ten hit?

| **Answers** | JK Rowling *(see Quiz 40)* |

1 1965. 2 1987. 3 Exeter. 4 French. 5 Christopher Little. 6 Bloomsbury Children's Books. 7 London. 8 Peter Needham. 9 Jessica. 10 Sean Harris. 11 July. 12 On a train (from King's Cross). 13 Of. 14 Amnesty International. 15 The Grey Lady. 16 Chris Columbus. 17 Edinburgh. 18 The Daily Prophet. 19 Philospher. 20 Goblet of Fire. 21 Parselmouth. 22 Hermoine Granger. 23 Gryffindor. 24 Portugal. 25 Year Six. 26 James & Lily. 27 Wydean. 28 Quaffle. 29 Left. 30 Gilderoy Lockhart.

Quiz 40 | JK Rowling

Answers – page 271

1 In which year was JK Rowling born?
2 In which year was the first Harry Potter book published?
3 At which University did she study?
4 Although she wanted to study English what did she study?
5 Who became her literary agent?
6 Which publisher and which division of it published her first book?
7 Both of JK's parents came from which city?
8 Who worked on the Latin translation of "Philosopher's Stone"?
9 What was the name of JK's first daughter?
10 Whom is "Chamber of Secrets" dedicated to?
11 The second, third and fourth Harry Potter books were published in which month?
12 Where did her parents meet?
13 All titles begin "Harry Potter and the" what other word is in titles two to five?
14 JK worked for a while in London for which worldwide organisation?
15 Who is the resident ghost of Ravenclaw House?
16 Who first directed a Harry Potter movie – Chris Columbus or Mike Newell?
17 Which Scottish city did JK Rowling move to when teaching English?
18 Which national wizarding newspaper did JK create in her books?
19 Which word was changed to Sorceror in the title of a US edition?
20 Which novel starts with Harry going to the Quidditch World Cup?
21 What is JK's word for a wizard that can talk to snakes?
22 Which character did JK once think of giving the surname Puckle?
23 Which Hogwarts House did JK say she would like to have been in the most?
24 In which mainland European country did JK teach English?
25 Harry Potter is in which year at Hogwarts for "The Half-Blood Prince"?
26 What were the names of Harry's parents?
27 Which secondary school did JK Rowling attend?
28 What is the name of the red ball used for scoring in quidditch?
29 On the cover of "Order of the Phoenix" does the bird look to its left or right?
30 Which character is the only one that depicts someone JK Rowling knew?

Answers | Pot Luck 19 *(see Quiz 39)*

1 Major Hugh Lindsay. 2 Colin Powell. 3 336. 4 Sir Ranulph Fiennes. 5 Reach. 6 Sir Francis Walsingham. 7 Mountaineering. 8 Philosopher's Stone. 9 Paraguay. 10 Abraham Darby. 11 Denise La Salle. 12 Daniel Day-Lewis. 13 Juventus. 14 Cockerel. 15 Sumatra. 16 Thin. 17 China. 18 Shay Given (Newcastle). 19 Julia Somerville. 20 Peacock. 21 Sphalerite. 22 Chess. 23 A stream. 24 President Truman. 25 Helston, Cornwall. 26 Ocean depths. 27 Sri Lanka. 28 Raw Meat. 29 Dieting. 30 How am I Supposed to Live without You.

1 What is a line joining any two points on a curve called in geometry?
2 What was Suzi Quatro's first UK Top Ten hit?
3 Which battle is remembered in the USA in April on Patriots' Day?
4 Who directed the films "Marathon Man" and "Billy Liar"?
5 Who was the eldest son of Henry III?
6 Who preceded Douglas Hurd as Foreign Secretary?
7 Which part of the body is affected by chorea?
8 Who was William Shakespeare's mother?
9 Which celeb chef spent nine years as head chef at the Long Room at Lord's?
10 Who founded the Outward Bound Trust?
11 What is Jonny Wilkinson's middle name?
12 How old was Klaus Barbie when he was sentenced to life for wartime atrocities?
13 What would you do with a kaki?
14 What are Purple Laver and Devil's Apron types of?
15 Where would ichor supposedly have flowed?
16 Which singing twins were Hal and Herbert?
17 In the Bible, what did Job suffer with?
18 Which straits separate India from Sri Lanka?
19 Who referred to international financiers as "gnomes of Zurich"?
20 Who was the second oldest Goon?
21 What was author John Buchan's real title?
22 Which country do the Hausa people live in?
23 What was the name of Don Quixote's horse?
24 Who wrote the opera "The Love for Three Oranges"?
25 Christopher Nolan was a Whitbread Book of the Year winner with what?
26 Which fur comes from the coypu?
27 Who wrote the travelogue: "I come from Des Moines. Somebody had to"?
28 Who became Minister of Defence when Churchill became PM in 1940?
29 Which tennis No. 1 in both 2001 and 2002 came from Long Island, USA?
30 In Tarantino's directorial debut, Harvey Keitel was White – who was Orange?

Answers	Food & Drink *(see Quiz 42)*

1 Type of grape. 2 Buck's Club in London. 3 Doner kebab. 4 Belgium. 5 The Dorchester. 6 Caraway seeds. 7 Australia. 8 Salt cod. 9 John Tovey. 10 Chocolate. 11 Top (garnish). 12 Chile. 13 Ullage. 14 Madame Harel, a French farmer's wife. 15 Chocolate. 16 Greece. 17 Bucket. 18 VDQS. 19 Cinzano, apricot brandy & angostura bitters. 20 Butter made from coconut. 21 Maths. 22 Biscuit. 23 Asparagus. 24 Tarragon, chervil. 25 Plums. 26 Geese or ducks. 27 Lime juice. 28 Mixed green salad. 29 Kebab. 30 Filled tortilla or pancake.

1 What is hanepoot?
2 Who or what was Buck's Fizz named after?
3 Which snack's name comes from the Turkish for rotating?
4 Where is the yeastless beer faro made?
5 Where was Anton Mosimann's first position as chef in the UK?
6 Kummel is a Russian liqueur extracted from what?
7 The macadamia is native to where?
8 What is the main ingredient of a brandade?
9 Who opened the Miller Howe restaurant in 1971?
10 In his diary what did Pepys call "jucalette"?
11 Where in a dish would you put gremolata?
12 Which country has a wine-growing area called O'Higgins?
13 Which term indicates the amount of wine by which a container falls short of being full?
14 Who is credited with creating camembert cheese in about 1790?
15 What is the base of a florentine biscuit made from?
16 Where did malmsey wine originate?
17 Balti is the Indian word for what?
18 Which abbreviation indicates wine between the qualities of vin de pays and appellation contrôlée?
19 What are the ingredients of a Mr Callaghan?
20 What is cocose?
21 What did TV cook Sophie Grigson study at university?
22 In Swiss cooking what is a leckerli?
23 What is added to an omelette to make an omelette Argenteuil?
24 Which herbs are put in a béarnaise sauce?
25 Which fruit is used to make slivovitz?
26 Foie gras is the liver of which creatures?
27 In ceviche raw fish is marinated in what?
28 What is a mesclun?
29 A brochette is another name for what?
30 In Mexican cookery what is a quesadilla?

---

1 What was Sting's debut movie?
2 What was Justin Henry's surname in a 70s Oscar winner?
3 In which film does railwayman Cleavon Little become sheriff?
4 "That's Entertainment" was a compilation of clips from which studio?
5 Who played Siegfried to Simon Ward's James in "All Creatures Great and Small"?
6 Which music plays in the background in "10"?
7 What was Alan Parker's first feature film?
8 Who starred in and produced "The China Syndrome"?
9 What was Tom Selleck's first film, in 1970?
10 Who played Winston's father in "Young Winston"?
11 Whose was the disembodied voice narrating Agatha Christie's "And Then There were None"?
12 Who wrote the music for "Shaft"?
13 Who was the landlord of "10 Rillington Place"?
14 Who sang the title song in "The Aristocats"?
15 For the trailer of which Hitchcock film was the director seen floating in the Thames?
16 Stacy Keach starred in "Fat City" after who turned it down?
17 Who directed "Death Wish"?
18 Who was the first director to cast Goldie Hawn in a non-comedy film?
19 Whom did Jane Fonda play in "Julia"?
20 Why did Peter Finch not collect his Oscar for "Network"?
21 Whose music did Malcolm McDowell like in "A Clockwork Orange"?
22 Who was the only female Oscar winner for "One Flew Over the Cuckoo's Nest"?
23 Who played the editor of the Washington Post in "All the President's Men"?
24 Which club features in "Cabaret"?
25 Who played the brother in "The Railway Children"?
26 Who was Maid Marian opposite Sean Connery in "Robin and Marian"?
27 What was the first film in which Julie Christie and Warren Beatty starred together?
28 What was Peter Ustinov's first film as Hercule Poirot?
29 What was the sequel to "Love Story"?
30 Which film of a Frederick Forsyth novel starred Jon Voight?

Answers	Pot Luck 21 *(see Quiz 44)*

1 Anything (omnivore). 2 Bankers. 3 Areas of equal rainfall. 4 Maria (Seas). 5 Kingston, Ontario. 6 Paranoid. 7 Britain. 8 Dujail. 9 Bran. 10 Diphtheria. 11 Woody Harrelson. 12 Smoke it (It's a strong cigar). 13 Three. 14 The Go Between (LP Hartley). 15 Jonathan Ross. 16 White. 17 1920s. 18 Ethiopia. 19 The Hopman Cup, Perth, Australia. 20 Cuban Rebel Girls. 21 1930s. 22 Mike Myers. 23 Officer Barraclough. 24 Gamophobia. 25 Army of Me. 26 Janet Street-Porter. 27 A ship. 28 Euphemism. 29 Lynsey de Paul. 30 17 games (of 19).

1 What is eaten by a pantophagist?
2 Who were the Fuggers?
3 What do isohyet lines indicate on a map?
4 What are the dark, lowland plains on the moon known as?
5 Where, in 1855, is ice hockey thought to have originated?
6 What was the only UK Top Ten hit for the group Black Sabbath?
7 In which country was musician Leopold Stokowski born?
8 Saddam's death sentence in Nov. 2006 related to a massacre in which town?
9 What was the name of Fingal's dog in Gaelic legend?
10 The Schich Test can be used to test for which disease?
11 In the Oliver Stone film "Natural Born Killers", who played Mickey?
12 What do you do with a maduro?
13 How many albums had Eva Cassidy made before the top-selling "Songbird"?
14 Which novel starts "The past is a foreign country: they do things differently there"?
15 Which TV celeb advertised pizza with Caprice?
16 What is the main colour on the cover of the album "Spice"?
17 In which decade was Betty Boothroyd born?
18 Coptic Christians are found in Egypt and which one other country?
19 Which 1996 tennis tournament saw the debut of a fluorescent ball?
20 What was Errol Flynn's last film in 1959?
21 In which decade was playwright Sir Alan Ayckbourn born?
22 Which son of English parents was the voice of the Scottish ogre in "Shrek"?
23 Which part did Brian Wilde play in the TV series "Porridge"?
24 Which phobia describes a fear of marriage?
25 What was Bjork's first UK Top Ten hit from 1995?
26 Which female media personality has been President of the Ramblers Association?
27 What was a carrack?
28 What term describes using a gentler expression to soften a hard one?
29 Who is the elder – Lynsey de Paul or Noel Edmonds?
30 How many games had Chelsea won halfway through their 2005–06 season?

Answers | 70s Films *(see Quiz 43)*

1 Quadrophenia. 2 Kramer. 3 Blazing Saddles. 4 MGM. 5 Anthony Hopkins. 6 Ravel's Bolero. 7 Bugsy Malone. 8 Michael Douglas. 9 Myra Breckinridge. 10 Robert Shaw. 11 Orson Welles. 12 Isaac Hayes. 13 John Reginald Christie. 14 Maurice Chevalier. 15 Frenzy. 16 Marlon Brando. 17 Michael Winner. 18 Spielberg (The Sugarland Express). 19 Lilian Hellman. 20 He died shortly after it was made. 21 Beethoven. 22 Louise Fletcher. 23 Jason Robards. 24 The Kit Kat Club. 25 Gary Warren. 26 Audrey Hepburn. 27 McCabe and Mrs Miller. 28 Death on the Nile. 29 Oliver's Story. 30 The Odessa File.

1 In what year was the first "Monty Python" show broadcast?
2 Who was the female presenter of "Tiswas"?
3 What was the final view at the end of "Blackadder Goes Forth"?
4 Which future Oscar nominee played Samantha Briggs in "Dr Who"?
5 Who was the only female on the first "Top of the Pops"?
6 In which TV pub did Vince Hill find fame?
7 On "The Golden Shot" who famously always got her sums wrong?
8 Who was the housekeeper in "All Creatures Great and Small"?
9 Who was the first presenter of "World of Sport" on ITV?
10 What was the booby prize on "Crackerjack"?
11 Who were the trio in "Take Three Girls"?
12 Who had the role of George Starling written for him in 1963?
13 Who originally shared a flat with Sandra in "The Liver Birds"?
14 Which comedian starred as himself in the Northern town of Woodbridge?
15 Who played the shop treasurer in "The Rag Trade"?
16 The lead singer of Herman's Hermits played whose son on TV?
17 Who was the first Teenage Mutant Hero Turtle alphabetically?
18 Who played Yosser in "Boys from the Blackstuff"?
19 Who was doing the asking in "Ask the Family"?
20 Who frequently appeared as Nymphia in "Up Pompeii"?
21 Who starred as Charley Farley, partner of Piggy Malone?
22 Who was the author played by Elaine Stritch in "Two's Company"?
23 Which sitcom began with a one-off play called "The Offer"?
24 Who played Nancy Astor's husband in the 80s series "Nancy Astor"?
25 As which character did David Cassidy shoot to fame in the 70s?
26 In "My Wife Next Door" which sitcom doyenne played George's mother?
27 Who was the only person the horse Mr Ed would talk to?
28 Which character shot Alan Rickman to fame in "The Barchester Chronicles"?
29 In "Fawlty Towers", what was Polly's surname?
30 Which corporal in "M*A*S*H" took to wearing women's clothes in order to be discharged?

Quiz 46 | Pot Luck 22

1 Which ex-World Bank chief economist reported about global warming in 2006?

2 In which year did Channel 4 start to broadcast?

3 What was the Scavenger's Daughter used for in the 16th century?

4 What can be sornick, nainsook and samite?

5 Who wrote "Life Before Man" and "The Edible Woman"?

6 Which country launched a strike against Russia's fleet in 1904 at Port Arthur?

7 What is the collective name for a group of rhinoceroses?

8 Who created the character Doctor Finlay?

9 Which British-born Hollywood star has children called Rafferty, Iris and Rudy?

10 "The Flame Trees of Thika" was set in which country?

11 What was Boney M's first UK Top Ten hit from 1976?

12 What was the Derby Scheme of 1915?

13 Who wrote "A Farewell to Arms"?

14 Who is the elder – Dawn French or Jennifer Saunders?

15 What name was given to George Stephenson's first locomotive?

16 At which ceremony are coins of the realm tested?

17 Who was Britain's first Minister for the Arts in 1967?

18 Which Northern city was given the Latin name Pons Aelius?

19 In "The Politician's Wife" who played the adulterer opposite Juliet Stevenson?

20 When was Exchange & Mart first published?

21 Whom did Buddha marry before searching for enlightenment?

22 Alphabetically what is the last of the Chinese Zodiac signs?

23 Did Geoff Hurst's World Cup final shirt fetch around £50,000, £92,000 or £130,000 at auction?

24 What was the profession of the pneumatic tyre patentee John Dunlop?

25 What, on 3 December 1923, gave its first broadcast?

26 Whose final movie as Q was in "The World is not Enough"?

27 Which Lord headed the investigating committee into "sleaze" in public life in 1995?

28 Who said, "Don't point that beard at me: it might go off"?

29 If someone was Rolfing you, what would they be doing?

30 What ceased to be legal at midnight, December 31, 1960?

Answers | TV Gold *(see Quiz 45)*

1 1969. 2 Sally James. 3 A poppy field. 4 Pauline Collins. 5 Dusty Springfield. 6 Stars and Garters. 7 Anne Aston. 8 Mrs Edna Hall. 9 Eamonn Andrews. 10 Cabbage. 11 Kate, Avril & Victoria. 12 Richard Briers. 13 Dawn. 14 Harry Worth. 15 Sheila Hancock. 16 Len Fairclough's son in Corrie. 17 Donatello. 18 Bernard Hill. 19 Robert Robinson. 20 Barbara Windsor. 21 Ronnie Corbett. 22 Dorothy McNab. 23 Steptoe & Son. 24 Pierce Brosnan. 25 Keith Partridge. 26 Mollie Sugden. 27 Wilbur Post. 28 Obadiah Slope. 29 Sherman. 30 Maxwell Klinger.

Quiz 47 | Girl Power

Answers – page 280

1 What are Celine Dion's first two words on "My Heart Will Go On"?
2 Which artist became the first to achieve one million paid downloads in the US?
3 What did Geri write by her signature on the cover notes of "Spice"?
4 Which sisters gave Stock/Aitken/Waterman their first No. 1 hit?
5 In which year was Diana Ross's first UK solo Top Ten hit?
6 Which hit made Helen Shapiro the youngest British artist to reach No. 1?
7 Who sang female vocals on the Beautiful South's first No. 1?
8 Belinda Carlisle and Bonnie Tyler both covered which 1970 No. 1?
9 Who partnered Janet Jackson on her UK No. 3 hit "Scream"?
10 Who was the first British female soloist to have three chart No. 1 hits?
11 Whose first UK Top Ten hit as a solo artist was "Light of My Life"?
12 Which character was played by Kylie Minogue in "The Delinquents"?
13 What is Enya's full name?
14 Which Bananarama star went on to join Shakespear's Sister?
15 What was Madonna's first UK No. 1?
16 Whose first UK Top Ten hit was "Love Resurrection"?
17 When did Shirley Bassey first reach the UK Top Ten?
18 Formed in 1981, girl band The Colours charted under which name?
19 What was Dina Carroll's first solo Top Ten hit?
20 Jacqui O'Sullivan left which girl group before a 2005 chart comeback?
21 Which film featured the Eternal hit "Someday" in 1996?
22 Whose first UK Top Ten hit was "My One Temptation"?
23 Which UK No. 3 for Stacy Lattisaw was a No. 8 for Dannii Minogue?
24 Which lady recorded the original "Midnight Train To Georgia"?
25 Which lady was "Rockin' Around the Christmas Tree" in 1987?
26 Lisa Scott-Lee and Faye Tozer were members of which top-selling pop quintet?
27 What was Geri Halliwell's first single with a one-word title?
28 Which star singer was born on 9 August in New Jersey?
29 In which girl group did Heidi Range replace Siobhan Donaghy?
30 Who was the first solo female to enter the UK charts at No. 1?

Quiz 48 Pot Luck 23

Answers – page 279

1 How did Marie Curie's husband Pierre die?
2 Which group of people were once known as Millennial Dawnists?
3 In which decade was musician Mark Knopfler born?
4 What are you like if you are described as being saurian?
5 Who was the father of Enoch in the Bible?
6 Who created the character Tristram Shandy?
7 2004 Olympic medals in 100, 200 and 400m went to men from USA and which country?
8 In which country is there a political party called Likud?
9 What was Tammy Wynette's real first name?
10 Which part did Carl Weathers play in the Rocky movies?
11 Where is a howdah normally found?
12 Which Spaniard painted the picture "The Rokeby Venus"?
13 Which River mouth was discovered by Amerigo Vespucci in 1499?
14 In "Corrie", what was the late Mike Baldwin's middle name?
15 What did PT Barnum allegedly say is born every minute?
16 Richard Kuhn, Jutus Liebig and Harold Urey were famous in which scientific field?
17 Who was the first undisputed heavyweight world champion boxer to be European?
18 Who is the elder – Ben Elton or Harry Enfield?
19 Which Diane featured in the original cult movie "The Wicker Man"?
20 Horace Saussure made the first ascent of where in 1787?
21 Which title is traditionally given to the second son of the monarch?
22 What sort of food is Dunlop?
23 What is a cow's first milk after calving called?
24 Which country celebrates the National holiday, the "Day of the Dead"?
25 Who wrote "A Handful of Dust"?
26 What's Geri Halliwell's middle name?
27 The train the Cornish Riviera ran from where to where?
28 In the Second World War what did the Germans send out in "wolf packs"?
29 What was Bow Wow Wow's first UK Top Ten hit?
30 Who wrote the poems "Maud" and "Locksley Hall"?

Answers	Girl Power *(see Quiz 47)*

1 Every Night. 2 Gwen Stefani. 3 Girl Power. 4 Mel and Kim Appleby. 5 1970. 6 You Don't Know. 7 Briana Corrigan. 8 Freda Payne's Band of Gold. 9 Michael Jackson. 10 Sandie Shaw. 11 Louise. 12 Lola Lovell. 13 Eithne Ni Bhraonain. 14 Siobhan Fahey. 15 Into the Groove. 16 Alison Moyet. 17 1957. 18 The Bangles. 19 Don't be a Stranger. 20 Bananarama. 21 Hunchback of Notre Dame. 22 Mica Paris. 23 Jump to the Beat. 24 Cissy Houston. 25 Kim Wilde. 26 Steps. 27 Desire. 28 Whitney Houston. 29 Sugababes. 30 Mariah Carey.

1 Which Grand National winner was the first to be trained by a woman?
2 David Broome was the first British showjumping champion on which horse?
3 Who had his spot kick saved in the first FA Cup Final decided on penalties?
4 How many deliveries were sent down in the final innings of the 2005 Ashes?
5 Jesse Owens was part of which university team when he set his three world records?
6 Who was the second player to hit a maximum 36 runs off one over?
7 In which road in Oxford did Roger Bannister run his four-minute mile?
8 How many people witnessed Brazil's defeat by Uruguay in the 1950 World Cup Final?
9 Who was the first athlete to break 13 minutes for the 5,000m?
10 Who made Chris Boardman's winning bicycle in Barcelona?
11 Which famous pacemaker founded the London Marathon?
12 Which Grand National horse was the first to cross the line the year the race was abandoned?
13 By what score did Steve Davis lose the World Professional Championship Final in 1985?
14 Who was the first man to break one minute for 100m breaststroke in a 25m pool?
15 With whom did Steve Redgrave take the second of his four Olympic golds?
16 Which British man ran the fastest mile in the 1980s?
17 Why did Susan Brown make history in 1981?
18 Which was the last horse before Lammtarra in 1995 to win the classic triple?
19 How many times did Nadia Comaneci score a perfect 10 at Montreal in 1976?
20 To the nearest 10 minutes, how long did it take Brian Lara to score his record 501 against Durham in 1994?
21 Who caddied for Tiger Woods on his first US Masters victory?
22 How many races out of the 16 did Nigel Mansell win to become World Champion?
23 Who was the first player since WWII to score more than 30 goals in three consecutive seasons?
24 Where was Harvey Smith when he made his infamous V sign?
25 Whom did Virginia Wade beat to win her Wimbledon Singles title?
26 How many League games had Stanley Matthews played before his final match aged 50?
27 Seb Coe simultaneously held three world records, at which distances?
28 To the nearest 100 what were the odds against Frankie Dettorri's seven Ascot wins?
29 Who broke the 1500, 3000 and 5000m records in 1994?
30 Whom did Mike Tyson beat to become the youngest WBC champion?

Answers	Pot Luck 24 *(see Quiz 50)*

1 50. 2 Polio. 3 A plant. 4 Ted Haggard. 5 Roads. 6 Hobson – the butler/valet. 7 An ornamental hanging in a church. 8 Norwich. 9 Proof of Life. 10 Chris Evans. 11 Vanessa Redgrave. 12 A small barrel. 13 Eight. 14 Cliff Richard. 15 Insects. 16 Priests. 17 Four. 18 Win golf's British and US Opens. 19 Toni Braxton. 20 Harold Wilson. 21 29 February. 22 Donald Coggan. 23 Usher. 24 Pierce. 25 Parsec. 26 Sir Matt Busby. 27 A silken fabric. 28 Artillery. 29 Athenia. 30 1940s.

Quiz 50 | Pot Luck 24

Answers – page 281

LEVEL 3

1 How many chapters are in the book of Genesis in the Bible?
2 The Salk vaccine was developed against which disease?
3 What is a Venus's Looking Glass?
4 Which White House ally said he had been a "deceiver and a liar" in 2006?
5 What were constructed in the Highlands by General Wade in 1724?
6 What was the name of the John Gielgud character in the film "Arthur"?
7 What is a dossal?
8 At which club did Nigel Worthington replace Bryan Hamilton?
9 What was Meg Ryan filming as her marriage to Dennis Quaid hit the rocks?
10 Who is the elder – Chris Evans or Paul Gascoigne?
11 In the film "Isadora" who played the role of Isadora Duncan?
12 What is a barrico?
13 How many American colleges and universities are in the Ivy League?
14 Who played the lead role in the film "Take Me High"?
15 Cicada are types of what?
16 Who are in charge in a theocracy?
17 How many lines has a clerihew?
18 What was Patty Sheehan the first woman to do in the same year?
19 "Breathe Again" was the first UK Top Ten hit for which female vocalist?
20 Who had been Britain's youngest cabinet member before William Hague?
21 Frederick is born on which date in "The Pirates Of Penzance"?
22 Who was Archbishop of Canterbury from 1974 to 1980?
23 In 2004, who set a new US record 28 weeks on top of the single charts?
24 What was the name of the first baby born to contestants who met on "Big Brother"?
25 Which unit of measurement is equal to 3.2616 light years?
26 Which Man Utd manager appeared in a film called "Cup Fever"?
27 What was sendal?
28 What is a firearm called if it has a calibre over 20mm?
29 Which British liner was the first to be sunk by a U-boat on the first day of the Second World War?
30 In which decade was actor David Jason born?

Answers | **Sport Moments** (see Quiz 49)

1 Corbiere. 2 Beethoven. 3 Paul Scholes (in 2005). 4 Four. 5 Ohio State University. 6 Ravi Shastri. 7 Iffley Road. 8 200,000. 9 Said Aouita. 10 Lotus. 11 Chris Brasher (pacemaker for Bannister). 12 Esha Ness. 13 18-17. 14 Adrian Moorhouse. 15 Andrew Holmes. 16 Steve Cram. 17 First woman to take part in the boat race. 18 Mill Reef (1971). 19 Seven. 20 7hr 54 mins. 21 Mike "Fluff" Cowan. 22 Nine. 23 Alan Shearer. 24 Hickstead. 25 Betty Stove. 26 700. 27 800m, 1000m, 1500m. 28 25,095-1. 29 Noureddine Morceli. 30 Trevor Berbick.

282

Quiz 51 | 20th Century

Answers – page 284

LEVEL 3

1 What was the last ruling dynasty of China?
2 Which oil field blow-out caused an 8.2 million gallon spill in April 1977?
3 Who became Europe's youngest head of state at 28 in 1993?
4 Where was Archbishop Makarios exiled by the British in the mid-50s?
5 Which Deputy Ministerial post did Winnie Mandela hold in Nelson Mandela's first government?
6 Which German Chancellor achieved post-war reconciliation with France in the 50s and early 60s?
7 Who became the youngest ever member of the GLC in 1969?
8 Which political parties linked in the UK in the 80s to form the Alliance?
9 Which Middle East leaders were awarded the Nobel Peace Prize in 1994?
10 Which film studio released the first talking film?
11 In the Watergate scandal, who or what was CREEP?
12 Who was the third-longest-serving Pope in history?
13 Wembley Stadium was completed for which event?
14 Harold Wilson became Baron of where on his elevation to the peerage?
15 Which quotation from "Richard III" was used to describe the end of 1978 and beginning of 1979?
16 What was nicknamed 'The Flapper Vote' in 1928?
17 Who succeeded the Ayatollah Khomeini as political leader of Iran?
18 Who was the first president of an independent Mozambique?
19 J. Arthur Rank entered films in the 30s to promote which cause?
20 In 1987, what did the Tower Commission investigate in the US?
21 Where was the Recruit Scandal of 1988?
22 Which minister in Thatcher's government shared his name with Henry VIII's chaplain?
23 What did the initials of film company RKO stand for?
24 Whose gang did Al Capone's men massacre on Valentine's Day 1929?
25 A shortage of which commodity was a major issue in the 1998 Indian election?
26 At what number Cromwell Street did Rose and Fred West live?
27 King Michael abdicated which throne in 1947?
28 Whom did Jacques Santer replace as President of the European Commission?
29 The 1964 Rivonia Trial involved those opposed to what?
30 What was the name of Franco's fascist party in Spain?

Answers | Pot Luck 25 *(see Quiz 52)*

1 Josie Jump. **2** Dublin. **3** Bookbinding. **4** Nelson Mandela. **5** James Joyce. **6** New York. **7** The flying shuttle. **8** Ken Boothe. **9** Cultivation of plants without soil. **10** Charles II. **11** A whip. **12** Mark Twain. **13** Handsome. **14** Stalin. **15** The Zaire. **16** Four. **17** Horses. **18** Arizona. **19** 1940s. **20** The Victoria Falls. **21** A pine cone. **22** Troops. **23** Muirfield. **24** King Baudouin (Belgium). **25** Esther. **26** September. **27** Ground-hog Day. **28** End of the Road. **29** Sian Lloyd. **30** Salmon.

1 What is the name of the fitness instructor in "Balamory"?
2 In which city in 1882 were the Phoenix Park murders?
3 What is Roxburghe a style of?
4 Which world leader married Graca Machel in 1998?
5 Which writer died in Zurich after an operation for an ulcer in 1941?
6 Which city's underground has more stations than any other?
7 Which weaving invention was invented by John Kay?
8 Who was first to take "Everything I Own" to No. 1 ?
9 What is hydroponics?
10 The Rye House Plot of 1683 was aiming to assassinate which king?
11 What is a quirt?
12 Who wrote "A Connecticut Yankee in King Arthur's Court"?
13 The Christian name Kenneth derives from the Gaelic for what?
14 Which Soviet dictator died on the same day as composer Prokofiev?
15 What is the unit of currency in The People's Republic of Congo?
16 How many No. 1 albums did Take That have?
17 Which animals can suffer the disease strangles?
18 Janet Leigh's car was registered in which American state in "Psycho"?
19 In which decade was Gloria Hunniford born?
20 What were discovered by David Livingstone in 1855?
21 What is a strobilus another name for?
22 The name Commandos comes from an Afrikaans word for what?
23 Where did Nick Faldo win his first British Open?
24 Which European King died in 1993?
25 Which Biblical woman is the Jewish festival Purim a celebration to?
26 In which month is Prince Harry's birthday?
27 In America what is 2 February called?
28 What was Boyz II Men's first UK Top Ten hit?
29 Which woman had the shortest name in the first two series of "I'm a Celebrity"?
30 Grilse, Alevins and Kelts are all forms of what?

---

1 Phi Phi Island is a popular holiday destination in which country?
2 Which eating house did Ruthie Rogers found?
3 Which soccer board game was launched by Terry Venables?
4 For what game is the Camrose Trophy awarded?
5 Who founded the Harlem Globetrotters?
6 How many tiles are there in a game of mah-jong?
7 Who designs clothes for younger people under the Emporio label?
8 What type of art was known as Jugenstil in Germany?
9 How long is the rope in water skiing?
10 In the early days of cinema how long would a "two reeler" last?
11 Serigraphy is also known as what?
12 What name is given to the style of skiing on a single broad ski?
13 Which type of outdoor spectacular was created by Paul Houdin and first shown at the Chateau de Chambord in 1952?
14 Which craft takes its name from the Arabic for "striped cloth"?
15 Where did canasta originate?
16 What are the two winning numbers made with two dice in craps?
17 Who opened Les Quat' Saisons in 1977?
18 If you follow FINA rules which sport do you practise?
19 How many dominoes are there in a double six set?
20 Southampton boast of having the first sports area of what type in the country?
21 Which sport would interest you if you followed the work of the ACS?
22 Ellem in Scotland is the oldest club of what type?
23 In the Role-Playing Game known as D&D, what does the second D stand for?
24 Where do cycle races called criteriums take place?
25 If you spent your leisure time in a sulky where would you be?
26 If you were spelunking in the US what would you be doing?
27 In 1976 the NBA and the ABA merged in which sport?
28 In sepek takrow you can hit the ball with any part of the body except which?
29 General Choi Hong Hi is responsible for the development of which martial art?
30 What position does the canoeist adopt in Canadian canoeing?

Quiz 54 | Pot Luck 26

Answers – page 285

1 Who composed the opera "The Bartered Bride"?
2 Who won the 1972 Olympic pentathlon title?
3 Paul Seaton was the first UK male to be European champion in what?
4 How old was Henry III when he became King?
5 Who said, "I look upon the world as my parish"?
6 In which performing art was Beryl Grey famous?
7 Where in Egypt did Cleopatra's needle originally stand?
8 The Silk Road ancient trade route ran between China and where?
9 Micky Finn played bongos in which pop group?
10 What is Sylvester Stallone's middle name?
11 Deuteroscopy is the common name for what?
12 Which actor links "Awakenings", "Toys" and "Cadillac Man"?
13 Who was the first admiral to pass through the Northwest Passage?
14 Who is the elder – Nicholas Lyndhurst or Gary Lineker?
15 Daniel Ortega was President of which country from 1981–90?
16 Where was the Encyclopaedia Britannica first published?
17 Why is Chinge Hall in Lancashire famous?
18 What name is given to the Runic alphabet?
19 What are affected by nystagmus?
20 What was Bobby Brown's first UK Top Ten hit?
21 Where were Frost Fairs held in London until 1831?
22 Which illustrator created the girls of St Trinians?
23 Which Premiership side featured D. Mills and M. Mills in 2005–06?
24 Which creature is represented in the year the Chinese call "ma"?
25 In which decade was pop superstar Mick Hucknall born?
26 Crockford's is a register of what?
27 Italy and Germany formed a military alliance in 1939 called what?
28 In the 2003 "Forsyte Saga", who played the role made famous by Kenneth More?
29 What is Dusty Springfield's real name?
30 What's the English name of the constellation Vulpecula?

Answers | Hobbies 1 *(see Quiz 53)*

1 Thailand. 2 River Cafe. 3 The Manager. 4 Bridge. 5 Abraham Saperstein. 6 144.
7 Armani. 8 Art Nouveau. 9 23m or 75 feet. 10 20 minutes. 11 Silk screen printing.
12 Monoboarding. 13 Son et lumière. 14 Macramé. 15 Uruguay. 16 7 & 11. 17
Raymond Blanc. 18 Swimming. 19 28. 20 Bowling green. 21 Cricket. 22 Angling.
23 Dragons. 24 Town or city centres. 25 Small cart in harness racing. 26 Potholing.
27 Basketball. 28 Arms and hands. 29 Taekwondo. 30 Kneeling.

1 In whose stately home was the Tarzan film "Greystoke" filmed?
2 What was Sharon Stone's first film, in 1980?
3 "Uncle Buck" was the debut of which movie star?
4 May Day was the Bond girl in which film?
5 What was the occupation of Madame Sousatzka in the Shirley Maclaine film?
6 Who had a lead role in the movie version of "Rising Damp" who wasn't in the TV sitcom?
7 Whom did Alan Rickman play in "Die Hard"?
8 Who are the two letter writers in "84 Charing Cross Road"?
9 Which son of a pop star appears as Jackson's friend in "Moonwalker"?
10 In which film did Jack Nicholson say the catchphrase "Here's Johnny"?
11 Who played Mrs La Motta in "Raging Bull"?
12 Which film all but bankrupted United Artists in 1980?
13 Which ailing actor's voice was dubbed by Rich Little in "Curse of the Pink Panther"?
14 Who played Meryl Streep's eccentric friend in "Plenty"?
15 Who won an Oscar for his first major role in 1982?
16 Who was Glenn Close's character in "Dangerous Liaisons"?
17 Which film included the song "It Might be You"?
18 Who was the only Cambodian Oscar winner of the 80s?
19 Who was the only winner of an Oscar and a BAFTA for "Platoon"?
20 Who was nominated as Best Supporting Actress for "The Color Purple"?
21 In the film "A Royal Love Story", who played Princess Diana?
22 "The Color of Money" re-created the character from which film?
23 Which father and son appeared in "Wall Street"?
24 Which role did Kevin Kline play in "A Fish Called Wanda"?
25 Which presidential candidate's cousin won an Oscar for "Moonstruck"?
26 Apart from Music and Visual Effects, which other Oscar did "E.T." win?
27 Who directed "Psycho III"?
28 Whose music features on the soundtrack of "When Harry Met Sally"?
29 Whose novel was Warren Beatty's "Reds" based on?
30 Who was the aerobics instructor in "Perfect"?

Answers | TV Times 1 *(see Quiz 56)*

1 Prince Edward. 2 Fiona Armstrong & Michael Wilson. 3 Blunder. 4 Bob Dylan. 5 Urquhart in House of Cards. 6 French & Saunders. 7 Greta Scacchi. 8 Tumbledown. 9 Frank Skinner. 10 Tony Hart. 11 Tutti Frutti & Fortunes of War. 12 First newsreader to be seen. 13 Ethel Merman. 14 Jack Lemmon. 15 Helen Hewitt. 16 Richard Branson. 17 Jean Marsh. 18 Clive Anderson. 19 Faith, Hope & Charity. 20 Mike Ahearne. 21 Alan Clark. 22 The Dead Good Show. 23 Phelan. 24 Westward. 25 Jimmy McGovern. 26 Hotel. 27 Lynne Franks. 28 Alec Baldwin. 29 Timothy Dalton. 30 Frank Muir.

1 Who set up the production company Ardent?
2 Which duo first presented the breakfast show on GMTV?
3 The characters Colonel Rudd and Franco Franco appeared in which 2006 sketch show?
4 Which legendary writer penned the song that became the "Ab Fab" theme?
5 Which character said, "You might very well think that, but I couldn't possibly comment"?
6 Who originally appeared in cabaret as the Menopause Sisters?
7 Who had a small role in "Bergerac" before starring in "Heat and Dust"?
8 Which play told of Falklands casualty Robert Lawrence?
9 How is comedian Chris Collins better known?
10 Who designed the original "Blue Peter" logo?
11 For which two series did Emma Thompson win best actress BAFTAs two years in succession?
12 Which BBC first will Kenneth Kendall always retain?
13 Which Hollywood actress played Lola Lasagne in "Batman"?
14 Who was Frank Ormand, the Pretzel man in "The Simpsons"?
15 What was the prison chief called in "The Governor"?
16 Which British entrepreneur once guested on "Friends"?
17 Who played Joanna in "Dr Who" and was the wife of a future Doctor?
18 Who said to Lord Archer, "There's no beginning to your talents, Jeffrey"?
19 Which pop band was Dani Behr a member of before her TV career?
20 What was Gladiator Warrior's real name?
21 Who wrote and presented a "History of the Tory Party"?
22 On which show did Caroline Aherne develop her Mrs Merton character?
23 Which brothers were played by the McGanns in "The Hanging Gale"?
24 Which TV company was founded by Peter Cadbury?
25 Who wrote the controversial series "The Lakes"?
26 In which series did Eileen Downey find fame?
27 "Ab Fab"'s Edina was based on which PR lady?
28 Who became narrator for "Thomas the Tank Engine" in the US in 1998?
29 Who played Rhett Butler in the TV sequel to "Gone with the Wind"?
30 A comedy writing award was introduced in 1998 in whose memory?

Answers | 80s Films *(see Quiz 55)*

1 Duke of Roxburghe's. 2 Stardust Memories. 3 Macaulay Culkin. 4 A View to a Kill. 5 Piano teacher. 6 Denholm Elliott. 7 Hans Gruber. 8 Helene Hanff & Frank Doel. 9 Sean Lennon. 10 The Shining. 11 Cathy Moriarty. 12 Heaven's Gate. 13 David Niven. 14 Tracey Ullman. 15 Ben Kingsley. 16 Marquise de Merteuil. 17 Tootsie. 18 Haing S. Ngor. 19 Oliver Stone. 20 Oprah Winfrey. 21 Catherine Oxenberg. 22 The Hustler. 23 Martin & Charlie Sheen. 24 Otto. 25 Olympia Dukakis. 26 Sound. 27 Anthony Perkins. 28 Harry Connick Jr. 29 John Reed's. 30 Jamie Lee Curtis.

1 In Oct. 2005, which UK politician travelled with Condoleezza Rice to her home state?
2 What was Brotherhood of Man's first UK Top Ten hit?
3 In which county did the battle of Edgehill take place?
4 Which country does chart-topping Eric Prydz come from?
5 In which decade was TV presenter Eamonn Holmes born?
6 Which theatre foundations were discovered in London in 1988?
7 Who was lead in the films "Man of the Moment" and "The Square Peg"?
8 Who became England cricket captain to replace Graham Gooch?
9 Which actor won Best Actor Oscar for "On Golden Pond" aged 76?
10 How many countries surround Botswana?
11 Barbara Trentham was the second wife of which English comic?
12 What is Bordeaux Mixture a blend of?
13 Which Spanish artist painted "The Persistence of Memory"?
14 Which film was remade as "Dirty Rotten Scoundrels"?
15 What is the middle name of knighted cricketer Gary Sobers?
16 What was Greta Garbo's last film?
17 The WWSU is the governing body of which sport?
18 What mass is measured in Criths?
19 In which city is the Verrazano Narrows Bridge?
20 Which profession did George Washington start out in?
21 To five, how many Premiership goals did Ruud van Nistelrooy score for Man, Utd?
22 Which country celebrates the crayfish with a party in August?
23 What was the title of the only UK Top Ten hit for James Brown?
24 Who is the elder – Joanna Lumley or Maureen Lipman?
25 What does the abbreviation 'fz' mean in music?
26 Spaniard Francisco Pizarro founded which city?
27 When was the magazine Cosmopolitan first published?
28 Which city was the first to erect a monument to Lord Nelson in Britain?
29 What was Angel Beast an old type of?
30 What is the county emblem of Lincolnshire?

Answers | Euro Tour *(see Quiz 58)*

1 Brenner's Park Hotel. 2 Romania. 3 Tbilisi. 4 Vienna. 5 Gulf of Riga. 6 Brussels. 7 Austria. 8 Koper. 9 Italy. 10 Baltic. 11 Netherlands. 12 Estonia. 13 Gulf of Finland. 14 Great Britain. 15 Mount Etna and Stromboli. 16 Grande Dizence in Switzerland. 17 Finland. 18 London. 19 Germany. 20 Liechtenstein. 21 Ormeli in Norway. 22 Belarus. 23 Assisi in Central Italy. 24 Germany. 25 Italy. 26 Roman Catholic. 27 Corfu. 28 Tourism and tobacco. 29 Spain. 30 Norway.

1 Which German hotel was home to the England WAGS during the 2006 World Cup?

2 Tarom Airlines are based in which country?

3 What is the capital of Georgia?

4 Which capital is further North – Budapest or Vienna?

5 Which Gulf is to the west of Estonia and Latvia?

6 Where is the news agency Centre d'Information Presse based?

7 In which country is Kranebitten International airport?

8 What is the chief port of Slovenia?

9 The Pelagian islands belong to which European country?

10 Bornholm is an island in which Sea?

11 Hoge Veluwe National Park is in which country?

12 Which European country has the internet code .ee?

13 St Petersburg is at the head of which gulf?

14 What is the largest island in Europe?

15 Which two Italian volcanoes erupted in 1994?

16 What is the world's highest dam?

17 Which country is called Suomen Tasavalta in its own language?

18 Which capital is further North – Berlin or London?

19 Aero Lloyd Airlines are based in which country?

20 Which European country has the highest life expectancy for men and women?

21 What is the highest waterfall in Europe?

22 Brest is a major town in which country other than France?

23 In which town did an earthquake claim nine lives in 1997?

24 In which country is the city of Bochum?

25 To which country do the islands of Stromboli and Vulcano belong?

26 What is the prominent religion of Lithuania?

27 Which is the northernmost and second largest of the Ionian islands?

28 What are Andorra's two main industries?

29 In which country is Sondica International airport?

30 Hardangervidda National Park is in which country?

Answers	Pot Luck 27 *(see Quiz 57)*

1 Jack Straw. 2 United We Stand. 3 Warwickshire. 4 Sweden. 5 1950s. 6 The Rose Theatre. 7 Norman Wisdom. 8 Mike Atherton. 9 Henry Fonda. 10 Five. 11 John Cleese. 12 Insecticide. 13 Dali. 14 Bedtime Story. 15 St Aubrun. 16 Two-Faced Woman. 17 Water skiing. 18 Mass of gases. 19 New York. 20 A surveyor. 21 95 goals. 22 Sweden. 23 Living in America. 24 Joanna Lumley. 25 Accented (Forzato). 26 Lima. 27 1972. 28 Glasgow. 29 A card game. 30 An imp.

1 What is No in Japan?
2 Who is the elder – David Mellor or Andrew Lloyd Webber?
3 What is a tulwar?
4 Who, with Paul McCartney, composed the "Liverpool Oratorio"?
5 What were Charles Dickens' two middle names?
6 Which team was the first to top the 50 points mark in a Super Bowl final?
7 In which city is Fettes College?
8 Where was the cloth used to make duffle coats first made?
9 On May 21, 1927, who landed at Le Bourget airport?
10 Where did Joseph of Arimathea's staff take root and bud, in legend?
11 Which song did Frank Sinatra feature in the film "Robin and the Seven Hoods"?
12 What is a skimmer to an American?
13 What name is given to the Greek letter that is the equivalent of letter O?
14 Which gulf is between the heel and sole of Italy?
15 Which famous leader brought an end to the Pharaohs in Egypt?
16 Which HG Wells novel is the musical "Half a Sixpence" based on?
17 To ten years, when was the magazine The Economist founded?
18 What is the final event in a Decathlon?
19 Which of the Manic Street Preachers was officially declared dead in 2002?
20 What was Mariah Carey's first UK Top Ten hit?
21 Which doctor played by Richard Wilson appeared in "Only When I Laugh"?
22 Who was the first wicket keeper to claim 50 stumping victims in Tests?
23 Which elegant white villa dating from the eighteenth century is situated on Hampstead Heath?
24 On which island is Bungee jumping said to have originated?
25 What were the Christian names of the showman Barnum?
26 To three years, in which year did Audrey Hepburn die?
27 Whose one and only hit was "Little Things Mean a Lot" in 1954?
28 Which monarch introduced the sedan chair into England?
29 What physical property lets a needle float on water?
30 Which country has the internet code .ua?

Answers | The Royals (see Quiz 60)

1 Anthropology. 2 Sir Robert Fellowes. 3 Marie Christine von Reibnitz. 4 Victoria Cross Heroes. 5 Viscount Linley. 6 Marina Olgivy. 7 Geelong Grammar. 8 Sports Science. 9 The Queen Mother. 10 Duke of Roxburghe. 11 Dame Kiri Te Kanawa. 12 Techno. 13 The Duke of Kent. 14 Diana. 15 Princess Margaret. 16 Eight. 17 Diana, Fergie. 18 Young England. 19 His wedding day. 20 Elizabeth Arden. 21 Les Jolies Eaux. 22 Barbara Daly. 23 The Rottweiler. 24 Sir George Pinker. 25 Ludgrove. 26 To ease traffic congestion. 27 Pulled the coach. 28 Martin Bashir. 29 Andrew and Alice. 30 Page boy to Fergie.

Quiz 60 The Royals

Answers – page 291

1 Along with Archaeology, which subject did Prince Edward read at Cambridge?
2 Who became the Queen's Private Secretary in 1990?
3 What was Princess Michael of Kent's maiden name?
4 In 2006 Prince Charles presented a TV series about what kind of heroes?
5 Which Royal had a financial interest in a chain of hamburger restaurants called Deal?
6 Who was the first unmarried Royal to announce her pregnancy in 1989?
7 Which school was attended by Prince Charles and Kerry Packer?
8 What did Peter Phillips study at Exeter University?
9 Who was portrayed as a school dinner lady on "Spitting Image"?
10 At whose home did Prince Andrew propose to Sarah Ferguson?
11 Who sang a Handel aria at Charles and Diana's wedding?
12 In a 16th birthday interview what type of music did Prince William say he preferred?
13 Who had the car registration plate K7?
14 Who was the first Royal bride to include her own family's coat of arms on her marital coat of arms?
15 Who retained the number plate 3 GXM for a new Rolls in 1972?
16 How many Princesses of Wales were there before Diana?
17 Who turned up with Pamela Stephenson at Annabel's on Prince Andrew's stag night dressed as police officers?
18 At which kindergarten did Diana Spencer work?
19 When did Prince Philip become Duke of Edinburgh?
20 The Duchess of Windsor employed a make-up artist daily from which cosmetics house?
21 What was Princess Margaret's house on Mustique called?
22 Who did Diana's make-up on her wedding day?
23 What was Diana's nickname for Camilla?
24 Who delivered Prince William?
25 What was William and Harry's first boarding school?
26 Why did the Queen change the Birthday Parade from Thursday to Saturday?
27 What part did Lady Penelope and St David play at Charles and Diana's wedding?
28 To which reporter did Diana admit her marriage was "a bit crowded"?
29 What were Prince Philip's parents called?
30 What was Prince William's first public duty?

Answers	Pot Luck 28 *(see Quiz 59)*

1 A type of theatre. 2 Lord Lloyd Webber. 3 A sword. 4 Carl Davis. 5 John Huffham. 6 San Francisco 49ers. 7 Edinburgh. 8 Duffel in Belgium. 9 Charles Lindbergh. 10 Glastonbury. 11 My Kind Of Town. 12 A straw hat. 13 Omicron. 14 Gulf of Taranto. 15 Alexander the Great. 16 Kipps. 17 1843. 18 1500 metres. 19 Richie Edwards. 20 Vision of Love. 21 Dr Thorpe. 22 Bert Oldfield (Australia). 23 Kenwood House. 24 Pentecost Island. 25 Phileas Taylor. 26 1993. 27 Kitty Kallen. 28 James I. 29 Surface tension. 30 Ukraine.

1 The discovery of which plot led to the death of Mary, Queen of Scots?

2 Who was England captain for Sven-Goran Eriksson's first game?

3 Which Duke commanded the English troops at Culloden?

4 Which letter is one dot and one dash in Morse Code?

5 Which Minister was murdered in 1990 outside his home by an IRA bomb?

6 Which Battle was the first in the Hundred Years War?

7 What is served at a Thyestean feast?

8 Who wrote "Goodbye to All That"?

9 Adam Faith's last TV drama role was in which occasional BBC series?

10 James Last was in the album charts this century playing music by which group?

11 Who is the elder – Desmond Lynam or Sir Paul McCartney?

12 In which year did Francis Drake complete the circumnavigation of the world?

13 How do you travel on the Devizes–Westminster race?

14 How old were both Anne Boleyn and Mrs Beeton when they died?

15 Who composed "Easter Parade"?

16 Which country gained independence in 1908 from Turkey?

17 What is the opening track on the Verve's "Urban Hymns"?

18 Which hymn was written by Augustus Toplady after sheltering from a storm?

19 In which decade was William Hague born?

20 Who wrote Dr Johnson's biography?

21 Who is the only English monarch to have won a flat race as a jockey?

22 Mary II died of which disease at the age of 32?

23 Whose only UK hit was "Patches"?

24 Marlon Brando, Clark Gable and Mel Gibson have all played which role?

25 Which drill gets women and children into lifeboats first?

26 Which greyhound was the first to win the Greyhound Derby twice?

27 The Sea of Marmara lies between the Bosporus and what?

28 Who designed The Monument in London?

29 Which scale other than the Richter scale measures earthquakes?

30 How many singles peaked at No. 2 for Elvis in his "comeback" year 2005?

Answers | Oldies & Goldies *(see Quiz 62)*

1 (How Much is) That Doggie in the Window? 2 Amazing Grace. 3 Oh Pretty Woman. 4 Honky Tonk. 5 I'm not in Love. 6 Rosemary Clooney. 7 If you're going. 8 So Gay. 9 Spirit in the Sky. 10 Little Jimmy Osmond. 11 I Can't Stop Loving You. 12 Terry Jacks. 13 Lily the Pink. 14 Adam Faith. 15 My Ding-a-Ling. 16 1973. 17 Needles and Pins. 18 Tab Hunter. 19 Lee Hazelwood. 20 Johnny Remember Me. 21 Jerry Keller. 22 Roy Wood. 23 Moon River. 24 The Good, the Bad and the Ugly. 25 Sunny Afternoon. 26 The Next Time/Bachelor Boy. 27 What a Wonderful World. 28 Land. 29 Zager & Evans. 30 You're My World.

Quiz 62 Oldies & Goldies

Answers – page 293

LEVEL 3

1 What was the first UK No. 1 in which the title posed a question?
2 Which traditional song provided instrumental and vocal versions that charted for 94 weeks?
3 What was Roy Orbison's final chart topper from 1964?
4 Which "Women" was the longest ever at No. 1 for the Rolling Stones?
5 Graham Gouldman and Eric Stewart wrote which 70s classic No. 1?
6 Which 1950s vocalist began singing with the Tony Pastor band?
7 What are the first three words of "San Francisco"?
8 How were the birds singing in the original title of the No. 1 "Why Do Fools Fall in Love"?
9 Which 1986 No. 1 was a cover of a 1970 No. 1?
10 Which artist took over the title of the youngest No. 1 hitmaker in 1972?
11 What is Ray Charles' only UK No. 1?
12 Which Canadian was next to No. 1 after Paul Anka?
13 Which hit gave producer Norrie Paramour his 27th and final No. 1?
14 Emile Ford shared his first week at No. 1 with which artist?
15 Which Chuck Berry hit was No. 1 at the same time in the UK and US?
16 Steve Miller's "The Joker" hit No. 1 in 1990 but when was it recorded?
17 Which hit gave The Searchers their second No. 1?
18 Who had a No. 1 with the original version of "Young Love"?
19 Who wrote and produced Nancy Sinatra's "These Boots are Made for Walking"?
20 Which John Leyton hit was covered in 1985 by Bronski Beat and Marc Almond?
21 Whose only UK hit was "Here Comes Summer"?
22 Who wrote "See My Baby Jive"?
23 What film theme gave Danny Williams his only No. 1 in 1961?
24 What was the first instrumental No. 1 after the Shadows' "Foot Tapper"?
25 What was the Kinks' third and final No. 1 hit in the summer of 1966?
26 What was the only Cliff Richard & the Shadows No. 1 double-A-side?
27 Which 1968 No. 1 was revived in the film "Good Morning Vietnam"?
28 What was Wonderful in the Shadows hit which stayed longest at No. 1?
29 Which act was the first beginning with a letter Z to have a No. 1 single?
30 What was Cilla Black's only US Top 40 hit?

Answers | Pot Luck 29 *(see Quiz 61)*

1 Babington Plot. 2 David Beckham. 3 Duke of Cumberland. 4 A. 5 Ian Gow. 6 Sluys. 7 Human flesh. 8 Robert Graves. 9 Murder in Mind. 10 Abba. 11 Sir Paul McCartney. 12 1580. 13 Canoe. 14 29 years. 15 Irving Berlin. 16 Bulgaria. 17 Bitter Sweet Symphony. 18 Rock of Ages. 19 1960s. 20 James Boswell. 21 Charles II. 22 Smallpox. 23 Clarence Carter. 24 Fletcher Christian. 25 Birkenhead Drill. 26 Mick the Miller. 27 The Dardanelles. 28 Christopher Wren. 29 Mercalli Scale. 30 Eight.

1 Which language do the words kiosk, tulip and caviar come from?

2 Whose Drum can be seen at Buckland Abbey in Devon?

3 Whose painting of the Liver Building fetched £1m at auction in June 2006?

4 What do the initials stand for in the name of ghost story writer MR James?

5 Which actor played Major Gowen in "Fawlty Towers"?

6 In which decade was Lloyd Grossman born?

7 Whose hymn book was first published in 1873?

8 A durmast is a variety of what?

9 Whose only UK Top Ten Hit was "Blue is the Colour" from 1972?

10 Which Europeans discovered Lake Tanganyika in 1858?

11 Who said, "I never hated a man enough to give him his diamonds back"?

12 Achulophobia is the fear of what?

13 Which brass instrument is wrapped around the player's body?

14 What colour appears with white and green on the Afghanistan flag?

15 In which US state was there a nuclear accident at Three Mile Island in 1979?

16 Who was the first woman to swim the English Channel in 1926?

17 What is the capital of Angola?

18 Under what pseudonym did Richard Horne write "The Last Polar Bears" and other children's books?

19 What is indium?

20 Who is the elder – Paul Merton or Richard Madeley?

21 Who lived at No. 1, London?

22 Where are the Aventine, Viminal and Quirinal Hills?

23 What nationality was Sir Robert Helpmann?

24 What is a clerihew?

25 In which country can you visit Espoo and Vantaa?

26 In which European country is the province of Brabant?

27 What was the title of Gloria Hunniford's book about her late daughter Caron Keating?

28 What was David Cassidy's first UK Top Ten hit?

29 Where did Kun's Red Terror exist in 1919?

30 Which actor was first to sign a $1 million deal for a single picture?

Answers | Olympics *(see Quiz 64)*

1 Singapore. 2 Ice hockey. 3 Yachting. 4 St Moritz. 5 Bars and beam. 6 Michael Johnson. 7 Long jump. 8 Al Oerter. 9 Five. 10 Two. 11 Retained 10,000m and won 5,000m and marathon. 12 Evander Holyfield. 13 Lake Lanier. 14 Simone Jacobs. 15 Michelle Smith. 16 Izzy. 17 Seoul. 18 Allan Wells. 19 Spain. 20 Soling. 21 Poland's Renata Mauer. 22 Tim Henman & Chris Broad. 23 Jayne Torvill. 24 4 x 400m relay. 25 1900. 26 Quarantine laws. 27 Denise Lewis. 28 Montreal. 29 Robin Cousins. 30 Japan.

Quiz 64 | Olympics

Answers – page 295

1 In which country did the final vote about hosting the 2012 Olympics take place?

2 At which sport did future tennis star Drobny win a medal in 1948?

3 Windsurfing is included in the Olympics as part of which sport's events?

4 Where were the Winter Olympics held in 1928 and 1948?

5 On which apparatus did Nadia Comaneci score perfect tens in 1976?

6 Who was the first man to win Olympic gold at 200m and 400m?

7 In which event did Carl Lewis win his ninth and final gold medal?

8 Who won the first of four discus golds in Melbourne in 1956?

9 How many silver medals did skier Raisa Smetanina win with her four golds and one bronze?

10 How many gold medals did Mark Spitz win in his first Olympics?

11 Which amazing treble did Emil Zatopek achieve at the 1952 Games?

12 Who carried the torch into the stadium at the Atlanta games?

13 On which lake did Steve Redgrave win his record-breaking fourth gold medal?

14 Who was the only British woman sprinter to compete in all Olympics between 1984 and 1996?

15 Under what name did Mrs Erik de Bruin win gold at Atlanta?

16 What was the name of the Olympic mascot in Atlanta?

17 Where did Linford Christie run his first Olympic race?

18 Who was the oldest Olympic 100m champion when he won in 1980?

19 Who won women's gold in hockey in Barcelona?

20 Which is the only Olympic yachting event for three-person crews?

21 Who won the first medal at the Atlanta games?

22 Who won Britain's first tennis medal since 1924 in Atlanta?

23 Who replaced her partner Michael Hutchinson before winning gold in 1984?

24 Other than 400m hurdles for which event did Sally Gunnell win a medal in Barcelona?

25 In which year did women first compete in the Olympics?

26 Why were equestrian events held in Sweden in 1956 when the Games were held in Australia?

27 Who was Britain's only female medallist at the Atlanta games?

28 Where did Daley Thompson compete in his first Olympics?

29 Which son of a former Millwall goalie won gold in the USA in 1980?

30 What was the first Asian country to have staged the Winter Olympics?

Answers | Pot Luck 30 *(see Quiz 63)*

1 Turkish. 2 Francis Drake's. 3 LS Lowry. 4 Montague Rhodes. 5 Ballard Berkeley. 6 1950s. 7 Sankey and Moody's. 8 An oak tree. 9 Chelsea F.C. 10 Richard Burton and John Speke. 11 Zsa Zsa Gabor. 12 Darkness. 13 Sousaphone. 14 Black. 15 Pennsylvania. 16 Gertrude Ederle. 17 Luanda. 18 Harry Horse. 19 A metallic element. 20 Richard Madeley. 21 Duke of Wellington. 22 Rome. 23 Australian. 24 A poem. 25 Finland. 26 Belgium. 27 Next to You. 28 Could It Be Forever/Cherish. 29 Hungary. 30 Marlon Brando.

Quiz 65 | Pot Luck 31

Answers – page 298

LEVEL 3

1 Whom did the Spice Girls sack as their manager in early 1998?
2 What is a porbeagle?
3 Which bandleader married both Ava Gardner and Lana Turner?
4 What was the family name of artists Jacopo and his sons Gentile and Giovanni?
5 Scottish solicitor William Mitchell drew up the rules for which sport?
6 Which group had a 70s hit with "Kiss You All Over"?
7 What is the first name of John Peel's widow?
8 What two colours go with black and yellow in printing's four-colour process?
9 What did Diana Princess of Wales describe as "a shameful friend"?
10 Who won an Oscar for her first screenplay "Silkwood"?
11 What was Bad Manners' first UK Top Ten hit?
12 What is a belvedere?
13 In which month is the feast day of St Cuthbert?
14 In which country are the mountains called the Stirling Range?
15 Which late politician was the first leader of the Scottish Parliament?
16 Which soccer club has been managed by both Jimmy Armfield and Brian Clough?
17 Whose one and only hit was "Float On" in 1977?
18 Who was the first Prime Minister of Israel?
19 Where is New York's Metropolitan Museum of Art?
20 In what year did the London Stock Exchange go computerised?
21 What is a gibus?
22 Who was the first man to hold the post of Astronomer Royal?
23 Who numbered Helen Menken and Mary Philips among his wives?
24 Who founded the record label Anxious Records?
25 Which Michelangelo statue is in Florence?
26 Vera Caslavska was Olympic and World Champion in which sport?
27 In which year was Wimbledon first televised?
28 Where was the first woman MP to enter the Commons born?
29 Who ceased to be queen when Victoria became queen?
30 What do you do if you siffle?

Answers | Hobbies 2 (see Quiz 66)

1 0 to 36. 2 Finland, playing football. 3 Chess. 4 Mahogany. 5 16lb. 6 Bilbao.
7 Steel links. 8 Tintin. 9 Alton Towers. 10 Giverny. 11 Clarice Cliff. 12 Military
combat. 13 10. 14 Baker Street. 15 Caman. 16 Tony Hancock. 17 Curling. 18
Tramp. 19 Aikido. 20 Four (11 and 7 respectively). 21 Stamp collecting. 22 Hang
gliding. 23 Harz Mountains (Germany). 24 Mogens Tholstrup. 25 Carry it. 26
Gothenburg, Sweden. 27 Nick Nairn. 28 Bungee jumping. 29 Kung fu. 30 Leiden.

Quiz 66 | Hobbies 2

Answers – page 297

1 What is the range of numbers on a roulette wheel?
2 Where would you watch FC Jazz and what would they be doing?
3 FIDE is the governing body of which game?
4 Which furniture-making wood can be Cuban, Honduras and San Domingan?
5 In athletics how much does a hammer weigh?
6 Where is the Guggenheim Museum in Europe?
7 In abseiling what are karabiners?
8 Who first appeared in a strip cartoon "in the Land of the Soviets"?
9 Which UK tourist attraction is on the site of an 8th-century fortress?
10 Where in Normandy would you visit Monet's garden?
11 If you collected Bizarre pottery whose work would you have?
12 Paintball is a simulation of what?
13 How many zones does an archery target have?
14 In which London street was the first artificial ice rink opened?
15 In shinty what is the curved stick called?
16 Which radio star appeared in films such as "The Wrong Box"?
17 In which sport does a match last for a certain number of heads?
18 John Gold was the owner of which night club for over 30 years?
19 Which activity has two main types, tomiki and uyeshiba?
20 How many more people are there in an outer handball team than there are in an indoor one?
21 John Tomlinson is credited with starting which hobby?
22 Which form of flying was perfected by Francis Rogallo in the 1970s?
23 In which mountains is the Brockenbahn steam railway?
24 Which restaurateur owned Daphne's and founded The Collection?
25 In cyclocross what do you do with your bike when you're not riding it?
26 Where is the Liseberg theme park?
27 Who opened the Braeval restaurant in Scotland in 1986?
28 In which activity do you "dive for the horizon"?
29 Wing Chun is a popular form of which art?
30 In which Botanic Gardens was the tulip first introduced in 1594?

Answers | Pot Luck 31 *(see Quiz 65)*

1 Simon Fuller. 2 A shark. 3 Artie Shaw. 4 Bellini. 5 Bowls. 6 Exile. 7 Sheila.
8 Cyan, magenta. 9 Bulimia. 10 Nora Ephron. 11 Special Brew. 12 A viewing
turret. 13 March. 14 Australia. 15 Donald Dewar. 16 Leeds. 17 The Floaters. 18
David Ben-Gurion. 19 Central Park. 20 1986. 21 A top hat. 22 John Flamsteed.
23 Humphrey Bogart. 24 Dave Stewart. 25 David. 26 Gymnastics. 27 1937. 28
America. 29 Adelaide. 30 Whistle.

1 Bernard Webb was a pseudonym used by which famous song writer?
2 In which country is the royal family the House of Bernadotte?
3 Acrophobia is the fear of what?
4 In which country is the city of Abidjan?
5 What was the only No. 1 UK hit for the Clash?
6 What colour is the circle on the Bangladesh flag?
7 A Brazilian Huntsman is a type of what?
8 Who played director Ed Wood in the 1994 film biography?
9 A Nutmegger is an inhabitant of which American state?
10 In which decade did South Africa resign from the Commonwealth?
11 How many locks are there on the Suez Canal?
12 What is Mrs Gordon Brown's first name?
13 Who composed Rhapsody on a Theme of Paganini for Piano?
14 What was the number of the British Armoured Division nicknamed the "Desert Rats"?
15 In which year did James Cook land at Botany Bay, Australia?
16 What is the correct form of address to begin a letter to a Baron?
17 In which country is the town of Nakhon?
18 Who is the elder – Caroline Quentin or Linda Robson?
19 What was Neneh Cherry's first UK Top Ten hit?
20 What was the Christian name of aeroplane manufacturer Mr Boeing?
21 In which European country are the provinces of Sofiya and Burgas?
22 What size is A4 paper in millimetres?
23 Australia hosted the 1956 Olympics but equestrian events were held in which other country?
24 Murderer Dr Harold Shipman worked in which Greater Manchester district?
25 Which artist painted "The Watering Place" in 1777?
26 INXS singer Michael Hutchence was born in and died in which city?
27 Who played Russell Crowe's wife in "Cinderella Man"?
28 Whose first novel was called "Glass Houses"?
29 Clarence House was built for which monarch when he was still Duke of Clarence?
30 What is the capital of Bahrain?

Answers	TV Times 2 *(see Quiz 68)*

1 Angus Deayton. 2 Po. 3 Andrew Lincoln. 4 Science. 5 Tinky Winky. 6 Ascot.
7 Sara. 8 Lakesiders. 9 Duffy (Cathy Shipton). 10 Papa, Bob. 11 Sorted. 12 Jane
Asher. 13 My Kind of People. 14 Dame Thora Hird. 15 Tantrums and Tiaras. 16
Francesca Annis. 17 Widows. 18 Helen Rollason. 19 James Naughtie. 20 Ian
Hislop. 21 Carla Lane. 22 Twin Peaks. 23 Bedrock (The Flintstones). 24 Heineken.
25 Warrington. 26 Gomez Addams. 27 Paul McGann. 28 Fiona Phillips. 29 1313
Mockingbird Heights. 30 The Woodentop twins.

Quiz 68 TV Times 2

Answers – page 299

1 Who played Mike Channel in "KYTV"?
2 Who is the smallest Teletubby?
3 Who found fame as Egg in "This Life"?
4 "Prove It!" was a CITV series about what?
5 Who is the largest Teletubby?
6 Where did the first outside broadcast on "Grandstand" come from?
7 Who is Postman Pat's wife?
8 In which docu soap did Emma Boundy find fame?
9 Which "Casualty" character played a midwife in "Spice World"?
10 Which two words has Nicole uttered to advertise Renault?
11 Which BBC drama series, first seen in 2006, was about a mailroom?
12 Which TV presenter made the cake when Jemima Goldsmith married Imran Khan?
13 What was Michael Barrymore's talent-spotting TV show called?
14 Which late actress won a BAFTA for "A Cream Cracker Under the Settee"?
15 What was the name of the David Furnish-directed documentary about Elton John?
16 Who played the Englishwoman in "Parnell and the Englishwoman"?
17 In which series did Lynda La Plante introduce Dolly Rawlings?
18 Who was the first woman presenter of "Grandstand"?
19 Who replaced Richard Baker as the presenter of the Proms?
20 Who presented Channel 4's religious series "Canterbury Tales"?
21 How is TV playwright Romana Barrack better known?
22 In which show was Harry S Truman the sheriff?
23 In which town would you read "The Daily Slate"?
24 The music from "Raging Bull" was used to advertise which lager?
25 Where is Chris Evans' home town?
26 Who had a pet octopus called Aristotle?
27 Who played the title role in Alan Bleasdale's "The Monocled Mutineer"?
28 Anthea Turner was replaced at GMTV by whom?
29 Where did the Munsters live?
30 On a Friday, on children's TV who were Jenny & Willy?

Answers | Pot Luck 32 *(see Quiz 67)*

1 Paul McCartney. 2 Sweden. 3 Heights. 4 Ivory Coast. 5 Should I Stay or Should I Go. 6 Red. 7 Spider. 8 Johnny Depp. 9 Connecticut. 10 1960s. 11 None. 12 Sarah. 13 Rachmaninov. 14 7th. 15 1770. 16 My Lord. 17 Thailand. 18 Linda Robson. 19 Buffalo Stance. 20 William. 21 Bulgaria. 22 210mm x 297mm. 23 Sweden. 24 Hyde. 25 Thomas Gainsborough. 26 Sydney. 27 Renée Zellweger. 28 Sandra Howard (wife of Michael). 29 William IV. 30 Manama.

1 In which decade was actor John Cleese born?

2 After which American General were sideburns named?

3 Freetown is the capital of which country?

4 Villinger and Couchepin have been Presidents of which country this century?

5 Which eating house was founded by Ruth Rogers?

6 What is the main language of Angola?

7 What happened to the Olympic flame during the 1976 games?

8 Hartford is the capital of which American State?

9 Which 18th-century artist painted "Peasant Girl Gathering Sticks"?

10 To five years, when was the News of the World founded?

11 What, other than "Amazing Grace", was a Top Ten hit for Judy Collins?

12 A fear of the cold is known as what?

13 In which county is the Rude Man of Cerne?

14 Which country has the dalasi as its currency?

15 What was done in an apodyterium?

16 Emperor Nero was the adopted son of which other emperor?

17 What is the international car index mark for a car from Libya?

18 The spice annatto is made from which part of a plant?

19 Other than Buckingham Palace, which venue sees the daily Changing of the Guard?

20 Which English county does actor Robert Lindsay come from?

21 What was the Commodores' first UK Top Ten hit?

22 In which movie did Harrison Ford play the character John Book?

23 Painter Georges Seurat was born, died and worked in which city?

24 What name is given to elements with atomic numbers 93 to 112?

25 What two colours appear with yellow on the Cameroon flag?

26 Who was the first woman to qualify for the Indy 500 motor race?

27 Which Latin phrase means, "Let the buyer beware"?

28 In which year did women gain the vote in Switzerland?

29 In which country is the city of Bamako?

30 As a child Jonathan Ross appeared in an ad for which food product?

Answers	90s Films *(see Quiz 70)*

1 Wag the Dog. 2 Francis Bacon. 3 Arnold Schwarzenegger. 4 River Phoenix. 5 Spanish Civil War. 6 Jean-Claude Van Damme. 7 That Thing You Do!. 8 Pretty Woman. 9 Seal. 10 Ellen Barkin. 11 Frank Drebin. 12 Banker. 13 Julia Roberts. 14 Kevin Kline. 15 Blue Sky. 16 Kennedy & Nixon. 17 James Earl Jones. 18 Abba. 19 Kirsty Alley. 20 Nine Months. 21 Emma Thompson. 22 Elizabeth Taylor. 23 Kevin McCallister. 24 Jim Carrey , who played The Riddler. 25 Ron Shelton. 26 Jude. 27 Christopher Walken. 28 Gonzo. 29 Nil by Mouth. 30 2000 AD.

1 Which Barry Levinson film was used to satirise the US presidency during the Lewinsky crisis?

2 Who is the subject of "Love is the Devil"?

3 Which tough guy directed "Christmas in Connecticut"?

4 Who died during the filming of "Dark Blood" in 1993?

5 Which war is depicted in "Land and Freedom"?

6 Who was Lyon Gaultier in "AWOL"?

7 In which film did Tom Hanks make his directorial debut?

8 Which film's initial title was "$3,000"?

9 Who or what is Andre in the film of the same name?

10 Who was Leonardo DiCaprio's mother in "This Boy's Life"?

11 Who is Leslie Nielsen in the "Naked Gun" films?

12 What is Jim Carrey's job before he finds the mask in the hit movie?

13 Who was Tinkerbell when Spielberg met JM Barrie?

14 Who was the butler in "Princess Caraboo"?

15 What was director Tony Richardson's final film?

16 Which US presidents does Gump meet in "Forrest Gump"?

17 Who was the voice of Mufasa in "The Lion King"?

18 Muriel is a fan of which band in "Muriel's Wedding"?

19 Whom did Woody Allen cast as his ex-wife in "Deconstructing Harry"?

20 What was Hugh Grant's first Hollywood movie?

21 Who was Oscar winning best screen writer for "Sense and Sensibility"?

22 Who was John Goodman's mother-in-law in "The Flintstones"?

23 What is Macaulay Culkin's full name in the "Home Alone" movies?

24 Who designed The Riddler's costume in "Batman Forever"?

25 Who directed "White Men Can't Jump"?

26 In which film did Kate Winslet have her first nude scene?

27 Who played rat catcher Caesar in "Mousehunt"?

28 Who was the author in "The Muppet Christmas Carol"?

29 Which film was Gary Oldman's directorial debut?

30 In which comic did Sylvester Stallone's '95 futuristic police character appear?

1 What is another name for the North American nightjar?
2 Who was the first woman to have a partial face transplant?
3 How is the disease trypanosomiasis also known?
4 What is meant by a haemorrhage which is "occult"?
5 Which protein is present in a hair?
6 What does it mean if a cell is haploid?
7 In addition to tea and coffee where is caffeine found?
8 Where is the flexor carpi radialis?
9 What is an erythrocyte?
10 How is the sand hopper also known?
11 Guano is used as fertiliser but what is it made from?
12 Cranes are found on all continents except which two?
13 What is an alternative name for leptospirosis?
14 Carragheen is a type of what?
15 Where is a caterpillar's spinneret?
16 Which bird flies highest?
17 What is an insect's Malpighian tubes?
18 How does a mamba differ from a cobra?
19 Which part of the brain controls muscular movements, balance and co-ordination?
20 Which bird can swim as fast as a seal?
21 An urodele is another name for which reptile?
22 Which bird builds the largest nest?
23 The world's largest spider is named after which Biblical character?
24 What is a bird's furcula?
25 Disulfiram is used in the treatment of what?
26 What is a hairstreak?
27 On which island would you find the bee hummingbird?
28 Which bird produces the largest egg in relation to its body size?
29 Why should you avoid a chigger?
30 How many hearts does an earthworm have?

Answers | Pot Luck 34 *(see Quiz 72)*

1 Louis Washkansky. 2 Denmark. 3 Bela Bartok. 4 Cliff Richard. 5 Terrorism. 6 George Bush. 7 Elephant. 8 Second or middle row. 9 Turkey. 10 Mackerel. 11 1985. 12 Blackheath. 13 Wallace & Gromit. 14 1940s. 15 One Day I'll Fly Away. 16 Helena Bonham Carter. 17 43,200. 18 Polish. 19 Sexual health in the Third World. 20 Martin Amis. 21 Dot, dot, dot. 22 Shakespeare. 23 Spencer Perceval (British PM). 24 Trumpet. 25 Edo. 26 Excessive growth. 27 New Zealand. 28 Indiana. 29 Kid Creole and the Coconuts. 30 Touch.

1 Who was the first person to receive a heart transplant?
2 In which European country are the counties of Viborg and Aarhus?
3 Who composed the music for the ballet "The Wooden Prince"?
4 Who played the lead role in the film "Two a Penny"?
5 As PM Tony Blair first lost a Commons vote on which high-profile subject?
6 Who was Vice President when Ronald Reagan was President?
7 Which animal head represents the Hindu god Ganesa?
8 Keying in the word DAMSON which row of letters is used the most?
9 In which country is the city of Adana?
10 Which type of fish gives its name to a particular patterning of the sky?
11 In which year did Roy Plomley last present "Desert Island Discs"?
12 The first men's hockey club in England was founded in which London suburb?
13 Who were the movie stars when Ralph Fiennes voiced Victor Quartermaine?
14 In which decade was Michael Gambon born?
15 What was Randy Crawford's first UK Top Ten hit?
16 Which Oscar and BAFTA nominee was a one-time face of Yardley cosmetics?
17 How many seconds are there in half a day?
18 What was the nationality of the astronomer Nicolaus Copernicus?
19 Geri Halliwell became a UN ambassador specialising in what?
20 Who wrote the novels "London Fields" and "Time's Arrow"?
21 How is the letter S formed in Morse Code?
22 The Globe Theatre's Dominic Dromgoole wrote "Will and Me" about whom?
23 Which public figure was shot dead by John Bellingham?
24 Bandleader Quincy Jones chiefly plays which instrument?
25 Changed in 1868, what was the former name of Tokyo?
26 What do you suffer from if you have acromegaly?
27 The yacht Black Magic won the America's Cup for which country?
28 A Hoosier is an inhabitant in which American state?
29 Who had hits with "Stool Pigeon" and "I'm a Wonderful Thing, Baby"?
30 Haphephobia is the fear of what?

Answers | Living World *(see Quiz 71)*

1 Whippoorwill. 2 Isabelle Diniore. 3 Sleeping sickness. 4 Internal. 5 Keratin. 6 Single set of chromosomes. 7 Kola nuts. 8 Human's forearm. 9 Red blood cell. 10 Beachflea. 11 Bird droppings. 12 South America & Antarctica. 13 Weil's disease. 14 Seaweed. 15 Head. 16 Ruppell's vulture. 17 Excretory organs. 18 Not hooded. 19 Cerebellum. 20 Penguin. 21 Salamander. 22 Male malle fowl. 23 Goliath. 24 Wishbone. 25 Alcoholism. 26 Butterfly. 27 Cuba. 28 Kiwi. 29 Harvest mite (which bites). 30 Ten.

Quiz 73 · Who was Who?

1 Who was known as the "father of the Soviet H-bomb"?
2 In which shipyards did Lech Walesa work before becoming Polish president?
3 Terry Waite was the envoy of which Archbishop of Canterbury when he was kidnapped?
4 Who founded the Police Memorial Trust after PC Yvonne Fletcher's death?
5 Who was the first US Ambassador in London?
6 Who recorded with the Hot Five and the Hot Seven in the 1920s?
7 Which David wrote "Bringing the House Down" about his father John?
8 Who was the 20th Prince of Wales?
9 Who succeeded Len Murray as TUC general secretary in 1984?
10 Who was the first Archbishop of Canterbury to be appointed by the Church Crown Appointments Commission?
11 Which children's author was Russian correspondent for the Daily News during WWI and the Revolution?
12 Which advocate of black rights left the US to live in England in the late 50s?
13 Who was the last British monarch to refuse royal assent of a Bill through Parliament?
14 Who was UK Deputy PM between 1942 and 1945?
15 Which UK PM was responsible for the purchase of US Polaris missiles?
16 Whom did Douglas Hurd replace as Foreign Secretary in 1989?
17 Who became President of the ANC in 1997?
18 Which Chancellor of the Exchequer introduced old-age pensions?
19 Which Fine Gael candidate did Mary McAleese defeat in the 1997 election for Irish President?
20 Which invention improved on Alexander Cumming's invention a century earlier?
21 What was Mikhail Gorbachev's wife called?
22 Who founded Standard Oil in 1870?
23 How was entrepreneur Roland Fuhrhop better known?
24 Which son of Findlaech was killed at Lumphanan?
25 Who was the first Archbishop of Canterbury?
26 Which former Enfield MP has the middle names Denzil Xavier?
27 The name of which UK PM was Ronald Reagan's middle name?
28 Who was shot at a rally in the US in 1972 while campaigning for the Democrats?
29 Which Baron began a continental pigeon post in 1849?
30 Who was German foreign minister during WWII?

1 The spice cayenne is made from which part of a plant?

2 Lincoln is the capital of which US state?

3 What was the only UK Top Ten hit from 1992 for Crowded House?

4 What was special about Robert Pershing Wadlow?

5 How many singles had Take That released before their first No. 1 "Pray"?

6 What is the international car index mark for a car from Botswana?

7 Which Costa Rican soccer player is their all-time top scorer?

8 Who was the Roman God of fire?

9 Which British journalist was involved in the Michael Jackson trial of 2005?

10 Mathematically speaking, what is an ALU?

11 In the 1920s who wrote "The Land that Time Forgot"?

12 How many stripes are on the national flag of Estonia?

13 Who is the only British prime minister to have been born outside the UK?

14 Which artist painted "Le Jardinier" in 1906?

15 In which year was the Battle of Edgehill?

16 Who directed the 1990 film "Dick Tracy"?

17 A Chief Constable is responsible for which uniformed force other than the police?

18 Lusaka is the capital of which country?

19 When does an MP apply for the Chiltern Hundreds?

20 What was Terence Trent D'Arby's first UK Top Ten hit?

21 What is the correct form of address to begin a letter to a Duke?

22 In which year did Frank Bruno first fight with Mike Tyson?

23 In which country is the city of Banjarmasin?

24 Who painted "The Rake's Progress" and "A Bigger Splash" in the 1960s?

25 Saint John Fisher was martyred during the reign of which English king?

26 Which ex-political leader wrote the book "Making Our Way"?

27 What's the English name of the constellation Pavo?

28 What size is A5 paper in millimetres?

29 What is the main language of the Republic of Benin?

30 What is the sum total of the spots on a set of dominoes?

Answers | Who was Who? *(see Quiz 73)*

1 Andrei Sakharov. 2 Gdansk. 3 Robert Runcie. 4 Michael Winner. 5 John Adams. 6 Louis Armstrong. 7 Profumo. 8 The future Edward VIII. 9 Norman Willis. 10 Robert Runcie. 11 Arthur Ransome. 12 Paul Robeson. 13 Queen Anne. 14 Attlee. 15 Macmillan. 16 John Major. 17 Thabo Mbeki. 18 Asquith. 19 Mary Bannotti. 20 Flushing toilet. 21 Raisa. 22 John D. Rockefeller. 23 Tiny Rowland. 24 Macbeth. 25 St Augustine. 26 Michael Portillo. 27 Wilson. 28 George Wallace. 29 Paul Julius Reuter. 30 Joachim von Ribbentrop.

1 What was Eddie Cochrane's next UK single after "Three Steps to Heaven"?

2 Who played Jerry Lee Lewis in the 1989 biopic of his life?

3 How does Roger Peterson figure in rock history?

4 What was Billy Fury's first UK Top Ten hit from 1960?

5 In which city were R.E.M. formed?

6 As a teenager Morrissey ran a fan club for which group?

7 Who wrote the Holly classic "It Doesn't Matter Anymore"?

8 Which Elvis No. 1 is the only one written solely by Leiber and Stoller?

9 Which hard-rock band did the Scottish Young brothers form in Australia?

10 "Rock Around the Clock" came out on which label?

11 Who did Keith Richard work for before coming a full-time Stone?

12 Which Slade hit was No. 1 when US soldiers left Vietnam in 1973?

13 What did Rick Allen of Def Leppard lose in 1984?

14 What did an electrician fitting a burglar alarm find in Seattle in 1984?

15 Who first charted with "Rip It Up"?

16 James Jewel Osterberg took the stage under which name?

17 At which studio did the "Million Dollar Quartet" get together in the 50s?

18 In which month did Jim Morrison die in 1971?

19 Where in London was the Sex Pistols' first concert?

20 Which Dickie Valentine hit replaced "Rock Around the Clock" at No. 1?

21 Which place used to form part of The Stranglers name?

22 Who was Francis Rossi's school mate and long-time bass player in Status Quo?

23 How were the Rolling Stones billed for their first live concert?

24 Which Jerry Lee Lewis hit is the only version of the Ray Charles classic to reach the British charts?

25 Who ran the Clovis, New Mexico studio where Buddy Holly recorded?

26 Who was Phil Lynott's father-in-law?

27 Who recorded the album "Ma Kelly's Greasy Spoon"?

28 Which Led Zeppelin drummer died in 1980?

29 Who ran the Chelsea clothes shop called Let It Rock?

30 Which 1955 Glenn Ford movie featured "Rock Around the Clock"?

---

1 In 2006 rugby union, who was captain for England's seventh defeat in a row?
2 In the 1980s, who wrote the short-story collection "A Twist in the Tale"?
3 What is the Parliament of Sark called?
4 What colour appears with white and red on the Faroe Islands flag?
5 In 1995 Hugh Grant got into trouble for performing a lewd act with whom?
6 What is the capital of Belize?
7 The North American Nebula is a region in which constellation?
8 What was The Damned's one and only UK Top Ten hit?
9 Which Inspector did Johnny Depp play in the movie "From Hell"?
10 What is a golomyanka?
11 Which singer with the Billy Cotton Band passed away in March 2005?
12 Bombay, Chartreux and Japanese bobtail are all types of what?
13 Which war is Stephen Crane's novel "The Red Badge of Courage" set in?
14 In which country is the city of Alma-Ata?
15 The writer Thomas Keneally comes from which country?
16 In which decade was actor Colin Firth born?
17 Prithwi Narayan Shah was the first King of which kingdom?
18 Where were William Hague, Jesse Owens and Pele brought together?
19 Homichlophobia is the fear of what?
20 Who became Chancellor of Hull University in 2006?
21 Who or what was a piggin?
22 In which year was the Women's International Bowling Board formed?
23 Which media presenter left his wife Carol McGiffin in 1993?
24 Which ex-Monkee was in a band called Shoe Suede Blues?
25 Among which hills does Chequers lie?
26 Who composed the opera "Noye's Fludde"?
27 The band Coldplay formed while attending which educational establishment?
28 Under which name did Leslie Charles sail to pop success?
29 Which city has the oldest stock exchange in the USA?
30 What does the musical term "giocoso" mean?

---

1 CIPS regulates which sport?
2 In which city were Haagen-Daz ice creams first sold?
3 Where is Rick Stein's famous seafood restaurant?
4 What is octopush?
5 In embroidery, what is the name for areas of raised decoration?
6 Who jointly opened La Gavroche in 1967?
7 Which venue was designed by George London and Henry Wise?
8 What colour might your balls be in croquet?
9 What is the nearest town to the Lightwater Valley Theme Park?
10 Which game was originally called Lexico?
11 The Toucan Terribles are prolific champions at what?
12 What is the name of England's smallest pub in Bury St Edmunds?
13 What did Andrew Forgan and Hugh Philp make?
14 Where was the Grand National run during WWI?
15 Who founded the London restaurants Quaglino's and Mezzo?
16 In judo which Dan grades are awarded a red belt?
17 How many points is the gold circle on an archery target worth?
18 In 1848 William Mitchell drew up the rules to which modern game?
19 In shinty what is the opponent's goal called?
20 Which musical instrument was the creation of Charles Wheatstone?
21 Which soccer club had a fanzine called Fly Me to the Moon?
22 Who opened his first restaurant Harveys in 1987?
23 In paddle tennis what is the ball made from?
24 Which game was derived from baggataway?
25 What is important dress code at France's Domaine de Lambetran?
26 What is a gricer?
27 Where is the UK's largest amusement park?
28 What name is given to the circular target in curling?
29 What is Denmark's Rutschebahnen?
30 What do you wear on your feet in street hockey?

Answers | Pot Luck 37 *(see Quiz 78)*

1 Francis Ford Coppola. 2 Earl of Liverpool. 3 The Valley of the Queens. 4 Alexander.
5 John Constable. 6 New Orleans. 7 Fruits. 8 1969. 9 The Ivy League (US colleges).
10 RC. 11 Doctor. 12 Wyclef Jean. 13 String. 14 Walter F. Mondale. 15 Sir William
Walton. 16 Lord Lovat (1747). 17 1970s. 18 Spartak Moscow. 19 The Hob. 20
Titanic. 21 The Milan – San Remo (Primavera). 22 The Times. 23 Solomon Islands. 24
Gordonstoun. 25 A black star. 26 Four. 27 Milk and Alcohol. 28 Buenos Aires. 29
Gordon setter. 30 Madagascar.

1 Who directed the 1992 film "Bram Stoker's Dracula"?
2 Robert Banks Jenkinson was British PM under which title?
3 Which cemetery is to the south of the Valley of the Kings?
4 What is Nick Faldo's middle name?
5 Which artist painted "The White Horse" in 1819?
6 The Lake Pontchartrain Causeway links Mandeville, Louisiana with where?
7 The spice coriander is made from which part of a plant?
8 When was The Sun newspaper founded?
9 Brown, Cornell and Dartmouth are all members of what?
10 What is the international car index mark for a car from Taiwan?
11 Neil Diamond started to train – but didn't qualify – as what?
12 Who featured on the first Top Ten hit for Destiny's Child?
13 What type of musical instrument is the Japanese koto?
14 Who was Vice President when Jimmy Carter was President of USA?
15 Which British composer died on the island of Ischia in 1983?
16 Who was the last person to be executed by beheading in the UK?
17 In which decade did Agatha Christie die?
18 Nemanja Vidic joined Man Utd from which club?
19 In quoits, what name is given to the target at which the rings are thrown?
20 What was the first movie to make $1,000 million at the box office?
21 In cycling what is the first major classic of the season?
22 Which newspaper in the UK was the first to publish a daily weather chart?
23 In which island group is Guadalcanal?
24 Prince Charles, Prince Edward and Prince Philip were all head boys at which school?
25 What appears in the centre of the national flag of Ghana?
26 How many symphonies did Brahms compose?
27 What was the title of Dr Feelgood's only Top Ten hit?
28 Which South American city has a name meaning "fair winds"?
29 Alexander Gordon 1743–1827 gave his name to what?
30 In which country is the city of Antananarivo?

Answers | Hobbies 3 *(see Quiz 77)*

1 Angling. 2 New York. 3 Padstow, Cornwall. 4 Underwater hockey. 5 Stumpwork.
6 The Roux Brothers. 7 Hampton Court maze. 8 Blue, red, yellow or black. 9 Ripon.
10 Scrabble. 11 Marbles. 12 The Nutshell. 13 Golf clubs. 14 Gatwick. 15
Terence Conran. 16 9th to 11th. 17 10. 18 Bowls. 19 Hail. 20 Harmonica. 21
Middlesbrough. 22 Marco Pierre White. 23 Sponge. 24 Lacrosse. 25 None (it's a
naturist site). 26 Trainspotter. 27 Blackpool. 28 House. 29 Roller coaster. 30 Roller
skates.

1 Which role does Mrs Trevor Eve play in "Holby City"?
2 Who played the British PM in "Suez" which commemorated the 50th anniversary of the crisis?
3 Who co presented "The Big Breakfast" with Zoe Ball?
4 Who played Kadi Toura in the drama series "Roots"?
5 Who was the antiques dealer in the "Paddington" stories?
6 Who used to say, "The next Tonight will be tomorrow night"?
7 Which was the English port in the "Triangle" drama series?
8 Mrs Robert Powell was a member of which famous dance group?
9 Who was the first Teletubby to have its alter ego sacked?
10 Who was Mrs Simpson when Stephen Campbell Moore played Edward VIII?
11 In which series did Charles Dance play Guy Perron?
12 On Channel 4 when Helen Mirren was Elizabeth I, who was Jeremy Irons?
13 Who directed a documentary called "Genderquake" after leaving a top soap?
14 Who followed Phillip Schofield as link man on Children's BBC?
15 Whose final TV role was as Daniel Reece?
16 In "May to December" what was Zoe's name before she married Alec?
17 Who played Dr David Kelly in "The Government Inspector"?
18 Who are the parents of "Live & Kicking"'s first female presenter?
19 What is the profession of Postman Pat's Mrs Goggins?
20 Which series took place in Lochdubh?
21 Who was Bamm Bamm's dad?
22 What was Alan B'Stard's constituency?
23 Which magazine did Amanda work for in "Girls on Top"?
24 Who were Father Ted's colleagues?
25 Which disgraced ex-MP is the uncle of Jack Davenport from "This Life"?
26 What did Angela Rippon dance to on "The Morecambe and Wise Show"?
27 George Baker aka Inspector Wexford appeared as which special agent in "Up Pompeii"?
28 What were the goldfish on "Playschool" called?
29 Who succeeded Amanda Burton in the lead role, in "Silent Witness"?
30 What did Peter do in "The Peter Principle"?

Answers | Pot Luck 38 *(see Quiz 80)*

1 Shetlands. 2 Signed, Sealed, Delivered, I'm Yours. 3 Plum. 4 Colombia. 5 £5.05. 6 Jill Balcon. 7 My Lord Mayor. 8 Three Coins In The Fountain. 9 Crowds. 10 Dog. 11 Bromley. 12 Piracy. 13 Benjamin Britten. 14 Gin and beer. 15 1880s. 16 Archbishop of Canterbury. 17 Argentina. 18 Rhodes. 19 Chess. 20 Arsenal. 21 Carl Douglas. 22 International Phonetic Alphabet. 23 69 goals. 24 Germany. 25 Melvyn Bragg. 26 Francis Coppola. 27 Peas. 28 Ireland. 29 Barry Sonnenfeld. 30 Blue and White.

1 Where is Baltasound Airport?
2 What was Blue's first single not to make the Top Ten?
3 Grand Duke, Stanley and Lombard are all varieties of which fruit?
4 In which country is the city of Cali?
5 In 2005 the hourly minimum wage for over-21s was fixed at what amount?
6 Who was the actress mother of actor Daniel Day-Lewis?
7 What is the correct form of address to begin a letter to a Lady Lord Mayor?
8 What was Frank Sinatra's first UK No. 1?
9 Demophobia is the fear of what?
10 Which creature is represented in the year the Chinese call gou?
11 What is the most southerly London borough?
12 Anne Bonney and Mary Read famously carried out which trade?
13 Who composed the opera "Death In Venice"?
14 What have you had if you've just had a dog's nose?
15 During which decade did the Orient Express first run?
16 The Court of Arches is the chief court of whom?
17 Which country has the austral as a unit of currency?
18 Which Island is the largest of the Dodecanese group?
19 Emanuel Lasker was undisputed world champion for over 26 years at what?
20 Which London football team did the author of "We All Live in a Perry Groves World" play for?
21 Whose one and only UK Top Ten hit was "Kung Fu Fighting"?
22 What are the initials IPA an abbreviation of, as well as being an ale?
23 How many league goals did Jimmy Floyd Hasslebaink score for Chelsea?
24 The landau carriage takes its name from a town in which country?
25 Who wrote the novel "A Time to Dance"?
26 Talia Shire is the sister of which film director?
27 What have you got with a plateful of Pisum satvium?
28 Which country left the Commonwealth in 1949?
29 Who directed the movie "Men in Black"?
30 Which two colours appear on the national flag of Honduras?

Answers | TV Times 3 *(see Quiz 79)*

1 Tricia Williams. 2 James Fox. 3 Mark Little. 4 OJ Simpson. 5 Mr Gruber. 6 Cliff Michelmore. 7 Felixstowe. 8 Pan's People. 9 Tinky Winky. 10 Joely Richardson. 11 Jewel in the Crown. 12 The Earl of Leicester. 13 Susan Tully. 14 Andy Crane. 15 Rock Hudson in Dynasty. 16 Angell. 17 Mark Rylance. 18 Bryan Forbes & Nanette Newman. 19 Postmistress. 20 Hamish Macbeth. 21 Barney Rubble. 22 Haltemprice. 23 Spare Cheeks. 24 Douglas & Jack. 25 Jonathan Aitken. 26 Let's Face the Music and Dance. 27 Jamesus Bondus. 28 Bit & Bot. 29 Emilia Fox. 30 Bank Manager.

1 Who has been an Irish international and the head of HJ Heinz?
2 In which decade of which century did the first league varsity match take place?
3 In which city were Barbarians RFC founded?
4 Which was the first league side to score 1,000 points in a season?
5 In 2006, who skippered Argentina when England lost their seventh game in a row?
6 Rob Andrew is qualified in what profession?
7 Where did Brian Moore begin his career?
8 How old was Will Carling when he played for Terra Nova Under 11s?
9 Against which side did Jeremy Guscott make his international debut?
10 Which league side was the first to win all its league games in a season?
11 In which month and year did Andy Robinson take over as England's head coach?
12 In 1986 St Helens beat Carlisle 112-0 in which competition?
13 Who was the first union player to kick eight penalties in an international?
14 What was Jason Leonard's first club?
15 Who were the beaten finalists in the first league Knockout Trophy?
16 Who captained Ireland in their centenary season?
17 Whom did the All Blacks beat 106-4 in 1987?
18 Where was the first floodlit rugby union match played?
19 What name was given to the breakaway clubs from the Rugby Union in 1895?
20 Which club won the first Middlesex Sevens at Twickenham?
21 What position did JJ Williams play for Llanelli?
22 Who returned to England from the Rugby World Cup in 2003 for the birth of daughter Eva?
23 Who recorded the then highest score draw 46-46 in 1994?
24 Who sponsored the rugby league before Courage?
25 In which country was the first rugby league World Cup held?
26 Who was the first UK rugby league club side to play in Australia?
27 Who played a record 17 appearances on five tours with the British Lions?
28 Which New Zealand fly half scored 26 points against England in Nov. 2006?
29 Who made the lowest score (0-0) in the BBC's Floodlit Rugby League competition?
30 Who were the first Scottish rugby union club champions?

Answers | Pot Luck 39 *(see Quiz 82)*

1 Hungary. 2 Oneirophobia. 3 Kiss Me. 4 100 miles (161 km). 5 Armoured Fighting Vehicle. 6 The Chicken Song. 7 I. 8 1960s. 9 Swaziland. 10 Marquis of Granby. 11 Green. 12 God willing. 13 Tessa Jowell. 14 North Carolina. 15 250mm x 353mm. 16 Portsmouth. 17 The Elephant Man. 18 Llandrindod Wells. 19 Bulgaria. 20 Under the Coronation Chair. 21 RCH. 22 1897. 23 Jerry Garcia. 24 China. 25 Orcus. 26 Winston Churchill's. 27 Seeds. 28 Love's Gotta Hold on Me. 29 A dolphin. 30 Joe DiMaggio.

1 Which country has the forint as its unit of currency?
2 A fear of dreams is known as what?
3 What was Stephen "Tin Tin" Duffy's only Top Ten hit?
4 How long is the Suez Canal?
5 In the military, what is an AFV?
6 Which UK No. 1 was written by Red Dwarf creators Robert Grant and Doug Naylor?
7 Which letter is two dots in Morse Code?
8 In which decade was Rory Bremner born?
9 Mbabane is the capital of which country?
10 What popular pub name comes from the title held by soldier John Manners?
11 What colour are the stars on the national flag of the Republic of Iraq?
12 What does the Latin deo volente mean?
13 Which high-profile politician won the Dulwich and West Norwood seat in 2005?
14 Raleigh is the capital of which US state?
15 What size is B4 paper in millimetres?
16 Ayegbeni Yakubu joined Middlesbrough from which club?
17 In which of his many movies did Anthony Hopkins play Dr Frederick Treves?
18 What is the administrative centre for the Welsh county of Powys?
19 Stotinki can be spent in which country?
20 Where in Westminster Abbey was the Stone of Scone?
21 What is the international car index mark for a car from Chile?
22 To five years when was the magazine Country Life founded?
23 Which late singer was the lead guitarist with the Grateful Dead?
24 In which country is the city of Dalian?
25 Who was the Roman God of death?
26 Whose top hat sold for £22,000 at Sotheby's in 1988?
27 The spice fenugreek is made from which part of a plant?
28 What was Dollar's first UK Top Ten hit in 1979?
29 In the film "Ace Ventura: Pet Detective" Ace is hired to find what?
30 Who was known as "Joltin Joe" and "the Yankee Clipper"?

1 What is the currency of Bolivia?
2 Between which two rivers does Manhattan lie?
3 Where in Russia was a school besieged by extremists in September 2004?
4 In which country is the city of Curitiba?
5 What is the capital of Brunei?
6 In which country is the deep-water port of Lobito?
7 The islands of Taipa and Coloane are part of which possession?
8 Pluna Airlines are based in which country?
9 Which capital is further North – Khartoum or Addis Ababa?
10 What is the official language of Bhutan?
11 In which country is Kakadu National Park?
12 Which country is due North of Uruguay?
13 Which two countries border Morocco?
14 Which desert lies between the Kalahari and the Atlantic Ocean?
15 Where is the news agency Colprensa based?
16 What is Madison Square Garden situated over?
17 On which island is Nassau, the capital of the Bahamas?
18 In which US state was the first National Park?
19 How is Denali in Alaska also known?
20 The Negev desert tapers to which port?
21 Who designed New Delhi?
22 What is the third longest river in Africa?
23 Which country has the largest oil resources in Africa?
24 Chandrika Kumaratunga was president of which country hit by the 2004 tsunami?
25 In which country is the city of Medan?
26 What is the capital of Burundi?
27 What is South Africa's judicial capital?
28 What is the most north-eastern US state?
29 SAHSA Airlines are based in which country?
30 Which island is situated between Sumatra and Bali?

Answers | Blockbusters *(see Quiz 84)*

1 It Happened One Night. 2 Elwood P. Dowd. 3 Lewis Gilbert. 4 Miracle on 34th Street. 5 Philadelphia Story. 6 A Night at the Opera. 7 Walter Pidgeon. 8 Dodi Fayed. 9 Robert Newton. 10 Dances with Wolves. 11 James Cameron. 12 Busby Berkeley. 13 Waterworld. 14 Gary Oldman. 15 Blenheim. 16 Amon Goeth. 17 Bruce Springsteen & Neil Young. 18 Ben Hur. 19 Gandhi. 20 Ellen Burstyn. 21 King Kong, 1933. 22 Bolivia. 23 Endora in Bewitched. 24 The Shadows. 25 Costume. 26 Liv Ullmann. 27 Cary Grant. 28 Mammy (Gone with the Wind). 29 The Full Monty. 30 How to paint.

1 Which 1930s classic was originally called "Night Bus"?
2 Whom does James Stewart play in "Harvey"?
3 Whom did Carol Reed replace at the last minute on "Oliver!"
4 In which 1940s classic did Edward Gwenn play Kris Kringle?
5 Katharine Hepburn bought the rights to a Philip Barry play to make which movie?
6 What was the Marx Brothers' first film for MGM?
7 Who played Mr Miniver in the Greer Garson Oscar winner?
8 Which film producer who died in 1997 co-produced "Chariots of Fire"?
9 Who played Bill Sikes when Alec Guinness was Fagin?
10 What was the first Western to win a Best Picture Oscar after a 60-year gap?
11 Who directed the first "Terminator" films?
12 Who choreographed "42nd Street"?
13 "Titanic" overtook which movie as the most costly ever made?
14 Which actor kidnapped Harrison Ford in "Air Force One"?
15 Which palace was used for Kenneth Branagh's "Hamlet"?
16 What is the name of Ralph Fiennes' character in "Schindler's List"?
17 Whose songs were on the soundtrack of "Philadelphia"?
18 Which 1950s film cost $4 million, twice the maximum of the time?
19 Which film begins with "No man's life can be encompassed in one telling"?
20 Which star of "The Exorcist" also used the name Edna Rae?
21 Which film has the quote, "It wasn't the airplanes. It was beauty killed the beast"?
22 Where were Butch Cassidy and Sundance finally tracked down?
23 What is the most famous TV role of actress Agnes Moorehead?
24 The composer of the only Oscar-nominated song from "Grease" was from which famous quartet?
25 John Mollo won an Oscar in "Star Wars" for what?
26 Who was the only woman to have top billing in "A Bridge Too Far"?
27 Who was originally sought for the role of Shears in "The Bridge on the River Kwai"?
28 Hattie McDaniel was the first black actress to win an Oscar, but for which role?
29 Which movie did "Titanic" overtake as a record UK earner?
30 The ex-GI is in Paris to learn what in "An American in Paris"?

1 Both Emma Bunton's dad and Robert Redford's dad worked as what?
2 London's Royal College of Music is in which regal-sounding road?
3 Which actress starred in "Thelma and Louise" and "Lorenzo's Oil"?
4 In which European country are the regions of Kitaa and Tunu?
5 Which Sale Sharks player fractured his left ankle playing for England in Nov. 2006?
6 What name is given to the Greek letter that is the equivalent of letter M?
7 Sophie Okonedo was Oscar-nominated for which film based on real life?
8 Who joined the European Union in 1995 with Finland and Sweden?
9 Which sea would you cross if you sailed from Corfu to Cephalonia?
10 Who has been married to Catherine Deneuve, Marie Helvin and Catherine Dyer?
11 Under which name did Aliaune Thiam top the single and album charts?
12 What was Celine Dion's first solo UK Top Ten hit?
13 Which US state is called the Bullion State?
14 What name did former Mayfair hairdresser Nigel Davies adopt in the 1960s ?
15 What colours appear with black and red on the Jordanian flag?
16 In which year did Dennis the Menace first appear in the Beano?
17 Which British army officer invented shells containing bullets to inflict more casualties?
18 Who was the longest-serving British PM?
19 What was Donovan's autobiography called?
20 What is the capital of Djibouti?
21 Which English seaside resort is associated with Count Dracula?
22 What was Donny Osmond's last UK No. 1?
23 Who wrote "Chicken Soup with Barley"?
24 Doraphobia is the fear of what?
25 What was the pirate Blackbeard's real name?
26 What is the name Blimp derived from in the character Colonel Blimp?
27 Which fund pays the Queen's private expenses as sovereign?
28 Martin Short played Franck Eggelhoffer in a 1990s remake of which movie?
29 Where was Captain James Cook killed in 1779?
30 Who composed the opera "Billy Budd"?

| **Answers** | **Plant World** *(see Quiz 86)* |

1 Ginkgo. 2 Oxalic. 3 Callus. 4 Cherokee leader. 5 It dissolves blood corpuscles. 6 Italy. 7 Rockies. 8 North & South Carolina. 9 Blue. 10 Ferns & mosses. 11 Pacific coast of North America. 12 Stalk. 13 African violet. 14 From insects. 15 It loses its green colour. 16 Matchbox bean. 17 Rose of Jericho. 18 Sloes. 19 Cactus. 20 Poppy. 21 General Sherman. 22 Lettuce. 23 On dung. 24 Sierra Nevada. 25 Belladonna. 26 Stalk. 27 By the sea. 28 Silver Fir. 29 Praslin & Curiense. 30 Giant waterlily.

Quiz 86 Plant World

Answers – page 317

LEVEL 3

1 How is the maidenhair tree also known?
2 Which acid makes rhubarb leaves poisonous?
3 What is a tissue which forms on a damaged plant surface called?
4 The Sequoia takes its name from what?
5 What makes the death cap mushroom so toxic?
6 Which European country produces more than half of Europe's rice?
7 Where would you find the home of the bristlecone pine?
8 The Venus flytrap is found naturally in which US states?
9 A meadow clary has flowers of what colour?
10 What sort of plants are cryptogams?
11 The world's tallest tree is native only to where?
12 If a leaf is sessile what is missing?
13 What is another name for the Saintpaulia?
14 How does a bladderwort receive its nourishment?
15 If a plant suffers from chlorosis what happens to it?
16 How is the entada known in Australia?
17 What is the only plant which can change its shape?
18 What is the fruit of the Blackthorn bush?
19 What type of plant is a saguaro?
20 To which family does the greater celandine belong?
21 The largest known giant redwood is named after whom?
22 How is the plant lactuca sativa better known?
23 If something is coprophilous where does it grow?
24 The tree sometimes known as Wellingtonia is native to which mountains?
25 Atropine is derived from which plant?
26 Which part of the flax plant is used to make linen?
27 If a plant is halophytic where does it grow?
28 Which tree is the tallest native to Europe?
29 On which two islands would you find the sea coconut?
30 Which plant has the largest leaves?

1 A sentence containing all the alphabet's letters is known as a what?
2 What is the international car index mark for a car from Singapore?
3 Who is the elder – Terry Wogan or Bill Wyman?
4 What was the most common surname of MPs after the 2005 general election?
5 In which decade did Fiji leave the Commonwealth?
6 Who wrote the novel "The Pathfinder"?
7 Columbus is the capital of which US state?
8 Who directed the 1991 film "The Silence of the Lambs"?
9 What was Duran Duran's first UK Top Ten hit?
10 Which post was held by William Gilbert at the courts of Elizabeth I and James I?
11 Which poet was awarded an Order of Merit in 1953, three years before his death?
12 Whose 2004 hit album "His Greatest Love Songs" came 37 years after his first hit?
13 Which river was explored by Scotsman Mungo Park?
14 Bill Robertie became the first person to win which World Championship twice?
15 Mogadishu is the capital of which country?
16 Where did the married Princess Elizabeth live before she came to the throne?
17 In music what does the expression "pesante" mean?
18 Who was the Greek goddess of victory?
19 On the first of which month is Canada Day celebrated?
20 What is the title of the head of the College of Arms?
21 In which movie did Hitchcock first appear in one of his cameo roles?
22 Which TV character drove a yellow car called Bessie?
23 In which country is the city of Douala?
24 Whose only UK Top Ten hit was "Jeans On"?
25 For which film did Geena Davis first win an Oscar?
26 In 1860 Willie Park became the first winner of which sporting trophy?
27 In 2005–06 Chelsea won their first nine Premiership games – who won their last nine?
28 What colour separates the black, red and green bands on the Kenyan flag?
29 What part of your body is initialised as the ANS?
30 Which artist painted "Dancer at the Bar" around 1900?

Answers	**Music Superstars** *(see Quiz 88)*

1 Tina Turner. 2 Tony Bennett. 3 Neil Diamond. 4 Girls! Girls! Girls! 5 Sorry Seems to be the Hardest Word. 6 When I Need You. 7 1960s. 8 Bohemian Rhapsody. 9 Bob Dylan. 10 Eleven. 11 Kate Bush. 12 Dancing Queen. 13 Turandot. 14 Barry, Robin & Maurice Gibb. 15 Let's Dance. 16 Jean Terrell. 17 Mark McGrath. 18 Madonna. 19 Epic. 20 1962. 21 Mick Jagger. 22 Roxy Music. 23 Rod Stewart. 24 Thunderclap Newman. 25 Celine Dion and Peabo Bryson. 26 Love Me for a Reason. 27 Zubin Mehta. 28 Hot Chocolate. 29 Blinded by the Light. 30 Rock On.

1 Which veteran singer's first No. 1 album was "Foreign Affair"?
2 Who included Bono, Paul McCartney and Sting on his 2006 album "Duets"?
3 Who wrote "I'm a Believer" for The Monkees?
4 From which film was Elvis Presley's 2005 hit "Return to Sender"?
5 What was Elton John's first solo hit on his own Rocket label?
6 Which Leo Sayer hit gave the Chrysalis label their first No. 1?
7 In which decade did Barbra Streisand first make the UK charts?
8 Which hit was the first to be No. 1 over two separate Christmases?
9 Which singer/songwriter penned the lines, "The carpet, too, is moving under you"?
10 How many consecutive UK No. 1 hits did the Beatles have?
11 Who duetted with Peter Gabriel on "Games without Frontiers"?
12 What was Abba's only No. 1 in the USA?
13 Which opera does Pavarotti's anthem "Nessun Dorma" come from?
14 Which of the Gibb brothers wrote their first UK No. 1 "Massachusetts"?
15 Which David Bowie hit was his fourth UK and second US No. 1 in 1983?
16 Who replaced Diana Ross when she left The Supremes?
17 Who was the first person to duet on a single with Shania Twain?
18 Stephen Bray and Patrick Leonard have both co-written No. 1s with which singer?
19 Michael Jackson's "Thriller" and "Bad" came out on which label?
20 When did Tony Bennett first record "I Left My Heart in San Francisco"?
21 Which group singer put out a solo album called "Primitive Cool"?
22 A John Lennon song gave which group their only UK No. 1?
23 Which singing superstar once had a trial for Brentford FC?
24 Pete Townshend's first No. 1 as a producer was for which group?
25 Who sang the theme song to the film "Beauty and the Beast"?
26 What was the final No. 1 by any of the Osmond family?
27 Who conducted the Three Tenors for their Italia 90 concert?
28 Who is the only group to appear in the charts in every year of the 1970s?
29 Which Springsteen song was a hit for Manfred Mann's Earth Band?
30 Which David Essex hit was the soundtrack for "That'll be the Day"?

Answers | Pot Luck 41 *(see Quiz 87)*

1 Pangram. 2 SGP. 3 Bill Wyman. 4 Smith. 5 1980s. 6 James Fenimore Cooper. 7 Ohio. 8 Jonathan Demme. 9 Girls on Film. 10 Royal Physician. 11 Walter de la Mare. 12 Engelbert Humperdinck. 13 River Niger. 14 Backgammon. 15 Somalia. 16 Clarence House. 17 Heavy, ponderous. 18 Nike. 19 July. 20 Earl Marshall. 21 The Lodger. 22 Dr Who. 23 Cameroon. 24 David Dundas. 25 The Accidental Tourist. 26 Golf's British Open. 27 Liverpool. 28 White. 29 Autonomic Nervous System. 30 Edgar Degas.

1 Which US state is called the Gopher State?
2 From which musical is the song "June is Bustin' Out All Over"?
3 In which decade was Frankie Dettori born?
4 The French physician Laennec invented which medical aid?
5 Nelophobia is the fear of what?
6 Who wrote the novel "Death In The Afternoon"?
7 In which country is the city of Fortaleza?
8 Which ex-Russian spy was in the news with claims of poisoning in Nov. 2006?
9 Which tree appears on the Lebanese flag?
10 What's the English name of the constellation Dorado?
11 Whose only UK Top Ten hit was "The Final Countdown"?
12 Who is the most photographed person to attend Riddlesdown High school, Croydon?
13 In which country are the regions of Liguria and Calabria?
14 Which studio produced the series of "Scream" slasher horror movies?
15 The majority of tourists to the USA are from which country?
16 Who composed the opera "The Golden Cockerel"?
17 Who was the youngest performer last century to win an Oscar open to adults?
18 Which country has the ngultrum as a unit of currency?
19 Who is the elder – Ruby Wax or Victoria Wood?
20 How old was James Herriot when he began writing books?
21 Which King of Spain was known as Charles the Mad?
22 Who joined the European Union in the same year as Portugal?
23 What is the Swedish plattar?
24 Which media celeb founded a magazine called "Passing Wind"?
25 Dying in 2005, Renaldo "Obie" Benson was a former member of which singing group?
26 What was Earth, Wind and Fire's first UK Top Ten hit?
27 The wall, bar and frog are all part of a horse's what?
28 What is the capital of the Dominican Republic?
29 What is Julie Andrews' full real name?
30 In which decade was the first Archery World Championship?

Answers | TV Times 4 *(see Quiz 90)*

1 Colin Firth. 2 AA. 3 Robert Lindsay. 4 Boyzone. 5 Nero. 6 Eric Idle. 7 British Rail. 8 Woodburn & MacKenzie. 9 Bella. 10 TISWAS. 11 Cedric Charlton. 12 Cricket St Thomas. 13 No one, he was never seen. 14 A moose. 15 Play Your Cards Right. 16 Letitia Dean. 17 The Winchester. 18 Michael Cole. 19 Alan Alda. 20 World's biggest one-man band. 21 Fleur. 22 Russell T. Davies. 23 Charlie Gimbert. 24 Seymour Utterthwaite. 25 Bullying. 26 Crimewatch UK. 27 Rathouse International. 28 It Ain't Half Hot Mum. 29 Purple. 30 Glenbogle.

1 Who played John McCarthy in "Hostages"?
2 Which emergency service did Anthea Turner work for before her media career?
3 Who played the scheming city council chief in "GBH"?
4 Whom did Andrew Lloyd Webber appear on "Top of the Pops" with in 1998?
5 What was the caterpillar called in "Dangermouse"?
6 Who founded Rutland Weekend Television?
7 Which company did Colin work for in "Colin's Sandwich"?
8 What are the surnames of Kim & Aggie in "How Clean is Your House?"?
9 In alphabetical order, who is the first of "The Tweenies"?
10 Which show had a punk dog called Spit?
11 In "The Darling Buds of May" what was Charley's real name?
12 "To the Manor Born" was set in which village?
13 Who played Joe Maplin in "Hi De Hi!"?
14 What strolled across the opening title in "Northern Exposure"?
15 How was the US series "Card Sharks" known when it transferred to the UK?
16 Who played Lucinda in "Grange Hill"?
17 What was the name of the pub in "Minder"?
18 Who left the employ of Mohammed Fayed to host a daytime chat show on satellite TV?
19 Who hosted "That was the Week that was" in the US?
20 What record did Roy Castle break on the very first "Record Breakers"?
21 What was Zoe and Alec's baby called in "May to December"?
22 Who wrote the "Doctor Who" spin-off which starred John Barrowman?
23 In "Lovejoy" who bough Felsham Manor after Lady Jane left?
24 Who replaced Foggy Dewhurst when Michael Aldridge joined the "Last of the Summer Wine" cast?
25 "See Something, Say Something" was a Nickleodeon feature about what?
26 Which series was based on Germany's "File XY Unsolved"?
27 Which company did Terence "Twiggy" Rathbone own in "Hot Metal"?
28 In which series were jungle sequences shot in Norfolk and desert scenes in Sussex?
29 What colour hair did Crystal Tipps have?
30 In which fictional place did Hector and Molly live?

Answers | Pot Luck 42 (see Quiz 89)

1 Minnesota. 2 Carousel. 3 1970s. 4 Stethoscope. 5 Glass. 6 Ernest Hemingway. 7 Brazil. 8 Alexander Litvinenko. 9 Cedar tree. 10 Swordfish. 11 Europe. 12 Kate Moss. 13 Italy. 14 Dimension Films. 15 Canada. 16 Rimsky-Korsakov. 17 Tatum O'Neal. 18 Bhutan. 19 Ruby Wax. 20 50 years old. 21 Charles II. 22 Spain. 23 Pancake. 24 Ian Hislop. 25 The Four Tops. 26 September. 27 Hoof. 28 Santo Domingo. 29 Julia Elizabeth Wells. 30 1930s.

Quiz 91 | Pot Luck 43

Answers – page 324

1 In which country is the city of Ibadan?
2 What do the initials for the chemical DDT stand for?
3 Who directed the film trilogy "Lethal Weapon"?
4 Arthur Scargill and the Duchess of York were removed from where in 1996?
5 What was Pigmeat Markham's only UK Top Ten hit?
6 What is the main language of the Republic of Chad?
7 Douroucouli, de Brazza's guenon and red colobus are types of what?
8 Which artist painted Black Paintings in the 1820s?
9 Who invented the word "frabjous"?
10 Salem is the capital of which US state?
11 What is Robson Green's middle name?
12 How old was Anna Paquin when she won her first Oscar?
13 Windhoek is the capital of which country?
14 A fear of fear is known as what?
15 What invaded the town of San Antonio de los Caballeros in June '98?
16 What was Rod Stewart's last UK No. 1?
17 Who was the Roman goddess of horses?
18 What does the green pentacle on the Moroccan flag depict?
19 What is the international car index mark for a car from Burundi?
20 What did the M stand for in JMW Turner's name?
21 Mrs Thatcher became Baroness Thatcher of where?
22 What is the drug thiopental used for?
23 Desmond Tutu's middle name is Mpilo, which means what?
24 Bernard Herrmann finished the score to which Scorsese film just before he died?
25 Who had an 80s hit with "She Means Nothing to Me"?
26 Beatriz Merino became PM of which South American country in this century?
27 In 1998 Tommy Dixon was arrested at home after what was mistaken for a gunshot?
28 In which city is the 305 metre long cable-braced Erskine bridge?
29 The spice sassafras is made from which part of a plant?
30 Who became Trade & Industry Secretary in 2006?

Answers | Performing Arts *(see Quiz 92)*

1 French & English. 2 Arlene Phillips. 3 English National Ballet. 4 A cappella. 5 Cell Mates. 6 Vanessa Mae. 7 Louis B. Mayer. 8 John Ogdon. 9 Rowan Atkinson. 10 Quintet du Hot Club de France. 11 Dash. 12 Mississippi. 13 Placido Domingo. 14 Phil Collins. 15 Popcorn. 16 Shostakovich. 17 Laurence Olivier. 18 Bournemouth Sinfonietta. 19 Tony Richardson. 20 Jerome Robbins. 21 Alan Ayckbourn. 22 The Who. 23 Jim Steinman. 24 Ronnie Barker. 25 Angela Gheorghiu and Roberto Alagna. 26 Hello Dolly. 27 Arpeggio. 28 Leslie Bricusse. 29 South Pacific. 30 Sir Peter Hall.

1 In which languages did Irishman Samuel Beckett write his plays?
2 Who choreographed the 2006 revival of "The Sound of Music"?
3 Princess Diana was patron of which ballet company?
4 Which type of singing means "in the style of the chapel"?
5 Which play did Stephen Fry walk out of in 1995?
6 Who went on a Red Hot world tour in 1996?
7 Who founded the American Academy of Motion Picture Arts and Sciences?
8 Who won the 1962 Tchaikovsky competition with Ashkenazy?
9 Who, in 1981, became the youngest star of a West End one-man show?
10 Grappelli and Reinhardt were leaders of which Quintet?
11 What was the name of Wayne Sleep's 1980 dance company?
12 Tennessee Williams was born in which US state?
13 Which opera singer sang with Sarah Brightman in "Requiem"?
14 Who played the Artful Dodger in the first stage production of "Oliver!"?
15 Which Ben Elton novel was the first to be adapted into a West End play?
16 2006's Last Night of the Proms had a Russian flavour for whose centenary?
17 Who shared management of the Old Vic between 1944 and 1950 with Ralph Richardson?
18 With which orchestra did Simon Rattle make his professional debut?
19 Who established the English Stage Company with George Devine at the Royal Court in 1955?
20 Who choreographed "West Side Story" and "Fiddler on the Roof"?
21 Who was in the Guinness Book of Records for having five plays running in the West End at one time?
22 Whose mini opera "Wire & Glass" was premièred at the 2006 Electric Prom?
23 Who wrote the lyrics for Lloyd Webber's "Whistle Down the Wind"?
24 Who wrote the radio drama "Mum" for his actress daughter Charlotte?
25 Which husband-and-wife team were in London's 2006 Proms in the Park Last Night?
26 Thornton Wilder's "The Matchmaker" was made into which musical?
27 Which musical term means "like a harp"?
28 Who wrote the songs for "Doctor Dolittle"?
29 Sean Connery's first West End appearance was in which chorus line?
30 Who founded the RSC aged 30?

Answers | Pot Luck 43 *(see Quiz 91)*

1 Nigeria. 2 Dichloro-diphenyl-trichloroethane. 3 Richard Donner. 4 Madame Tussaud's displays. 5 Here Comes the Judge. 6 French. 7 Monkey. 8 Goya. 9 Lewis Carroll. 10 Oregon. 11 Golightly. 12 11 years (The Piano). 13 Namibia. 14 Phobophobia. 15 Butterflies. 16 Baby Jane. 17 Epona. 18 The Seal of Solomon. 19 RU. 20 Mallord. 21 Kesteven. 22 General anaesthetic. 23 Life. 24 Taxi Driver. 25 Phil Everly and Cliff Richard. 26 Peru. 27 A balloon bursting. 28 Glasgow. 29 Root bark. 30 Alistair Darling.

1 In which Hawaiian island is Pearl Harbor?
2 What was Cliff Richard's first 1980s No. 1?
3 JF Kennedy was one of how many children?
4 Under what name did Helen Porter Mitchell sing her way to success?
5 What was John Schlesinger's first US film?
6 In which month is the US holiday President's Day?
7 In which European country are the areas of Telemark and Troms?
8 Joe Fagin's 1980s hit was a theme tune for which TV series?
9 Which country has the pula as a unit of currency?
10 What is the correct form of address to begin a letter to an Earl?
11 Which US state is called the Bay State?
12 Who were Jessica, Kelli, Kevin, Michelle and Tony collectively?
13 Hypegiaphobia is the fear of what?
14 Whom did Joe Louis beat to first become world heavyweight champ?
15 What was Eva Braun working as when she met Adolf Hitler?
16 Adrian Vowels was the first Man of Steel winner from which rugby club?
17 Which Battle was the last in the Hundred Years War?
18 Who joined the European Union in the same year as UK and Denmark?
19 Who composed the opera "Punch and Judy"?
20 What was American hero Paul Revere's day job?
21 Who founded the Pakistan People's Party?
22 In which country is the city of Guayaquil?
23 What was the name of the Queen's first corgi?
24 Who played Sally Bowles in the 1955 film "I am a Camera"?
25 Which rock star had a major stake in the production company that made "Enigma"?
26 Kurt Weill and Henrik Ibsen were born in which month?
27 Who was the first Austrian to top the UK charts?
28 In which well-known building did the late George Best spend Xmas in 1984?
29 Which Frank L. Baum story provided the inspiration for a 2006 new musical?
30 To five either way, how many weeks did Sinatra's "My Way" spend in the UK charts between 1969 and 1971?

Answers	Tennis *(see Quiz 94)*

1 Borotra, Brugnon, Cochet & Lacoste. **2** Vijay Amritraj. **3** Martina Navratilova. **4** Arthur Ashe. **5** Gabriela Sabatini. **6** Pete Sampras. **7** French Open. **8** Margaret Smith. **9** Plus an Olympic gold medal. **10** Karen Hantze. **11** 1968. **12** Michael Stich. **13** Richard Krajicek. **14** Andy Roddick. **15** Justine Henin Ardenne. **16** Russia. **17** The Queen. **18** Men's doubles. **19** French. **20** French Open. **21** Michael Stich. **22** Lindsay Davenport. **23** Kevin Curren. **24** Tony Pickard. **25** Stefan Edberg. **26** Tim Gullikson. **27** Roger Taylor. **28** Kosice, Slovakia. **29** Sue Barker. **30** Sukova.

Quiz 94 | Tennis

Answers – page 325

1 Who were tennis's "Four Musketeers"?
2 Which tennis player appeared in "Octopussy"?
3 Who had the car number plate X CZECH?
4 Who won the first US Men's Open?
5 Who, in 1986, became the youngest woman semi-finalist at Wimbledon for 99 years?
6 Who won the inaugural Grand Slam Cup in Munich in 1990?
7 What was Monica Seles's first Grand Slam title?
8 Who was the first Australian woman to win the Wimbledon Singles?
9 How does a Golden Grand Slam differ from a Grand Slam?
10 With whom did Billie Jean Moffitt win her first Wimbledon Doubles title?
11 What year was the world's first Open tournament?
12 Who was the first German to win the Wimbledon Men's Singles after reunification?
13 At Wimbledon who won an unseeded men's final in the 90s?
14 Whom did Roger Federer beat to win his third US Open?
15 In 2005, who won the women's German Open for the third time?
16 Who were the winners of the 2006 Davis Cup?
17 Who gave Virginia Wade her trophy when she won Wimbledon?
18 Which new competition was included in the Wimbledon championships in 1884 along with the Women's Singles?
19 Which Grand Slam title has Boris Becker never won?
20 Which Grand Slam title did Roger Federer not win in 2006?
21 In 1992 John McEnroe won the Wimbledon Doubles title with whom?
22 Who replaced Martina Hingis as World No. 1 in October 1998?
23 Whom did Boris Becker beat to become Wimbledon's youngest Men's Singles winner?
24 Whom did Greg Rusedski sack as his coach during Wimbledon 1998?
25 Who won his first Open title in 1985 two years after winning the Junior Grand Slam?
26 Which mentor of Pete Sampras died in May 1996?
27 Who was the last British man before Tim Henman to reach a Wimbledon quarter-final?
28 Where was Martina Hingis born?
29 How is Wimbledon semi-finalist Mrs Lampard better known?
30 Which Helena won two titles in one day at Wimbledon 1996?

Answers	Pot Luck 44 *(see Quiz 93)*

1 Oahu. 2 Mistletoe and Wine. 3 Nine. 4 Nellie Melba. 5 Midnight Cowboy. 6 February. 7 Norway. 8 Auf Wiedersehen, Pet. 9 Botswana. 10 My Lord. 11 Massachusetts. 12 Liberty X. 13 Responsibility. 14 James Braddock. 15 Photographer's assistant. 16 Castleford. 17 Castillon. 18 Republic of Ireland. 19 Harrison Birtwistle. 20 Silversmith. 21 Zulfikar Ali Bhutto. 22 Ecuador. 23 Susan. 24 Julie Harris. 25 Mick Jagger. 26 March. 27 Falco (Rock Me Amadeus). 28 Pentonville Prison. 29 The Wizard of Oz (Wicked!). 30 122.

Quiz 95

Pot Luck 45

Answers – page 328

LEVEL 3

1 What was the christian name of chocolate founder Mr Cadbury?
2 In which country is the city of Gwangju?
3 Bill Perks the son of a bricklayer became known as who?
4 What does the Latin mea culpa mean?
5 Which creature is represented in the year the Chinese call "long"?
6 Which country has the rufiyaa as a unit of currency?
7 2000 saw the first "X-Men" film – which decade saw the comic characters first appear?
8 What was Enrique Iglesias's first US No. 1 single?
9 What was Foreigner's first UK Top Ten hit in 1981?
10 Who is the elder – Bob Geldof or Nigel Kennedy?
11 Which Hitchock film title ties in with his father's field of work?
12 Who first appeared for England – Joe Cole or Owen Hargreaves?
13 Whose nickname was "Stormin' Norman"?
14 Who directed the 1987 film "Good Morning Vietnam"?
15 Columbia is the capital of which US state?
16 What is a honey locust?
17 Born Marie Grosholtz, under what name is this French lady remembered?
18 What could be signed by Hardy Bros of Ainwick or Charles Forlan?
19 Which saints share their names with three of the five inhabited Scilly Isles?
20 Maputo is the capital of which country?
21 What does the medical term D & C stand for?
22 Who played Marsellus Wallace in "Pulp Fiction"?
23 Which artist painted "Toledo Landscape" around 1610?
24 How is the letter O formed in Morse Code?
25 How many square chains make one hectare in surveying?
26 In which county was Sir Humphry Davy, inventor of the miner's safety lamp, born?
27 What did Terry Wogan study at Belvedere College, Dublin?
28 Who was the Greek god of vegetation and rebirth?
29 Which seasonal rose is from the genus Helleborus?
30 What is the international car index mark for a car from Lebanon?

Answers | Famous Names *(see Quiz 96)*

1 39. 2 Joan Plowright. 3 Antony Worrall Thompson. 4 George Michael. 5 Helen Mirren. 6 Vic Reeves. 7 His hair was too long. 8 Duchess of Kent. 9 Mountbatten's. 10 Bernard Ingham. 11 David Hasselhoff. 12 Catherine Walker. 13 Marco Pierre White. 14 Malcolm McLaren. 15 Jane and Jonathan Ross. 16 Anne-Sophie Mutter. 17 Samira Khashoggi. 18 Duke of Westminster. 19 Ryan Giggs. 20 Michael Grade. 21 Sir Peregrine Worsthorne. 22 Gary & Michelle Lineker. 23 Sean Bean. 24 Soft drinks. 25 Chloe. 26 First cousin. 27 Her favourite restaurant. 28 Ralph Fiennes. 29 Swansea. 30 Alexander McQueen.

Quiz 96 Famous Names

Answers – page 327

1 How old was David Cameron when he was elected Tory leader?
2 Who was Sue Lawley's final guest on "Desert Island Discs"?
3 Which celeb chef appeared in "Adrian Mole: The Cappuccino Years" and "Footballers' Wives"?
4 Who is known to his family as "Yog"?
5 Who became Mrs Taylor Hackford in 1997?
6 Who changed his name from Jim Moir so it didn't clash with the BBC's Head of Light Entertainment?
7 Why was Cliff Richard banned from entering Singapore in 1972?
8 How is the former Miss Katharine Worsley better known?
9 In whose family home did Charles and Diana spend the first night of their honeymoon?
10 Who was Margaret Thatcher's Press Secretary when she resigned?
11 Which "Baywatch" star's autobiography was called "Making Waves"?
12 Who founded the Chelsea Design Company in 1976?
13 Which Leeds-born chef won three Michelin stars by his early thirties?
14 Who opened the punk boutique Seditionaries in the 70s with Vivienne Westwood?
15 Who have children called Betty Kitten, Harvey Kirby and Honey Kinny?
16 Who was André Previn's fifth wife?
17 Who was Mohammed Fayed's first wife and Dodi Fayed's mother?
18 Who is London's largest landowner?
19 Who is the son of former rugby league international Danny Wilson?
20 Who was raised by his grandmother Olga Winogradsky?
21 Which former editor is Lady Lucinda Lambton's third husband?
22 Who are the parents of George, Harry, Tobias and Angus?
23 Who has "100% Blades" tattooed on his left arm?
24 William Hague's father's business produced what?
25 In 1998 Stella McCartney designed for which fashion house?
26 What relation is Natasha Richardson to Jemma Redgrave?
27 After who or what did Lady Helen Taylor (née Windsor) name her first son?
28 Which Hamlet ran off with his mother Gertrude in 1995?
29 Where was Michael Heseltine born?
30 Who succeeded John Galliano at Givenchy in 1996?

Answers Pot Luck 45 *(see Quiz 95)*

1 John. 2 South Korea. 3 Bill Wyman (Rolling Stones). 4 Through my fault. 5 Dragon. 6 Maldives. 7 1960s. 8 Bailamos. 9 Waiting for a Girl Like You. 10 Bob Geldof. 11 The Birds (Dad a poultry trader). 12 Joe Cole. 13 US General Norman Schwarzkopf. 14 Barry Levinson. 15 South Carolina. 16 A tree. 17 Madame Tussaud. 18 Fishing reel. 19 Agnes, Mary & Martin. 20 Mozambique. 21 Dilation and Curettage. 22 Ving Rhames. 23 El Greco. 24 Dash, dash, dash. 25 Ten. 26 Cornwall. 27 Philosophy. 28 Adonis. 29 Christmas Rose. 30 RL.

Quiz 97 | Pot Luck 46

Answers – page 330

1 Which occupation was shared by the fathers of Roger Moore and Burt Reynolds?
2 What are the two colours of the national flag of Pakistan?
3 Who was the elder – Liam Gallagher or Ryan Giggs?
4 What was Gerald Ford's middle name?
5 What was the profession of escapologist Harry Houdini's father?
6 Over 700 people died in Greece in July 1987 due to what?
7 Who composed the opera "The Rape of Lucretia"?
8 Ian Thorpe announced his retirement from swimming at what age?
9 Which gallery is located at Bankside, London SE1 9TG?
10 Who was the "Big Brother" winner following Craig Phillips?
11 Which prince was born in the year Ted Hughes became Poet Laureate?
12 If a wine is said to be flabby what does it lack?
13 What is the capital of Greenland?
14 In music, what does the expression "strepitoso" mean?
15 For a role in which film did Vanessa Redgrave shave her head?
16 Which country has the lev as a unit of currency?
17 For what offence did Sophia Loren spend 17 days in prison in 1982?
18 In which decade was Richard Branson born?
19 In which European country are the regions of Beja and Guarda?
20 Which playwright was born in Whiston on Merseyside in 1947?
21 Which American state is called the Hawkeye State?
22 Which vitamin is also known as biotin?
23 Which singer played a bouncer in "Wayne's World"?
24 In this millennium, who first won the University Boat Race in successive years?
25 Who played Ron Jenkins in "Coronation Street"?
26 "Lost Souls" was the first chart album for which act?
27 Which hit got to No. 2 simultaneously in November 1995 with two separate groups?
28 On TV, James Bolam's Arthur and Michael French's Tom came from which town?
29 Who in Gilbert and Sullivan is "a dealer in magic and spells"?
30 Alphabetically, what is the first English parliamentary constituency?

Answers | Screen Greats *(see Quiz 98)*

1 None. 2 Betty Grable. 3 Peter Lorre. 4 Goldfinger. 5 Errol Flynn. 6 20th Century-Fox. 7 Charles Bronson. 8 Tony Curtis. 9 Barbara Stanwyck's. 10 Bela Lugosi. 11 Gene Kelly. 12 Audrey Hepburn. 13 Marlon Brando. 14 Ingrid Bergman. 15 Rita Hayworth. 16 Rebecca. 17 Sophia Loren. 18 One Night in the Tropics. 19 Dustin Hoffman. 20 George C. Scott. 21 Julie Andrews. 22 Lola-Lola. 23 His wife Carole Lombard. 24 Ginger Rogers. 25 Charlotte Brontë. 26 Twenty. 27 Anchors Aweigh. 28 The Big Broadcast. 29 The Barkleys of Broadway. 30 Making a Living.

1 What is the total number of Oscars won by Errol Flynn, Peter Cushing and Richard Burton?

2 Who once had her name changed to Frances Dean by Goldwyn?

3 Who is mentioned by name in Al Stewart's song "The Year of the Cat"?

4 Which Bond film did Sean Connery make prior to Hitchcock's "Marnie"?

5 Eric Porter played Soames on TV but who played Soames in "That Forsyte Woman"?

6 Which was the first US studio Richard Burton worked for?

7 Who was known in Italy as "Il Brutto"?

8 Who changed Bernie for Tony in his first film "Criss Cross"?

9 Bette Midler re-created whose 1930s role in "Stella"?

10 Which screen great did Martin Landau play in "Ed Wood"?

11 Who was lent to Columbia by MGM for "Cover Girl"?

12 Sean Ferrer was the son of which Hollywood Oscar winner?

13 Whose first Oscar was for playing Terry Malloy in a 1950s classic?

14 Who was the mother of actress Isabella Rossellini?

15 Whose pin-up was pinned to the atomic bomb dropped on Bikini?

16 What was Hitchcock's first Hollywood film?

17 Who was the first performer to win an Oscar for a performance entirely in a foreign language?

18 What was Abbot and Costello's first feature film?

19 Who played Sean Connery's son in "Family Business"?

20 Who was the first actor ever to refuse an Oscar?

21 Who was the first British-born British actress of British parents to win an Oscar?

22 What was the name of Marlene Dietrich in "The Blue Angel"?

23 Whose death in 1942 spurred Clark Gable to join the US Air Corps?

24 Whose first film was "Campus Sweethearts" with Rudy Vallee?

25 Which author did Olivia de Havilland play in "Devotion"?

26 How old was Debbie Reynolds when she made "Singin' in the Rain"?

27 What was the first film which teamed Gene Kelly with Frank Sinatra?

28 In which film did Bob Hope find his theme tune?

29 In which 1949 film were Rogers and Astaire reunited after a 10-year break?

30 In which film did Chaplin make his screen debut, in 1914?

Answers | Pot Luck 46 *(see Quiz 97)*

1 Police officers. 2 White and green. 3 Liam Gallagher. 4 Rudolph. 5 A Rabbi. 6 Heatwave. 7 Benjamin Britten. 8 24. 9 Tate Modern. 10 Brian Dowling. 11 Prince Harry. 12 Acidity. 13 Godthab. 14 Noisy, boisterous. 15 Playing for Time. 16 Bulgaria. 17 Tax evasion. 18 1950s. 19 Portugal. 20 Willy Russell. 21 Iowa. 22 B6. 23 Meat Loaf. 24 Oxford. 25 Ben Kingsley. 26 Doves. 27 Wonderwall. 28 Ormston (Born & Bred). 29 John Wellington Wells (The Sorcerer). 30 Aldershot.

Quiz 99 | World History

1. Who was the first post-war German Chancellor to have been brought up in the former DDR?
2. The Isle of Man belonged to which two countries before it came under UK administration in 1765?
3. What name meaning "achievement of universal peace" is given to the reign of Emperor Akihito?
4. How did the former Princess Alix of of Hessen meet her death?
5. Who did not seek re-election as Austrian President in 1991 after revelations about his activities in WWII?
6. Who was the first President of Israel?
7. How many days after Waterloo did Napoleon resign?
8. Which governor of Sumatra was responsible for the founding of Singapore?
9. What did the Rarotonga Treaty secure in 1987?
10. What does Rasputin mean, as a name given to Grigory Efimovich?
11. Where were all but six French kings crowned?
12. Which country had a secret police force called the securitate which was replaced in 1990?
13. Which President Roosevelt was Republican?
14. What name was given to the incorporation of Austria into the Third Reich?
15. What did Haile Selassie's title Ras Tafari mean?
16. Who was Nazi minister of eastern occupied territories from 1941–44?
17. Who was secretary of state to Kennedy and Johnson?
18. Which French Prime Minister asked Anthony Eden to have the Queen as head of state?
19. In which country was the Rosetta Stone found in in 1799?
20. What name was given to the socialist movement which carried out the Nicaraguan Revolution?
21. Which Conference drew up the United Nations Charter?
22. How many German Popes were there before Benedict XVI?
23. In which year did Baroness Elliott become the first woman to address the House of Lords?
24. Who succeeded Ian Smith as Prime Minister of Rhodesia which then became known as Zimbabwe?
25. Where was the first Marxist state in Africa created?
26. Where was the Maoist guerrilla group Sendero Luminoso active in the 1980s?
27. Who became New Zealand PM in December 1997?
28. Who was joint secretary general of the ANC with Mandela in 1964?
29. Who were the first three states to break away from Yugoslavia in 1991?
30. Where did the Hundred Flowers Movement encourage government criticism in the 50s?

Answers | Pot Luck 47 *(see Quiz 100)*

1 U2. 2 Brighton & Hove Albion. 3 South Dakota. 4 Joan Crawford. 5 Edward Heath. 6 Boa snakes. 7 Rosemary Conley. 8 Anita Lonsborough. 9 She fell down a flight of stairs. 10 Ouranophobia. 11 Ben E. King. 12 MC. 13 Henri Matisse. 14 Ronnie Barker. 15 Myalgic Encephalitis. 16 Eltham. 17 Steven Spielberg. 18 Mali. 19 Hugh Grant. 20 Catherine Zeta Jones. 21 Delia Smith. 22 Sunderland. 23 Mauritania. 24 Samuel. 25 Balamory. 26 Lewis Carroll. 27 Taiwan. 28 American. 29 Winifred Holtby. 30 2,197.

1 Some England cricketers went to which band's 2006 Sydney concert?
2 Which football team does Des Lynam support?
3 Pierre is the capital of which American State?
4 Which actress was also known as Lucille Le Sueur?
5 Which ex-PM died on 17 July 2005?
6 Which reptiles come from the family Boidae?
7 Who produced a fitness video called "Ultimate Fat Burner"?
8 Who was the first female winner of the BBC Sports Personality of the Year?
9 How did fashion empress Laura Ashley die?
10 A fear of heaven is known as what?
11 Which singer's real name is Benjamin Earl Nelson?
12 What is the international car index mark for a car from Monaco?
13 Which artist painted "La Desserte" in 1908?
14 Who presented David Jason with his BAFTA Fellowship?
15 What is the full name for the medical condition known as ME?
16 Where in the UK did Bob Hope have a theatre named after him?
17 Who directed the 1992 film "Hook"?
18 Bamako is the capital of which country?
19 Who links the movies "Extreme Measures" and "The Remains of the Day"?
20 Who duetted with David Essex on "True Love Ways" in 1994?
21 Whose first book was "How to Cheat at Cooking"?
22 David Bellion joined Man Utd from which club?
23 Which country has the ouguiya as a unit of currency?
24 What was the christian name of shipowner Cunard?
25 In which town was Edie McCredie the minibus driver?
26 Which children's author appeared on the cover of "Sgt Pepper"?
27 In which country is the city of Kaohsiung?
28 What is the nationality of writer and chef Ken Hom?
29 "Testament of Friendship" is about Vera Brittain's friendship with which author?
30 What is 13 cubed?

Answers	World History *(see Quiz 99)*

1 Angela Merkel. 2 Norway & Scotland. 3 Heisei. 4 Shot with her husband Tsar Nicholas II. 5 Kurt Waldheim. 6 Chaim Weizmann. 7 Four. 8 Thomas Stanford Raffles. 9 Nuclear-free South Pacific. 10 Dissolute. 11 Reims. 12 Romania. 13 Theodore. 14 Anschluss. 15 Lion of Judah. 16 Alfred Rosenberg. 17 Dean Rusk. 18 Guy Mollet. 19 Egypt. 20 Sandanista. 21 San Francisco. 22 Seven. 23 1958. 24 Bishop Abel Muzorewa. 25 Mozambique. 26 Peru. 27 Jenny Shipley. 28 Walter Sisulu. 29 Slovenia, Macedonia & Croatia. 30 China.

1 Who starred with Steve Coogan on "The Dead Good Show"?
2 Who was the real-life husband of the first girl in the famous Nescafe commercials?
3 How was comedy writer Gerald Wiley better known?
4 Who found fame with Emma Thompson playing Danny McGlone?
5 Who starred in and produced a mini-series called "Sins"?
6 Who was a regular in "Crown Court" as barrister Jeremy Parsons QC?
7 Who is the mother of the actor who played Mr Rochester in the 2006 "Jane Eyre"?
8 What was presenter Matthew Wright's job before moving to TV in 2000?
9 Whose first pop TV series was called "The Power Station"?
10 Which Moll Flanders lost husband Ralph to Francesca Annis?
11 Who was the first male presenter of "Live & Kicking"?
12 What was Lenny Henry's Rastafarian community police officer called?
13 Who came to fame as "Q" of "The Little Ladies"?
14 Who was Cherie Lunghi's character in "The Manageress"?
15 Who played Fletch's son Raymond in "Going Straight"?
16 Which Andy was the 32nd presenter of "Blue Peter"?
17 Who are the two youngest McGann brothers?
18 Who was the first female presenter of "Top Gear"?
19 Who wrote the "Magic Roundabout" scripts when they were first broadcast in the UK?
20 Which actresses created "The House of Eliot"?
21 Who appeared in "Dixon of Dock Green" aged 10 and found fame as Mrs Theodopolopoudos?
22 Who introduced a famine report with the words, "A biblical famine, now in the twentieth century"?
23 Which "EastEnders" star used to be better known by his catchphrase "Terr-i-fic"?
24 Who played Marjory in "The Outside Dog" in the "Talking Heads" series?
25 Who won "New Faces" and went on to present it?
26 Who is the real-life mum of Grace and Henry Durham?
27 Still popular, who broke into TV with the 1986 series "Pet Watch"?
28 Who adapted his novel of the same name into "Men Behaving Badly"?
29 Who played the seventh Doctor Who?
30 Who was the only female presenter at the Live Aid concert?

1 Betty Joan Perske. 2 Margaret Thatcher. 3 Tennyson. 4 Jeweller. 5 Spice Up Your Life. 6 Scilly Isles. 7 RM. 8 Iran. 9 Oops Up Side Your Head. 10 Conakry. 11 Karpov. 12 Oriental rug. 13 Liberator. 14 Bolivia & Peru v. Chile. 15 Little Sioux River. 16 Children. 17 Conservatives. 18 Michael Ramsey. 19 Brighton. 20 Jane Seymour. 21 Trans-Canada Highway. 22 Kris Kristofferson & Rita Coolidge. 23 Complete works of Shakespeare. 24 Maine. 25 Phil Collins. 26 Myanmar. 27 Sir Edward Heath. 28 Gannex. 29 Romania. 30 2nd (2001–02).

1 What is Lauren Bacall's full real name?

2 About whom did Cliff Richard say, "She really is a woman just like my Mum"?

3 Who wrote the poem "The Idylls of the King"?

4 What was the profession of fizzy drinks maker Jacob Schweppes?

5 What was the fifth No. 1 single for the fab five Spice Girls?

6 Saint Mary's airport serves which Isles?

7 What is the international car index mark for a car from Madagascar?

8 Which country did Hollywood director Barbet Schroeder come from?

9 What was the Gap Band's first UK Top Ten hit?

10 What is the capital of Guinea?

11 Whom did Kasparov beat to become world chess champion in 1985?

12 What is a kelim?

13 What was the by-name for the B24 bomber?

14 Which countries fought the Pacific War in the 19th century?

15 On which river does the US city of Cherokee lie?

16 What or who does UNICEF benefit?

17 Which political party did Mrs Pankhurst join in 1925?

18 Who was the first Archbishop of Canterbury to meet a Pope since the 16th century?

19 The first Bodyshop opened in which town?

20 Who was Elizabeth I's first stepmother?

21 What runs for 4,860 miles from St John's to Victoria?

22 Which husband-and-wife team had a hit with "A Song I'd Like to Sing"?

23 What was the first text to be 'bowdlerised' by Thomas Bowdler?

24 Which American state is called the Pine Tree State?

25 Who is taller – Mick Jagger or Phil Collins?

26 Which country has the kyat as a unit of currency?

27 Who according to Denis Healey, "represented the sensible wing of the Tory party"?

28 What make of raincoat did Harold Wilson popularise?

29 In which European country are the counties of Arad, Arges and Cluj?

30 What was the highest Premiership position of Gerard Houllier's Liverpool?

1 What was Bob Geldof's TV production company called?
2 When were downloads added to physical sales in the UK singles chart?
3 Who led the protest about Murdoch's buying of ITV shares in Nov. 2006?
4 What was the first INR radio station?
5 Kelly's Directories catalogue what?
6 Which female Russian journalist was murdered in a high-profile case in 2006?
7 What was the first magazine in the UK in 1691?
8 In which magazine did the Addams Family first appear?
9 Which American syndicated a newspaper column called "My Day"?
10 Who founded the Daily Mail?
11 Where is the newspaper ABC from?
12 Which two UK national newspapers were founded in 1990?
13 Apart from the Tribune, which other US newspaper has Chicago in its name?
14 Which press agency has the abbreviation IRNA?
15 Which newspaper proprietor was born Jan Ludvik Hoch?
16 In 1989 Richard Murdoch bought a 50% stake in which Hungarian tabloid?
17 Which Sunday Times editor made headline news himself regarding details of his affair with Pamella Bordes?
18 Lloyd Grossman was restaurant critic of which magazine in the 1980s?
19 Who took over The Observer in 1981?
20 Apart from the Guardian, which other newspaper did James Naughtie work for before joining the BBC?
21 What type of correspondent for the BBC was Michael Cole before he went to work for Mohammed Fayed?
22 Who was chairman of Saatchi & Saatchi when they took over the Tory Party account?
23 Which agency did the Saatchi brothers found in 1995?
24 Which famous columnist is married to Lady Camilla Harris?
25 Whose affair with David Mellor brought media man Max Clifford into the public gaze?
26 Which media man's sons all have the middle name Paradine?
27 Which track became the first to achieve one million paid downloads in the US?
28 Which co-founder of TV am was married to a future Leader of the House of Lords?
29 What was Ted Turner's family business before he turned to TV?
30 Which media magnate has owned AC Milan and been his country's PM?

1 What two colours appear on the flag of San Marino?
2 Male is the capital of which country?
3 In which century was Dame Barbara Cartland born?
4 What is the international car index mark for a car from Barbados?
5 Who directed the 1992 film "A Few Good Men"?
6 What was Twickenham's new record crowd on Nov. 5, 2006?
7 Which Persian word means "pleasure garden"?
8 Which film production company began as the Famous Players Film Company?
9 In which country is the port of Lubango?
10 Which painting did Arthur Scargill choose as his luxury on "Desert Island Discs"?
11 Paul Kagame became President of which country plagued by internal fighting?
12 Which country has the tugrik as a unit of currency?
13 When was the Piccadilly line fully operational after the July 7, 2005 bombing?
14 In which Canadian province is the novel "Anne of Green Gables" set?
15 What was painter Tintoretto's real name?
16 Which 1968 Scottish Cup winners did not make another final until 2004?
17 Which Sea, after the Coral Sea, is the largest in area in the world?
18 From which countries do the Mende people originate?
19 Who was the Greek Goddess of the rainbow?
20 What does BUPA stand for?
21 What trade did playwright Brendan Behan learn on leaving school?
22 Who played Paul Verlaine in the film "Total Eclipse" to Leonardo DiCaprio's Rimbaud?
23 What is the only US state to have been an independent republic?
24 In monetary and banking terms, what do the initials SIB stand for?
25 The Gladys Porter Zoo in Texas is noted for its collection of what?
26 Thalassophobia is a fear of what?
27 What was Peter Gabriel's first UK Top Ten hit?
28 What was Usher's first single to top both the UK and US charts?
29 Who wrote the screenplay for the 1963 film "Tom Jones"?
30 What is the main language of the Dominican Republic?

Answers | The Media *(see Quiz 103)*

1 Planet 24. 2 April 2005. 3 Richard Branson. 4 Classic FM. 5 Towns and cities. 6 Anna Politkovskaya. 7 Compleat Library. 8 New Yorker. 9 Eleanor Roosevelt. 10 Lord Northcliffe. 11 Madrid. 12 The Independent on Sunday & The European. 13 Chicago Sun-Times. 14 Islamic Republic News Agency. 15 Robert Maxwell. 16 Reform. 17 Andrew Neil. 18 Harpers and Queen. 19 Tiny Rowland. 20 The Scotsman. 21 Royal. 22 Tim Bell. 23 M & C Saatchi. 24 Nigel Dempster. 25 Antonia de Sancha. 26 David Frost. 27 Hollaback Girl. 28 Peter Jay. 29 Advertising. 30 Silvio Berlusconi.

Quiz 105 | Whose Music?

Answers – page 338

LEVEL 3

1 Who was knocked off No. 1 position by "Wannabe"?
2 Whose record has the longest playing time of any to make No. 1?
3 Howie Dorough was in which best-selling boy band?
4 Whose one-hit wonder replaced "Honky Tonk Women" at No. 1 in US and Britain?
5 Which singer left school in 1961 to appear in the film "It's Trad, Dad"?
6 Which No. 1 singer was born Arnold George Dorsey in Madras?
7 Which top musician produced Shakin' Stevens' "Merry Christmas Everyone"?
8 Who sang lead vocal on the chart topper "Babe"?
9 Who wrote the lines, "All alone, without a telephone"?
10 Who has recorded singles with Paul McCartney, Julio Iglesias and Diana Ross?
11 Who was the first drummer with The Stone Roses?
12 Joyce Vincent and Thelma Hopkins were the girls in which 1970s group?
13 Who joined Wendy Richard in the No. 1 from 1962 "Come Outside"?
14 Craig David's "Woman Trouble" featured Robbie Craig and who else?
15 Which chart topper started life at Leigh, Lancashire as Clive Powell?
16 Who set up the DEP record label?
17 Which 60s artist was the first British-born artist with three No. 1 hits?
18 To two years, when did Tony Christie's "Amarillo" first hit the charts?
19 Who wrote "Chain Reaction" for Diana Ross?
20 Who joined the Beatles on their first hit to enter the charts at No. 1?
21 Who recorded the 1993 No. 1 written and produced by Shaw and Rogers?
22 Which actor was talking to the trees on the B side of "Wand'rin' Star"?
23 Who was No. 1 in the UK and US singles and album charts at the same time in 1971?
24 How many versions of "Spirit in the Sky" had made No. 1 before Gareth Gates did?
25 Which Creation Records boss signed Oasis?
26 Which duo made up the Righteous Brothers?
27 Who joined the Beautiful South after being roadie for The Housemartins?
28 Whose death moved Don McLean to write "American Pie"?
29 The Beatles apart, who first took a Lennon & McCartney song to No. 1, with the Dakotas?
30 In the 1950s who was the first instrumentalist to achieve two No. 1s?

Answers | Pot Luck 50 *(see Quiz 106)*

1 Liberia. 2 Arnold Wesker. 3 Man City. 4 Five. 5 Gillian Shephard. 6 G8. 7 God.
8 Alaska. 9 John Donne. 10 Dreams. 11 Physics. 12 Spain. 13 An antelope.
14 Colombia. 15 1900. 16 The Red House Mystery. 17 Five. 18 Drowning. 19
Romania. 20 Charles Buchinski. 21 MA. 22 San Quentin prison. 23 Rho. 24
Veterans Day. 25 Great Ultimate Boxing. 26 British Open 2006. 27 Mozambique. 28
Brian Johnston. 29 Michael Tippett. 30 Paul Cattermole.

Quiz 106 Pot Luck 50

Answers – page 337

LEVEL 3

1 Which country has the ports of Buchanan and Grenville?
2 Who wrote "Chips with Everything"?
3 Who were the first English team outside London to claim the European Cup Winners' Cup?
4 In Scrabble what would the word DOG score without any bonus points?
5 Which politician stood down from the Norfolk South West seat in 2005?
6 Which major conference took place at the Gleneagles Hotel, July 2005?
7 Theophobia is the fear of what?
8 Which American state is called the Last Frontier?
9 "For whom the bell tolls" is a quote from whom?
10 What was Gabrielle's first UK Top Ten hit?
11 What did Olivia Newton-John's grandfather win a Nobel Prize for in 1954?
12 In which European country are the regions of Vigo and Murcia?
13 What type of animal is a kudu?
14 Peter Crouch made his England debut against which country?
15 In which year did Michelin produce the first of its Red Guides?
16 Which detective novel did AA Milne write in 1922?
17 How many stripes are there on the Thai flag?
18 What was the first Backstreet Boys' hit with a one-word title?
19 In which country is the town of Constanta?
20 What was Charles Bronson's full real name?
21 What is the international car index mark for a car from Morocco?
22 Where had Jim Rockford been in the years preceding "The Rockford Files"?
23 What name is given to the Greek letter that is the equivalent of letter R?
24 What is Remembrance Sunday called in the US?
25 What does "tai chi chuan" mean in Chinese?
26 What was the first Major won by Tiger Woods after his father's death?
27 In which country is the city of Maputo?
28 Which cricket commentator was awarded the Military Cross in WWII for his "cheerfulness under fire"?
29 Who wrote the opera "The Knot Garden"?
30 Who was the first person to leave S Club 7?

Answers | Whose Music? (see Quiz 105)

1 Gary Barlow. 2 Meat Loaf. 3 Backstreet Boys. 4 Zager and Evans – In the Year 2525. 5 Helen Shapiro. 6 Engelbert Humperdinck. 7 Dave Edmunds. 8 Mark Owen. 9 Marc Bolan (Metal Guru). 10 Stevie Wonder. 11 Alan "Remi" Wren. 12 Dawn. 13 Mike Sarne. 14 Artful Dodger. 15 Georgie Fame. 16 UB40. 17 Frank Ifield. 18 1971. 19 The Gibb Brothers. 20 Billy Preston on Get Back. 21 Mr Blobby. 22 Clint Eastwood. 23 Rod Stewart. 24 Two versions. 25 Alan McGhee. 26 Bill Medley and Bobby Hatfield. 27 Dave Stead. 28 Buddy Holly. 29 Billy J. Kramer. 30 Eddie Calvert.

1 Who beat Jahangir Khan's five-year unbeaten record in 1986?
2 Who had the car number plate 1 CUE?
3 How was Walker Smith better known?
4 Who was Man Utd's only Premiership ever-present in 2005–06, his debut season?
5 Whom did Andy Robinson name as his first captain when appointed head coach?
6 What was the nickname of baseball player Ty Cobb?
7 Which woman was undefeated over 400m between 1977 and 1981?
8 Which horse did Willie Shoemaker ride in his last race?
9 Who was the only person to beat Sugar Ray Leonard in a professional fight?
10 Which athlete was nicknamed "The Flying Finn"?
11 Who beat Babe Ruth's long-standing record of 714 home runs in 1974?
12 Who was the first jockey to saddle more than 8,000 winners?
13 Who was the first skier to overtake Pirmin Zurbriggen's four overall world championship titles?
14 Which American football player was nicknamed "Sweetness"?
15 Who in 1985 was the first man for 30 years to hold the 1500m and 5000m world records at the same time?
16 Whose Triple Jump World Record did Jonathan Edwards break?
17 Who was the first South African to win the Benson & Hedges Masters snooker title?
18 Where did Nelson Piquet win his first Grand Prix?
19 Who were the 2006 European women's doubles champions in badminton?
20 Who won the Moto Cross des Nations for the first time in 1975?
21 Who was dubbed the Louisville Lip?
22 Whose record of 24 Grand Prix wins was broken by Jim Clark?
23 Who was the first non-European to win the Tour de France?
24 Who won the 1988 Jesse Owens Award as the year's most outstanding athlete?
25 Fiona May represents which country at which sport?
26 Who was the British Superbike Champion of 2006?
27 Which French cyclist's nickname means "The Badger"?
28 Gene Tunney was only beaten once, by whom?
29 Who was the first Australian to win the Women's World Open Snooker Championship?
30 Who was the first racing driver to win 500 points in Formula 1?

| **Answers** | Pot Luck 51 *(see Quiz 108)* |

1 What's the most number of raised dots in a single letter of Braille?
2 Which 'E' number is used to represent riboflavin in products?
3 Who was actress Jane Seymour's first father-in-law?
4 In which country is the city of Maracaibo?
5 In which decade was Mohammed Fayed born?
6 Who, on the cover of "Sgt Pepper", was known by his three names?
7 What is Sven-Goran Eriksson's star sign?
8 What was David Gray's next Top Ten single hit after "Babylon"?
9 Which two colours form the background for the Vatican City flag?
10 What is the capital of the American state of Wisconsin?
11 Who was Henry IV's father?
12 In Bangladesh what is kabaddi?
13 Which actress links "Goldeneye" and "X-Men"?
14 Which Spice Girl once appeared as an extra in "Emmerdale"?
15 What's the English name of the constellation Pictor?
16 Which former Chechen president was killed by Russian troops in 2005?
17 Which country has the dirham as a unit of currency?
18 What is the main food of baby whales?
19 What is the international car index mark for a car from Tanzania?
20 In which US state is a university endowed by Cornelius Vanderbilt?
21 Which comedian played Tollmaster in "Doctor Who" in 1987?
22 What is the main language of Ethiopia?
23 Who played the black film detective Shaft?
24 Which Nobel Prize was won in 1975 by Andrei Sakharov?
25 Who had a No. 1 UK hit with "Seven Tears" in 1982?
26 Who is the elder – Jemima Khan or Kate Moss?
27 Who wrote the "Leatherstocking Tales"?
28 Tegucigalpa is the capital of which country?
29 What was the Christian name of frozen food man Mr Birdseye?
30 Who directed the 1991 film "JFK"?

1 What is chiefly grown in Alabama's Canebrake country?
2 The Julian and Dinaric Alps extend into which two countries?
3 The Amur river forms much of the boundary between which two countries?
4 What is the Maori name for New Zealand?
5 Which two main metals are found in the Atacama Desert in Chile?
6 What is the currency of Malaysia?
7 Which country has the highest density of sheep in the world?
8 Which African country takes its name from the Shona for "House of Stone"?
9 Which volcanic peak is west of Cook inlet in Alaska?
10 San Miguel is the main island of which group?
11 What is the capital of the Lazio region of Italy?
12 What is the former name of the capital of Dominica?
13 Which Brazilian state is the centre of Amazonian tin and gold mining?
14 Aqaba is which country's only port?
15 On which island of the Philippines is Manila?
16 What is the world's flattest continent?
17 Which former fort in New York State is the home of the US Military Academy?
18 Which US state capital lies on the river Jordan?
19 In which country is Africa's lowest point?
20 What is the largest primeval forest left in Europe?
21 The Red Sea is the submerged section of which valley?
22 Regina in Saskatchewan was originally called what?
23 How many countries do the Andes pass through?
24 In which country do the Makua live?
25 What is the highest peak of the Apennines?
26 Which city south east of St Malo was the old capital of Brittany?
27 Which Alps lie north east of the Sea of Showers?
28 Robben Island is a prison in which Bay?
29 What is Malawi's largest city?
30 Which south American port's name means River of January?

Answers | Pot Luck 52 *(see Quiz 110)*

1 Robert Altman. 2 Wood not metal resonators. 3 Indonesia. 4 Tippett. 5 Dick Tracy.
6 Amy Grant. 7 Tea. 8 Geoffrey Boycott. 9 Argentina. 10 Henry. 11 Crimean. 12
Doris Kappelhoff. 13 Kansas. 14 Z. 15 Jawaharlal (Pandit) Nehru. 16 Man City. 17
Sousaphone. 18 Journalism, literature & music. 19 Turkey. 20 Ghosts. 21 Czech
Republic. 22 Light My Fire. 23 Max. 24 Ice cream. 25 Muscat. 26 The Phantom.
27 Laura Moffatt. 28 Puppetry. 29 Kidney. 30 William I.

1 Which famous movie director died in Los Angeles in Nov. 2006?

2 How does a marimba differ from a xylophone?

3 In which country is the city of Surabaya?

4 Who composed the opera "The Ice Break"?

5 Which comic strip character was played by Warren Beatty?

6 Whose first UK Top Ten hit was "Baby Baby"?

7 What would you drink from a cha-no-yu?

8 Who said they'd hang their MBE round their cat's neck when they got back home after the 2006/07 Ashes whitewash?

9 Nestor Kirchner became President of which South American country in 2003?

10 What did the last emperor of China Hsuan Tung ask to be called after he was deposed?

11 In which war was the Battle of Inkerman?

12 What is Doris Day's full real name?

13 Which American state is called the Sunflower State?

14 Which letter is two dashes and two dots in Morse Code?

15 Who preceded Lal Shastri as Prime Minister of India?

16 Which club moved from M14 7WN to M11 3FF?

17 According to the Bonzo Dog Doo-Dah Band's "The Intro and the Outro" what is Princess Anne playing?

18 The Pulitzer Prize is awarded in which three categories?

19 In which European country is the region of Anatolia?

20 Phasmophobia is the fear of what?

21 Which country has the koruna as a unit of currency?

22 Which song links UB40 and Will Young?

23 Who is the male hero of the children's book "Where the Wild Things are"?

24 What is cassata a type of?

25 What is the capital of Oman?

26 In the first "Pink Panther" film what was the professional jewel thief called?

27 Which politician had the smallest majority after the 2005 general election?

28 In Japan what type of entertainment is bunraku?

29 Pyelitis affects which organ of the body?

30 Which king of England was crowned on Christmas Day?

Answers | Exploration *(see Quiz 109)*

1 Cotton. 2 Albania & Yugoslavia. 3 China & Russia. 4 Aotearoa. 5 Silver & copper. 6 Ringgit. 7 Wales. 8 Zimbabwe. 9 Mount Redoubt. 10 Azores. 11 Rome. 12 Charlotte Town. 13 Rondonia. 14 Jordan. 15 Luzon. 16 Australia. 17 West Point. 18 Salt Lake City. 19 Djibouti. 20 Hainburg in Austria. 21 Great Rift Valley. 22 Pile of Bones. 23 Seven. 24 Mozambique. 25 Gran Sasso d'Italia. 26 Rennes. 27 Lunar Alps. 28 Table Bay. 29 Blantyre. 30 Rio de Janeiro.

1 Who were the opposition in Sven's first game?
2 Which secretary of the FA alleged having an affair with Sven?
3 Which player scored the first goal in Sven's reign?
4 Wayne Rooney made his debut against which team?
5 World Cup 2006's first qualifier was a 2-2 against which side?
6 What was the half-time score in Sven's last game?
7 At which ground was the Swede's first game?
8 Who was right-back for 2002's World Cup Final tournament?
9 Which England player touched the ball last in Sven's reign?
10 To three, how many goals did England let in during the Sven years?
11 Which FA director of communications resigned in 2004?
12 Who was the first keeper to feature in Sven's first game?
13 In which German city was his last game?
14 Sven had a good start, winning how many games?
15 Peter Crouch was at which club when he made his England debut?
16 Which caretaker boss did Sven take over from?
17 The Fake Sheikh scam linked Eriksson with moving to which club?
18 Did Frank Lampard appear for England before Sven took over?
19 What was Sven's last club side as boss before joining England?
20 Who won his 51st and last cap in 2002's World Cup game v. Brazil?
21 How many games did England lose under Sven?
22 Which 31-year-old Chris won a cap in Sven's first game?
23 To five, how many goals did England score for Sven?
24 Which team were the first to beat Sven's England?
25 Who scored the last goal in open play in Sven's reign?
26 Did Gareth Southgate win over half his caps with Sven or before him?
27 Who was the last substitute used by Sven?
28 Who acted as Sven's assistant coach during his period in change of England?
29 To three, how many games did Sven's England win?
30 Who was the only player throughout Sven's first and last games?

1 What was film producer Ismail Merchant's final film?
2 Which two actors rejected "Bridge on the River Kwai" before Alec Guinness got the lead role?
3 How is actor/director Nobby Clarke better known?
4 Who played the first cinema vampire in "Nosferatu"?
5 Who was Daniel Day-Lewis' actress mother?
6 Who has a production company called Edited?
7 Which TV hero played a movie villain in "Beethoven"?
8 Who walked off the set of "10" and gave Dudley Moore a movie break?
9 Who did Schwarzenegger's love interest in "Twins" marry after the movie was made?
10 Who links TV's "Yes Minister" and the film "Nuns on the Run"?
11 Who was the voice of Zazu in "The Lion King"?
12 Whose legs were insured for more – Fred Astaire's or Betty Grable's?
13 Whom did Val Kilmer replace as "Batman"?
14 Who had the title role in the remake of "The Absent Minded Professor"?
15 What was the name of the Bond girl in Pierce Brosnan's first outing as 007?
16 In which film did Bing Crosby first play Father O'Malley?
17 Who adapted the play "Cyrano de Bergerac" Into the movie "Roxanne"?
18 Who appeared in her father's "Godfather Part III"?
19 Who directed the first two films in which Dianne Wiest won Oscars?
20 The movie "A Good Year" was based on whose novel?
21 Which American soul singer played a black lesbian assassin in her film debut, "Smokin' Aces"?
22 Who adapted Agatha Christie's "Evil Under the Sun" for the big screen?
23 Which production company was set up by Hugh Grant and Elizabeth Hurley?
24 Who is the president played by Anthony Hopkins in "Amistad"?
25 Who played Prinny In "The Madness of King George"?
26 Which were the first two films for which Brenda Blethyn was Oscar-nominated?
27 Which 1966 World Cup star shares his name with the writer of "American Beauty"?
28 Who played Streisand's son in "Prince of Tides"?
29 Who won supporting actor Oscar for "Jerry Maguire"?
30 Who directed "Mrs Doubtfire"?

How to Set Up Your Own
Pub Quiz

It isn't easy, get that right from the start. This isn't going to be easy. Think instead of words like "difficult", "taxing", "infuriating", consider yourself with damp palms and a dry throat and then, when you have concentrated on that, put it out of your mind and think of the recognition you will receive down the local, imagine all the regulars lifting you high upon their shoulders dancing and weaving their way around the pub. It won't help but it's good to dream every once in a while.

What you will need:

- A good selection of Biros (never be tempted to give your own pen up, not even to family members)
- A copy of *The Best Pub Quiz Book Ever! 3*
- A set of answer sheets photocopied from the back of the book
- A good speaking voice and possibly a microphone and an amp
- A pub
- At least one pint inside you
- At least one more on your table
- A table

What to do:

Choose your local to start with; there is no need to get halfway through your first quiz and decide you weren't cut out for all this and then find yourself in the roughest pub in Christendom 30 miles and a long run from home.

Chat it through with the landlord and agree on whether you will be charging or not; if you don't then there is little chance of a prize for the winners other than a free pint each and this is obviously at the landlord's discretion – if you pack his pub to bursting then five free pints won't worry him, but if it's only you and a couple of others then he may be less than unwilling, as publicans tend to be.

If you decide on an entry payment keep it reasonable; you don't want to take the fun out of the quiz; some people will be well aware that they have very little hope of winning and will be reluctant to celebrate the fact by mortgaging their house.

Once location and prize are all sorted then advertising the event is paramount. Get people's attention, sell, sell, sell or, alternatively, stick up a gaudy-looking poster on the door of the bogs. Be sure to specify all the details, time, prize and so on – remember you are selling to people whose tiny attention span is being whittled down to nothing by alcohol.

After this it is time for the big night. If you are holding the event in the "snug" which seats ten or so you can rely on your voice, if not you should get hold of a good microphone and an amplifier so that you can boom out your questions and enunciate the length and breadth of the pub (once again, clear this with the landlord and don't let liquid anywhere near the electrical equipment). Make sure to practise and get comfortable with the sound of your own voice and relax as much as possible, try not to rely on alcohol too much or "round one" will be followed by "rown' too" which will eventually give way to "runfroe". Relax your voice so that you can handle any queries from the teams, and any venomous abuse from the "lively" bar area.

When you enter the pub make sure you take everything listed above. Also, make sure you have a set of tie-break questions and that you instruct everybody who is taking part in to the rules – and be firm. It will only upset people if you start handing out impromptu solutions, and let's face it the wisdom of Solomon is not needed when you are talking pub quiz rules; "no cheating" is a perfectly healthy stance to start with. Keep people happy by double-checking your questions and answers; the last thing you need is a mix-up on the prize-winning question.

Finally, keep the teams to a maximum of five members, hand out your answer papers and pens and, when everybody is good and settled, start the quiz. It might not be easy and it might not propel you to international stardom or pay for a life of luxury but you will enjoy yourself. No, really.

ANSWERS

1 _____	16 _____
2 _____	17 _____
3 _____	18 _____
4 _____	19 _____
5 _____	20 _____
6 _____	21 _____
7 _____	22 _____
8 _____	23 _____
9 _____	24 _____
10 _____	25 _____
11 _____	26 _____
12 _____	27 _____
13 _____	28 _____
14 _____	29 _____
15 _____	30 _____

ANSWERS

1 _____

2 _____

3 _____

4 _____

5 _____

6 _____

7 _____

8 _____

9 _____

10 _____

11 _____

12 _____

13 _____

14 _____

15 _____

16 _____

17 _____

18 _____

19 _____

20 _____

21 _____

22 _____

23 _____

24 _____

25 _____

26 _____

27 _____

28 _____

29 _____

30 _____

ANSWERS

1 _____

2 _____

3 _____

4 _____

5 _____

6 _____

7 _____

8 _____

9 _____

10 _____

11 _____

12 _____

13 _____

14 _____

15 _____

16 _____

17 _____

18 _____

19 _____

20 _____

21 _____

22 _____

23 _____

24 _____

25 _____

26 _____

27 _____

28 _____

29 _____

30 _____

ANSWERS

1 _____

2 _____

3 _____

4 _____

5 _____

6 _____

7 _____

8 _____

9 _____

10 _____

11 _____

12 _____

13 _____

14 _____

15 _____

16 _____

17 _____

18 _____

19 _____

20 _____

21 _____

22 _____

23 _____

24 _____

25 _____

26 _____

27 _____

28 _____

29 _____

30 _____